THE DISABLED READER

EDUCATION OF THE DYSLEXIC CHILD

THE DISABLED READER

Education of the Dyslexic Child

JOHN MONEY
Editor

GILBERT SCHIFFMAN
Advisory Editor in Education

THE JOHNS HOPKINS UNIVERSITY PRESS
Baltimore and London

Manufactured in the United States of America

The Johns Hopkins University Press, Baltimore, Maryland 21218
The Johns Hopkins University Press Ltd., London

Library of Congress Catalog Number 66-20713
ISBN 0-8018-0465-5 (cloth)

Originally published, 1966
Second printing (cloth), 1967
Third printing (cloth), 1974

Library of Congress Catalog Card Number 66-20713

PREFACE

The disabled reader is one whose condition is that of being unable to thrive pedagogically, unable to profit from standard methods of instruction, and unable to learn to read. The resultant illiteracy or defective literacy is to be distinguished from that which results simply from educational neglect or inadequate instruction. Characteristically, the disabled reader is arrested at the beginner or near-beginner level, making the typical beginner's mistakes. Thus, reading disability can be suspected and recognized in the first and second grades. In the higher grades, it is a rule of thumb to identify the disabled reader as one who is two or more grade levels retarded in reading relative to his schoolmates who have been exposed to the same educational system as he. In severe reading disability, a child has at no stage of his schooling been able to achieve at grade level. There is no single cause of reading disablement. The different causes lead to the same final result, namely, impairment or arrest of maturation.

The title of this book, *The Disabled Reader*, was deliberately chosen to reflect the fact that it is not about any one type of reading disability of any one origin or cause. It is about all reading disability, and about the possible teaching methods that may ameliorate it. The volume was assembled by inviting original chapters from thirteen contributors and then by asking four others for permission to reprint already published material. Each contributor thus worked independently of the others.

There is no chapter on the whole word or look-and-say method of teaching. This is the method routinely in use in the majority of American schools, and is therefore widely known. It is also the method under which most disabled readers have failed to prosper. Therefore, it was decided to present in this book the alternative methods that might be tried. The methods all pertain literally to the teaching of reading. There are no chapters on the current fashions in perceptual training and visual-motor coordination because these methods have not yet been proved to have any direct effect on the learning of reading. One may well be perplexed that the various methods are presented sometimes with a partisanship and finality that seem to preclude alternatives or to suggest that comparison with a rival method and empirical evaluation of the two would be superfluous. For better or for worse, it was decided to allow these disjunctions in today's methodology of the teaching of reading to be accurately reflected. The working teacher may formulate his own synthesis, borrowing what he can use from each system.

It may well be that the era of competitive methodological systems is about to end and to be replaced by empirical evaluation and scientific testing. In a few years, it may be hoped, the reading teacher may expect to be diagnostically precise in tailoring the method of teaching to an individual's special handicaps and abilities. The combination of medical, psychological, and pedagogical points of view found herein aims to demonstrate the application of research and to encourage the spread of the experimental method to the study of disabled readers, while at the same time encouraging an evaluation of the methods used to teach them. The age of scientific evaluation and experimental test is upon us, and the education of the disabled reader is a part of that age.

In the case illustrations, all traces of personal identity have been eliminated, and the names, of course, are fictitious.

JOHN MONEY
Department of Psychiatry and Behavioral Sciences
Department of Pediatrics
The Johns Hopkins University School of Medicine
Baltimore, Maryland 21205
January, 1966

ACKNOWLEDGMENTS

This volume had its beginnings in a grant from the Association for the Aid of Crippled Children, which also was instrumental in originating the book's predecessor: *Reading Disability: Progress and Research Needs in Dyslexia.* Gifts from the Henry Foundation, New York, from Marion Tuttle Colwill, and from Hershel and Levonna Herzog also indirectly supported the book's appearance.

Mrs. Mary Loper shouldered a heavy burden of responsibility as secretary. Mrs. Christine Wang assisted with checking and consolidating the bibliography, and Mrs. Harry Schindler volunteered many hours of her time to type the bibliography and to proofread the glossary.

Dr. Bannatyne acknowledges a debt of gratitude to the late Edith Norrie, founder of the Ordblinde Institute in Copenhagen and inventor of the Composition Box; to Helen Arkell, Anne Church, Esther Hirsch, Moya Horder, Gudrun McCowen, and Thilde Stern, the teachers and staff at the Word Blind Centre for Dyslexic Children, London; and to the Invalid Children's Aid Association, the organization of which the Centre is a part, for the provision of facilities and financial help.

Doctors Kinsbourne and Warrington wish to thank Dr. J. St. C. Elkington, Dr. W. Gooddy, Dr. P. H. Sandifer, Professor O. L. Zangwill, and the physicians and surgeons of the National Hospital for permission to study patients under the Hospital's care.

Acknowledgment of financial support of their research is made by the following contributors to this volume: Dr. Philip Drash, to the National Institute of Child Health and Human Development, Public Health Service, U.S. Department of Health, Education and Welfare, for Research Grant #HD–00126; Dr. Leon Eisenberg, to the Grant Foundation, for a research fund for the study of early cognitive development in culturally disadvantaged children; Dr. Eleanor Gibson, to the Cooperative Research Program of the Office of Education, U.S. Department of Health, Education and Welfare, for a research grant; and Dr.

John Money, to the National Institute of Child Health and Human Development, Public Health Service, U.S. Department of Health, Education and Welfare, for Research Grant # HD–00325 and Research Career Development Award # HD–K3–18635.

Permission to reproduce the following copyrighted material is gratefully acknowledged:

American Academy of Pediatrics, for L. Eisenberg, Reading Retardation, Psychiatric and Sociologic Aspects. *Pediatrics*, 37 (1966): 352–65.

American Association for the Advancement of Science, for E. J. Gibson, Learning to Read. *Science*, 148 (May 21, 1965): 1066–72. (Copyright 1965 by the American Association for the Advancement of Science.)

American Medical Association, for M. Kinsbourne and E. K. Warrington, The Developmental Gerstmann Syndrome. *Archives of Neurology*, 8 (May, 1963): 490–501. (Copyright 1963 by the American Medical Association.)

British Psychological Society, for M. Kinsbourne and E. K. Warrington, Developmental Factors in Reading and Writing Backwardness. *British Journal of Psychology*. 54 (1963): 145–56.

Encyclopedia Britannica Educational Company, for the color plates used in Chapter 11.

Dr. W. Ritchie Russell, Editor, for M. Kinsbourne and E. K. Warrington, Disorders of Spelling. *Journal of Neurology, Neurosurgery and Psychiatry*, 27 (1964): 224–28.

W. W. Norton and Company, Inc., for quotations from S. T. Orton, *Reading, Writing and Speech Problems in Children*. New York, 1937.

CONTENTS

PART II: TEACHING METHODS AND PROGRAM ORGANIZATION

PART III: ILLUSTRATIVE EXAMPLES

CONTRIBUTORS

ALEX D. BANNATYNE, PH.D. Research and Educational Psychologist-in-Charge, Word Blind Centre for Dyslexic Children, Coram's Fields, 93 Guilford Street, London, W.C. 1, England; at present Senior Specialist in Education, Institute for Research on Exceptional Children, University of Illinois

PHILIP W. DRASH, PH.D. Instructor in Pediatrics, The Johns Hopkins University School of Medicine; Pediatric Psychologist, The Johns Hopkins Hospital, Baltimore, Maryland 21205

JARL E. DYRUD, M.D. Principal Investigator, Institute for Behavioral Research, 2426 Linden Lane, Silver Spring, Maryland 20910

THOMAS J. EDWARDS, PH.D. Senior Language Arts Consultant, Science Research Associates, Inc., 259 East Erie Street, Chicago, Illinois 60611

LEON EISENBERG, M.D. Professor of Child Psychiatry, Psychiatrist-in-Charge, Child Psychiatry Service, The Johns Hopkins Hospital, Baltimore, Maryland 21205

CALEB GATTEGNO, D.E.S., DR.PHIL., D. ES L. Director, Schools for the Future, P.O. Box 349, Cooper Station, New York, New York 10003

ELEANOR J. GIBSON, PH.D. Senior Research Associate in Psychology, Graduate Psychology Laboratory, Cornell University, Research Park, Ithaca, New York 14850

ISRAEL GOLDIAMOND, PH.D. Executive Director, Institute for Behavioral Research, 2426 Linden Lane, Silver Spring, Maryland 20910

DOROTHEA E. HINMAN, ED.D. Assistant in the United States to Dr. Caleb Gattegno, Schools for the Future, P.O. Box 349, Cooper Station, New York, New York 10003

MARJORIE SEDDON JOHNSON, ED.D. Associate Professor of Psychology and Educational Psychology and Associate Director, The Reading Clinic, Temple University, Broad and Montgomery, Philadelphia, Pennsylvania 19122

LOYAL W. JOOS, PH.D. Director of Systematic Studies, Oakland Schools, 109 Ottawa Drive, Pontiac, Michigan 48053

MARCEL KINSBOURNE, D.M., M.R.C.P. Lecturer in Psychology, Institute of Experimental Psychology, University of Oxford, 1 South Parks Road, Oxford, England

VIOLA G. LEWIS, B.S. Assistant in Medical Psychology, Department of Psychiatry and Behavioral Sciences, The Johns Hopkins University School of Medicine, Baltimore, Maryland 21205

ALBERT J. MAZURKIEWICZ, ED.D. Associate Professor of Education and Director of the Reading and Study Clinic and i/t/a Studies Center, Lehigh University, 230 W. Packer Avenue, Bethlehem, Pennsylvania 18015

JOHN MONEY, PH.D. Associate Professor of Medical Psychology and Pediatrics, Department of Psychiatry and Behavioral Sciences, Department of Pediatrics, The Johns Hopkins University School of Medicine; Psychologist, The Johns Hopkins Hospital, Baltimore, Maryland 21205

JUNE L. ORTON, M.SS. Director, Orton Reading Center, 106 North Hawthorne Road, Winston-Salem, North Carolina 27104

GILBERT SCHIFFMAN, ED.D. Supervisor of Reading, State of Maryland, Department of Education, State Office Building, 301 W. Preston Street, Baltimore, Maryland 21201

ELIZABETH K. WARRINGTON, PH.D. Principal Psychologist, The National Hospital, Queen Square, London, W.C. 1, England

PART I

Phenomenology and Theory

THE EPIDEMIOLOGY OF READING RETARDATION AND A PROGRAM FOR PREVENTIVE INTERVENTION

LEON EISENBERG

Fully half the world's adults are wholly illiterate, and not one third are "functionally" literate by the criterion of a fourth-grade reading level (Gray, 1956, p. 29). By that standard in 1956, 11 per cent of U.S. citizens could not read, the proportions varying by states from 3.9 to 28.7 per cent (Gray, 1957, p. 2). This is a measure of our failure and their failure, for to them are denied the riches of literature and the necessities of life. Employability is increasingly contingent upon literacy; those who fail to learn to read today will be the disadvantaged of tomorrow, impoverished in body and in soul.

What is the magnitude of the reading retardation problem in our school population? How many children are defective readers, and where are they to be found? What personal and familial characteristics are associated with reading difficulty? If the answers to these questions are to be interpretable, we must first consider methods of measurement of reading competence.

METHODS

Surveys of reading performance are based upon group tests of reading such as the Iowa, Stanford, California, Gates, and others. Typically, the test is standardized by scoring the results of its administration to a sample of children drawn from selected and presumably representative communities throughout the United States. Practical considerations demand that the test be given to groups of children rather than individually administered. The test must be relatively brief in order to avoid fatiguing the child and in order to commend it to school administrators for periodic system-wide surveys. Scoring must be simple; thus the reliance on multiple-choice answers, which permit machine scoring. In general, the tests that are given to upperclassmen assume reading competence at the elementary level, again in keeping with the necessity for brevity; consequently, a child may receive a minimum non-zero score simply by appearing for the test and signing his name to it. To this basement grade score may then be added additional credit for successful guessing at answers; most standard tests do not penalize for errors (the Gates is an exception). As a result, clinical reading specialists usually report functional reading levels based upon individual examination that are one or more grades lower than those derived from the group tests.

The skills measured by the elementary reading tests differ from those demanded for successful completion of the intermediate and advanced batteries. At the lower levels, little more is required from the child than the ability to decode the visual symbols into recognizable words. At intermediate and advanced levels, comprehension is called much more directly into play; in consequence, performance will vary with vocabulary, level of reasoning, and general intellectual facility. One would expect, therefore, that the child with limited exposure to intellectual stimulation would be penalized more and more at ascending grade levels. One final caveat is in order. The great variability in individual response at primary grade levels, together with the limited discrimination of the test instrument at the lower end of the scale, restricts the confidence to be placed in group testing methods in the first grades of school.

Epidemiology

With these general considerations in mind, and the further restriction that comparisons between systems employing different tests must be made with caution, let us look at the facts and figures that we can summon. In Figure 1, I have plotted the reading performance on the Stanford test of the entire sixth-grade population of a large urban center, here named "Metropolis." (It should be noted that children in special classes for mental retardation are not included.) Though the figures in this graph are precise and based upon actual figures from a single city, I shall not name the city. Naming would invite invidious comparisons, and the findings are in fact comparable to those from any major American city with a large indigent population. Of the sixth-grade students, 28 per cent are reading two or more grades below expected grade level, the conventional definition of severe reading

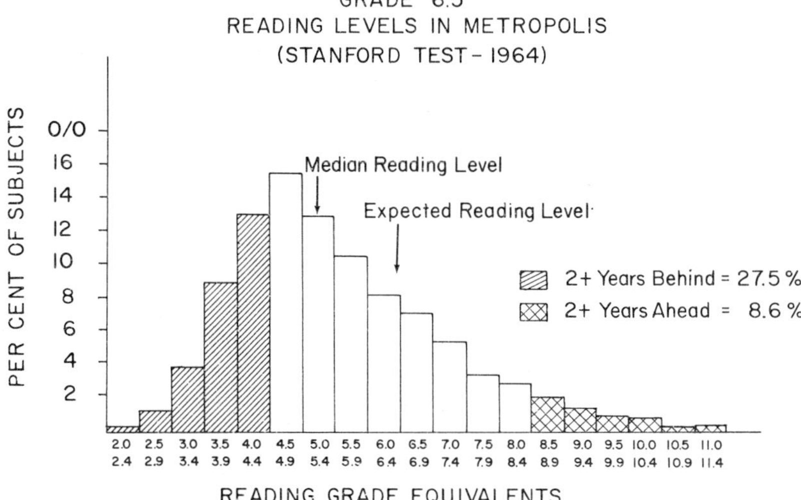

Figure 1. Reading levels for all sixth-grade children (except those in special classes for the retarded) in a large city in the eastern United States. The data are based on 12,000 children. On the abscissa are plotted reading scores by half-year intervals; on the ordinate, the percentage of the total sample scoring in each range.

retardation! With a median reading level of 5.2, the distribution is shifted significantly to the left; by definition of test construction, the median should lie at 6.5, the grade and month at which the test was administered.

Group intelligence tests administered to these children at the same time revealed a median IQ of between 94 and 95. This may appeal to school personnel as a rationalization for the reading scores on the grounds that, had the children had the expected IQ median of 100, the theoretically constructed reading curve would be shifted well toward a more normal distribution. Before we buy this reassurance that all is well with the educational establishment, let us remember that the group IQ test requires reading for its comprehension, and success with it, no less than with the reading test, is a function of the educational experience of the child. It would be more accurate to state that both group IQ and reading levels are depressed in contemporary American urban school populations, given the circumstances of education and of life for the children who reside in the gray areas of our cities.

The epidemiological significance of these data can be heightened by comparing them with those from other population groups. Figure 2 plots the reading scores for Metropolis, for "Suburbia" (a county immediately outside Metropolis), and for children attending independent (that is, private) schools in Metropolis. So enormous are the differences that one could almost believe that three different biological populations are represented here; yet with the exception of the greater burden of brain damage in the indigent, consequent upon the more frequent complications of pregnancy and parturition, the children of Metropolis have the potential to do at least as well as those of Suburbia and, I would add, almost as well as those of the independent schools.[1] If this be so, or even approximately so, then we have herein the difference between what the children of Metropolis do do and what they could do—a scathing indictment of the indifference of our cities to the education of their children.

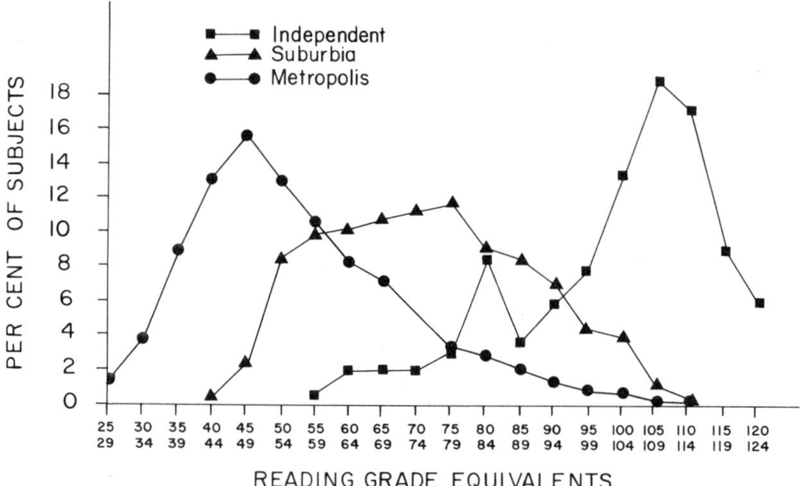

Figure 2. Reading levels in 1964 for sixth-grade children in Metropolis, Suburbia, and Independent. Plot is as in Figure 1. Number of subjects in each sample: 12,000 for Metropolis, 8,000 for Suburbia, and 200 for Independent. Expected mean based on national sample is 6.5 (i.e., 5 months into the sixth grade).

Table 1 sets forth key reading parameters for the school populations of Metropolis, Suburbia, the independent schools, and "Commuter County," a bedroom county (for exurbanite white collar workers) that includes pockets of rural, largely Negro, poverty. If we focus our attention on the percentage of children who are more than one year

[1] The use of entrance examinations in the private schools serves to exclude some children vulnerable to learning disability.

retarded in reading, Metropolis has failure rates two thirds higher than Commuter County, three times higher than Suburbia, and more than fifty times higher than the independent schools. Similar discrepancies obtain at the other end of the reading spectrum. Success rates, as measured by the percentages of children more than two years advanced in reading, are nine times higher in the independent schools than in Metropolis or Commuter County and 2.4 times higher than in Suburbia.

Table 1. Sixth-grade reading levels by school system

School System	Test	% Retarded > 2 yrs.	% Retarded > 1 yr.	% Advanced > 2 yrs.
Metropolis	Stanford	28	57	9
Commuter County	California	15	35	8
Suburbia	Iowa	3	19	34
Independent	Stanford	0	1	82

Let us now turn to other demographic characteristics as a basis for comparative analysis of population groups. Rates by sex (for Commuter County) reveal that the number of retarded readers among boys (19.5 per cent) is more than twice as high as that for girls (9.0 per cent), a finding consistent with other surveys of reading performance (Bentzen, 1963; Miller, Margolin, and Yolles, 1957) and a point to which we shall return.

We have thus far examined rates by area of residence and by sex. What of rates by race? This question is not readily answerable for many urban school systems, for, although the schools may not be fully integrated, the records are, much, one suspects, to the relief of administrators when irate citizen groups raise questions about the adequacy of education for Negro children. The data from Commuter County, however, did permit computation of rates by race. Whereas 12 per cent of the white children were two or more years retarded in reading, a failure rate alarming enough in itself, the corresponding figure for Negro children was 36 per cent, three times as great. (Within each ethnic group, the male rate remains significantly higher than the female rate—16.8 per cent to 7.1 per cent for whites and 42 per cent to 26 per cent for Negroes.) These figures become somewhat more explicable when we add the information that only 7 per cent of the white families in Commuter County, as against 62 per cent of the Negro families, fall into social class V, the very bottom of the economic heap.

Sources of Retardation in Reading

Epidemiological surveys employing a crude measure like group reading levels suffer from the inherent limitation that they treat by a common statistic cases that vary widely in the nature of the underlying pathology. We would not expect to learn much that is useful about the epidemiology of infections if we studied the distribution of fever in a population without regard to its source. Yet this has been the common practice in respect to reading. It is not surprising, therefore, that competent investigators have been led to contrary conclusions about the role of handedness, heredity, perceptual handicap, and the like, when each has examined a heterogeneous sample of cases defined only by its reading performance.

To order our further inquiry, it is convenient to divide the sources of retarded reading into two major groups: the sociopsychological and the psychophysiological, in the full realization that this dichotomy is both arbitrary and inaccurate. Given the differential distribution by social class of the complications of pregnancy and parturition and of the availability of adequate nutrition and medical care, one could equally well classify brain injury under the heading, sociophysiological. However, the axis of classification employed in Table 2 can provide a useful basis for a preliminary examination of the types of retarded readers.

Table 2. Provisional classification: the sources of reading retardation

Sociopsychological Sources:

1. Quantitative and qualitative defects in teaching
2. Deficiencies in cognitive stimulation
3. Deficiencies in motivation
   a. Associated with social pathology
   b. Associated with psychopathology ("emotional")

Psychophysiological Sources:

1. General debility
2. Sensory defects
3. Intellectual defects
4. Brain injury
5. Specific (idiopathic) reading disability

Sociopsychological Sources

Defects in Teaching. We would not expect that a child who had not been taught would learn to read. Yet there are children in the United States who are late in beginning school, who attend irregularly, whose school year is foreshortened to conform to the farming season, and who therefore experience a significant loss of exposure to teaching. These are the children of sharecroppers and of migratory workers. Similar academic ills befall children of disorganized families who move from one tenement, and hence one school district, to another.

But even those urban or rural children of the poor who attend school more or less as required by law suffer a serious deficit in teaching. The schools they attend are likely to be overcrowded, are more often than not staffed by poorly qualified teachers, are beset by problems of discipline to the detriment of teaching time, and employ traditional methods of teaching that, however adequate they may be for the middle-class child, are highly inappropriate to the special educational needs of the disadvantaged. No less devastating is the pessimistic conviction of many teachers and many administrators that such children lack the necessary wherewithal to learn. This belief may be couched in terms of the restricted intellectual stimulation in the child's home or may be more nakedly racist in adhering to beliefs in biological inferiority. Whatever the source of the conviction, it influences the performance of the teacher, the expectations he sets for the child, and the ultimate attainment in the classroom. Without a direct challenge to these conventional beliefs, educational progress will not be possible.

Under the heading of teaching defects, most physicians will expect to hear some discussion of the "look-say" (whole word) method versus phonics. Attacks on the look-say method have their fad; they appeal to traditionalism and suggest a cheap and easy answer to contemporary problems by returning to the ways of the good old days. Such evidence as there is indicates that the average first grader learns equally well by either method but somewhat faster by look-say, whereas the potentially dyslexic child may have his disability magnified by exclusive reliance on the whole word method. That the look-say primers have been full of drivel—"Here, Tip! Run, Jane! Look, look, look!" (Damn, damn, damn!)—is not inherent in the whole word method but must be attributed to the vacuousness of the uninspired authors of these non-books. Pending the accumulation of definitive evidence based upon controlled studies, we can only conclude that the excellence of the teacher and a class size small enough for individualization of instruction are far more important than the choice of method. An either/or formulation is in any event absurd; a competent teacher should know the several ways of teaching reading in order to capitalize on the ability profile of the particular child. Nostalgia for the McGuffey Reader and a "no nonsense" approach to education will not solve the reading problem.

Deficiencies in Cognitive Stimulation. Although the formal education of the child by definition begins when he enters school, there has in fact been a quite extraordinary transformation in his mental function during the first six years of life at home. From a largely vegetative, only intermittently conscious newborn with a limited repertoire of reflexes, he has become a self-conscious, speaking, reasoning, and imaginative being. This developmental explosion accompanies a tripling of brain weight and an uncountable proliferation of dendrites and synapses, but it is in no sense a mere unfolding of a process predetermined from within. How fast it happens and how far it goes are, within limits, direct functions of the amount and variety of patterned stimulation supplied by the environment (Hunt, 1961).

We know that if a child does not hear language, he will not speak. We tend to overlook the corollary proposition that if he is exposed to a less differentiated language experience, he will speak and understand less well. The slum child, on the average, has had less training in listening to sustained and grammatically complex speech, has had less exposure to the extensive vocabulary of our language, and has had less reinforcement for his own verbal efforts. He exhibits defects in auditory attention and perception, performs less well on vocabulary tests (especially when challenged by abstract words), and is less responsive to verbal instructions in the classroom (John, 1963; Deutsch, 1965).

Many inner city children have never been more than a few blocks from their home; the museums, symphony halls, and even the zoos and amusement parks of their communities are foreign territory to them. Books, magazines, even newspapers are infrequent companions; such children are not often read to. Exercises with paper and pencil, puzzles, and sedentary games with formal rules are uncommon. They have been short-changed of experiences that, for other children, serve to build concepts and set the ground for learning to learn (Harlow, 1949). Yet their lives have in no sense been blank. Scrounging in the streets, dodging cars for a game of stick ball, avoiding the police, defending themselves from youthful and adult predators alike, they have had to learn the complex arts of survival in the slums. In so doing, they acquire behavior traits that interfere actively with the acquisition of the patterns required for success in the classroom. To note that these children are different is not to convict them of being defective. The figures from Metropolis make appallingly clear their failure to learn as they have been taught. This, however, is a failure of the teaching, not of the children (Gordon, 1965).

Deficiencies in Motivation. Intelligence tests have been the best available single predictors of academic success, but the highest correlations obtained between IQ and grade averages have been on the order of 0.5 and 0.6. Statistically, then, "intelligence" (or whatever IQ tests measure) accounts at best for one quarter to one third of the variance in academic performance. This is hardly surprising; we all recognize it when we choose students and colleagues by estimating their motivation as well as their talent. Motivation, like intelligence, is shaped by the environment; in this shaping, both social class values and idiosyncratic life experiences play a role.

When parents fail to reinforce a child for good school performance or to chastise him for academic misbehavior, when they convey a belief that school success bears little relationship to ultimate occupational attainment, and when they share with the child a view of school authorities as repressive agents employed by a society hostile to their values, they provide little support for the development of achievement motivation. The beliefs on which these behaviors are predicated are not myths; they are constructed from the social reality of the slum dweller. These beliefs may lead—indeed, they do lead—to the self-perpetuation of defeat and alienation, but that does not make them untrue. The Negro high school graduate is more often unemployed, and, when employed, earns less, than the white graduate. Unemployment rates for young workers, white and Negro, are disproportionately high; unchecked, the crisis will grow worse as population trends lead to an increase in this age group (Freedman, 1965). The examples of success that sustained previous generations of immigrants from abroad have been replaced by the examples, in homes and on street corners, of failure, and all but the hardiest of today's domestic immigrants from farm and mine are discouraged. The solution for this problem will not lie in the schools but in the creation of job opportunities to which all have equal access.

However, teacher attitudes may serve to consolidate a conviction of the hopelessness of it all. Educators are satisfied with less from the lower-class child because they expect less; their expectations form part of the social field that molds the child and determines, in part, what he does. He arrives at school ill prepared; his initial poor performance leads to "streaming" in low-ability sections; the limited teaching further retards his learning; he completes his "education" less able than others; ironically, the terminal product is used to justify the system (Wilson, 1963). But is it not apparent that the operation of the system has guaranteed fulfillment of the prophecy? Schiffman (personal communication), in a study of eighty-four elementary school children referred for placement in classes for "slow learners" because of academic failure, found that 78 per cent had Wechsler performance quotients in the average or better range. Yet only 7 per cent of their teachers identified them as other than dull, and only 14 per cent of their parents recognized their potential. Need it surprise us that 86 per cent of the children rated themselves as dull or defective? With such a self-image, affirmed at school and at home, what shall it profit a child to try?

With or without social disadvantage, though all too commonly associated with it, individual psychopathology is a frequent concomitant of retardation in reading. On the one hand, school difficulties are among the major presenting complaints at every psychiatric clinic for children; on the other, physicians who have studied retarded readers have uniformly noted a high association with emotional disturbance (Missildine, 1946; Fabian, 1951; Blanchard, 1935). The correlation with antecedent family pathology (Ingram and Reid, 1956) indicates that, in a substantial number of cases, the psychiatric disorder is the source of the reading problem. No single pattern of psychopathology is characteristic: among the more common patterns are anxiety states that preclude attention to academic tasks, preoccupation with fantasy such that the child is psychologically absent from class, passive-aggressive syndromes in which resistance to parental coercion is subtly executed by a hapless failure to learn, low self-esteem based upon identification with an inadequate parent, and schizophrenic thought pathology in which letters and words become invested with idiosyncratic meanings. Reading failure is a final common pathway for the expression of a multiplicity of antecedent disruptions in learning.

At the same time, it must be recognized that the reading difficulty is in itself a potent source of emotional distress. Embarrassed by fumbling recitations before his peers, cajoled, implored, or bullied by his parents and his teachers to do what he cannot, the retarded reader is first disturbed and finally despondent about himself. His ineptness in reading penalizes him in all subjects and leads to his misidentification as a dullard. With class exercises conducted in what for him is a foreign language, he turns to other diversions, only to be chastised for disruptive behavior. However begun, the psychiatric disturbance and the reading disability are mutually reinforcing in the absence of effective intervention. For such children, psychiatric treatment may be necessary before response to remedial techniques can be expected (Eisenberg, 1959).

Psychophysiological Sources

General Debility. The psychophysiological sources of reading retardation can be divided into five major categories: general debility, sensory defects, intellectual defects, brain injury, and idiopathic or specific reading disability. Overlap and multiple conjunction of causes are common.

Discussions of reading retardation do not list general debility among its causes, but this is a serious oversight. The child who is chronically malnourished and the child who is chronically ill can hardly be expected to perform adequately in school. I mention these factors here only to stress the importance of a thorough pediatric examination as the first step in the evaluation of any child with a learning failure.

Sensory Defects. Defects in seeing and hearing impede information transmission over the primary channels whose integration is required for reading. Visual defect leads to reading handicap only when acuity is reduced by half or more (Irvine, 1941). With respect to hearing, however, there is increasing evidence that children with normal pure tone auditory thresholds may nonetheless suffer from perceptual handicaps in discriminating speech sounds (Goetzinger, Dirks, and Baer, 1960) and defective intersensory integration, as in the task of converting auditory to visual signals (Birch and Belmont, 1964), both disorders being associated with poor reading. These deficits may stem from central nervous system pathology or from faulty auditory experience. In either case, corrective training to minimize this source of difficulty would appear logical, though the effectiveness of such training remains to be established.

Intellectual Defects. Intellectual defect can be expected to limit reading achievement in proportion to its severity. The assessment of this factor requires individual clinical examination by a competent psychologist and cannot be based upon group testing. The prognosis will, of course, vary with the nature of the underlying disorder as well as the degree of mental deficiency. However, even moderately retarded children can learn to read enough to transact the ordinary business of life if teaching methods take into account the learning characteristics of the defective child.

Brain Injury. Children with chronic brain syndromes are at high risk for learning disabilities, though there is no simple one-to-one relationship between amount or locus of damage and ultimate academic achievement (Eisenberg, 1964). Whether the category "brain injury" or its various extensions—"minimal cerebral dysfunction," "diffuse brain damage," etc.—are useful concepts has been challenged (Herbert, 1964), but the clinician should be alerted to the search for learning problems and to the importance of special teaching techniques for children with borderline as well as overt neurological findings. Occasional children with brain tissue damage sufficient to result in mental deficiency of moderate degree are nonetheless able, in the elementary grades, to attain above average fluency in oral reading, although their comprehension of what they have read is minimal. Such instances are instructive in several respects. They serve to remind us of the variability of the clinical patterns observed in brain-injured children; they indicate the complex nature of the reading process, in which word recognition and sentence comprehension are separable skills; and they emphasize the importance of a thorough reading analysis as a complement to a comprehensive pediatric assessment in the workup of each case of reading retardation.

Specific Reading Disability. We turn now to the important residual category of specific reading disability, also known as congenital word blindness (Morgan, 1896), primary reading retardation (Rabinovitch *et al.*, 1954), and developmental dyslexia (Critchley, 1964). The adjective "specific" calls attention both to the circumscribed nature of the disability and to our ignorance of its cause. Operationally, specific reading disability may be defined as the failure to learn to read with normal proficiency despite conventional instruction, a culturally adequate home, proper motivation, intact senses, normal intelligence, and freedom from gross neurological defect. Hinshelwood's (1917) statement is not less relevant today than when it was originally written in 1902: "It is a matter of the highest importance to recognize the cause and the true nature of this difficulty in learning to read which is experienced by these children, otherwise they may be harshly treated as imbeciles or incorrigibles, and either neglected or punished for a defect for which they are in no wise responsible."

There are no reliable data on which to base a secure estimate of the prevalence of specific reading disability. Such surveys as exist record only the extent of retardation in reading on group tests without differentiation as to cause. Clinical reports indicate a much higher rate of occurrence among boys, the male:female ratio generally exceeding four to one (Critchley, 1964). This disproportion is similar to, but higher than, the surplus of boys among retarded readers from all causes, among children designated as academically backward (Bentzen, 1963), and among children referred to psychiatric clinics (Bahn, Chandler, and Eisenberg, 1961). Some have sought to explain these figures on the grounds of greater cultural pressure upon boys for academic success; this may account for some differential in rates of identification, insofar as standards for boys may be more exacting. But it is noteworthy that boys are in general slower to acquire verbal facility and are more prone to exhibit behaviors in the early school grades that teachers label "immature." It would seem more appropriate to relate these disproportions to the greater biological vulnerability of the male to a wide variety of ills; from the moment of conception onwards, there is a highly significant differential in morbidity and mortality between the sexes, such that an original surplus of males is converted to its opposite by the time adulthood is attained (Childs, 1965; Washburn, Medearis, and Childs, 1965).

Many authorities have called our attention (as though such phenomena were diagnostic of specific reading disability), to reversals (**was** for **saw**, **gril** for **girl**), mirror writing, confusion of certain letters (**b, d, p, q, g**), omitted or added words, perseverations, skipped or repeated lines, and the like. These very same errors occur as the normal child learns to read; what distinguishes the dyslexic is the frequency and persistence of these errors well beyond the time at which they have become uncommon in the normal child.

The failure of many investigators to adhere to defined criteria for diagnosis and to recognize the importance of the age variable accounts for some of the contradictory findings reported in the literature. It does seem that sinistrality and, more especially, delayed or inconsistent laterality occur more often among dyslexics (though many are typical dextrals), but it is quite another matter to suggest that "incomplete cerebral dominance" accounts for the reading problem. The determination of laterality is not so simple a matter as was once thought (Benton, 1959), nor is "brainedness" so readily to be inferred from handedness (Mountcastle, 1962). The apparent association between delayed establishment of laterality and the reading defect seems more probably related to a common underlying developmental antecedent than to be one of cause and effect. The confusion about the proportion of dyslexics with perceptual deficits takes on some pattern when it is realized that perceptual handicaps are more often found in younger than in older dyslexics (Benton, 1962). This change with age may reflect the developmental course of perception (Birch and Belmont, 1965). The older child may no longer exhibit the handicap which may have been prominent at a critical stage in the learning process and contributed to his failure to learn to read.

Etiological studies have also led to apparently contradictory conclusions. Kawi and Pasamanick (1959) have presented evidence of a much greater frequency of pregnancy complications and premature births in the obstetrical histories of retarded readers than in those of control cases. The differences are well beyond chance expectancy. However, the index cases were selected from school records because of retarded reading and screened only for an IQ above 84. It seems probable that cases with a variety of reading disorders were included, the proportion of specific dyslexia being unknown. On the other hand, many clinicians have been impressed with the regularity with which a history of reading difficulty is obtained from the parents and collateral relatives of children with specific reading disability. In the most comprehensive study of its kind, Hallgren (1950) concluded that the data from a genetic survey of 276 cases support a dominant mode of inheritance.

We are left with the unanswered question of the nature of the defect, even if we accept the proposition that it is biological. Critchley supposes it to be due to "specific cerebral immaturity" but adds that he doubts the existence of "a structural lesion recognizable by present day techniques" (Critchley, 1964, p. 80). Geschwind (1965) has advanced the notion that there is "delayed maturation of the angular gyrus region, probably bilaterally." From the evolutionary standpoint, this region is not recognizable in the macaque and is only imperfectly developed in the higher apes. The human inferior parietal lobule (including the angular and supramarginal gyri) matures very late cytoarchitectonically, often not until late childhood (Geschwind, 1965). Geschwind argues that, since lesions of the angular gyrus in the adult result in word blindness, delay in its development might account for specific reading disability in childhood. Against this thesis is the opinion of other neurologists that pure word blindness is neither so "pure" nor so consistently associated with specific lesions as classical doctrine alleges. Autopsy material being unavailable, the arguments rest upon its plausibility and upon the way in which the clinical evidence is evaluated.

The Development of Reading Skill: A Pediatric Action Program

The evidence marshaled in this chapter has, I trust, persuaded you of the integral relationship between reading and intellectual development, of the appalling extent of retardation in reading among American school children, of the multiple sources of interference with the acquisition of literacy, and of the relevance of the foregoing to the pediatrician's role in the maintenance of health and the correction of disability. In this final section, I shall outline the areas in which there are indications for social action to promote the healthy development of children. Those areas, as I see them, are maternal and child health programs, health and education programs for the preschool child, and revised curricula and classroom conditions throughout the years of public schooling.

Maternal and Child Health Programs

At the level of primary prevention, there is a clear need for comprehensive maternal and child health programs to diminish the complications of pregnancy, parturition, and the neonatal period that lead to insult to the central nervous system of the infant (Eisenberg, 1962). Malnutrition, poor hygiene, and inadequate medical care are among the causal factors subject to control if we but have the determination to apply present knowledge and resources (Pasamanick, 1956; Scrimshaw and Behar, 1965; Craviato and Robles, 1965). Current federal legislation provides us with a splendid opportunity for progress, but money and initiative from Washington alone will not suffice to guarantee quality of services. Pediatricians in every community will have to participate in the planning and the execution of new and imaginative programs. More is needed than the customary three-minutes-per-child schedule of traditional health department well baby clinics—more than the mere advertisement to the community of their existence. Medical interest will have to extend beyond vaccinations and cursory physical examinations to sensitive concern with cognitive as well as physical development: notices of clinic hours must be augmented by an active recruitment of the families not now making use of these services. The index patient may be the pregnant woman or the infant, but the physician's curiosity must extend from them to the welfare of all members of the family unit. Special programs will be necessary for mothers at highest risk: the unmarried, the very young and the old, the Negro, the mother with prior history of obstetrical difficulty. We should not tolerate the simple dismissal of the pregnant high school student from school; health care and provision for supplementary education are essential. In these tasks medical specialists and generalists, nurses, social workers, health educators, nutritionists, and others will have to function as a team if the disadvantaged family is to be rehabilitated.

Preschool Programs

The emphasis on preschool enrichment, via Project Headstart, opens the vista of large-scale efforts to foster early cognitive development. Pilot studies indicate that inner city children exposed to nursery enrichment programs function more effectively than their peers when they enter first grade. For the first time, funds are available to extend this opportunity to several hundred thousand children. Funds, though necessary, are not sufficient to ensure quality. Thought and effort will have to be devoted to curricula that promote intellectual growth rather than provide babysitting services. The shortage of professional personnel requires that we must use talent imaginatively wherever it exists in the community without getting hung up on formal criteria created to preserve the educational power structure and without opening the doors to politically controlled job handouts. If the children are to be served with greatest effect, there must be parallel educational programs for parents, couched in terms that make sense to urban slum dwellers. They love their children no less than we; what they need to understand is how they can help their children to achieve the goals they long for but see as unattainable. The preschool program will serve as a catchment area for pediatric identification of medical defects and the mobilization of corrective measures. If these are to be more than the mere compilation of records, vigorous pediatric procedures for follow-up, together with the establishment of medical responsibility, will be required.

Improved School Programs

If preschool enrichment is not augmented by substantial revision of traditional school services, there is little reason to anticipate significant long-run benefit. None of us would expect that a good diet at the age of three should protect us against malnutrition at the age of six. The brain requires alimentation, both biological and psychological, at each stage of the life cycle; early nourishment is necessary but is not sufficient to guarantee its development. The precedent-shattering federal aid to education bill recognizes for the first item a national responsibility to improve the quality of education; the funds made available are but a token of what will be required ultimately. If we allow them to be used merely to supplant state funds or to be spread thinly throughout the system, no palpable changes will result. The best teachers must be attracted to slum area schools; class size must be reduced to the private school levels of fifteen to twenty pupils per class;

curricula must be modified, school programs must be extended to include after-school tutoring and recreational activities. What I am emphasizing is capital investment in human renewal, the very principle that has paid off so handsomely in our industrial enterprise. These proposals will not be welcomed by those school boards and those professional educators threatened by any change in the *status quo*.

I would urge upon the reader one final task. Most school systems introduce remedial reading instruction at the third grade or later (if they have it at all). The justification is one of economy. Of those children not reading at the end of first grade, perhaps half manage to pass muster by the end of the second grade, a few more learn to read by standard instruction by the end of the third grade. These children are the "late bloomers," youngsters who, for unknown reasons, acquire late, but do acquire, the capacity to profit from conventional teaching. By waiting till the third grade, the school system has spared itself the cost of extra teaching for children who were going to make it on their own. This "economy," however, must be balanced against the cost to those children who, by the third grade, are deeply imprisoned in faulty learning habits, have become convinced of their ineptness, and now respond poorly to any but the most expert individual clinical instruction. Surely this country can afford to do better by its children. It is essential that we early identify the child who will not succeed to read on time (De Hirsch, Jansky, and Langford, 1965). The child not beginning to read by the second semester of the first grade needs diagnostic study and the appropriate remedial education. If to achieve this means that we will be giving extra help to a child who does not need it for every child who does need it, then I urge that we do so. The surplus child will not be harmed and may be benefited; the dyslexic child will be reached at a time the chance of success is greatest. We would not hear of delaying therapy for rheumatic fever because not every patient incurs a valvulitis; we would not consider deferring laparotomy for a suspected appendicitis because diagnosis is imprecise and not every appendix perforates. How, then, can we tolerate a view that is equivalent to saying, let us make certain that the child cannot read and is really in trouble before we give him extra help? An effective program for early identification and treatment might even produce long-run savings if we take into account the cost of prolonged treatment and the ultimate loss in economic productivity of handicapped readers. But my argument places no weight on such matters. Where the healthy development of children is concerned, financial considerations are simply irrelevant.

CHAPTER 2

ON LEARNING AND NOT LEARNING TO READ

JOHN MONEY

THE LAW OF CAMOUFLAGE OR OBJECT CONSTANCY

The prereader lives like a spy in a jungle of camouflage, learning during all the years of his preschool experience that objects retain their same identity and meaning irrespective of transformations and disguise. Without changing its name or significance, an object may take on a different visual form by rotation to any point of the compass, fall upside down, recede into the distance, or approach. It may be dismembered, disassembled, or subtracted from. It may be embellished and added to. Or its salient characteristics may change, as in the many species of dog or types of chair (Fig. 1). Nonetheless, despite any of

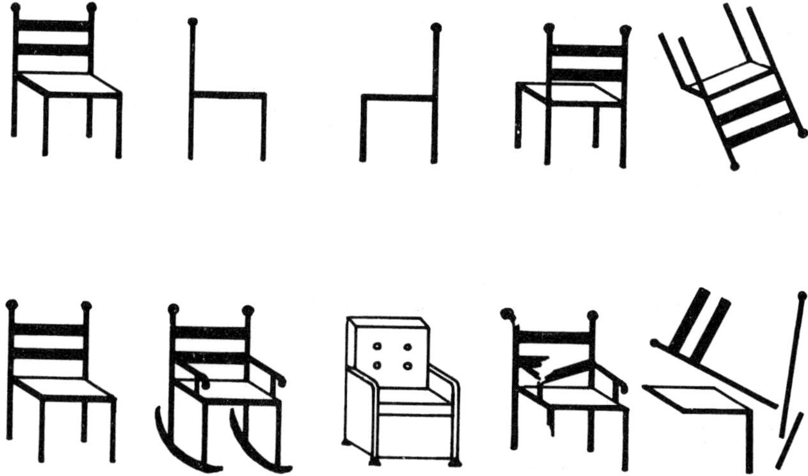

Figure 1. Persistence of object constancy versus rotational (top) and form (bottom) change. (Drawn by Duane Alexander.)

these possible changes, the object has the same designation and meaning. It obeys the law of object constancy. Learning to read turns the prereader's conceptual world of object constancy into chaos, for it supplements and supplants the law of object constancy with the law of directional constancy and the law of form constancy.

The Law of Directional or Positional Constancy

The law of directional constancy may also be called the law of positional constancy. In learning to read and write, this law applies both to letters, the alphabetic symbols, and to their arrangement in words. An alphabetic character, to retain its name and meaning, must always be directionally oriented the same way.

There are three dimensions of rotation: the bottom-to-top clockwise rotation, the push-pull (near-far or fore-aft) mirror rotation, and the right-to-left mirror rotation. These three transformations, applied to the word **READ**, are as follows:

Bottom-to-top	**ᗡ∀Ǝᴚ**
Right-to-left	**ᗡAƎЯ**
Near-to-far	**ᴚE∀D**

These three dimensions of rotation give three directional rules to obey:

1. Letters may not be rotated clockwise (or anticlockwise). Thus, **u** is the same shape as **n** upside down, or rotated 180°, but each has a different name, and likewise **h** and **ɥ**. Rotations of 90°, as in **ɷ** – **B** – **ϖ**, or **Z** – **N** – **Z**, are also forbidden.

2. Letters may not be near-far (fore-aft or push-pull) mirror-rotated. This is the type of mirror rotation obtained when you write on the flat surface of a table while looking at a mirror propped up in front of you. Examples are **5** – **ƻ** and **f** – **t**; **S** – **Ƨ**, **Z** – **Σ**, and **N** – **И** are also near-far rotations, though in addition they may be right-left rotations as well.

3. Letters may not be right-left mirror-rotated. This is the type of mirror rotation obtained if you imagine your name tattooed on your own forehead and yourself trying to read it while standing before a mirror. Everyone is familiar with right-left rotations from trying to read from the reverse side a sign written on glass, as when one is inside a store. **R** – **Я** and **3** – **Ɛ** are examples of right-left mirror rotation. The notorious offenders are **b** – **d** and **p** – **q**.

The characters **b**, **d**, **p**, and **q** are the most directionally confounding in the alphabet, for **b** – **p** and **d** – **q** are both near-far mirror rotations and **b** – **q** and **d** – **p** are both clockwise, upside-down rotations of one another. To confound still further, **9** not only is nine, but almost que (**q**) and almost gee (**g**).

A mirror rotation is not only a visual phenomenon, but also a motor or kinetic one of the act of writing. The movements that produce a mirror image are different from those that produce a correct one. The perceptual-motor discriminations necessary for the child who is learning to read and write are conceptually confounded by the fact that some characters of the alphabet can be formed with mirror image movements without changing their visible appearance. **H** and **O** can be written in either normal or right-left or near-far mirror script with results that look identical. Any letter that is symmetrical about a vertical midline can be subject to right-left mirror rotation without looking erroneously formed—for example, **A**, **H**, **V**, **W**, **X**. When symmetrical about the horizontal axis, letters may be written with the kinetics of near-far mirror writing without looking altered—for example, **B**, **C**, **D**, **E**, **3**. It is little wonder that the beginning reader, able to rotate some but not others of his graphic movements without producing an erroneous symbol, gets tangled in the confusion of this new experience in concept formation.

Beyond the alphabet, the law of directional or positional constancy applies also to the serial arrangement of letters in words. To have the same meaning, a word must invariably have its letters in the same serial position. It is not sufficient simply to have all the letters included, though jumbled by transposition, as in **distrubance** for **disturbance, ychat** for **yacht, preceed** for **precede,** or **procede** for **proceed.** Transpositions may change the meaning. **Sacred god** does not mean the same as **scared dog.**

Directional constancy in serial arrangement also applies to the syntactical arrangement of words in sentences, insofar as linguistic laws dictate the conventions of word order. Many of these conventions have already been assimilated aurally by the prereader, and these he is ready to translate into written language. Supported by the familiarity of usage, his errors are likely to be not so much transpositions as omissions of words, particularly when the syntactical unit is too lengthy to be grasped quickly.

The Law of Form or Shape Constancy

The law of form constancy supplants the law of object constancy insofar as it dictates that an alphabetic object or character, to retain its meaning, must not transform its shape except within certain prescriptions. Omissions or additions are likely to change one letter into another in such transformations, for example, as

c–e	**f–r**	**i–j**	**k–R**	**y–j**
c–o	**f–t**	**i–T**	**n–m**	**y–g**
C–G	**F–E**	**I–L**	**n–h**	**y–u.**

The trouble with the law of form constancy is that its application is extremely inconstant. The beginning reader is ensnared at the outset into differentiating capitals from lower case, and also variations of font, of which an outstanding discrepancy is the variation between **g** and **g**. To round off the confusion, it is necessary to distinguish and equate print and cursive script. Recognition of all these differences and equalities, added to those pertaining to directional orientation, constitutes a very complex conceptual task. Children bring to it a wide range of competence and preparedness.

The law of form constancy applies also to words since, within the limits of script changes, a word must always have the same lexical form. Transpositions, as already mentioned, are disallowed. So also are additions or omissions: **preceding** may not be expanded to **preceeding,** nor, capriciously, may **proceeding** be condensed to **proceding.** Additions and omissions may change not only the form but also the meaning, as when **scared** becomes **scarred** and **cared,** respectively.

The beginner's difficulty with the law of form constancy can be gauged by the experienced reader if he tests himself with proofreading, especially if the material has previously been read. Then it is fatally easy to miss errors, as **though** for **through, menustration** for **menstruation,** and so forth.

The sources of error in form constancy are often paired look-alikes or sound-alikes such as **their–there, to–too, witch–which,** or **weather–whether.** Behind such an error, one can construe a mental process of conceptual discrimination that can be formulated this way: "One is positive and one is negative, but I cannot select which is which." This same difficulty with discriminating between alternatives can be inferred as lying behind errors of rotation also. Moreover, it reappears at a more complex level of conceptual meaning, namely in such confusions as **into–out of, yesterday–tomorrow, front–back, older–younger,** and **brother–sister,** which are often encountered in young children and in those with reading disability.

In the act of handwriting, errors of form constancy derive from the phenomenon that may be called motor or kinetic overshoot (or undershoot). To illustrate: the initial hand movements and kinesthetic sensations are the same for writing a **b** and a **p** (or *b* and *p*). Though the subsequent movements are different, as may be the positioning on the line, it is easy to see how the habit patterns of the one may translocate inappropriately to the other. This example, **b** and **p**, is unusually instructive because it illustrates the multiple sources of confusion to which a learner is exposed. They are said alike. They sound alike. Visually and graphically they are rotations of each other. Motorically, they begin with the same sweep, downward in print script and upward in cursive script.

Phonemic-Graphemic Matching

Remembering the lexigraphic form of English words is not the same as remembering a random assortment of objects or a vocabulary of Egyptian hieroglyphs or Chinese ideographs. Because written English, despite multiple redundancies and irregularities, is phonetically based, its spelling follows certain predictable regularities. For example, the letters **kw** at the beginning of a word typically signal that the word is Chinese or American Indian in origin, or perhaps African, all other words beginning with this sound being spelled with **qu**. Moreover, the permutations and combinations of phonemic elements to be transposed into phonetic spelling themselves follow the laws of philological and linguistic usage. According to these laws, some phonemic combinations are more probable or more frequent than others, and some are nonoccurring. For example, the chances that the sound **qu** will be followed by a vowel and never a consonant are overwhelmingly strong. Thus, the misprint **qunine** is readily read as **quinine.** Even those who are unfamiliar with the word can guess that one of the five vowels, or a diphthong combination, must be missing, provided that they already have the concept or "feel" of linguistic and orthographic probabilities following **qu**.

The rules of linguistic probabilities in actual usage and the orthographic probabilities by which they are transformed into writing can be explicitly codified and taught. The fact is, however, that no such complete system is actually employed in the teaching of reading and spelling. Reference to rules is, at most, piecemeal—as in teaching the rule of the silent *e*; of dropping a terminal *e* before adding *-ing*; of doubling the terminal consonant in forming the past tense and other derivatives of monosyllables or words accented on the last syllable; the rule of spelling *i* before *e* except after *c*, and so forth. For the most part, the learning process is one of assimilating linguistic-orthographic rules pragmatically as "subliminal concepts"; that is to say, the learner gets a conceptual "feel" of how the written language should look from experience in reading, writing, or spelling it orally.

The development of concepts of what looks right orthographically presupposes the development of ability to analyze the spoken language into component elements. Words are relatively easy to isolate, though the uninitiated may easily write **would of** for **would have,** for example. The real difficulty for the beginner comes in isolating the components of spoken words, the syllables and their sound units, and writing them, that is, turning the phonemes into graphemes. The experiences of everyday life, up to the point of learning to read, do not require such minute attention to the elemental sounds of language. Skill in the principles of how to analyze words phonetically develops simultaneously, therefore, with going to school and becoming skilled in orthographic concepts. The more one knows about the principles of spelling and which words look alike, the easier it will be to syllabify an unfamiliar word and sound out its phonic elements. Conversely, the more one knows of the principles of vocal syllabication and sounding of unfamiliar words, the easier it will be to read or spell them. The two processes are mutually reinforcing.

Development of skill in making the transition back and forth between the two processes, matching the phonetic and the graphic, the acoustic and the visual, is accompanied by a steady increment of words for which the matching has been fully accomplished. These words become part of an inventory of vocabulary that is subject first to instant recognition and, slightly later, to instant recall. This is the vocabulary available for fluent reading and spelling. The words no longer need to be analyzed. They have become unit *gestalten* or configurations in themselves. The size of the inventory will be a function of the speed and efficacy partly of orthographic concept formation and partly of rote or inventory memory.

In a language like Spanish or Polynesian, more phonetically accurate in its spelling than English, the orthographic concepts involved are fewer and more highly generalized, and the number of deviant cases is less numerous. Thus the demands on inventory memory are fewer. It would greatly simplify life for reading teachers and pupils alike if English were to reform to a phonetic script—in much the same way that arithmetical drudgery for British school children will be greatly alleviated by conversion to the decimal system. Perfect phoneticism does not, however, rule out the possibility of reading disability. Dyslexia exists in Latin America. The basic task of oral-visual matching and inventory memory still remains, even though simplified.

Oral-visual matching is the ability to see what one hears and hear what one sees, which is a special instance of the psychological phenomenon of synesthesia, or transfer between the senses. Individual differences in ability to conform to the law of synesthesia in oral-visual (or aural-visual) matching of words are extremely varied. At one extreme are the precocious readers, already able to read at the third- or fourth-grade level by the time they enter school. They work out for themselves the principles of alphabetical notation and the syllabication of words. They do it by matching the printed symbols with the oral narration of stories in their children's books, and by matching voice and script in television commercials, and then matching the script with its replication in magazine advertisements and product-package labels.

At the other extreme are children who have extraordinary difficulty with the matching process, so that their academic progress is retarded, or at least hindered. Such difficulty may exist independently of otherwise superior achievement. The manuscripts of F. Scott Fitzgerald are quite extraordinary for their makeshift phonetic spelling. High-level graduates in medicine and science may have similar difficulty. Here are some typical examples from a young medical student who was by no means inferior in research and clinical performance: **disserpoint** for **disappoint, phisiology** for **psychology, physcian** for **physician, temperal** for **temporal, varibles** for **variables.** Errors of this type were produced more frequently when the student was tired or wrote hurriedly under pressure, but his writing was never entirely free of them; at the time of making them he did not recognize them as errors.

Left-Right and the Body Schema

Among all the possible rotations, the right-left mirror rotation is the most common and creates the most difficulty for the beginner in reading and writing. Why? The answer lies in the basic neuropsychological functioning of the human body and relates to two facts of the body schema: (1) that we are able with our hands to perform operations on ourselves, especially the face, which we cannot see except in the mirror; and (2) that we are partially constructed more or less symmetrically about a midline, with one side being a mirror image of the other.

If you try to write your name with greasepaint or lipstick on your abdomen, your hand will be held in approximately the same position as when you write at a desk. Your name will be legible to you, looking down at it, but to anyone else standing in front of you, it will be upside down.

Now try the experiment of writing your name on your forehead. You are righthanded. First you must rotate your right forearm 180°, exactly as if you had put it through a half-opened window and were trying to write on the glass outside. Imagine yourself writing not on your forehead but on the outside of the pane, so that what you see as you stand on the inside is not rotated, but normally progressing from left to right. Your rotated right arm will feel clumsy, and the kinesthetic sensations will be unfamiliar as your hand reaches to your left to begin writing. When you have finished, what you have written will be in right-left mirror script to anyone standing in front of you—as you can easily prove by holding a piece of card to your forehead, writing on it, then taking it down to inspect the result.

If you try now to write on your forehead, starting from right to left, the unfamiliar feeling of the rotation of your right arm will be offset by the right-to-left rotation of your line of writing. It is the visual image of what you are doing that will seem strange. If you imagine yourself on the inside of an imaginary pane of glass, what you see will be unfamiliar and right-left mirror-rotated, but to a person standing on the outside, facing you, the writing will look normal, as you can prove by using a piece of card again.

If, as a righthanded person, you try this device of writing on your forehead with your left hand, then writing from left to right will usually produce a feeling of unexpected ease and familiarity of movement and muscular sensation. The image of the writing will be in right-left mirror rotation to a person facing you to read it.

If, in the actions of everyday life, one hand replicates the movements of what the other hand might be doing, then automatically both hands move either toward or away from the midline, each mirroring the other in right-left rotation. You may demonstrate to yourself the right-left mirror-image phenomenon in the movements of the two hands if you take a pencil in each hand, place them near the center of the page and begin writing outwards, simultaneously. Without special effort or thought, your left hand will produce a left-right mirror script as:

THGIЯ–TꟻƎ⅃ LEFT–RIGHT

The same facility of the hands to mirror each other can be demonstrated on a musical keyboard, if you begin with the thumbs between, say, two black notes and pay no attention to discord as you move each hand symmetrically outward.

The legs and feet, though able to mirror each other in motion, are less accustomed to it, since they usually move forward or back. Consequently, you will in all likelihood find it easier to trace your name with the toe of your left foot than to write it with your left hand.

The phenomenon of mirrored symmetry about the midline carries through to the cerebral cortex, where the general rule is that the primary sensory and motor representation of each limb is in the opposite cerebral hemisphere, though there are subsidiary cross-connections. Each ear sends connections to both hemispheres, with predominantly fewer to the ipsilateral than the contralateral side. Each eye also connects with each hemisphere. The left half of each retina (and the right half of the visual field) is represented in the occipital lobe of the left hemisphere and the right half of each retina (and the left visual field) in the occipital lobe of the right hemisphere—which means that only half of each retina is represented in the opposite cerebral hemisphere (a fact which is overlooked in a good deal of loose talk about lateral dominance and crossed lateral dominance with reference to use of the eyes versus the hands).

A curious situation exists in the cerebral hemispheres with regard to language. There are two ears to hear with, but there is only one mouth, one tongue, one set of lips, and one set of vocal cords to talk with. The muscles of these organs of speech are separately innervated on the left and right and are separately represented in the contralateral cerebral hemisphere. But the act of speech in the production of words is a unitary act requiring perfect coordination of the left and the right sides of the speech-producing organs. An utterance is produced as a unit entity, not as a right half and a left half that become fused together as the sounds entering each ear become fused together. Nothing in the vocal production of speech corresponds to the binocular effect in vision or the binaural effect in hearing.

It is not too surprising, therefore, that the cerebral representation of utterances is in one hemisphere of the cortex only, by virtue of which this hemisphere is known as the dominant hemisphere. At birth neither hemisphere is dominant, and in the event of injury to, or removal of, one, the other can take over the function of language as maturation and experience increase. After one hemisphere has become dominant, however, damage to the speech and language centers severely impairs language usage and comprehension, as in the varied symptoms of aphasia.

Ordinarily, in the human race the left hemisphere assumes dominance. The determinant is, presumably, hereditary. In some family trees there appears to be a hereditary tendency for the right hemisphere to assume dominance. In these cases, the affected individuals are usually lefthanded, though not invariably so. Among lefthanded people, approximately one third have been found to be right cerebral dominant and two thirds left cerebral dominant for language; and among the righthanded people, 1 per cent have been found to be right cerebral dominant, on the bases of surgical findings in cases of aphasia (Gloning, Gloning, and Hoff, 1963; see also Hécaen and Ajuriaguerra, 1964). Presurgically, the Wada sodium amytal test is a test for language dominance. This is a test in which an injection of amytal sodium into the carotid artery produces brief, transient, aphasic symptoms when injected into the side of the dominant hemisphere, but not into the contralateral side. So far as is known, language is always represented dominantly in one hemisphere and never ambihemispherically, though lefthanders with left cerebral dominance may, following aphasic damage to the dominant hemisphere, recover more successfully than do most aphasics.

This peculiar circumstance of the monohemispheric representation of language usage and comprehension stands in contrast to the bihemispheric ipsi- and contralateral representation of acoustic reception. It stands also in contrast to the contralateral bihemispheric representation of the motor expression of language in left- and righthanded writing. Even more complexly, it stands in contrast to the partially contralateral, partially ipsilateral, bihemispheric representation of visually perceived language, namely, reading.

The theoretical literature on specific language disability, including reading disability, pays a good deal of attention to the fact of cerebral dominance in language representation. Orton proposed the idea that in the linguistically handicapped child the dominance of one hemisphere is not fully established, there being a competition between the two hemispheres or a mixed lateral dominance. He further proposed that each hemisphere linguistically reflects the other in mirror image, the nondominant hemisphere being a weakened copy of the dominant. Thus could he explain the appearance of mirror-image writing as a product of rivalry between the two hemispheres in cases of mixed lateral dominance. There are many problems in this theory. Empirically, it cannot be demonstrated that the language functions of the dominant hemisphere are mirror-replicated in the nondominant hemisphere. It can be shown only that the motor representations of the left and right limbs are mirrored copies of each other in the right and left hemispheres, respectively.

Further, it is not possible to demonstrate that mixed dominance of the two hemispheres exists for language per se. Mixed dominance must be inferred from motor movements, as when a person is right-handed but leftfooted. Traditionally, sighting tests are combined with tests of handedness and footedness, which is completely unscientific, since each hemisphere of the brain receives part of the optic nerve and part of the eye-muscle nerve supply of both the left eye and the right eye.

Yet further, it cannot always be demonstrated that mixed lateral preference exists, according to the tests used, in cases of specific language disability.[1] The obverse also holds, namely, that children may show mixed lateral preference without having speech or reading problems. According to the theory, completely ambidextrous people ought to be gravely beset by developmental language and reading problems, but that is not the case either.

All in all, it is clear that the attempt to relate reading disability to cerebral dominance should not be in terms of a theory of simple hemispheric rivalry or mixed dominance. It makes more sense to see the issue as one of the relationship between unilateral versus bilateral representation of functions related to language in its many facets.

Hypothetically, it can be readily recognized that there are places of potential dysjunction between the unilateral representation of language usage and comprehension versus the bilateral representation of (a) the acoustic reception of language and (b) the kinetic, manual expression of language in writing, and versus (c) the semi-crossed, semi-uncrossed representation of visually perceived language in reading. It is, perhaps, little wonder that these places of potential dysjunction sometimes, and for a variety of reasons not always known, permit the development of symptoms of impaired speech, as in stuttering and cluttering, and of impaired reading skill, as in reading retardation and specific developmental dyslexia.

Deficits and Impairments

It takes time for a beginning reader to make a successful accommodation to the demands of rendering oral language visual. The alert observer

[1] Balow, 1963; Belmont and Birch, 1963, 1965; Coleman and Deutsch, 1964; Flescher, 1962; Malmquist, 1958; Spitzer, Rabkin and Kramer, 1959; Silver and Hagin, 1960; Vickery, 1962.

will catch many examples of a beginner's rotations, transpositions, omissions, additions, and phonetic-graphic matching errors. He may also miss them, for some children make exceptionally rapid progress, like those who teach themselves to read with minimal tutoring before they enter school.

By contrast, there are other children who procrastinate at the beginner's level, unable to come to terms with the conceptual demands and rules of rendering oral language visual. Some few of these slow ones will stay stuck at the beginner's level for very long periods of time, perhaps indefinitely, handicapped by some intractable impediment to learning.

There are many sources of impediments to learning, whether learning of school subjects in general or of reading in particular. They range from the specific, as in poor vision or hearing, to the general, as in chronic debility or mental deficiency. They include divergencies as great as localized malfunction of, or injury to, the brain versus life history-generated learning blocks. In fundamental etiology they may be genetic, or the result of physiological insult to the developing fetus, or of traumatic fetal injury at birth. After birth, infections or trauma may have an adverse effect. Or lack of exposure to the proper experiential stimulation at the proper time (the critical period) in behavioral and linguistic growth and differentiation may leave a lasting handicap. Later deprivation may take the form of inadequate teaching. A continuing merry-go-round of pathological family relationships may also have a deleterious effect on learning. Within the family and beyond, the social traditions of the community may include an approval of illiteracy or quasiliteracy, or at least a tolerance of incomplete schooling and inadequate pedagogy. Supplanting the standards of family and community, the ideals and traditions of the peer group may also put no premium on academic survival, so that to be a "big shot" means to have achieved status as a nonlearner and perhaps to be a graduate in delinquency as well.

However varied the ultimate sources or origins of learning blockage, in learning to read the outcome is the same. There is a failure to get started or to continue to make progress—constant failure to progress beyond the beginner's tell-tale errors, which typically are rotations, inaccuracies of form, wrong sequence, and phonetic faults. Later, if partial progress is made despite the blockage, the beginner's stage and its errors may be surpassed, the chief symptom then being retarded achievement relative to age.

Errors of rotation, form, sequence, or phonetic transcription are not pathognomic of any particular diagnosis, etiologically. They are indicative only of developmental dyslexia with arrest at an immature level. Whether developmental dyslexia will be qualified as specific or not will depend on whether there is a discrepancy between the level of achievement in reading and that in other activities of life (including earning power) or other school subjects. It will depend also, by and large, on whether there is a discrepancy between reading achievement and IQ level.

In the etiology of developmental dyslexia, the eyes are sometimes implicated as the primary offenders. Typically, however, the retarded reader has no optical problem that can be corrected by wearing glasses and, if he does, then the wearing of glasses is not followed by reading improvement. Should the problem be one of the ocular muscles, then eye fatigue and headache may have an adverse effect on learning, though not only on learning to read. There may be improvement following orthoptic therapy or surgical correction. There are many cases, nonetheless, of severe optic or ocular defect in which reading progress is average or even superior.

The ears, like the eyes, also have been implicated as primary offenders. On the face of it, it seems reasonable to suppose that the child who is hard of hearing will have difficulty with visual language that he cannot properly discriminate aurally. The fact is, however, that visual language is a substitute for auditory. It is the academic salvation of some children with defective hearing. Moreover, it is rare that the child who is retarded in reading can be shown to be acoustically impaired. He may, however, have been slow in general language development, with unduly prolonged persistence of baby talk and other errors of articulation. Developmentally, he may have had trouble integrating speech heard with speech spoken, just as he later has difficulty integrating auditory-spoken language with visual-written language. Yet, such is by no means invariably the case.

It is fashionable today to talk of minimal brain damage in relation to reading disability. This is really begging the question. In the majority of cases no kind of brain damage can be demonstrated by today's techniques. It is simply inferred from the phenomena of the learning block itself and from the fact that some children with other symptoms of suspected minimal brain damage (hyperactivity, distractibility, labile emotionality) are also retarded learners relative to IQ.

Electroencephalographic abnormalities are sometimes called upon in support of the hypothesis of minimal brain damage. It is true that some studies of retarded readers have shown an overabundance of minor EEG anomalies relative to age, especially the persistence of infantile wave patterns. These same anomalies are seen in other children with quite different developmental diagnoses, and they are also seen in children with no diagnosis at all. They do not, therefore, strongly support a specific relationship between abnormal brain function and reading disability. Rather, they should be construed as indicating a maturational anomaly, most commonly a maturational lag.

By far the most useful hypothesis, in this matter of brain function and reading disability, is not a quasineurological one at all, but a neuropsychological one of maturational lag. Then it can be allowed that some cases of maturational lag in reading may be a sequel to known, demonstrable brain pathology, even though disability specific to reading is rare in cases of brain pathology in childhood. The great majority of reading disability cases will be classifiable not on the basis of brain pathology, but simply as representative of a lag in the functional development of the brain and nervous system that subserves the learning of reading.

Functional Maturational Lag

Functional maturational lag may show itself in a variety of ways and at various stages of development. Thus, a child may be behind in reaching the milestones of motor development, like sitting and walking. Later, in infancy and childhood, he may be clumsy and unskilled in coordination. Language development may be slow, articulation, vocabulary, and syntax all being affected. Control of the body may also be tardy, as in poor food habits, poor sleeping and waking habits, and poor toilet control. Perhaps there may be persistence of infantile rocking and swaying movements and of head-banging or temper tantrums. Sensory discrimination, if tested, may be found immature, as may pattern recognition. Hoffman (1964) applied an ingenious mathematical model to the retinal explanation of visual pattern recognition and erroneous recognition, as in dyslexia. Immaturity may also be found in intersensory transfer. Intersensory transfer is the ability to transfer a stimulus from one sensory modality to the other, as, for example, the ability to recognize the same Morse code signal in print, on the air, or tapped onto one's hand. Delayed maturation or impairment of intersensory transfer is believed to be the factor responsible for some cases of language disability, including reading disability (Birch and Belmont, 1964; see also Bridger and Blank, 1966).

Functional lag in relation to reading may on occasion be traced to family tree heredity (as contrasted with sporadic or mutational heredity), for there is sometimes multiple occurrence of reading disability in families. Such multiple occurrence does not in itself prove inheritance, however, since various members of the same family line may have been exposed to the same antiacademic influences, and younger ones may have identified themselves with and patterned themselves after older, dyslexic ones. Only a detailed clinical history and psychological test record will provide the data for a balanced judgment as to etiology in such a family. Test data alone, without the clinical history, do not permit a diagnosis to be established.

Functional maturational lag in learning to read may in some cases be attributed to a specific neuropsychological deficit analogous to the type of deficit found in color blindness or in tone deafness. Color blindness is not grossly incapacitating, though it would be disastrous for a color-blind person to take up interior decorating, fabric designing, fashion, paint mixing, or other occupations requiring the use of color or the decipherment of color signals. Even in the fine arts, however, a color-blind artist is not necessarily disqualified. He may achieve fame, as Daumier did, by concentrating on drawing with monochromatic rather than polychromatic tinting.

Like color blindness, the neuropsychological disabilities that may underlie reading retardation are not grossly incapacitating for all activities and accomplishments in life. The dyslexic boy, scarcely able to read road signs, may be able to earn a living as a truck driver or mechanic, relatively well skilled in the maintenance of automobile engines, provided that his reading disability is not secondary to a problem in conceptualizing shapes and form relationships.

There are, by contrast, some cases of developmental dyslexia that are apparently derived specifically from a disability for, or developmental slowness in, conceptualizing shapes in two or three dimensions. Neuropsychologically, this difficulty may be labeled space-form dysgnosia. Case 1 in Part III is an example of such a boy. It is not possible, however, to maintain that all people with space-form dysgnosia will have difficulty with reading. Girls with Turner's syndrome, a condition characterized by various birth deformities and by a hereditary defect, namely, absence (or mosaicism) of one of the X chromosomes, frequently exhibit a degree of space-form blindness and also of disability for right-left directional sense,[2] yet they have no corresponding reading

[2] Alexander, Ehrhardt, and Money, 1966; Alexander and Money, 1965, 1966; Alexander, Walker, and Money, 1964; Money, 1963; Money and Alexander, 1966; Shaffer, 1962; Walker, 1965.

deficit. Evidently, therefore, a space-form deficit creates reading problems only if in the brain it is related to the areas and circuits that mediate language, and the same holds for directional sense deficit.

Some cases of developmental dyslexia appear to be derived from a directional sense disability, or developmental slowness in conceptualizing the position of the body in space, particularly in relation to the left-right dimension. Children with this kind of handicap are slow to distinguish their own left and right. They are slow to pass to the next stages of ability to identify left and right on a person standing before them, to walk (or draw) an imaginary block plan following oral instructions to turn left or right, and to read a road map with left and right turns both going away and coming back. These same children are prone, at a late age in development, to be unable to write in a straight line, being unable to resist the rivalry of right over left or vice versa, if they are lefthanded. They are pulled diagonally up or down the page, even to the point of writing in a clockwise direction (anticlockwise, if they are lefthanded). In a very minor way, their writing adumbrates the whirling of autistic and schizophrenically defective children, who also have problems of orienting their bodies in space. Case 2 in Part III is an example of this type of disability, though it is complicated also by severe pathology of intrafamilial relationships.

Directional sense disability is in some cases associated with another problem of conceptualizing the body in space, namely, finger agnosia (or dysgnosia). Affected children are slow in developing the ability to discriminate whether two adjacent or two nonadjacent fingers are touched, in a finger gnosis test, or whether a single finger is touched simultaneously in two places. They are also slow in achieving ability to match the feel of a shape, held but not seen, with its matching twin which is seen but not held. Examples of this symptom, among others, in cases of reading disability are given in the studies by Kinsbourne and Warrington in Part III.

Autism, already mentioned, or an autistic tendency may itself be the basic disability underlying failure to make progress in reading, since all of language and communication is likely to be affected. Case 3 in Part III is an illustrative example. In this case, the child's eccentric and bizarre private conceptual world contaminated all of her academic development. Unable to abide consistently by the symbolic codes and conventions of the speech and writing that other people live by, the girl inevitably became retarded educationally, yet not in the manner of simple mental deficiency.

In a case like this it is quite to be expected that antithetical opinions will be found regarding the cause of the condition. Psychiatric research has itself not been able to settle the issue of life-history and social versus genetic, metabolic, and somatic determinants of schizophrenia. In Case 3, the child had been very early adopted into a family that, on the face of things, did not appear to be unwittingly conspiring to reinforce schizoid tendencies and/or learning disability problems in the child—a conspiracy that can readily be observed in some families.

Case 2 is a case of family-reinforced disability. In the saga of this family, it is easy to see that the mother and father were hopelessly disaligned, as were the father and only son. Mother and son were close. The mother unwittingly maneuvered to maintain her son's closeness by acts presumably beneficial to, but actually of sabotage against, his school progress. Her protection of him entailed feuding with school authorities. Symbolically, she was saving her son from growing up to be sexually abnormal like the man she erroneously interpreted her husband to be. There is a possibility, in such a pathological complementarity of family relationships, that something adverse happens maturationally in infancy during a critical period that will have a chronic and deleterious effect on subsequent learning. Thus the problems of directional confusion already mentioned in Case 2 might not have been congenital but the result of a persistently enduring imprint. Alternatively, they may have been congenital (a paternal uncle was allegedly a complete dyslexic) and simply capitalized upon within the interpersonal pathology of the family, in much the same way as a newborn baby's hydrocephalus might be used to separate estranged parents still further.

The problem of congenital disposition versus a critical period imprint appears also in cases of school failure (often ending as school dropouts) associated with delinquent irresponsibility and antisocial acting out. The boy in Case 4, Part III, is from a disturbed family, and he himself appeared to be particularly disturbed by the acquisition of a stepfather at the time when he should have been consolidating basic reading skills. At the age of fourteen he still had persistent disability in the concept of phonetic-graphic matching and the syllabication of words. It is possible that he became fixated at an immature level and became an underachiever as a side effect of his home problems. In the absence of a good longitudinal record of school achievement levels and the onset of failure, the issue cannot be properly decided, for a genetic factor is also possible. This patient has an underachieving half-sister, and he is the cousin of the boy in Case 1, so some common hereditary factor may be shared. Case 4 did not, however, share Case 1's space-form conceptual problems.

Case 4 raises the cart-and-horse controversy of whether the boy became delinquent in response to being an academic nonentity needing recognition and a sense of being somebody, or whether, having developed or established the temperamental traits essential to the irresponsible or antisocial personality, he was in essence a nonlearner from the beginning.

The same cart-and-horse problem arises with regard to Case 5 in Part III. This boy also is an all-round nonachiever. The question is whether he is functionally illiterate at age nine because of lack of schooling, or whether he managed to maneuver within his gifted but psychologically disturbed family to be exempted from schooling because he himself was too neurotically disturbed to put forth the effort to become literate. If the latter, then the next question is whether his own personality development has proceeded in such a way that he will always have a blockage against learning. Here is yet another of the series of questions that will be answered only as the result of painstaking record-keeping in longitudinal research, which is still pitifully insufficient.

Sex Ratio: A Hypothesis

It has long been known that reading retardation is more common in boys than girls (Bentzen, 1963), the ratio being as many as four or six to one. This discrepancy is, of course, easy enough to explain away as simply a by-product of the expectancies of the cultural pattern and the values that boys, as opposed to girls, live by. Yet so simple an explanation does not take account of the fact that the culture has traditionally defined literacy as a male prerogative and renown in literature as a male privilege. While not ignoring the cultural pattern, it is necessary to look beyond it to a factor that may indeed have helped to shape it. This factor is a sex difference in itself and pertains to the fact that in the human species, as in various other mammalian species, it is the male, in contrast to the female, who establishes territory rights in mating. Relative to other species, territoriality as phylogenetically stereotyped behavior is not strongly or rigidly determined in the human male, and in some individuals it is much weaker than in others. That it is present, however, can be seen even in the play of children. From early infancy onward, more boys than girls get killed at play, according to the statistics of widely disparate countries. They do so because they expend more energy, explore further, encroach on more dangerous places and creatures, and engage in more lethal activities. In middle childhood, while girls are playing house and mothers and fathers with dolls, boys are making dens, forts, camps, and tree houses, and are scouting territory. In late childhood and adolescence comes the gang age, when boys rove in troops, pitting their wits against other troops, even challenging them to cross territorial boundaries.

Developmentally, boys, according to a recent study (Money, Alexander, and Walker, 1965), have a slight edge over girls in the development of right-left discrimination in map reading—which may conceivably be related biologically to the male trait of territoriality. Moreover, a group of boys in summer school classes for dyslexia showed themselves developmentally retarded on this same map-reading test.

Now it is known in embryology that the making of a male embryo is more complex than the making of a female, in the sense that something must be added before the male embryo can develop male organs. This something is male sex hormone (or organizer substance), and without it the genetic male embryo will develop a female sexual morphology. One may say it is more difficult for nature to make a male. It is also more difficult for her to keep him alive. The birth ratio is 106 males to 100 females. The males die off more quickly, so that the sex ratio is equalized by the fifth decade. It also appears more difficult for nature to effect a male than a female psychosexual differentiation after birth, for males, more than females, develop psychosexual anomalies—the exact ratio being unascertained.

Perhaps, therefore, it is not unreasonable to suggest that it is also difficult for nature to effect a development of territoriality and direction sense in the male. Those males who encounter difficulty and who, at the same time, encounter a strong social challenge to succeed are, it might one day be shown, unable to attend to this task and to school learning as well, and so they may become nonlearners, disabled readers, school dropouts, and delinquents. By contrast, the males who either encounter no difficulty or respect no challenge from a demanding social environment in this matter of territoriality and its corollary of direction sense encounter no difficulty with literacy. From their ranks are drawn the literary greats.

Summary

The law of object constancy must, in the visual symbolism of reading, be partially replaced by the laws of directional constancy and form constancy. Until he has accomplished this transition, the beginning learner is liable to make errors of rotation and wrong form of letters and of their serial sequence. Of all possible rotations, those of right-left mirror rotation are the most common. This circumstance can be related to the fact that mirror rotation occurs when with our hands we do things on certain parts of our own bodies, notably the face. It can also be related to the fact that we are constructed on a midline, so that when the left and right hand replicate each other, they automatically perform in right-left mirror rotation.

The hands and arms are cerebrally represented on the contralateral hemispheres, though with subsidiary cross-connections, as are the left and right sides of the face and the organs of speech. But speech itself and language comprehension, which do not have two halves, are unitarily represented in one, the dominant cerebral hemisphere. The dominant hemisphere is usually the left in righthanded persons, though not invariably so, and vice versa for lefthanded persons. Each ear sends connections to each hemisphere and each eye also is cerebrally represented in both cerebral hemispheres, the left half of each retina (and therefore the right half of the visual field) in the left hemisphere and vice versa in the right hemisphere. Complexities of cerebral interrelationship between these different schemes of cerebral localization are more likely to account for language and reading disability than is a simplistic hypothesis of imperfect cerebral dominance.

Visual or acoustic impairment cannot as a matter of course be implicated as etiological factors in reading retardation. Nothing is gained by postulating the disability as an effect of minimal brain damage. It is more sensible to use a hypothesis of functional maturational lag. This maturational delay does not necessarily have only one single cause. It may be the end result of several different responsible agents. Two possible neuropsychological deficits that may tie in with reading disability are disability for conceptualizing space-form relationships and disability for right-left orientation in space—though both disabilities may exist without concomitant reading disability.

The sex difference in children with reading disability, with a preponderance of boys, is largely unexplained. One hypothesis relates it to the greater vulnerability of the male than of the female in sexual differentiation, whether in embryonic development, childhood psychosexual development, or adolescent territoriality behavior.

CHAPTER 3

EXPERIMENTAL PSYCHOLOGY OF LEARNING TO READ

ELEANOR J. GIBSON

Ever since free public education became a fact, educators and the public have exhibited a keen interest in the teaching of reading, historically reviewed by Fries (1963). Either because of or despite their interest, this most important subject has been remarkably susceptible to the influence of fads and fashions and curiously unaffected by disciplined experimental and theoretical psychology. The psychologists have traditionally pursued the study of verbal learning by means of experiments with nonsense syllables and the like—that is, with materials carefully divested of useful information. And the educators, who found little in this work that seemed relevant to the classroom, have stayed with the classroom; when they performed experiments, the method was apt to be a gross comparison of classes privileged and unprivileged with respect to the latest fad. The result has been two cultures, the pure scientists in the laboratory, and the practical teachers ignorant of the progress that has been made in the theory of human learning and in methods of studying it.

That this split was unfortunate is clear enough. True, most children do learn to read. But some learn to read badly, so that school systems must provide remedial clinics; and a small proportion (but still a large number of future citizens) remain functional illiterates. The fashions which have led to classroom experiments, such as the "whole word" method, emphasis on context and pictures for "meaning," the "flash" method, "speed reading," revised alphabets, and the "return to phonics," have done little to change the situation.

Yet a systematic approach to the understanding of reading skill is possible. The psychologist has only to treat reading as a learning problem in order to apply ingenuity in theory construction and experimental design to this fundamental activity on which the rest of man's education depends. A beginning has recently been made in this direction, and it can be expected that a number of theoretical and experimental studies of reading will be forthcoming.[1]

Analysis of the Reading Process

A prerequisite to good research on reading is a psychological analysis of the reading process. What is it that a skilled reader has learned? Knowing this (or having a pretty good idea of it), one may consider first how the skill is learned, and next, how it could best be taught. Hypotheses designed to answer all three of these questions can then be tested by experiment.

There are several ways of characterizing the behavior we call reading. It is receiving communication; it is making discriminative responses to graphic symbols; it is decoding graphic symbols to speech; and it is getting meaning from the printed page. A child in the early stages of acquiring reading skill may not be doing all these things, however. Some aspects of reading must be mastered before others and have an essential function in a sequence of development of the final skill. The average child, when he begins learning to read, has already mastered to a marvelous extent the art of communication. He can speak and understand his own language in a fairly complex way, employing units of language organized in a hierarchy and with a grammatical structure. Since a writing system must correspond to the spoken one, and since speech is prior to writing, the framework and unit structure of speech will determine more or less the structure of the writing system, though the rules of correspondence vary for different languages and writing systems. Some alphabetical writing systems have almost perfect single-letter-to-sound correspondences, but some, like English, have far more complex correspondences between spelling patterns and speech patterns. Whatever the nature of the correspondences, it is vital to a proper analysis of the reading task that they be understood. And it is vital to remember, as well, that the first stage in the child's mastery of reading is learning to communicate by means of spoken language.

[1] In 1959, Cornell University was awarded a grant for a Basic Research Project on Reading by the Cooperative Research Program of the Office of Education, U.S. Department of Health, Education and Welfare. Most of the work reported in this chapter was supported by the grant. The Office of Education has recently organized "Project Literacy," which will promote research on reading in a number of laboratories, as well as encourage mutual understanding between experimentalists and teachers of reading.

Once a child begins his progression from spoken language to written language, there are, I think, three phases of learning to be considered. They present three different kinds of learning tasks, and they are roughly sequential, though there must be considerable overlapping. These three phases are learning to differentiate graphic symbols, learning to decode letters to sounds ("map" the letters into sounds), and using units of structure of a progressively higher order. I shall consider these three stages in order and in some detail and describe experiments exploring each stage.

Differentiation of Written Symbols

Making any discriminative response to printed characters is considered by some a kind of reading. A very young child, or even a monkey, can be taught to point to a patch of yellow color, rather than a patch of blue, when the printed characters *YELLOW* are presented. Various people, in recent popular publications, have seriously suggested teaching infants to respond discriminatively in this way to letter patterns, implying that this is teaching them to "read." Such responses are not reading, however; reading entails decoding to speech. Letters are, essentially, an instruction to produce a given speech sound.

Nevertheless, differentiation of written characters from one another is a logical preliminary stage to decoding them to speech. The learning problem is one of discriminating and recognizing a set of line figures, all very similar in a number of ways (for example, all are tracings on paper) and each differing from all the others in one or more features (as, straight versus curved). The differentiating features must remain invariant under certain transformations (size, brightness, and perspective transformations, as well as less easily described ones produced by different type faces and handwritings). They must therefore be relational, so that these transformations will not destroy them.

It might be questioned whether learning is necessary for these figures to be discriminated from one another. This question has been investigated by Gibson, Gibson, Pick, and Osser (1962). In order to trace the development of letter differentiation as it is related to those features of letters which are critical for the task, we designed specified transformations for each of a group of standard, artificial, letter-like forms comparable to printed Roman capitals. Variants were constructed from each standard figure to yield the following twelve transformations for each one: three degrees of transformation from line to curve; five transformations of rotation or reversal; two perspective transforma-

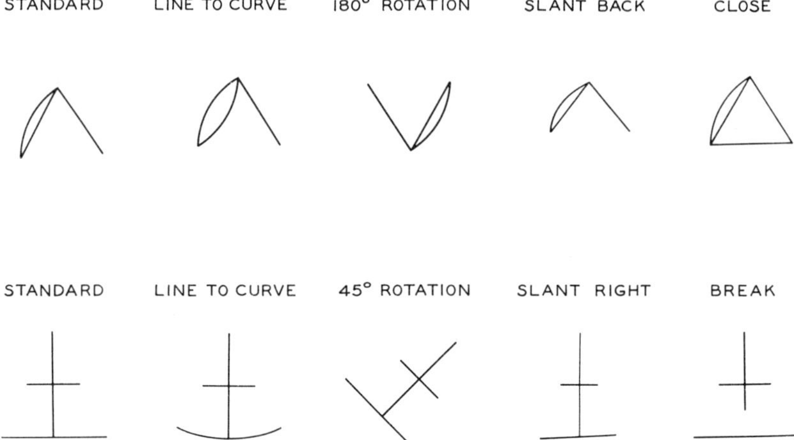

Figure 1. Examples of letter-like figures illustrating different types of transformation.

tions; and two topological transformations (see Fig. 1 for examples). All of these except the perspective transformations we considered critical for discriminating letters. For example, contrast **v** and **u**; **c** and **u**; **o** and **c**.

The discrimination task required the subject to match a standard figure against all of its transformations and some copies of it and to select only identical copies. An error score (the number of times an item that was not an identical copy was selected) was obtained for each child, and the errors were classified according to the type of transformation. The subjects were children aged four through eight years. As would be expected, the visual discrimination of these letter-like forms improved from age four to age eight, but the slopes of the error curves were different, depending on the transformation to be discriminated (Fig. 2). In other words, some transformations are harder to discriminate than others, and improvement occurs at different rates for different transformations. Even the youngest subjects made relatively few errors involving changes of break or close, and among the eight-year-olds these errors dropped to zero. Errors for perspective transformations were very numerous among four-year-olds and still numerous among eight-year-olds. Errors for rotations and reversals started high but dropped to nearly zero by eight years of age. Errors for changes from line to curve were relatively numerous (depending on the number of changes) among the youngest children and showed a rapid drop among the older ones—almost to zero for the eight-year-olds.

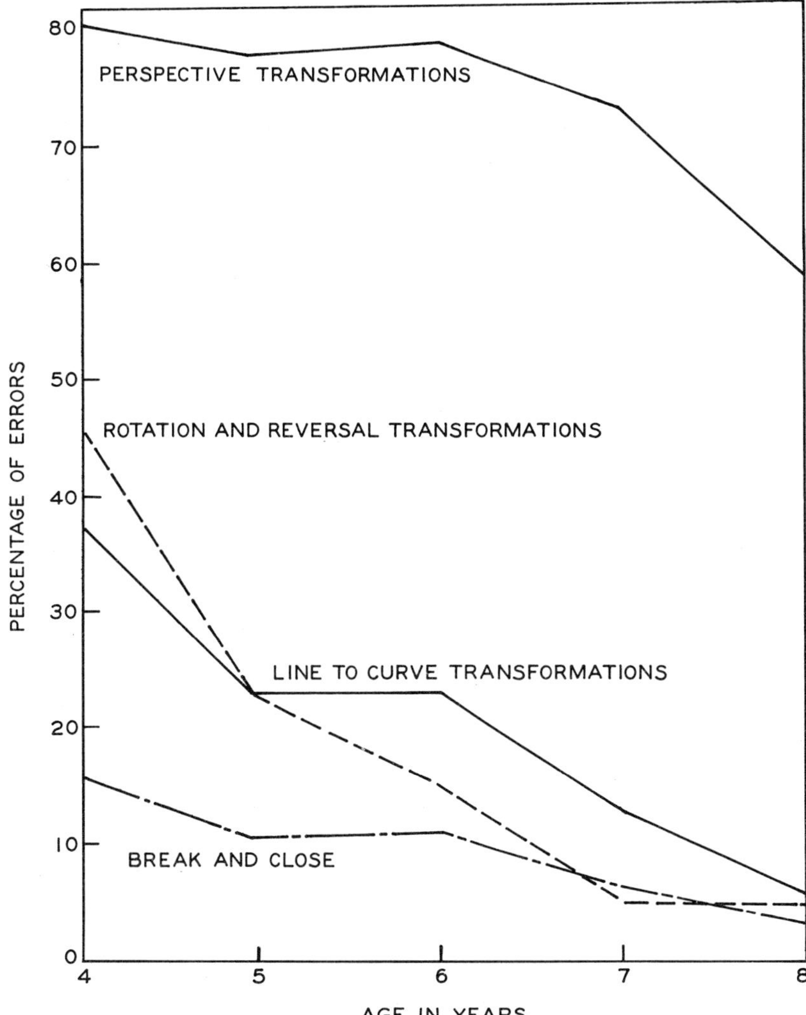

Figure 2. Error curves showing rate of improvement in discriminating four types of transformation.

The experiment was replicated with the same transformations of real letters on the five-year-old group. The correlation between confusions of the same transformations for real letters and for the letter-like forms was very high ($r = +0.87$), so the effect of a given transformation has generality (is not specific to a given form).

What happens, in the years from four to eight, to produce or hamper improvement in discrimination? Our results suggest that the children have learned the features or dimensions of difference which are critical for differentiating letters. Some differences are critical, such as break versus close, line versus curve, and rotations and reversals, but some, such as the perspective transformations, are not, and must in fact be tolerated. The child of four does not start "cold" upon this task because some of his previous experience with distinctive features of objects and pictures will transfer to letter differentiation. But the set of letters has a unique feature pattern for each of its members, so learning of the distinctive features goes on during the period we investigated.

If this interpretation is correct, it would be useful to know just what the distinctive features of letters are. What dimensions of difference must a child learn to detect in order to perceive each letter as unique? Gibson, Osser, Schiff, and Smith (1963) investigated this question. Our method[2] was to draw up a chart of the features of a given set of letters, test to see which of these letters were most frequently confused by prereading children, and compare the errors in the resulting "confusion matrix" with those predicted by the feature chart.

A set of distinctive features for letters must be relational in the sense that each feature presents a contrast which is invariant under certain transformations, and it must yield a unique pattern for each letter. The set must also be reasonably economical. Two feature lists which satisfy these requirements for a specified type face were tried out against the results of a confusion matrix obtained with the same type (simplified Roman capitals available on a sign-typewriter).

Each of the features in the list in Table 1 is or is not a characteristic of each of the twenty-six letters. Regarding each letter, one asks, for example, "Is there a curved segment?" and gets a yes or no answer. A filled-in feature chart gives a unique pattern for each letter. However, the number of potential features for letter shapes is very large and would vary from one alphabet and type font to another. Whether or not we have the right set can be tested with a confusion matrix. Children should confuse with greatest frequency the letters having the smallest number of feature differences, if the features have been chosen correctly.

[2] The method was greatly influenced by the analysis of distinctive features of phonemes by Jakobsen and Halle (1956). A table of twelve features, each in binary opposition, yields a unique pattern for all phonemes, so that any one is distinguishable from any other by its pattern of attributes. A pair of phonemes may differ by any number of features, the minimal distinction being one-feature opposition. The features must be invariant under certain transformations and essentially relational, so as to remain distinctive over a wide range of speakers, intonations, and so on.

Table 1. Tabulations of a "feature chart." Whether the features chosen are actually effective for discriminating letters must be determined by experiment.

Features	A	B	C	E	K	L	N	U	X	Z
Straight segment										
Horizontal	+			+		+				+
Vertical		+		+	+	+	+			
Oblique /	+				+				+	+
Oblique \	+				+		+		+	
Curve										
Closed		+								
Open vertically								+		
Open horizontally			+							
Intersection	+	+		+	+				+	
Redundancy										
Cyclic change		+		+						
Symmetry	+	+	+	+	+			+	+	
Dicontinuity										
Vertical	+				+				+	
Horizontal				+		+	+			+

We obtained our confusion matrix from four-year-old children, who made matching judgments of letters, programmed so that every letter had an equal opportunity to be mistaken for any other, without bias from order effects. The "per cent feature difference" for any two letters was determined by dividing the total number of features possessed by either letter, but not both, by the total number possessed by both, whether shared or not. Correlations were then calculated between per cent feature difference and number of confusions, one for each letter. The feature list of Table 1 yielded twelve out of twenty-six positive significant correlations. Prediction from this feature list is fairly good, in view of the fact that features were not weighted. A multidimensional analysis of the matrix corroborated the choice of the curve-straight and obliqueness variables, suggesting that these features may have priority in the discrimination process, and perhaps developmentally. Refinement of the feature list will take these facts into account, and other methods of validation will be tried.

Detecting Distinctive Features

If we are correct in thinking that the child comes to discriminate graphemes by detecting their distinctive features, what is the learning process like? That it is perceptual learning and need not be verbalized is probable (though teachers do often call attention to contrasts between letter shapes). An experiment by Pick (1965) was designed to compare two hypotheses about how this type of discrimination develops. One might be called a "schema" or "prototype" hypothesis and is based on the supposition that the child builds up a kind of model or memory image of each letter by repeated experience of visual presentations of the letter; perceptual theories which propose that discrimination occurs by matching sensory experience to a previously stored concept of categorical model are of this kind. In the other hypothesis it is assumed that the child learns by discovering how the forms differ, and then easily transfers this knowledge to new letter-like figures.

Pick employed a transfer design in stage 1 in which subjects were presented with initially confusable stimuli (letter-like forms) and were trained to discriminate between them. In stage 2 (the transfer stage) the subjects were divided into three groups. One experimental group was given sets of stimuli to discriminate which varied in new dimensions from the same standards discriminated in stage 1. A second experimental group was given sets of stimuli which deviated from new standards, but in the same dimensions of difference discriminated in stage 1. A control group was given both new standards and new dimensions of difference to discriminate in stage 2. Better performance by the first experimental group would suggest that discrimination learning proceeded by construction of a model or memory image of the standards against which the variants could be matched. Conversely, better performance by the second experimental group would suggest that dimensions of difference had been detected.

The subjects were kindergarten children. The stimuli were letter-like forms of the type described earlier. There were six standard forms and six transformations of each of them. The transformations consisted of two changes of line to curve, a right-left reversal, a 45° rotation, a perspective transformation, and a size transformation. Table 2 gives the errors of discrimination for all three groups in stage 2. Both experimental groups performed significantly better than the control group, but the group that had familiar transformations of new standards performed significantly better than the group given new transformations of old standards.

We infer from these results that, while children probably do learn prototypes of letter shapes, the prototypes themselves are not the original basis for differentiation. The most relevant kind of training for discrimination is practice which provides experience with the characteristic differences that distinguish the set of items. Features which are actually distinctive for letters could be emphasized by presenting letters in contrast pairs.

Table 2. Number of errors made in transfer stage by groups with three types of training

Group	Type of Training		Errors
	Standards	Transformations	
E1	Same	Different	69
E2	Different	Same	39
C	Different	Different	101

Decoding Letters to Sounds

When the graphemes are reasonably discriminable from one another, the decoding process becomes possible. This process, as common sense and many psychologists would tell us, is simply a matter of associating a graphic stimulus with the appropriate spoken response—that is to say, it is the traditional stimulus-response paradigm, a kind of paired-associate learning.

Obvious as this description seems, problems arise when one takes a closer look. Here are just a few. The graphic code is related to the speech code by rules of correspondence. If these rules are known, decoding of new items is predictable. Do we want to build up, one by one, automatically cued responses, or do we want to teach with transfer in mind? If we want to teach for transfer, how do we do it? Should the child be aware that this is a code game with rules? Or will induction of the rules be automatic? What units of both codes should we start with? Should we start with single letters, in the hope that knowledge of single letter-to-sound relationships will yield the most transfer? Or should we start with whole words, in the hope that component relationships will be induced?

Bishop (1964) investigated the question of the significance of knowledge of component letter-sound relationships in reading new words. In her experiment, the child's process of learning to read was simulated by teaching adult subjects to read some Arabic words. The purpose was to determine the transfer value of training with individual letters as opposed to whole words, and to investigate the role of component letter-sound associations in transfer to learning new words.

A three-stage transfer design was employed. The letters were twelve

Arabic characters, each with a one-to-one letter-sound correspondence. There were eight consonants and four vowels, which were combined to form two sets of eight Arabic words. The twelve letters appeared at least once in both sets of words. A native speaker of the language recorded on tape the twelve letter sounds and the two sets of words. The graphic form of each letter or word was printed on a card.

The subjects were divided into three groups—the letter training group (*L*), the whole-word training group (*W*), and a control group (*C*). Stage 1 of the experiment was identical for all groups. The subjects learned to pronounce the set of words (transfer set) which would appear in stage 3 by listening to the recording and repeating the words. Stage 2 varied. Group *L* listened to and repeated the twelve letter-sounds and then learned to associate the individual graphic shapes with their correct sounds. Group *W* followed the same procedure, except that eight words were given them to learn, rather than letters. Learning time was equal for the two groups. Group *C* spent the same time interval on an unrelated task. Stage 3 was the same for the three groups. All subjects learned to read the set of words they had heard in stage 1, responding to the presentation of a word on a card by pronouncing it. This was the transfer stage on which the three groups were compared.

At the close of stage 3, all subjects were tested on their ability to give the correct letter sound following the presentation of each printed letter. They were asked afterward to explain how they tried to learn the transfer words.

Figure 3 shows that learning took place in fewest trials for the letter group and next fewest for the word group. That is, letter training had more transfer value than word training, but word training did produce some transfer. The subjects of group *L* also knew, on the average, a greater number of component letter-sound correspondences, but some subjects in group *W* had learned all twelve. Most of the subjects in group *L* reported that they had tried to learn by using knowledge of component correspondences. But so did twelve of the twenty subjects in group *W*, and the scores of these twelve subjects on the transfer task were similar to those of the letter-trained group. The subjects who had learned by whole words and had not used individual correspondences performed no better on the task than the control subjects.

It is possible, then, to learn to read words without learning the component letter-sound correspondences. But transfer to new words depends on use of them, whatever the method of original training. Word training was as good as letter training if the subject had analyzed for himself the component relationships.

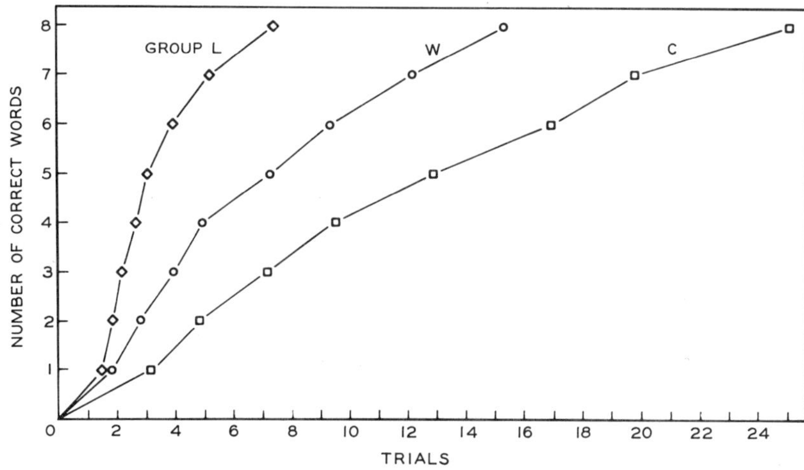

Figure 3. Learning curves on transfer task for group trained originally with whole words (*W*), group trained with single letters (*L*), and control group (*C*).

Learning Variable and Constant Component Correspondences

In Bishop's experiment, the component letter-sound relationships were regular and consistent. It has often been pointed out, especially by advocates of spelling reform and revised alphabets,[3] that in English this is not the case. Bloomfield (1942) suggested that the beginning reader should, therefore, be presented with material carefully programmed for teaching those orthographic-phonic regularities which exist in English, and should be introduced later and only gradually to the complexities of English spelling and to the fact that single letter-to-sound relationships are often variable. But actually there has been no hard evidence to suggest that transfer, later, to reading spelling patterns with more variable component correspondences will be facilitated by beginning with only constant ones. Although variable ones may be harder to

[3] As detailed in Chapter 10, current advocates of a revised alphabet who emphasize the low letter-sound correspondence in English are Sir James Pitman and John A. Downing. Pitman's revised alphabet, called the Initial Teaching Alphabet, consists of forty-four characters, some traditional and some new. It is designed for instruction of the beginning reader, who later transfers to traditional English spelling. See Pitman (1961), Downing (1962), and Downing, "Experiments with Pitman's Initial Teaching Alphabet in British Schools," paper presented at the Eighth Annual Conference of the International Reading Association, Miami, Florida, May, 1963.

learn in the beginning, the original difficulty may be compensated for by facilitating later learning.

A series of experiments directed by Harry Levin (Levin and Watson, 1963; Levin, Baum, and Bostwick, 1963) dealt with the effect of learning variable, as opposed to constant, letter-sound relationships on transfer to learning new letter-sound relationships. In one experiment, the learning material was short lists of paired associates, with a word written in artificial characters as stimulus and a triphoneme familiar English word as response. Subjects (third-grade children) in one group were given a list which contained constant graph-to-sound relationships (one-to-one component correspondence) followed by a list in which this correspondence was variable with respect to the medial vowel sound. Another group started with a similarly constructed variable list and followed it with a second one. The group that learned lists with a variable component in both stages was superior to the other group in the second stage. The results suggest that initiating the task with a variable list created an expectation of learning set for variability of correspondence which was transferred to the second list and facilitated learning it.

In a second experiment, the constant or variable graph-sound relation occurred on the first letter. Again, the group with original variable training performed better on the second, variable list. In a third experiment adult native speakers of English and Spanish were compared. The artificial graphs were paired with nonsense words. Again there was more transfer from a variable first list to a variable second list than from a constant to a variable one. Variable lists were more difficult, on the whole, for the Spanish speakers, perhaps because their native language contains highly regular letter-sound relationships.

A "set for diversity" may, therefore, facilitate transfer to learning of new letter-sound correspondences which contain variable relationships. But many questions about how the code is learned remain to be solved, because the true units of the graphic code are not necessarily single letters. While single letter-sound relations in English are indeed variable, at other levels of structure regularity may be discovered.

Lower and Higher Order Units

For many years, linguists have been concerned with the question of units in language. That language has a hierarchical structure, with units of different kinds and levels, is generally accepted, though the definition of the units is not easily reached. One criterion of a unit is recodability—

consistent mapping or translation to another code. If such a criterion be granted, graphic units must parallel linguistic units. The units of the writing system should be defined, in other words, by mapping rules which link them to the speech code at all levels of structure.

What then are the true graphic units? What levels of units are there? Exactly how are they mapped to linguistic units? In what "chunks" are they perceived? We must first try to answer these questions by a logical analysis of properties of the writing and speech systems and the correspondences between them. Then we can look at the behavior of skilled readers and see how units are processed during reading. If the logical analysis of the correspondence rules is correct, we should be able to predict what kinds of units are actually processed and to check our predictions experimentally.

Common sense suggests that the unit for reading is the single grapheme, and that the reader proceeds sequentially from left to right, letter by letter, across the page. But we can assert at once and unequivocally that this picture is false. For the English language, the single graphemes map consistently into speech only as morphemes—that is, the names of the letters of the alphabet. It is possible, of course, to name letters sequentially across a line of print ("spell out" a word), but that is not the goal of a skilled reader, nor is it what he does. Dodge (1905) showed, over sixty years ago, that perception occurs in reading only during fixations, and not at all during the saccadic jumps from one fixation to the next. With a fast tachistoscopic exposure, a skilled reader can perceive four unconnected letters, a very long word, and four or more words if they form a sentence (Cattell, 1885). Even first graders can read three-letter words exposed for only 40 milliseconds, too short a time for sequential eye movements to occur.

Broadbent (1958) has pointed out that speech, although it consists of a temporal sequence of stimuli, is responded to at the end of a sequence; that is, it is normal for a whole sequence to be delivered before a response is made. For instance, the sentence "Would you give me your ———?" might end with any of a large number of words, such as "name" or "wallet" or "wife." The response depends on the total message. The fact that the component stimuli for speech and reading are spread over time does not mean that the phonemes or letters or words are processed one at a time, with each stimulus decoded to a separate response. The fact that *o* is pronounced differently in *boat* and *bomb* is not a hideous peculiarity of English which must consequently be reformed. The *o* is read only in context and is never responded to in isolation. It is part of a sequence which contains constraints of two kinds, one morphological and the other the spelling patterns which are characteristic of English.

If any doubt remains as to the unlikelihood of sequential processing letter by letter, there is recent evidence (Newman, 1965; Kolers and Katzman, 1963) on sequential exposure of letters. When letters forming a familiar word are exposed sequentially in the same place, it is almost impossible to read the word. With an exposure of 100 milliseconds per letter, words of six letters are read with only 20 per cent probability of accuracy; and with an exposure of 375 milliseconds per letter, the probability is still well under 100 per cent. But that is more than 2 seconds to perceive a short, well-known word! We can conclude that, however graphemes are processed perceptually in reading, it is not a letter-by-letter sequence of acts.

If the single grapheme does not map consistently to a phoneme, and furthermore, if perception normally takes in bigger "chunks" of graphic stimuli in a single fixation, what are the smallest graphic units consistently coded into phonemic patterns? Must they be whole words? Are there different levels of units? Are they achieved at different stages of development?

Spelling Patterns

It is my belief that the smallest component units in written English are spelling patterns.[4] By a spelling pattern, I mean a cluster of graphemes in a given environment which has an invariant pronunciation according to the rules of English. These rules are the regularities which appear when, for instance, any vowel or consonant or cluster is shown to correspond with a given pronunciation in an initial, medial, or final position in the spelling of a word. This kind of regularity is not merely "frequency" (bigram frequency, trigram frequency, and so on), for it implies that frequency counts are relevant for establishing rules only if the right units and the right relationships are counted. The relevant graphic unit is a functional unit of one or more letters, in a given

[4] Spelling patterns in English have been discussed by Fries (1963, p. 169 ff.). Hockett (1963) has made an analysis of English graphic monosyllables, which presents regularities of spelling patterns in relation to pronunciation. This study was continued by Venezky (1962), who wrote a computer program for obtaining the regularities of English spelling-to-sound correspondence. The data obtained by means of the computer permit one to look up any vowel or consonant cluster of up to five letters and find its pronunication in initial, medial, and final positions in a word. Letter environments have now been included in the analysis as well. See also Weir (1964).

position within the word, which is in correspondence with a specified pronunciation.[5]

If potential regularities exist within words—the spelling patterns that occur in regular correspondence with speech patterns—one may hypothesize that these correspondences have been assimilated by the skilled reader of English (whether or not he can verbalize the rules) and have the effect of organizing units for perception. It follows that strings of letters which are generated by the rules will be perceived more easily than ones which are not, even when they are unfamiliar words or not words at all.

Several experiments testing this prediction were performed by Gibson, Pick, Osser, and Hammond (1962). The basic design was to compare the perceptibility (with a very short tachistoscopic exposure) of two sets of letter-strings, all nonsense or pseudo-words, which differed in their spelling-to-sound correlation. One list, called the "pronounceable" list, contained words with a high spelling-to-sound correlation. Each of them had an initial consonant spelling with a single, regular pronunciation; a final consonant spelling having a single, regular pronunciation; and a vowel spelling, placed between them, having a single regular pronunciation when it follows and is followed by the given initial and final consonant spellings, respectively—for example, **gl/ur/ck**. The words in the second list, called the "unpronounceable" list, had a low spelling-to-sound correlation. They were constructed from the words in the first list by reversing the initial and final consonant spellings. The medial vowel spelling was not changed. For example, **glurck** became **ckurgl**. There were twenty-five such pseudo-words in each list, varying in length from four to eight letters. The pronunciability of the resulting lists was validated in two ways, first by ratings, and second by obtaining the number of variations when the pseudo-words were actually pronounced.

The words were projected on a screen in random order, in five successive presentations with an exposure time beginning at 50 milliseconds and progressing up to 250 milliseconds. The subjects (college students) were instructed to write each word as it was projected. The mean

[5] For example, the cluster **gh** may lawfully be pronounced as an **f** at the end of a word, but never at the beginning. The vowel cluster **eigh** pronounced **ā (ej)** may occur in initial, medial, and final positions, and does so with nearly equal distribution. These cases account for all but two occurrences of the cluster in English orthography. A good example of regularity influenced by environment is **c** in a medial position before **i** plus a vowel. It is always pronounced **s**, as in **social, ancient, judicious.**

percentage of pronounceable words correctly perceived was consistently and significantly greater at all exposure times.

The experiment was later repeated with the same material but a different judgment. After the pseudo-word was exposed, it was followed by a multiple-choice list of four items, one of the correct one and the other three the most common errors produced in the previous experiment. The subject chose the word he thought he had seen from the choice list and recorded a number (its order in the list). Again the mean of pronounceable pseudo-words correctly perceived significantly exceeded that of their unpronounceable counterparts. We conclude from these experiments that skilled readers more easily perceive as a unit pseudo-words which follow the rules of English spelling-to-sound correspondence—that spelling patterns which have invariant relations to sound patterns function as a unit, thus facilitating the decoding process.

In another experiment, Gibson, Osser, and Pick (1963) studied the development of perception of grapheme-phoneme correspondences. We wanted to know how early, in learning to read, children begin to respond to spelling patterns as units. The experiment was designed to compare children at the end of the first grade and at the end of the third grade in ability to recognize familiar three-letter words, pronounceable trigrams, and unpronounceable trigrams. The three-letter words were taken from the first-grade reading list; each word chosen could be rearranged into a meaningless but pronounceable trigram and a meaningless and unpronounceable one (for example, **ran, nar, rna**). Some longer pseudo-words (four and five letters) taken from the previous experiments were included as well. The words and pseudo-words were exposed tachistoscopically to individual children, who were required to spell them orally. The first graders read (spelled out) most accurately the familiar three-letter words but read the pronounceable trigrams significantly better than the unpronounceable ones. The longer pseudo-words were seldom read accurately and were not differentiated by pronunciability. The third-grade girls read all three-letter combinations with high and about equal accuracy, but differentiated the longer pseudo-words; that is, the pronounceable four- and five-letter pseudo-words were more often perceived correctly than their unpronounceable counterparts.

These results suggest that a child in the first stages of reading skill typically reads in short units, but has already generalized certain regularities of spelling-to-sound correspondence, so that three-letter pseudo-words which fit the rules are more easily read as units. As skill develops, span increases, and a similar difference can be observed for longer items. The longer items involve more complex conditional rules and longer clusters, so that the generalizations must increase in complexity. The fact that a child can begin very early to perceive regularities of correspondence between the printed and spoken patterns and to transfer them to the reading of unfamiliar items as units suggests that the opportunities for discovering the correspondences between patterns might well be enhanced in programming reading materials.

I have referred several times to levels of units. The last experiment showed that the size and complexity of the spelling patterns which can be perceived as units increases with development of reading skill. That other levels of structure, both syntactic and semantic, contain units as large as and larger than the word and that perception of skilled readers will be found, in suitable experiments, to be a function of these factors is almost axiomatic. As yet we have little direct evidence better than Cattell's original discovery (1885) that when words are structured into a sentence, more letters can be accurately perceived "at a glance." Developmental studies of perceptual "chunking" in relation to structural complexity may be very instructive.

Where does meaning come in? Within the immediate span of visual perception, meaning is less effective in structuring written material than good spelling-to-sound correspondence, as Gibson, Bishop, Schiff, and Smith (1964) have shown. Real words which are both meaningful and, as strings of letters, structured in accordance with English spelling patterns are more easily perceived than non-word pronounceable strings of letters; but the latter are more easily perceived than meaningful but unpronounceable letter strings (for example, **bim** is perceived accurately, with tachistoscopic exposure, faster than **ibm**). The role of meaning in the visual perception of words probably increases as longer strings of words (more than one) are dealt with. A sentence has two kinds of constraint, semantic and syntactic, which make it intelligible (easily heard) and memorable (Miller and Isard, 1963; Marks and Miller, 1964). It is important that the child develop reading habits which utilize all the types of constraint present in the stimulus, since they constitute structure and are, therefore, unit formers. The skills which the child should acquire in reading are habits of utilizing the constraints in letter strings (the spelling and morphemic patterns). We could go on to consider still superordinate ones, perhaps, but the problem of the unit, of levels of units, and of mapping of rules from writing to speech has just begun to be explored with experimental techniques. Further research on the definition and processing of units should lead to new insights about the nature of reading skill and its attainment.

Summary

Reading begins with the child's acquisition of spoken language. Later he learns to differentiate the graphic symbols and to decode these to familiar speech sounds. As he learns the code, he must progressively utilize the structural constraints which are built into it in order to attain the skilled performance which is characterized by processing of higher order units—the spelling and morphological patterns of the language.

Because of my firm conviction that good pedagogy is based on a deep understanding of the discipline to be taught and the nature of the learning process involved, I have tried to show that the psychology of reading can benefit from a program of theoretical analysis and experiment. An analysis of the reading task—its discriminatory and decoding aspects as well as the semantic and syntactical aspects—tells us what must be learned. An analysis of the learning process tells us how. The consideration of formal instruction comes only after these steps, and its precepts should follow from them.

CHAPTER 4

DEVELOPMENTAL FACTORS IN READING AND WRITING BACKWARDNESS

MARCEL KINSBOURNE AND
ELIZABETH K. WARRINGTON

INTRODUCTION

Some children of normal intelligence meet unexpected difficulties in learning to read and write. These difficulties have been explained in a wide variety of mutually exclusive ways.

Morgan (1896) postulated congenital word blindness as an isolated defect of cerebral cortical functioning. Subsequently, many other workers, though repeatedly renaming the condition and differing as to the nature of the underlying functional disorder and the extent to which it may be regarded as pure or isolated, have agreed that "There exists, within the community of poor readers, a specific syndrome wherein particular difficulty exists in learning the conventional meaning of symbols—[which] is of constitutional and not of environmental origin, and is often genetically determined" (Critchley, 1961).

This syndrome has been regarded as the result of a "developmental lag with ultimate spontaneous maturation" (Olson, 1949) of the dominant cerebral hemisphere in the region of the angular gyrus in "otherwise normal and undamaged brains" (Hinshelwood, 1917), though in the absence of anatomical verification this remains purely speculative. The resulting impairment of function has been regarded as limited to reading and writing (Hinshelwood, 1917; Orton, 1937), or as related to retarded development in the language sphere (McCready, 1910; Ewing, 1930). It has been explained as due to a more general disorder of visual perception, in terms implying acceptance of *gestalt* hypotheses (Schilder, 1944; Drew, 1956; Hermann, 1959), or as due to defective visual discrimination (Bronner, 1917), auditory discrimination (Tamm, 1943), or both (Fildes, 1921).

Others, admitting a constitutional basis for selective difficulty in learning to read and write, have regarded it as representing one extreme of normal variation (Meyer, Norgaard, and Torpe, 1943; Malmquist, 1958). This attitude has been thought to dispose of the concept of congenital word blindness (Collins, 1961), a view based upon the naive assumption that impairment due to disease states is necessarily total and irremediable (Burt, 1935; Murray and Gulliford, 1960). A contrasting interpretation, in terms of emotional disorder, was offered by Gates (1922), Blau (1946), and Lynn (1957), while multifactorial causation was invoked by Robinson (1947). Ilg and Ames (1950) and Collins (1961) looked beyond the individual to his social setting, and the latter pointed out that "more slow learning is due to bad teaching than is generally admitted."

Most workers have searched for some abnormality common to a group of children with selective retardation in reading and writing. By definition, reading and writing retardation is common to these children, but it cannot in itself be regarded as evidence for any view of causation. It has also not proved possible to isolate any common primary distinguishing factor that is definitely not secondary to the educational deficit. This suggests that the group of backward readers (variously defined and selected by different workers) included children not of one type but of several, so that the test procedures were being applied to a heterogeneous population. Test results might then fail to reach statistical significance on account of dilution of the relevant population by the inclusion of one or more contrasting types of case.

If backwardness in reading and writing in any given case may be due to one or more of several causes, then the need is for test procedures by means of which the various causes can be distinguished. A suitable test procedure would be applicable to children of school age and standardized on this age group. It would not be empirical but would be based on present knowledge of psychological function. It would not tap abilities which might be secondarily affected by the fact of reading retardation, but would relate to some aspect of function uninfluenced by the level of achievement in reading. Preferably, it would not appear to bear on the child's educational disability, thus minimizing the spread to the test situation of emotional resistances.

Among the syndromes of cerebral cortical disorder in adults is one manifested in difficulty in naming the fingers (finger agnosia), in right-left discrimination, and in writing and calculating (Gerstmann, 1924). Analysis of finger agnosia has shown it to be based on an inability to differentiate between the fingers in terms of their relative positions on the hand (Kinsbourne and Warrington, 1962). The essential ingredient of the writing difficulty relates to the order of letters within the word (Kinsbourne and Warrington, unpublished data), and of the difficulty in calculation of the rank of the numbers as determined by their relative positions (Stengel, 1944). In each instance, the difficulty relates to a task involving sequential ordering. These symptoms find their parallels in some children with reading retardation. Thus, in such children "the major interference with the process of recognizing or recalling the word is a failure to reproduce the exact order of its constituent letters" (Orton, 1937). Right-left disorientation in backward readers has frequently been described (Hermann, 1959; Gooddy and Reinhold, 1961), and congential word blindness has been regarded as analogous to the Gerstmann syndrome in adults (Hermann and Norrie, 1958). If some children have trouble in learning to read and write on account of specific difficulty in sequential ordering, they might also have finger agnosia, the most characteristic element of the Gerstmann syndrome.

Tasks involving the naming of fingers (Gerstmann, 1924) are unsuitable for use with children who cannot normally be relied upon to know these names (Hermann, 1959). Tasks of finger localization (Strauss and Werner, 1939; Benton, 1959) have not been shown to bear any relationship to the clinical sign of finger agnosia. The tests of finger differentiation and finger order of Kinsbourne and Warrington (1962), however, were shown by them to be specific for the diagnosis of finger agnosia in adults. They were then standardized on a group of children in a primary school. Success on these tests was achieved by more than 95 per cent of the children over the age of seven years (Kinsbourne and Warrington, 1963). These test procedures, therefore, seemed suitable for the detection of finger agnosia in children with reading and writing retardation who are over seven years of age.

Children with reading or writing retardation who fail on the test of finger differentiation and order would be predicted also to exhibit other elements of the Gerstmann syndrome. They might show a particular type of difficulty in reading or writing which would distinguish them from patients who are backward in reading and writing for other reasons. In particular, they might show selective impairment on those WISC subtests with high spatial loading (Maxwell, 1959).

Children who succeed on the tests of finger differentiation and order might have reading or writing retardation because they are emotionally disturbed, inadequately taught, or have a cerebral deficit of a type other than the Gerstmann. Again, correlations within patient groups might help in this differentiation. In particular, retardation in language development would be expected to delay the acquisition of reading and writing skills (Ingram, 1959). Indeed, insofar as reading and writing make as much demand on the language abilities of a young child as anything else he is likely to encounter, reading and writing retardation might prove to be a sensitive index of language impairment. Such a deficit should be detectable by clinical assessment of the patient's speech reception and expression and might also result in selective difficulty on those WISC subtests with high verbal loading (Maxwell, 1959).

These possibilities were tested by selecting from a series of patients retarded in reading or writing those who showed a wide verbal-performance discrepancy on the WISC or WAIS and determining whether the direction of discrepancy correlates with success or failure on the finger tests and on other tasks relevant to the syndromes under consideration.

Clinical Study

Subjects

The patients in this series fell into two groups. These were, respectively, Group 1, in which the score on the nonverbal section of the WISC or WAIS exceeded that of the verbal section by at least 20 points, and Group 2, in which the converse was true. There were six patients in Group 1 and seven patients in Group 2. Their ages ranged from eight to fourteen years, with the exception of one patient in Group 1 who was thirty-one years old. The six patients in Group 1 were male; five of the seven patients in Group 2 were female.

Each patient was examined by the methods customary in neurological practice. These included routine history-taking and general and neurological examination, as well as such special investigations as seemed indicated. This was done under the direction of the consultant neurologist in charge of the case.

Attention was paid to the efficiency of verbal comprehension and expression (word choice, syntax, and articulation). Right-left orientation was assessed by direct questioning, tasks involving personal right and left, and observation of any right-left confusion during the test interview. Constructional skill was assessed by the ability to copy drawings and matchstick patterns. The procedures were comparable with those in use for the examination of cerebral cortical function in adults (Critchley, 1953). As these tests are as yet largely unstandardized in children, the results represent no more than a clinical impression.

Standard Procedures

1. Wechsler Intelligence Scale for Children (details of tests administered are given below). The one adult in the series was tested on the Wechsler Adult Intelligence Scale.

2. Tests of graded reading and spelling (Schonell and Schonell, 1956).

3. Tests of finger differentiation and order (Fig. 1). These finger tests are described in detail by Kinsbourne and Warrington (1963).

In Test 1, two points on the fingers are simultaneously touched. These may be on one, or on two, adjacent fingers. The patient is required to say whether one or two fingers are being touched. Touch is maintained till a response is made.

In Test 2, two fingers are simultaneously touched and the patient is required to say how many fingers there are between the ones being touched. Touch is maintained till a response is made.

In Test 3, four wooden blocks, shaped as shown in Figure 1, are placed in front of the patient. While his eyes are closed, the patient's fingers are moulded around one of four corresponding blocks. He is then asked to open his eyes and, without looking at the block in his hand, to pick out the corresponding one on the table.

The tests were carried out in the standard manner described by Kinsbourne and Warrington (1963). Patients who failed to satisfy the criteria for pass were all re-examined on another occasion before the results were accepted for purposes of the present communication.

Results

Verbal and performance IQs, together with individual test scores, are given in Table 1. The patients in Group 1 show a discrepancy between verbal and performance scores ranging from 23 to 45 IQ points in favor of the performance score ("negative discrepancy index"—Seashore, 1951). Individual test scores within the performance scale are on the whole consistent. Within the verbal scale, the scores on the Vocabulary and Digit Span tests, which make relatively high demands on language ability (Maxwell, 1959), tend to be low.

The patients in Group 2 show a discrepancy ranging from 20 to 35 IQ points between the verbal and the performance scores, in favor of the verbal score ("positive discrepancy index"—Seashore, 1951). Within the

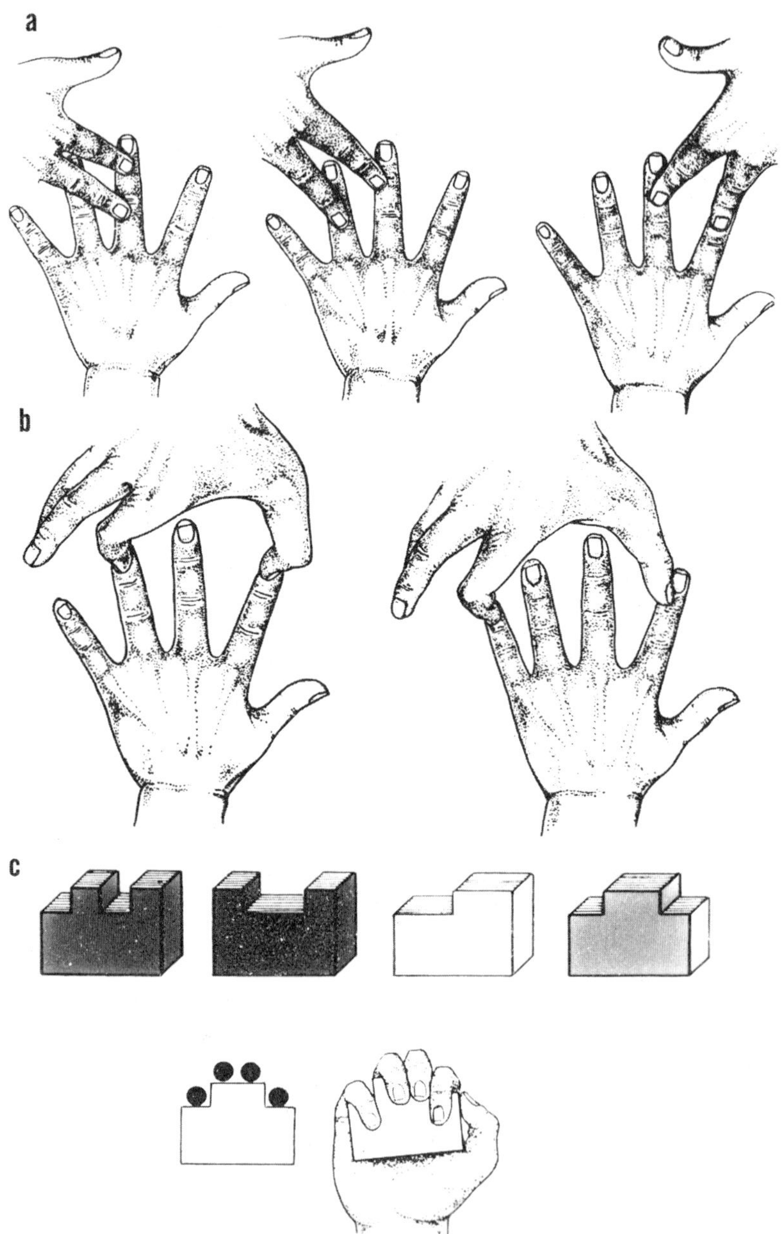

Figure 1. Testing for finger differentiation.

Table 1. Intelligence test scores and individual subtest scores

Test	Group 1 1	2	3	4	5	6	Group 2 7	8	9	10	11	12	13
Verbal IQ	72	105	75	86	101	77	89	97	81	128	84	116	86
Performance IQ	107	150	107	115	142	101	64	62	58	108	53	93	58
Subtest:													
Information	6	11	4	9	11	–	4	10	6	16	5	12	7
Arithmetic	6	13	5	8	10	5	4	5	8	12	8	12	4
Similarities	8	16	10	7	13	7	13	11	7	16	10	13	10
Vocabulary	4	9	6	6	9	7	14	13	7	15	5	13	6
Digit Span	6	10	5	9	9	6	–	–	5	13	10	–	7
Picture Completion	9	19	12	14	14	10	10	5	5	15	10	10	9
Picture Arrangement	7	15	14	14	15	9	3	6	5	14	3	8	2
Block Design	10	20	9	12	17	11	4	3	6	10	5	9	5
Object Assembly	16	20	9	11	18	–	2	4	0	6	0	–	0

performance scale, the scores on block design and object assembly were the lowest in every case. These are tests with high spatial loading (Maxwell, 1959). In this group, the discrepancy between the verbal and performance IQs holds in spite of the disproportionate difficulty some of these patients showed on the test of arithmetic.

Table 2 presents the reading and spelling ages (Schonell and Schonell, 1956) and the arithmetic ages (calculated from the score on the WISC subtest of arithmetic). In Group 1, the language-retarded patients,

Table 2. Educational attainment levels and chronological age

Age (*yrs.-mos.*)	Group 1 1	2	3	4	5	6	Mean
Chronological	14-8	9-0	13-6	11-0	10-6	31-0	-
Reading	6-0	7-6	6-6	6-0	7-0	5-0	6-4
Spelling	5-0	7-6	6-0	6-0	7-0	7-6	6-6
Arithmetic	10-0	10-6	8-6	10-0	10-6	-	9-11

Age (*yrs.-mos.*)	Group 2 7	8	9	10	11	12	13	Mean
Chronological	9-5	8-5	10-3	9-6	14-6	11-7	12-1	-
Reading	7-0	6-0	6-0	12-0	8-0	8-0	11-0	8-3
Spelling	8-0	5-0	6-0	9-0	7-0	8-0	9-0	7-5
Arithmetic	6-0	6-0	8-6	10-6	11-0	12-0	7-9	8-10

the mean reading and spelling ages are very nearly the same, 6 4/12 and 6 6/12 years, respectively, while in Group 2, the patients with selective difficulty on performance tests, the mean spelling age is lower by one year than the mean reading age. The mean arithmetic age in Group 1, 9 11/12 years, is very much higher than either the mean reading or mean spelling age. This is not the case in Group 2, where the mean arithmetic age is very nearly the same as the mean reading age. It is not possible to compare the absolute values between the two groups, as they are not matched for severity of disability.

Table 3 presents the clinical psychological findings and the results on the tests of finger differentiation and order. All patients in Group 1 showed evidence of language impairment on tests of naming and verbal learning, and three of these patients showed impairment on tests of speech reception. In contrast, no patient in Group 2 had such difficulty. Patients in Group 2 all had difficulty on constructional tasks, while no patient in Group 1 had this difficulty. Though all the patients in Group 1 were poor at spelling, they were able to write neatly and copy written words. Four patients in Group 2 had impaired script in that they were unable to form and copy letters properly. The arithmetic age quoted in Table 2 was based on the ability to solve arithmetical problems. To test mechanical arithmetic, the patients were asked to perform written additions and subtractions. Two patients in Group 1, and all in Group 2, found this difficult. Patients 9 and 10, and all patients in Group 2, had more difficulty with additions and subtractions than with solving arithmetical problems. One patient in Group 1 was disorientated for right and left on himself, as were four patients in Group 2. Systematic reversals (Benton, 1958) were not found. No patient in Group 1 failed the tests of finger differentiation and order, while all the patients in Group 2 failed these tests.

There was a high incidence of lefthandedness and mixed laterality in both groups. However, three patients in Group 1 were fully right-handed. Three patients had a family history of reading or writing backwardness; two of these were in Group 1. Six patients had a history suggestive of birth injury; five of these were in Group 2. Motor development was normal in all but one of the six patients in Group 1 but was delayed in three of the seven patients in Group 2. Speech development was delayed, or very much delayed, in the five patients in Group 1 about whom this information was available. In contrast, speech development was delayed in only one of the patients in Group 2.

Three patients were entirely normal neurologically; these were all in Group 1. Three further cases were normal on examination but not

Table 3. Summary of clinical psychological tests

Test	Group 1 1	2	3	4	5	6
Language functions:						
Expressive	+	+	+	+	+	+
Receptive	+	−	−	−	+	+
Constructional ability	−	−	−	−	−	−
Writing ability (letter formation)	−	−	−	−	−	−
Right-left orientation	−	−	+	−	−	−
Addition and subtraction	−	−	+	+	−	−
Finger differentiation and order	−	−	−	−	−	−

Test	Group 2 7	8	9	10	11	12	13
Language functions:							
Expressive	−	−	−	−	−	−	−
Receptive	−	−	−	−	−	−	−
Constructional ability	+	+	+	+	+	+	+
Writing ability (letter formation)	+	+	−	+	−	+	−
Right-left orientation	+	+	−	−	−	+	+
Addition and subtraction	+	+	+	+	+	+	+
Finger differentiation and order	+	+	+	+	+	+	+

+ Indicates abnormality.

electroencephalographically; two of these patients were in Group 2. There was a higher incidence of neurological abnormality in Group 2 than in Group 1.

Discussion

A group of patients (Group 2) who showed selective impairment on the performance subsection of the WISC also failed the standard tests of finger differentiation and order and had difficulty in arithmetic, while the other group (Group 1), who did less well on the verbal subsection of the WISC or WAIS than on the nonverbal, passed tests of finger differentiation and order and showed no selective impairment of arithmetical abilities. Furthermore, in Group 1 clinical testing revealed significant impairment of language ability, outside reading and writing.

An analogy may be drawn between these two groups and two syndromes of cerebral cortical disorder in adults, the Gerstmann syndrome and aphasia. In Group 2 the finger agnosia of the Gerstmann syndrome is represented by poor performance on the tests of finger order and differentiation. Significant retardation in right-left orientation and in mechanical arithmetic was also found, as well as constructional difficulty comparable to that which accompanies the Gerstmann syndrome in adults (Ajuriaguerra and Hécaen, 1960). On the other hand, the patients in Group 1, in their delay in acquisition of speech and in their clinically apparent difficulties in verbal comprehension and expression, provide a picture analogous to that of aphasia in the adult.

It appears that among backward readers and writers there exist two groups with developmental defects reminiscent of acquired cerebral syndromes in adults. Group 1 will be called the language retardation group and Group 2 the Gerstmann group.

The two groups are readily distinguishable by use of the finger tests. The Gerstmann group is further characterized by a positive discrepancy score (Seashore, 1951) on the WISC greater than that occurring naturally in 95 per cent of the population. This cannot be regarded as a secondary consequence of failure to acquire reading skill, as this, if anything, gives rise to a discrepancy in the opposite direction, with performance scores exceeding verbal scores (Strang, 1943; Holmes, 1954; Vernon, 1957; Collins, 1961). Indeed, Rabinovitch, Drew, De Jong, Ingram, and Withey (1954) were so sure that the retarded readers would have a lower verbal than performance IQ that they excluded from their study all children who did not fulfill this criterion.

The selectively depressed verbal scores of the language retardation group could more easily be regarded as nonspecific and secondary to the lack of reading skill. However, the marked degree of discrepancy, in association with a history of retarded speech development and, in some cases, with persisting evidence of inadequate verbal expression and reception, distinguishes this group from the rest. With regard to their discrepancy index on the WISC, these patients resemble those of Rabinovitch *et al.* (1954), and clinically they conform to the description by Ingram (1959) of developmental dyslexia secondary to retardation of language development. The analogy between these syndromes of acquired cerebral deficit in adults and developmental cerebral deficit in children is solely at the level of function, with due allowance for the widely different settings involved—the loss of an ability previously possessed, as opposed to the failure to acquire that ability. No anatomical correspondences may be assumed. The fact that a lesion in a certain part of the brain may cause a particular syndrome in the adult in no way implies that the child with an analogous developmental syndrome has a similarly localized cerebral lesion, or, indeed, any gross cerebral damage at all. Nevertheless, at the functional level the similarities are striking. Sequential ordering may be regarded as one of the basic activities of the cerebral hemispheres (Lashley, 1951), and it appears that the ability to recall and manipulate sequences (at least in relation to the fingers) is not as a rule developed much before the age of six years (Kinsbourne and Warrington, 1963)—even much later in some instances (the present work, Group 2)—and is impaired by damage to the dominant parietal lobe in some adults (Kinsbourne and Warrington, 1962). Thus, the young child, the older child with the developmental Gerstmann syndrome, and the adult with the acquired Gerstmann syndrome all lack the same basic ability, each in a quite different setting and with somewhat different consequences.

A different ability, this time in the verbal sphere, was delayed in its full development in the cases in Group 1. If the ability, once acquired, is then lost on account of a disease process in adult life, aphasia will result. Again, the same disorder of function will express itself differently in the different setting.

The full syndrome need not be present in every Gerstmann or language case. The manifestations will depend not only on the deficit (which may be at any level of severity) but also on the compensation to it. This may be so good as to permit above-average reading ability in a case with the developmental Gerstmann syndrome (Case 10). The arbitrarily selected criterion of a discrepancy of 20 or more points in favor of the WISC verbal subscale need not be regarded as essential for the diagnosis. Less striking discrepancies exist and are not inconsistent with defective performance either on reading and spelling or finger tests.

Conversely, the presence of such a discrepancy—in favor of the WISC Verbal score—is not in itself sufficient reason to expect the finger tests to be failed. Nor is it sufficient reason for diagnosing the developmental Gerstmann syndrome, although the seven cases of this series all happened to fall into this category. There are other conceivable disorders (of perception as well as of movement) which might lead to difficulty in certain performance tests, including reading or writing. These have still to be looked for.[1]

Which, if either, of the two syndromes corresponds to the condition variously named congenital word blindness or specific dyslexia? If the condition is regarded as strictly limited to the use of visual symbols (Hinshelwood, 1917; Orton, 1937), then neither group may be thus

[1] Since submitting this manuscript we have seen a nine-year-old boy who was quite unable to read and, in spite of a performance deficit of 25 points, passed the finger tests.

identified. Indeed, the existence of such a pure defect would be more readily acceptable had its protagonists given details of test results outside the reading and writing spheres. But even if it is agreed that the condition is found in a setting of associated defects (Hermann, 1959; Critchley, 1961), the answer is still not obvious, as each group contains features which have at times been stated to characterize specific dyslexia. Thus, selective impairment on the spatial subtests of the WISC was stressed by Galifret-Granjon (1952) and Lachmann (1960), while selective impairment on the verbal scale was found by Rabinovitch *et al.* (1954) and Drew (1956). Right-left disorientation has been frequently observed in children with reading retardation. The association of delayed speech development with reading retardation was asserted by McCready (1910). It is therefore hardly possible to select either group as representing the syndrome of specific dyslexia or congenital word blindness. Failure to distinguish between two quite different types of developmental cerebal deficit causing reading and writing retardation has led to the attribution of a large variety of associated defects to children retarded in reading and writing. At the same time, it has made it difficult for the results of systematic testing of reading and writing deficits to reach significance. Rather than regarding specific dyslexia as a single condition, it would seem preferable to allow that in the population of backward readers and writers there are cases arising from developmental cerebral deficit. Insofar as the acquisition of reading and writing skill is a complex procedure involving a variety of cerebral functions, it is not surprising to find that retarded development of one or other of the functions subserved by the cerebral hemispheres may delay this acquisition, and that it may do so in different ways, depending upon the exact nature of the function which is insufficiently developed. The Gerstmann and the language-retardation types of case should be regarded not as representing a single disease condition, but rather as each corresponding to a syndrome of retarded cerebral development, however caused. Among the patients here studied, six suffered perinatal trauma; the others may be regarded as delayed in development of the relevant functions on account of constitutional factors ("biological variation"—McCready, 1910). The presence of brain lesions or active cerebral disease is not a necessary condition for the genesis of either syndrome, though an active disease process affecting the brain may lead to disabilities indistinguishable from those due to simple constitutional factors. The present study includes three patients in whom reading and writing deficit was a familial feature and three instances in which it may have been the consequence of delayed cerebral maturation on a genetic basis (Hallgren, 1950). Finally, although there is no such case in the present series, the two types of defect may coincide in the same patient. In such cases, the WISC discrepancies would to some extent reciprocally cancel out, and the WISC profile would lack characteristic diagnostic features. There might be special difficulties in distinguishing them from cases with uniform mental retardation.

Syndromes of cerebral cortical deficit causing reading retardation may be associated with a variety of neurological deficits or may occur in relative isolation, but it is knowledge of the nature of the underlying disorder of function, whatever its accompaniments, which is of most immediate importance for treatment. It has been questioned whether the empirical methods presently in use in remedial reading centers offer any advance over competent teaching in the first instance (Collins, 1961), and it may well be, as Ilg and Ames (1950) and Collins (1961) suggest, that the bulk of children in such classes are there on account of shortcomings in their schools rather than in themselves. Children such as those described in this communication probably represent only a minority among the population of backward readers. Nevertheless, this minority might benefit if taught along lines which take cognizance of the nature of the disorder of cerebral cortical function. The present study is an attempt at a classification of backward readers and writers into groups which could then be made the subject of controlled experiments involving a variety of teaching methods.

Summary

Two groups of patients referred on account of backwardness in reading or writing, or both, were studied. These were selected on the basis of a discrepancy of more than 20 points between verbal and performance IQs on the WISC or WAIS, the verbal IQ being the lower in Group 1 (six cases) and the performance IQ the lower in Group 2 (seven cases). Other clinical evidences of language disorder were found in Group 1 but were almost completely absent in Group 2. A specific difficulty with tests of finger differentiation and order, as well as impairment on constructional tasks and mechanical arithmetic, was found in Group 2 but not in Group 1. These two groups represent syndromes of developmental cerebral deficit based on difficulties in sequential ordering and in the language sphere, respectively. Each syndrome may give rise to a characteristic type of delay in learning to read and write. Children with such cerebral cortical deficits probably represent a minority within the population of retarded readers and writers.

DISORDERS OF SPELLING

MARCEL KINSBOURNE AND
ELIZABETH K. WARRINGTON

The writing process may be regarded as compounded of spelling (requiring correct choice and sequence of letters) and of script (demanding correct formation of letters). Impairment in each activity may be studied separately and assessed relative to a clinically apparent writing disorder. If performed orally, spelling, with which we are here concerned, can be studied in isolation from script.

A spelling disorder may be a feature of central or expressive aphasia. In the writing of a series of aphasic patients, Weisenburg and McBride (1935) found errors of choice of letter to be prominent.

Gerstmann (1924) reported a disorder of writing in association with finger agnosia. Many subsequent case reports of the Gerstmann syndrome present examples of misspelling, among which errors of order of letters are prominent.

Clinical observations thus suggest that patients with finger agnosia tend to make spelling errors involving letter order, while aphasics characteristically make errors of letter choice. The present study was designed to test this possibility in a formal manner.

Clinical Study

Methods of Testing

Finger agnosia. Tests of finger differentiation and order (Kinsbourne and Warrington, 1962) were used. These test for the same defect as Gerstmann's (1924) tests for finger agnosia but do not require the patient to know the names of the fingers.

Aphasia. Clinical tests of comprehension of speech and expression were used. These included naming common objects, explaining common sayings, carrying out single and double instructions, and learning a simple sentence.

Spelling disorder. Spelling was tested orally, using Schonell's graded word spelling lists (Schonell and Schonell, 1956). The words were read aloud, beginning with the easiest. The patient's first attempt at spelling the word was recorded. No time limit was imposed, but efforts at self-correction were not taken into account. As the procedure differed from that customary when the test is given to children, no attempt was made to score it in terms of spelling age. Instead, an over-all error score was obtained.

Intellectual status. All patients except those in Control Group 4 (extracranial lesions) were tested on the Wechsler Adult Intelligence Scale. Further clinical tests for the presence of selective defects referable to cerebral hemisphere dysfunction were employed. These included tests of reading, writing, drawing, and memory.

Selection of Patients

Four groups of patients were included in this study. These were selected as follows:

Group 1. Patients with finger agnosia. This group was drawn from patients referred to the psychology department between February, 1962, and April, 1963, on suspicion of cerebral cortical disease. Twelve patients fell into this category, for which failure on the tests of finger differentiation and order was the sole and sufficient criterion.

Group 2. Patients with aphasia. This was a group of patients with a clinically obvious speech impairment of an aphasic type (apart from spelling), who had been referred in a similar manner between February, 1962, and April, 1963. The only additional criterion for selection was a pass on the tests for finger agnosia. Aphasic patients who failed the finger tests were included in Group 1 (Cases 3, 7, 9, 10, 11). The size of the group of aphasics tested was sixteen.

Group 3. Patients with right hemisphere lesions. This was a group of fifteen righthanded patients with evidence of right hemisphere lesions.

Group 4. Patients with extracranial lesions. This group consisted of patients none of whom had evidence of disease affecting the brain, and contained thirteen patients.

All patients were tested on oral spelling, as described above. The test contained one hundred words. Patients who spelled fewer than twenty words correctly were excluded from the analysis, as were those who made fewer than ten errors and thus provided insufficient data. Table 1 gives the size of the original groups of patients, together with the number of patients excluded and the final size of the groups used in the analysis that followed. Table 2 presents psychological findings on the patients finally included in Group 1 (finger agnosia) and Group 2 (aphasia but no finger agnosia), respectively.

Table 1. Selection of groups of patients

	Number of Patients			
Patient Group	Originally Tested	With Fewer than 20 Wds. Correct	With Fewer than 10 Wds. Incorrect	In Final Group
1	12	1	0	11
2	16	3	0	13
3	15	0	2	13
4	13	0	3	10

Method of Analysis of Spelling Errors

The spelling of patients with cerebral cortical lesions may be wildly incorrect. Multiple errors may occur within one word, and at times such errors might be classifiable in more than one way. It was therefore decided to let each misspelled word appear only once in the analysis and to establish a "hierarchy" of spelling errors to determine the category of error where more than one type of error was present.

The particular method of analysis described below was suggested by clinical observations of extraneous letter errors in aphasic spelling and of order errors in association with finger agnosia. Omission errors were also often noted in the presence of finger agnosia. Vowel substitutions and reduplications were not uncommon in normal people, and perhaps often reflect educational shortcomings.

Types of Error

Types of error were classified as follows:

1. *Extraneous letters.* Any word contaminated by an extraneous letter (defined as one that does not in fact occur anywhere in it) was classified under the heading, "extraneous letters." Irrespective of the presence of any other errors in the word, it was then excluded from further analysis.

Table 2. Psychological findings in patients in Groups 1 and 2

	Group 1										
	1	2	3	4	5	6	7	8	9	10	11
Initials	G. L.	M. B.	S. C.	R. F.	J. G.	C. H.	L. W.	J. K.	S. S.	I. R.	A. F.
Age	52	48	55	58	43	56	57	38	34	31	64
Sex	F	M	M	F	M	M	F	F	F	F	M
Handedness	R	R	R	R	R	R	R	R	L	L	R
Verbal IQ	91	87	80	98	104	123	92	96	76	84	86
Performance IQ	40	n. t.	40	87	91	68	71	83	80	86	78
Spelling score	B	A	B	A	A	A	A	B	A	A	A
(out of 100)	42	47	27	82	77	70	81	74	67	40	59
Aphasia	–	–	+	–	–	–	+	–	+	+	+
Disordered script	+	+	+	–	–	–	–	–	–	–	+
Right-left disorientation	+	+	+	+	+	+	+	–	–	+	+
Dyscalculia	+	+	+	–	–	–	+	+	+	+	+
Constructional apraxia	+	+	+	+	–	+	+	n. t.	–	+	+

	Group 2												
	1	2	3	4	5	6	7	8	9	10	11	12	13
Initials	D. B.	S. R.	A. H.	A. K.	R. N.	O. B.	L. M.	H. J.	J. H.	C. G.	W. S.	L. G.	A. M.
Age	59	71	54	59	58	55	59	64	38	53	52	55	55
Sex	M	M	M	M	M	M	M	M	M	M	M	M	M
Handedness	R	R	R	R	R	R	R	R	R	R	R	R	R
Verbal IQ	93	69	68	87	96	n. t.	95	122	67	90	73	91	86
Performance IQ	123	82	96	101	84	n. t.	97	n. t.	80	97	n. t.	97	61
Progressive matrices	40/60	n. t.	n. t.	n. t.	n. t.	32/60	28/60	41/60	n. t.	n. t.	41/60	n. t.	n. t.
Disordered script	–	–	n. t.*	n. t.*	–	+	–	–	–	n. t.	n. t.	–	+
Spelling score (out of 100)	78	25	32	73	64	53	89	83	21	65	31	74	23
Right-left disorientation	–	–	–	–	–	–	+	–	–	–	–	+	–
Dyscalculia	–	+	–	–	–	–	+	–	+	–	+	–	+
Constructional apraxia	–	–	n. t.*	n. t.*	+	–	–	–	–	–	–	–	–

* Not tested on account of right hemiplegia.

2. *Letter order errors.* Of the residue, every word in which there occurred (a) an interchange in position of two letters or letter groups, or (b) a letter out of turn (unless it represented an immediate repetition of the letter, error type 5, or was limited to vowels, error type 4) was classified as containing an order error and excluded from further analysis.

3. *Letter omissions.* Of the residue, every word in which one or more letters were omitted was classified as containing an "omission" error and excluded from further analysis.

4. *Vowel substitution.* Of the residue, each word in which there was substituted for a vowel another one that also occurred elsewhere in the word was classified as a "vowel substitution."

5. *Reduplications.* This left only the erroneous reduplications of a letter, which were classified under this heading.

The first ten misspellings produced by each patient were subjected to analysis. Further errors (on more difficult words) were not included, as when a person is tested on words well outside his range his efforts become wilder and less specific. Each patient, therefore, was represented in the calculations by ten misspelled words, irrespective of the over-all severity of the disability or the presence of multiple errors within one word.

Results

The Spelling Analysis

The spelling score (number of words correct out of 100) obtained on the Schonell word lists for each patient in Group 1 and Group 2 is given in Table 2. The mean spelling scores were as follows: Group 1, 60.5; Group 2, 54.7; Group 3, 71.0; and Group 4, 79.4. The scores obtained by the four groups do not directly represent their relative spelling efficiency, as spelling achievement was equated to the extent of demanding a score of between 20 and 90 for inclusion in the study. A number of patients had, therefore, to be excluded from each of the four groups because they made too few errors (in the case of the control groups 3 and 4, Table 1). Even after selection on this basis, the two control groups obtained a higher mean score than either the aphasia or the finger agnosia group, but only in the case of the aphasia group does the difference reach significance. If the initial selection were taken into account, the differences would be greater.

Analysis of Spelling Errors

Ten misspelled words from each patient were classified as described above. The incidence of each type of error, for each group of patients, was estimated as a percentage of the total errors made. The percentage of each type of error for each group is given in Table 3.

Table 3. Distribution of spelling error types in the four groups of patients

Errors	Extraneous Letter	Order	Vowel Substitution	Omission	Reduplication
Group 1: finger agnosia	19	35	11	44	1
(N = 11)	(17%)	(32%)	(10%)	(40%)	(1%)
Group 2: aphasics	63	9	14	38	7
(N = 13)	(49%)	(7%)	(11%)	(29%)	(4%)
Group 3: right hemisphere	33	22	27	43	5
(N = 13)	(25%)	(17%)	(21%)	(33%)	(4%)
Group 4: extracranial	22	17	15	38	8
(N = 10)	(22%)	(17%)	(15%)	(38%)	(8%)
Combined control (3 + 4)	55	39	42	81	13
(N = 23)	(24%)	(17%)	(18%)	(35%)	(6%)

Only order errors and extraneous letter errors occurred with significantly different frequencies in the four groups. This inequality of distribution was the result of aphasic patients making more extraneous letter errors and fewer order errors and finger agnosia patients making more order errors. As regards the incidence of omission errors and vowel substitution errors, the finger agnosia and the aphasia groups did not differ significantly from the control group.

Discussion

The finger agnosia and the aphasia group each showed a distinctive pattern of incidence of the various types of spelling errors. These patients occupy the opposite ends of a spectrum, with the two control groups in an intermediate position. Each group made errors of every kind; the difference lay in the relative proportion.

In brief, the aphasic group yielded a high proportion of extraneous letter errors, and the finger agnosia group a high proportion of letter order errors. Errors of omission and vowel substitutions did not discriminate between the groups. Reduplications were too few to permit conclusions to be drawn (Table 3).

The results show that at least two factors may limit oral spelling ability in the presence of cerebral pathology. While in one group of cases the spelling disability reflects a more general language disorder, in the other group it is related to deficits not limited to the verbal sphere.

Gerstmann's (1924) patient with finger agnosia wrote in a virtually illegible scribble. Subsequent more detailed analyses of comparable cases have been reported as showing, among other things, errors of letter order (Herrmann and Pötzl, 1926; Lange, 1930), extending also to oral spelling (Wagner, 1932). In the present study of oral spelling, this type of error was prominent in a group of patients with finger agnosia. In view of the double dissociation between the finger agnosia and the aphasia groups in respect to order errors and extraneous letters, the spelling disability of the finger agnosia group cannot be due to aphasia. The high proportion of order errors suggests a difficulty in evoking the letters in correct sequence. As Critchley (1953) remarked in another context, "Some disorders of spelling can be regarded less as grammatical errors than as a spatiotemporal disability." Such a disability might extend beyond spelling so as to embarrass, in an analogous manner, the recall of nonverbal information.

The classifying of stimuli (both verbal and nonverbal) in terms of their relative positions in space and time was thought by Lashley (1951) to represent a distinctive mode of cerebral functioning. Finger agnosia, which has been shown to be associated with order errors in spelling, is based on an underlying difficulty in classifying the fingers in terms of their relative positions (Kinsbourne and Warrington, 1962). Finger agnosia and order errors in spelling may thus be manifestations of an underlying disorder of cerebral functioning of the type suggested by Lashley.

Belief in the integrity of the Gerstmann syndrome has been challenged by a study with negative outcome (Benton, 1961), which, however, failed to take account of the distinctive features of its elements. In the present study, for example, it was the type of the spelling errors, rather than their mere occurrence, which distinguished the finger agnosia group. If only a total error score had been obtained, the distinction from the aphasic group would have been missed. It may be that further attempts at establishing the coherence of the syndrome regarded as the expression of a disorder of spatiotemporal sequencing will meet with more success.

The presence of an oral spelling disability of order-error type in association with finger agnosia is not indicative of a more general language disorder. To regard it as such would lead to a spuriously high estimate of the incidence of aphasia in association with finger agnosia (Heimburger, De Myer, and Reitan, 1964).

The patients with finger agnosia (Group 1) included five who had a coincident aphasia (Table 1). Nevertheless, as a group they produced a pattern of spelling error of types differing widely from that of the aphasics (Group 2). An alternative approach would have been to exclude from the analysis all cases with both aphasia and finger agnosia, but it was thought that to use failure on the finger tests as the sole criterion for inclusion in Group 1 would be the more objective method.

Attention was confined to the first ten misspelled words produced by each patient when tested on the graded word list. Had care not been taken in each case to use for analysis words only just beyond the patient's spelling capacity, the correlations might well have been obscured by nonspecific errors on words with which the patient had perhaps never been really familiar. The method used showed also that the pattern of errors may point to a disability not revealed by the overall score for spelling errors. Patients 4 and 7 in Group 1, and 7 and 8 in Group 2, produced tell-tale patterns of error in spite of a total score well within the limits sets by the control population. Presumably, their premorbid spelling ability was still higher, but this cannot usually be accurately determined in retrospect, and in a mild case only the error pattern may reveal a spelling disability.

The relative proportions of the error types produced by the patients with right hemisphere lesions (Group 3) closely approximated those found with control Group 4. If any variety of right (minor) hemisphere lesion gives rise to a specific impairment of oral spelling, this was not brought out by the present study.

The features of spelling performance which have been discussed relate to groups of patients. They are statistical findings and cannot be directly applied to the individual case. There may be a considerable difference not only in total error score but also in patterns of error between individual members of a group, as well as overlapping between groups.

Of the eleven patients in Group 1, selected on account of the presence of finger agnosia, nine had right-left disorientation, four had disorders of script, and eight had dyscalculia. In Group 2 (thirteen patients with aphasia but without finger agnosia), there were two instances of right-left disorientation, two (out of nine cases able to be tested) of disordered script, and six of dyscalculia. The incidence of the classical Gerstmann elements is seen to be higher in the finger agnosia group. Whether the instances of right-left disorientation and dyscalculia in Group 2, in the absence of finger agnosia, are, in fact, strictly comparable to those that occur in its presence (Group 1) or whether, as with oral spelling errors in the two groups, they are referable in each instance to a different type of underlying disability is not yet known.

Summary

Oral spelling ability was tested by means of a standard spelling test in four groups of patients. It was found that aphasic patients and patients with finger agnosia each showed a distinctive pattern of spelling error when compared with control groups consisting of patients with right hemisphere and extracranial lesions, respectively. Aphasic misspellings included a high proportion of extraneous letters. Patients with finger agnosia produced a high proportion of errors relating to letter order. The control groups took up intermediate positions in these respects and did not differ significantly from one another.

It was concluded that patients with aphasia and with finger agnosia misspell in different ways and for different reasons. The association of aphasic speech and extraneous letter errors in spelling seems to reflect the underlying disorder of language functions, while the association between finger agnosia and order errors in spelling appears to reflect an underlying more general difficulty in processing information (both verbal and nonverbal) in terms of spatiotemporal sequence.

CHAPTER 6

LINGUISTICS FOR THE DYSLEXIC

LOYAL W. JOOS

Language and the Nonreader

By the time that a child has been identified as retarded in reading, it is highly probable that he will be at least 7 years of age, and by that time he is the possessor of considerable language ability—that is, he can and does communicate with others, and they with him, through the use of audible language. It is necessary to establish, as a basis for this discussion of linguistics, that the spoken language, together with the usual accompaniment of gestures and facial expressions (paralanguage), constitute the essential totality of a language. Written symbols—the alphabet, words, sentences, numbers—are not the language, but only the graphic representations of language.[1] Our seven-year-old (or older) child, then, is usually the possessor of language ability. He may not have much language, in which case he will not possibly learn to read much. Talking must come first; reading ability cannot (at first) proceed beyond the language ability possessed.

In order to possess language ability, the child must have thoughts and the ability to understand the thoughts of others. His language is a system of communicating with other people—they "say" things to him, and if he communicates with language, he replies in kind. The communication is (it must be) systematic; that is, an audible communication must mean the same thing each time it is used in a given way. In order to convey meaning, language must be systematic; and because meaning is contained, conveyed, and received by language signals, the language ability possessed and used by a human being is an excellent index, not only of intelligence, but of mental health and functioning.

[1] However, it must be noted that printed language is usually much different than spoken, having been altered to the style and rhythm which the author believes suitable to his purposes. Some people "talk like a book," but very few write like they talk.

It should not be inferred from these remarks that a poor reader is not able to read because he has little or no language ability, or because of low intelligence, or because of emotional disturbance; rather, the intention is to convey the idea that the reading ability of a given individual must be viewed in the light of the language ability he possesses.

Any linguistic approach to the remediation of dyslexia must be predicated on the assumption that appropriate steps have been or are being taken to alleviate physical difficulties which may be contributory to reading failure, such as hearing loss and visual difficulties of all kinds. The appropriateness of any method of teaching reading is of course relative to the amount of language ability possessed by the learner, but this truth is the very foundation of linguistically oriented teaching. Remedial reading classes often include pupils with a wide range of intellectual and physical disabilities, yet the success of reading instruction is often judged as if all were equal. Worse still, the materials and methods used in reading remediation often seem designed for the immature and intellectually backward.

Unless the nonreader is actually in or above the normal range of language ability and skill, he is not dyslexic. If he is actually dyslexic, then reading instruction must proceed at his language level, giving all credit for otherwise normal abilities possessed.

It is not usually possible for the teacher to make an accurate estimate of the language ability a child has because in the school environment he may well be reluctant to speak, and if he doesn't speak, his language is not directly observable. There are a few very good, ordinary reasons why a child with considerable language ability may refuse to use it in school. Most often, his refusal is based on bad experiences he has had in trying to understand and to be understood. Of course, this kind of experience is very likely to be emotionally disturbing, because human beings very much need to understand and be understood.

It should be obvious, too, that the retarded reader has had some of these frustrating experiences with his language, and it is quite probable that these experiences have left him much more affected than might be the case with another sort of child. It is often observed that children who have reading disabilities have had nonschool experiences which have (presumably) induced emotional disturbances. However true this may be, the best therapy for the nonreader is going to be something which results in a confident use of language as he understands it. Of course this means that book language and teacher language must be compatible with his language in enough points to result in successful communication.

Linguistics and the Teacher

The teacher of reading is concerned with the human intelligence which can talk, but not read. From a linguistic point of view, the pupil has already mastered the language; he has its grammar and a part of its vocabulary. He can send and receive thoughts by voice signal.

The task of the teacher of reading is to show the child how he may translate printed language into spoken language. If the printed language, spoken aloud, does not convey a language meaning to the child, there can be no use in his attempting to read it. It does not necessarily follow that the beginning reader should be taught to read only those sentences which he has previously spoken; that is too confining a limitation, because the language which can be comprehended is of greater scope than the language which can be spoken.

The teacher, then, must begin with language which the child can comprehend when he hears it. The child is to be taught how to read this language. How can this be done? If the teacher will remember that the child already knows the system of the language, in its oral form, then the process can be considered to be that of discovering the same system in the graphic form.

This, of course, is the rationale behind the use of chart stories and language experience methods in general: "What I can say, I can write. What I can write, you can read. Then you can say what has been written." But this sort of remark, though useful, is only the least of the system of English. The order of words in an English sentence and the patterns of sounding in English words are the proper study of all who would read or teach reading.

When the child has mastered the language system, he is not, of course, aware of it as a system. He has learned to talk and to listen with understanding, but he has done this naturally, in a kind of growth process, and without the conscious formulation of rules. Of course, the rules are there, in the grammar and syntax of the language, but the child uses the rules without knowing them as such.

The teacher also learned his language in the same way as did the child. The teacher must learn more than this about the language; she must see it as a system and demonstrate that system, little by little, in teaching the child.

It is indeed unfortunate that many reading teachers do not believe that English has any system. Perhaps that is too strong a remark, but how else could one interpret the following advice to teachers:

> All reading matter, no matter how simple, is made up of words. Therefore, before a child can read anything, he must know some words. If he looks at a sentence or paragraph, he must recognize some of the words, or most of the words, before he can begin to get the meaning. That is, he must have a stock of sight words to "work with." Just as no merchant can do business without some stock, so the child can do nothing until he has some sight vocabulary, and a considerable sight vocabulary at that. It will be noted that there are no reading tests of connected sentences until the second grade. That is because the first grade must be spent in getting a stock of sight words with which sentences can be read (Dolch, 1945).

Dolch goes on to say that sight words are learned in three ways—by hearing words read aloud (oral reading), by asking to have a strange word pronounced, and by studying word lists. Nowhere does he admit that the linguistic structure of words is useful to the learner; in fact, he says, "Usually the child should learn to recognize the common words instantly by sight before he begins to think of sounding. There is a danger that the habit of sounding, if taught too early, will cause him to look only at the *first letters* of common words when he should look at the whole word at once" (Dolch, 1945; italics added).

It is possible (linguists have done it) to discover a good deal more system in language than is needed by a child learning to read. So the teacher must exercise some discretion in making use of English language patterns; the discretion should be based on practical utility. For example, one linguistic reading approach identifies the pattern found in the word **pot** (consonant-vowel-consonant) and then proceeds to ring all the changes on **p__t**: **pat, pit, put, pot, pet**. This device is not practical because it does not lead to generalization in word attack skills. In short, English words do contain closed patterns like **p__t**, but since they are closed, they are not useful in word linkages.

Linguistics and Learning to Read

English is a language which consists of closed-pattern units called words, which are arranged in a closed pattern called a sentence. A closed pattern is a unit with a definite beginning and a definite end. English words are closed at both ends; when they are arrayed together to form a sentence, they are not normally changed by linking between words.[2]

[2] From a linguistic point of view, the terms "word" and "sentence" are rela-

English sentences, too, are closed. They start in a definite way, continue in one of a very few patterns, and end in a definite manner. The use of the child's unconscious knowledge of sentence patterns in reading is usually called "obtaining meaning from context." Unfortunately, many reading texts make use of rather artificial sentence patterns—shortened (for simplicity?) so much that little or no pattern remains. The very short sentences in beginning books offer so little of pattern clues that pictures must be resorted to.

Thus "Run, Jane, run" must be reinforced with a picture of Jane running, while in the longer sentence, "When Jane wants to go very fast, she must run," the meaning of "run" is clear from context.

There is a popular misconception about language difficulty which holds that long sentences are more difficult to read than shorter ones. The basis of this idea seems to be that long sentences have more words, and each added word is thought to add to the weight of the reading task. But, as a matter of fact, the longer the sentence—if it is a good sensible remark within the listening vocabulary of the child—the more the linguistic clues and cross-checks which the reader may use to obtain meaning from context.[3]

The use of pictures as a substitute for, or a supplement to, printed language is a mistake and is often a serious handicap to the beginning reader. Pictures are not the graphic representation of the language sounds that he knows; printed words are. Of course, pictures are useful to introduce the topic for the reading lesson—so are objects, music, and common experiences. After all, reading is a communication of ideas. But, once the stage is set for reading (which in the classroom means telling the teacher what the book says), attention must be directed to the printed words. A child who is having difficulty may, and often does, bluff his way along on picture clues when he should be studying the words.

So, in the beginning of learning to read, one starts by looking at words—English words. English words are composed, for the most part, of syllables which are closed, or stopped, by the fact that they end with

---

tively undefined. It should be noted, therefore, that we are using them in the same sense that an English teacher would. A word is the smallest language unit which has meaning; a sentence is a language unit which conveys a complete thought.

[3] We are aware of some research which appears to indicate a positive relationship between sentence length and reading difficulty. There is also some evidence that increasing sentence length reduces reading difficulty if the reader makes use of linguistic clues in reading. Since a linguistic approach would give the reader use of linguistic clues, longer sentences tend toward less reading difficulty than very short sentences. Obviously, if very short sentences have only limited vocabulary, an apparent low difficulty level would seem to be associated with such sentences.

a consonant or a semi-vowel. Every English syllable has a vowel sound in it. Some syllables also begin with a consonant sound. Every syllable, however, which begins with a consonant, can be pronounced even if the initial consonant were not there. Consonants are relatively invariant in sounding, particularly initial consonants. Hildreth says that "The vowels are the more important elements because they govern the pronunciation of the consonants and are usually more distinct characteristics in spoken words. A consonant sound depends upon the following vowel; it can be accurately pronounced only in conjunction with vowels. Consider the different sounds of the letter *b* in *bursting*, *bench*, *balloon*" (Hildreth, 1958).

This is a bit of nonsense, a really classic example of the cart before the horse. It would take a discriminating ear, indeed, to detect any difference in the consonant **b** among the three words cited, or among any words in which **b** is the initial sound. Of course, if Hildreth insists on sounding **bu**, **be**, **ba**, the sounds are greatly different; but it is the vowel which changes, not the **b** sound. Beginning **b** sound is invariant; let us therefore remove it from **bursting**, thus: **ursting**. Can this be pronounced? Indeed yes; the loss of the **b** leaves nonsense, but it is pronounceable nonsense, and it has the same sound it had before. Just so does one get **ench** from **bench** or **alloon** from **balloon** or **all** from **ball**. Is the sound of **b** changed by the vowel, then? No, but the vowel sound is greatly affected by the consonants which follow it.

The basic pronouncing unit of English words is a pattern which begins with a vowel and ends in a consonant or semi-vowel. This unit is open at the vowel and closed at the consonant. Because this pattern has an open end, it is easily used in building words. The English-speaking person does this without thinking—this is the way he talks.

If it were possible for English-reading people to have all printed matter instantaneously re-spelled in some standard and sensible way, we would no doubt arrange matters so that words would be phonetically spelled. Of course, this would not change the nature of English words—they would still conform, in their pronunciation, to the standard patterns mentioned above. In the preceding remarks I have been discussing vowels and consonants quite without reference to the printed representations of vowels or of consonants. Linguistically speaking, the spelling of words is not important; the sound-sense pattern is important.

Our beginning reader has the task of finding the sound-sense pattern in words as they are spelled and in sentences as they are printed. We are persuaded that the accomplishment of this task can proceed quite as well without tampering with traditional spelling or printing as it might if a phonetic spelling were used, provided that the teacher and pupil direct their attention to the discovery of the sound-sense pattern in whatever way it is spelled.

Phonogram Word Analysis

For convenience in discussing the sound-sense pattern (vowel-consonant) in its graphic form, we shall define a phonogram as a closed syllable (grapheme) which begins with a vowel and which usually produces the same sound. Some examples of phonograms will make this definition more clear:[4]

Phonograms	*Words Containing Phonograms*
and	**sand slander stand**
ill	**will illusion still**
ate	**late plate fate**

As pointed out above, phonograms are closed only at the terminal end. The beginning vowel provides an open connector to which we can and do attach beginning consonants or (frequently) the consonant which ends a preceding phonogram, as in the word **along**, which contains **al** and **ong**. When we pronounce **along**, the **l** links with the **o** very neatly to make a practically seamless joint; yet there are two vowels and two syllables in **along**, and the linguistic division would be between the **l** and the **o**.

This kind of word analysis is extremely practical for beginners in reading because the division of words (for analysis of sound) based on the phonogram unit results in phoneme-grapheme modules which have two characteristics essential to a language system—phonetic stability and coding generality. By phonetic stability we mean the quality of regularity in sounding; that is, the phonogram **ill** sounds the same no matter where in a word it is used. By coding generality we mean that the unit can be used in many different language patterns to produce as many meanings, yet it remains an identifiable unit.

Perceptually, the phonogram unit provides a middle-ground symbol, not as long as the total word, not as short as single letters. It resists

[4] By coincidence, the example phonograms are also words, but the definition is broader than the examples. Some phonograms are words; most are not. A phonogram is always a syllable, but to reduce a syllable to a phonogram, initial consonants are removed. Note, also, that each of the example phonograms can be stripped to a simpler form, e.g., **an** from **and**. The learner begins with the simple forms and builds toward the more complex forms.

perceptual reversal, as frequently happens when individual letters are identified as reading units. Being shorter than the word which contains it, the phonogram acquires the very useful quality of being a sound symbol rather than a meaning symbol. This means that a child who learns a new word by phonogram analysis sees that word as being composed of sound-symbol units; the individual perceptual parts of the word correspond to sounds.

Since the phonogram unit is longer than a single letter, yet perceptually is used as a composite symbol, each phonogram contains the definition of the vowel sound to be associated with the vowel symbol contained. It is a characteristic of English vowels that their sounding is regulated (in most cases) by the letter pattern which follows the vowel. Since the phonogram has the vowel plus its following letter pattern, the reader soon learns to see the entire pattern as a unit. Experience has shown that this is exactly what happens; pupils taught to analyze words into phonograms quickly learn to read sound-symbol patterns and are safely past letter-by-letter perception.

It should be noted that phonogram analysis avoids the traps which have beset proponents of phonic methods. In phonic methods the learner is taught a number of rules about vowel sounding, and to each rule there are exceptions; as Frostig says, "It is even difficult to teach rules of exceptions, since there are exceptions to the exceptions. For instance, when the letter **i** appears in short syllables, it is pronounced as in the word **bit** except when it appears before the letters **nd** when it is pronounced with a long sound (as in **kind**), except in the word **wind** referring to air in motion" (Frostig, 1965).

But in phonogram analysis, **ind** is a phonogram, and the **i** is long or short depending upon linguistic (language) clues. Linguistic clues are built into the oral language—the speaker of English cannot say **ind** with a long **i** if **ind** is in the initial position, but he always uses a long **i** in saying **find**, **kind**, etc., because the initial sound is a consonant other than **w**. Reading students using phonogram analysis instinctively change the vowel sound when the phonogram is preceded by a **w**.

The linguistic clues are not rules to be taught in school; they are learned along with the rest of the language. The advantage of phonogram word analysis is that it enables the child to use the built-in rules that he has.

Notice that linguistic clues to the best choice among alternative soundings of such phonograms as **ind** depend partly upon the reader's knowing the proper sounding of initial consonants, so these must be well taught.

Teaching the Child

A linguistically sound approach to the teaching of reading must be one which reveals to the learner enough about the graphic system of his language to make it possible for him to learn how to teach himself to read. The learner must have not merely a reading vocabulary, but a system of word attack which he can use to increase his vocabulary. The system of word attack must be based on some understanding of graphic language as a sound-symbol system.

For the beginning work in reading, a few carefully selected words are taught as sight words. These words are selected because they contain very common phonograms and high-incidence consonants. Of course, even at the beginning words are not to be taught in isolation but in meaningful sentences.

The next step is to call to the attention of the pupil the structure of the words already learned. Phonogram units are identified by underlining. The pupil is told that he will see these same patterns again in other words. Other simple words with the same phonograms are read—again only in sentences.

After the initial lessons, new words are always introduced as being related, in some sound-symbol way, to words previously learned. Thus, a new phonogram is taught in a word which has the same initial consonant sound as one previously learned.

Even at the beginning of reading, some words will be encountered which seem to be exceptions to the above pattern of English words. Those which cannot be avoided through vocabulary-controlled materials are best taught as sight words, and they must always be taught in sentences. Also, words like **I**, **my**, **me**, **he**, **she**, **two**, **too**, and **to** are easily learned as simple patterns involving only the long vowel sound, preceded (usually) by a consonant sound, and belonging to a familiar set of this English sound-sense pattern.

After the child has developed some confidence in his ability to attack new words by phonogram analysis, he is ready to encounter words which seem to violate the established pattern. Experience shows that children have no difficulty in learning the exceptions, provided that the usual pattern has been learned. Thus, in the initial teaching, the words **neat**, **heat**, and **treat** may be used, but **great** is taught later as an exception.

As much as possible, the teaching must be centered around language as a conveyor and container of meaning. Oral reading is useful when it can proceed as reading rather than as imitation of sounds made by others. Asking the child to read a passage aloud provides a useful check on his interpretation of letter patterns. The teacher must listen closely for good sounding of initial consonants and consonant blends, because any really wrong pronunciation of a consonant sound (unless it be due to a speech defect) indicates that the pupil is attempting a pronunciation which has no language meaning.

One should avoid the teaching of sound-symbol patterns in isolation. Further, it is a mistake to teach a single pattern exhaustively. This means that a child must learn to associate **at** with the sound found in **hat** or **rat**, but the teacher must not teach all the words ending in **at** as a complete lesson or set. Language simply does not come to us sorted out. In any case, the value of understanding that **an** has a certain sound (as in **man** or **ran**) should not be confused and debased by allowing the child to practice such drivel as "Nan has a tan fan." Instead, the reader is encouraged to discover **an** in **any**, in **annual**, in **banana**, **pancake**, etc. The goal is to have the child learn the linguistic principle, rather than the example which illustrates it.

Summary

Dyslexia can be fully understood only in the context of oral linguistic usage. Language structure must be studied as a basis for teaching of reading. Linguistics applies to the teaching of reading in the analysis of words into useful sound-sense patterns. The basic sound-sense pattern is called a phonogram. Word attack skills should be built around phonogram analysis. English sound-sense patterns are independent of spelling; reading consists of discovering the English sound patterns in their graphic coding. It is erroneous to teach reading as if English conforms to arbitrary or artificial patterns, or as if it has no pattern at all.

CHAPTER 7

READING AS OPERANT BEHAVIOR

ISRAEL GOLDIAMOND AND JARL E. DYRUD

Our experience of the words in the title of a book is often almost as compelling as its color. Each word is experienced as a unit rather than being read as a collection of letters or being perceived as an interpretation of forms. That the compelling reading experience is the result of a complex learning history is evident if the book is in an alphabet with which we are not yet thoroughly familiar, or have not yet overlearned. Further, our recollections of our own learning and our observations of children learning to read also indicate that although our present reading may be simple and immediate, the course of its acquisition may have been otherwise. The appearance of a disability where there may have been none before suggests that the maintenance of reading may also be under the influence of complex variables. Their previous effortless control over reading has now deteriorated.

The present discussion will be concerned with the contributions which an operant analysis of behavior may make to the acquisition of reading and the variables which maintain it, with specific reference to reading disabilities.

A report involving a specific deficit may serve as a convenient starting point, since it touches upon a number of points we shall raise. The report is by Hofsteater (1959), whose deaf parents were determined that their prospective child, if deaf, would not suffer the conceptual retardation which often characterizes deaf children. Language, of course, classifies and categorizes our observations as well as the rules for relating them, and different languages classify in different manners and supply different rules (cf. Whorf, 1956). The congenitally deaf child is normally excluded from the spoken language and therefore is initially excluded from many of its relations to his own behavior and that of others, including those involved in classification. This conceptual retardation often affects reading as well. Hofsteater's parents felt that the deficits were outcomes of differential treatment accorded to deaf children, and they decided to treat their child exactly as normal children are treated; they would speak and listen to him as though he were normal—using the finger alphabet. Their child was born normal but shortly after birth developed an illness which produced deafness. The parents conversed with each other and also with the child in the finger alphabet, holding up the bottle and spelling it out exactly as normal parents would talk about it. Fingering by the child was encouraged, and doing things for him was often made contingent upon appropriate fingering, in what we presume involved an implicit program of approximation and requirement of increasing approach to adult norms.

The child lisped and babbled—with his fingers. The lisping consisted of such letter combinations as "mk" for milk, and the babbling involved lettering "bo-bo-bo-bottle." This suggests that many of the developmental anomalies found in speech and currently assigned to speech mechanisms may be independent of the response modality, and may be related to general learning procedures. For example, the babbling may serve the same function as prompting in programmed instruction, with the child's behavior being described as self-prompting (Skinner and Holland, 1960). Language developed very rapidly, within the range considered normal for speaking children.

Hofsteater's father read to him regularly. With the child beside him, he opened the book, and fingered in accord with the printed text. One day, when the child was four, his father returned home tired and refused to read. The child cried, the mother supported him, and the father then acquiesced. He read in a desultory manner, and the child then pushed his father's hands aside and *read the material himself.* Stated formally, the textual stimuli were now controlling appropriate fingering behavior (rather than vocal behavior); further, the fingering behavior had been established in a linguistic context. Thereafter, he was required to do his own reading.

This unusual report deserves greater attention than it has thus far received. For one thing, it suggests that the conceptual and reading difficulties of deaf children are not in all cases products of the auditory sensory deficit *qua* deficit, but rather of deficit in the environment which responds to them in a specially deficient way. It raises the question as to what extent reading deficits in other populations, normally attributed to a peculiarity of the population, are not attributable to our reacting to that peculiarity in a way which sets up an environment which does not establish and maintain reading (cf. Goldiamond, 1958). It further suggests procedures for preventing such deficiencies from occurring and for overcoming them.

The report also reiterates what may be the basic behavioral unit for language in general. This would be (a) behavior which the organism emits, which (b) stimulates the behaving organism the same way that (c) similar behavior by a different organism stimulates it, the other organism being treated analogously to the behaving one. Speech by the child produces auditory stimuli for him which are similar to the auditory stimuli he gets when other people speak (Skinner, 1961). In the report cited, fingering behavior by the child produced visual stimuli for him similar to the visual stimuli produced by his parents when they fingered. His behavior, of course, affected them in the same way that their own analogous behavior did.

This formulation requires refinement. For one thing, after a while, the child need not look at his fingers; presumably proprioceptive stimuli replace the visual ones. Analogously, after a while, we need not listen to ourselves read; we read silently. Secondly, the child's hand, being closer, is perceptually larger and therefore different from the hand stimuli of others. Analogously, the sound of our own voice differs from the sounds of others, by virtue of such differences as bone conduction and intensity, and the like. Jersild (1947) cites the three-year-old who told her younger sister: "Don't say yook, say wook." Needless to say, a sound spectograph would record "yook", "wook," and "look" differently. Yet the different stimuli have the same meaning.

This introduces the concept of stimulus class. Operant laboratory research, with people as well as animals, indicates that physically different stimuli become members of the same stimulus class when the same consequences are attached to similar behaviors in their presence (Holland and Skinner, 1961). Thus, the red traffic light, the octagonal stop sign, and the policeman's whistle, discriminative stimuli which are quite different, all control the same behavior of putting on the brake, since the same consequences are attached to this behavior, and the consequences differ from those attached to pressing the accelerator (Goldiamond, 1966b). It is these similarities, rather than any in the discriminative stimuli themselves or in their neural pathways, which define them as having the same meaning. Herrnstein and Loveland (1964) recently selected several thousand commercially available slides, which were singly presented to a pigeon. Some contained no people, others might be a face, one or two people, or a crowd. The people were in different states of dress and undress and differed in race. If the pigeon responded (pecking at the key into which the slide was projected) when a person was present, food was presented; if no person was present, and he so responded, the apparatus was temporarily inactivated. In short order the pigeons differentiated people from non-people, a differentiation difficult to define in terms relating the physical stimulus differences, but definable conceptually. The similar "meaning" was established by similar consequences. Incidentally, among the mistakes the pigeons made was that of classifying as people a house with smoke rising from the chimney, but not a house without such smoke!

Reading involves bringing the linguistic behavioral unit under the control of textual stimuli, and the basic procedure for systematically bringing any behavior under the control of discriminative stimuli has just been presented. Through systematically relating different consequences (called differential reinforcement [Holland and Skinner, 1961]) to different behaviors in the presence of different discriminative stimuli, we can get behavior of one kind in the presence of green, and of another kind in the presence of red. We can extend this to twenty-six letters of the alphabet, with twenty-six systematically different responses attached. The pigeon may be taught to peck an A way, a B way, and so on, like the finger alphabet. This is called stimulus control; to call it reading would require that the responses so controlled be the linguistic behavior units discussed. Stated otherwise, since Finnish is written in the Latin alphabet, the authors could do a creditable job of responding appropriately in a verbal manner to Finnish text, exactly as the pigeons might do, using vocalization, of course. For the authors to be considered as reading (with understanding), the words they read should affect their other behaviors (or potential behaviors) in the same way that words similar to the text words, when uttered by a Finn, would affect the authors or other members of the Finnish community. The Finnish equivalent of "Look at the footprints on the ceiling" might be expected to occasion either such looking behavior or a grin which signified that we were not going to be caught by the gag again (Goldiamond and Pliskoff, 1965).

Operant behavior may be defined as behavior whose rate or form is affected by its consequences (Skinner, 1953). It is consequential behavior. Most behaviors of consequence are operants. The consequences and the behavior are so often intertwined in the natural setting as to obscure their relation. The consequence of pedaling a bicycle, for example, is to move forward. Turning in the direction of a fall breaks the fall, but has the additional consequence of not moving forward. The learner who instead straightens the wheel winds up with the bicycle on top of him. The relation between behavior and its consequences here is so invariant that almost every child learns to ride a bicycle, as do numerous circus animals (Goldiamond and Pliskoff, 1965). In operant laboratories, the behaviors are separated from the consequences which normally maintain them. Thus, the pigeon normally pecks on the ground for food. In the laboratory, presentation of food is made contingent upon the entirely different response of stretching, then standing upright and extended, then walking toward and pecking a disc, and the pigeon is transformed into a woodpecker. The conditions of occurrence are varied, so that in the presence of a red light one response is required and in the presence of green, yet another, as described previously. Through careful control and manipulation of conditions, lawful relationships have been discovered which have not been observed in the more natural ecology, or which have been assumed to be capricious.

An outgrowth of such research has been the development of a body of procedures to maintain and alter behavior toward a goal specified by the investigator. Indeed, such control is a major investigative tool. If the behavior desired can be produced at will, then relevant variables are obviously being manipulated. Their elucidation may contribute to our lawful understanding of behavior, as well as provide practical procedures for changing it. Space precludes discussion of other features of operant investigation which differentiate it from more traditional behavioral research. They do, however, deserve mention. In addition to using control as a procedural and analytical tool, operant investigations typically involve analysis of the behavior of individual organisms over extended periods of time, rather than of groups run for short and fixed periods. The differential effects of procedures upon the ongoing behavior of the individual, where it may be instated, attenuated, reinstated, etc., substitute for a control group differently treated from an experimental group, and procedural control and analysis is substituted for statistical control and analysis. It is evident from the foregoing that the research behaviors of the operant investigator are often close to the professional behaviors of the practitioner, who teaches individual children over extended periods of time, who varies his procedures in accord with changes in the child's behaviors, and who would like to bring each child's behaviors toward a specified criterion, rather than doing better, on the average, with one group of children than another (Goldiamond, Dyrud, and Miller, 1965). The analysis makes it possible to generalize lawfulness and procedures obtaining in one situation to another, from one species to another, from one behavior to another, and so on. For example, a pigeon subjected to certain procedures will produce curves which are identical to those produced by a child. The behavior in one case is pecking and in the other it is reading; the discriminative stimuli in one case are colors and in the other, words; the reinforcements in one case are food and in the other, progression through the program. The species differ, yet similar lawful relations obtain, and procedures developed which change the relations in one case may be extended to the other case to change the behaviors there. Thus, a variety of procedures developed in the laboratory are available for a technology of human behavioral change and maintenance.

Programs have been developed which make it possible to alter, without disrupting the behavior, the reinforcers which maintain it. For example, Cohen (1965), working with institutionalized delinquents, started out maintaining learning (going through programmed instructional material) by supplying points which were convertible to admission to a lounge containing jukeboxes and pinball machines, the initial reinforcers. Changes were gradually introduced, and algebra has now become a reinforcer! Stated otherwise, the opportunity to study advanced material has replaced the opportunity to play pinball machines in the value system of the delinquents. The temporal relation between reinforcement and behavior can also be altered by explicit procedures. In the study cited, the points were initially delivered immediately. The students are now paid weekly. The behavioral rate required can also be programmed. Initially, the organism is reinforced for every appropriate response (continuous reinforcement). This schedule can be altered so that twenty-five thousand responses are required to produce one reinforcement (Finley, personal communication), and the behavior is maintained! Reinforcements may be delivered irregularly; under these conditions, the behavior persists for extended periods of time without reinforcement (Holland and Skinner, 1961). Perseverance has been built in.

Other programs have been established so that behaviors of one kind replace the initial behaviors, as in the case of the woodpecking behavior cited, a procedure called "shaping," or the Method of Successive Approximations (Keller and Schoenfeld, 1950; Isaacs, Thomas, and Goldiamond, 1960). In yet other programs, the discriminative stimuli are shifted. For example, normally thousands of trials are required to get a pigeon to differentiate successfully between a vertical rectangle which is almost a square and a horizontal one which is almost a square, even though behavior to one is reinforced, and is not to the other. Pigeons, however, can rapidly establish discrimination between red and green. One of the rectangles is always embedded in red, and the other in green. The discrimination is rapidly acquired. The colors are then faded out gradually, and in very few trials, the behavior is transferred to the appropriate rectangle. Where thousands of trials were hitherto required, far fewer are now required; where thousands of errors were hitherto required, none are now made. This procedure is called "fading" (Terrace, 1963a, b) and suggests that it was not necessarily the task itself that was difficult for the pigeon, nor the pigeon that was difficult; it was the way we tried to teach the pigeon that caused the difficulty.

The current performance of the student may be to a considerable extent a function of the procedures used to establish that behavior; we should look to deficits in our own procedures before ascribing deficits to the student or difficulty to the problem. These procedures have been extended by Sidman (personal communication) to teaching complex discrimination of ellipses and circles to a Mongolian idiot (Skinner, 1965) and difficult form discrimination to preschool children, where, without such procedures, continual errors were made (Moore and Goldiamond, 1964). The authors were able to demonstrate control by the fading procedures themselves; when they were removed, the correct behavior collapsed; when they were reinstated, it returned. Since the interest of the authors was in demonstrating such control, some pretests with letter discrimination were not reported. The letters produced learning so rapidly that withdrawing the procedures, within the limitations of the experiment, produced no reversal; hence they were not pursued. The establishment of discrimination along a dimension of word meaning (male and female names) using similar procedures has also been demonstrated (Goldiamond, 1964b).

All of these programs, whether they relate to reinforcers, behaviors, or discriminative stimuli, have in common that they start out with and accept the level the organism starts out with, and then gradually alter it, in steps to produce the level that the investigator desires. This is done virtually without error, each step being sufficiently similar to the preceding one to maintain the relation of behavior to its ecology, but with a difference introduced which is so slight that it does not disrupt it; the differences gradually move in one direction to produce a totally new relationship. We may learn from our errors, but the notion that error is intrinsic to the learning process may be related to procedures in which error is so much a part of learning that the number of errors before learning or the number of trials to criterion (which incorporates errors) is the measure of learning. Such studies, which form the experimental basis for much of current learning theory, typically provide the organism with alternatives (going left or right in a maze, selecting the cup with the circle or square), one of which is reinforced (food is at the left turn, or the raisin is in the cup on which there is a square), but the organism is left to his own devices to discover which is correct. In the form discrimination task, for example, if the organism responds correctly when the correct form is on the left, it may be switched in position to make sure that a position preference has not been taught; other changes may also be made to ensure control only by the appropriate form. The organism may be required to unlearn incorrect bases for discrimination (produced by reinforcement when the irrelevant basis was coupled with the relevant one). These studies may be characterized by the fact that the terminal choice is presented initially and throughout, and the behavior is not programmed in terms of its current repertoire and led up to the criterion. Accordingly, there are errors, and these may be idiosyncratic to the organism and the particular experimental design that it encounters. Considerable individual differences may ensue, whose variance may override that contributed by the experimental variable, thus requiring groups, averages, and complex statistical analysis (Goldiamond, 1966b). In operant research, the terminal choice situation may not be presented initially. The choice situation initially presented may be quite far from the terminal one but so close to the organism's current repertoire as to make the correct choice highly likely. This is changed in the next presentation, and so on.

The rationale of small steps, shaping, and fading is incorporated into programmed instruction (e.g., Lumsdaine and Glaser, 1960), which is gradually being applied to reading (Martin, 1965; Summers, 1965; Birnbrauer, Kidder, and Tague, 1964; Cohen, 1964; McNeil, 1962; Silberman, 1964; Buchanan, 1964; Smith and Kelingos, 1964), and even to music instruction, which involves a different repertoire, but has functional similarities, as indicated in the term "reading music" (Maltzman, 1964). Many of the programs in programmed instruction assume that being correct is the major reinforcer, i.e., that immediately supplying information regarding accuracy will maintain the behavior in strength. Such reinforcement must, however, be examined in its larger context. Stated in common terms, why should a child want to be correct? Why should being correct keep him learning?

Research by Staats and Staats has experimentally addressed itself to the question of such intrinsic reinforcement as opposed to "extrinsic" reinforcement, and to the development of reading procedures which incorporate and advance operant technology. In an initial study (Staats, Staats, Schutz, and Wolf, 1962), social reinforcers such as saying "Good" or "That's fine" for correct behavior were compared with presentation of extrinsic reinforcers such as a trinket or a piece of candy, on identical programs. The series started with a picture presented by the investigator, with the child asked to select the same picture from a card containing others as well. This series was followed by matching a printed word, in the same manner. The child was then shown a printed word, such as "monkey," it was read to the child, and he was then required to select the corresponding picture from a card; the word was then presented again for him to say aloud. At a much later stage, sentences were introduced for him to read aloud, without such matching. The children were prekindergarten children, four years of age. These programs accompanied by social reinforcers did not maintain behavior very long. In fact, "they quickly produced escape behaviors of many kinds. The introduction of the additional reinforcers (i.e., trinkets, candy) contingent on the reading behavior reversed this . . . . they strengthened the behaviors of staying in the situation and working," which was accompanied by learning. It should be noted that the behaviors could be manipulated—that is, could be increased, attenuated, and reinstated—by the experimenter's procedures, thereby not only indicating to him when he was successful and when unsuccessful, but also immediately suggesting which variables were relevant to the child's behavior. Indeed, making such relationships explicit is one of the major contributions of operant research: in the course of doing basic research and trying to isolate the relevant variables, the experimenter becomes more skilled as a behavioral practitioner.

The foregoing procedures have since been rationalized further and automated (Staats, Minke, Finley, Wolf, and Brooks, 1964). Automation makes possible immediate reinforcement. More important, it forces the experimenter or teacher to translate the transactions between child and his environment into explicit terms, which are comprehensible, so to speak, to the machine. This provides not only for explicit analysis of effectiveness and the variables contributing to it but also provides a more readily communicable language to train others in the procedures. The basic paradigm currently used is the match to sample procedure (Skinner, 1950), which has proven to be singularly effective in training animal discriminations. Here, a stimulus presentation, say, a triangle, is presented in a small window. The child touches this window, and windows underneath the sample then light up as a consequence. One contains the triangle, while the others contain other figures, and the child matches the sample previously presented by touching the triangle window or pressing a button underneath it. Reinforcement is then presented immediately by the apparatus. The sample may contain geometric figures, letters of the alphabet, words; it may be accompanied by sound. The match may literally match the sample, or may be a word when the sample was a picture, and so on. The response may be merely a button press, may require verbalization, and so on. The procedure is quite flexible and allows for the development and testing of patterns, programs, and sequencing of programs, as for example, whether it is preferable to teach the child first to match written words to sample sounds, or vice versa.

Another discrimination procedure borrowed from the animal laboratory is the "oddity" program, where several stimuli which are similar are presented along with one which is different, the task being to select the different one. This can be related to auditory and other presentations and is being applied to teaching reading for mentally retarded deaf mutes (Candland and Conklyn, 1962).

A reinforcement program which maintains sustained behavior beyond that normally obtained is reported by Staats, Finley, Minke, and Wolf (1964). Each correct response immediately dispenses a marble from a dispenser. The child may keep the marble, or may drop it into a machine which dispenses in turn a trinket or candy. At the side are several transparent plastic cylinders, varying in size. Above each is a toy which the child had hitherto selected. The toys vary in cost, and the child may save for a toy by dropping his marble into the plastic container, getting the toy when it is filled. The sustained behavior developed raises the question of the extent to which the low attention spans assigned to preschool children are functions of the procedures used, rather than developmental. The procedures developed are being extended to teaching reading and other academic subjects to mentally retarded children (Birnbrauer, Bijou, Wolf, and Kidder, 1965).

The use of extrinsic reinforcers is related by Staats and Staats (1962) to the strength of the behavioral repertoire. Where the repertoire is weak, they argue, it may require a variety of reinforcers to maintain it. As it develops in strength, however, other reinforcers may gradually be brought into play, including those which the task itself produces.

The scheduled relation of the consequence to behavior has also been tested (Staats, Finley, Minke, and Wolf, 1964). For example, each correct testing response initially produced a reinforcer. The reinforcer was then presented only after each sixth response (called Fixed Ratio 6 in the laboratory literature), and the child's behavior disintegrated. The continuous reinforcement schedule was then returned; the behavior was reinstated. A Fixed Ratio 2 schedule (reinforcement after every second response) was then introduced, and when the behavior was stabilized here, the ratio was again increased and was soon maintained by the FR 6, which initially had disrupted it. Other schedules developed in the laboratory have also been assayed and have been found to hold relations to reading behavior in children similar to those observed in laboratory animals for other behaviors and other reinforcers.

One implication of this systematic research is that we may apply to the maintenance of human behavior some powerful techniques developed in the laboratory. In the variable schedules, the reinforcement is presented somewhat randomly, but on the average after a certain number of responses or time dictated by the schedule. An example of this schedule is where the reinforcement is presented, on the average, every three minutes, sometimes being presented after five seconds, sometimes after ten minutes (Ferster and Skinner, 1957). Behavior programmed in this manner has proven extremely difficult to extinguish; a pigeon was put on such a schedule for a short time, the reinforcement was shut off, and he was then observed to peck five hundred thousand times without reinforcement! One might state that the pigeon had character and perseverance and was proceeding despite disappointments. Someone unfamiliar with the procedures might argue that the pigeon was working for internalized or intrinsic reinforcers, since none were being presented. Be the interpretation as it may, such internal control was not present initially and is the product of explicit procedures which produce similar results wherever they are applied. There would seem to be considerable promise in the application of this technology to human reading behavior; its principles have long been applied to slot machines, which, in contrast to the gum dispenser, maintain extended behavior without continual reinforcement.

The reinforcing properties of an electric typewriter enter into procedures being developed by O. K. Moore. In the initial studies, an electric typewriter was placed in a nursery school; pressing the keys had the immediate familiar consequence of operating the strokes. The fingernails of the child were then painted in different colors, corresponding to colors on the keyboard. When the fingernail-keyboard color matched, the current was put on and the machine worked, but when there was a mismatch, the current was turned off. Appropriate fingering was thereby established (Pines, 1965). Initially, a teacher sat by with an on-off switch in her hand. She has since been replaced by a versatile computer, which can be programmed to allow the typewriter to operate only when responses defined as correct are made; correctness may be related to presentations on a screen or from auditory tape. The relations may be programmed in advance, with the entire system being labeled a "responsive environment."[1] An example of one of the units of the program is the presentation of a picture of a cow on the screen, along with the printed letters **c–o–w**. The appropriate keys on the keyboard are also illuminated, and the typewriter will work only when they are struck. The illumination on the keyboard, as well as the letters **c-o-w** on the screen, gradually fades, and the child may then type **cow** when the cow appears, or **the boy runs** when a brief motion picture appears, and so on (Moore, 1963). The child is responding with words when nonverbal material is presented, and the typewriter thus replaces the finger alphabet of the deaf. The approach has possibilities in teaching deaf children language, as well as reading and writing, and some pretests with deaf children at Gallaudet are encouraging (Roy, Schein, and Frisina, 1964). It should be noted that the procedures can be used not only to teach reading and writing of English but to develop artificial languages and study linguistics in general (Schein, personal communication), since any material may be put on the screen and the relationship programmed by the experimenter.

The program of the responsive environment may not only occasion writing when pictures are presented, but writing from dictation, as when orally dictated words and sentences are presented. The words themselves may be presented on the screen and the child required to produce the appropriate typing or verbal response; he is now reading. Penciled and blackboard-type letters are introduced both as stimuli and as behavior. Creative writing is programmed: having typed from someone else's dictation, the child may be asked to say some words and type from his own dictation. The first graders put out a newspaper (Moore, 1963).

Reading and writing can be intrinsically related: our own reading is normally a critical feedback for our own writing. Stated otherwise, our reading is contingent upon our writing and will maintain or alter it, as is evident when we misspell a word and correct it by seeing it; reading may reinforce writing. Goldiamond (1966a) reports a high school senior who was failing because his writing was illegible. When legibility was produced, numerous spelling errors were discovered which had not been amenable to correction before because the writing was illegible. Cohen (1964) required college freshmen to type everything so that spelling errors could not be fudged by sloppy writing.

The separate teaching of the interwoven behaviors of reading and writing is related to the fact that writing involves the acquisition of

[1] The commercial version is obtainable through Responsive Environments Corporation, 21 East 40th Street, New York, New York 10016.

complex muscular coordination and must be part of a separate program for young children. The electric typewriter overcomes this difficulty and makes it possible to teach these two intrinsically related behaviors together, more in accord with their relationship in the natural ecology.

In this context, the possible use of Hawken Letters for programming reading should be noted. These are letters and letter combinations printed on small rectangles. A dot underneath each aids in orientation. The tabs are orange for vowels and white for consonants; they can be coordinated with a flash-card, textual, and oral program, as reported by Friedlander, Lightbody, and Schwartz (1965). Moving the tabs around requires the child to learn no new muscular coordinations but does produce words, that is, writing.

Needless to say, the establishment of discrimination is facilitated if the stimuli to which systematically different responses will be reinforced are different, and the stimuli related to similar behaviors are similar. Such an orderly relation unfortunately does not strictly obtain in English. The development of an orderly alphabet by Pitman (Downing, 1964) is relevant to this problem. Interestingly, children taught in the Initial Teaching Alphabet are reported to transfer to the conventional alphabet—an example of the effects of the larger ecology.

If reading and writing are intrinsically related, so that the consequence of reading maintains and alters our own writing, then listening and speaking are similarly related. Stated otherwise, listening maintains and alters the sounds we speak, as was discussed earlier in the definition of the basic linguistic response. The child who has hurt himself may be heard telling himself: "There, there, don't cry." The sound of his own voice presumably affects him the way such vocalizations by parents have affected him in the past. This relationship may be capitalized upon in the teaching of language. A match-to-sample device for German may include in its matches such choices as **vier**, **for**, **fuhr**, **für.** If the sample to be matched is an auditorily presented **fy:r**, or **fu:r**, or **fi:r**, correct matching requires distinguishing between these often confused sounds, and the ear may thereby be trained; that is, differential listening is of consequence (Rocha e Silva and Ferster, 1964). Once the child has learned to discriminate these sounds, he may check his own speech production against the sounds it produces, which is analogous to our checking of our own spelling against our reading, and may shape his own verbal patterns. The use of a card-changing device based on such match-to-sample procedures for teaching beginning reading is reported by Doehring and Lacy (1963); the card contains a sample on top and matches below. Three types of matches were investigated: a visual match to auditory sample, which the authors consider a form of silent reading, and which is directly relevant to the point just made, since the child's correct behavior is contingent upon auditory discrimination, visual match to visual sample, where the same written word or sentence appears both in match or sample and may be accompanied by a spoken word; and oral match to visual sample, or reading aloud. A more detailed analysis of the reinforcing properties of the auditory stimuli produced by the speaker's own speech is presented by Goldiamond (1965), who attributes the disruption of speech under delayed auditory feedback to disruption in the normally immediate temporal relation obtaining between speech and its reinforcing sound; the delayed feedback is used as a consequence attached to specified speech patterns. Among the variables manipulated is reading rate, which is altered to produce prolonged speech; the rate is then gradually increased by explicit procedures. The analysis has been used in the establishment of fluent and rapid patterns of speech which replace the stuttering of clinical cases.

Procedures for measuring and altering silent and oral ongoing reading rate are reported by Goldiamond (1962a), who required the reader to press a button to present himself with a few words of reading material. A cumulative recorder is thereby activated and consequences may be attached to alter rate. The use of a lever pull for similar purposes is reported by Raygor, Wark, and Warren (1964). Shaping procedures were applied to intervals between such responses. A similar principle has been applied by Lindsley (1962) to television viewing. The screen fades out unless the child presses a button to keep it bright, and the rate curves obtained relate to the viewer's interest and to whether the humor in the presentation is carried by visual or auditory stimuli. These procedures might well be adapted to measuring interest of reading material.

Doehring and Lacy (1963) report that correctness was an adequate reinforcer; however, they also report that the behavior was established in the context of much socialization between teacher and child. Indeed, laboratory investigations indicate that the effectiveness of a reinforcer is dependent upon a variety of other variables, so that punishment may even be arranged in such a way as to maintain the behavior upon which it is contingent (Holz and Azrin, 1961). Stimuli which initially had no reinforcing properties may be established as reinforcers through a variety of procedures (Kelleher & Gollub, 1962); the marbles used so effectively by the Staatses require a "back-up" reinforcer to maintain their properties (the candy and large toys to which they can be converted). The issue of correctness alone, as opposed to trinkets and the like, may be related to other such reinforcers. Moore, who tries to keep adults away from the child's relation with the responsive environment, does have a class to which the child later goes and where the behavior acquired is consequential. Behaviors such as puzzle solving, in which the consequence (solution) stems directly from the behavior, are defined as "autotelic" (an end in itself) by Moore (1963; cf. Skinner, 1961), who considers rewards and punishments as distractions from the learning process, since the child may try to discover how these relate to his behavior. As has been suggested, the decision as to whether these are distracting or necessary to learning may depend upon the strength of the repertoire and the general ecology of behavior, rather than being inherent in any general properties of reward (which is only one form of reinforcement) *per se*.

One of the classical consequences maintaining reading is, of course, finding out what happened; this is involved in reading for its own sake. The rhythm of a written poem cannot be produced unless the poem is read, and if verbal rhythm and other effects of poetry are not reinforcing, there will be little reading of poetry. Such books as *Alice in Wonderland* are read by Moore's children, in marked contrast to the limited possibilities open to children taught by the *Go Dog Go* readers. Procedures based upon word recognition must limit the number of words which the child learns to read, and his reading vocabulary will, accordingly, not only be much smaller than his spoken vocabulary but will also be inadequate for many stories, including the children's classics, which have sustained children's behaviors for many years. The legendary power of such reinforcers is demonstrated in the *Arabian Nights*, where the discovery of what happened next in Scheherezade's stories was contingent upon the king's keeping her alive. This he did for more than a thousand and one nights, rather than killing her immediately, as was his original intention. The power of the storyteller over adults is as great as over children, and it is questionable whether whatever advantages adhere to the word-recognition reading procedures, in pure or phonics-adulterated form, outweigh the elimination from reading of this proven reinforcer. Further, making the reading vocabulary smaller than the child's spoken vocabulary decreases the likelihood of presenting material which ties in with other reinforcers stemming from the ecology in which the child has acquired his spoken vocabulary.

Reinforcers which can be manipulated are quite varied. They range from the immediate feedback of the sounds of one's own voice (Goldiamond, 1965), to the presentation of auditory and visual patterns

(Friedlander, 1965), to making a typewriter work (Moore, 1963) or a musical instrument play (Maltzman, 1964); to presentations of food, candy, trinkets (Staats *et al.*, 1964); to being correct (Doehring and Lacy, 1963); to tokens (Ayllon and Azrin, 1965; Birnbrauer and Lawlor, 1964); to obtaining social approval and the like, which, like marbles or money, is dependent upon the larger ecology; to other consequences such as finding out what happened next, to solving a puzzle, or putting a kite together by following the instructions. In the latter cases, one behavior is contingent upon another (cf. Premack, 1959)—that is, is reinforced by another—and this too may depend upon the larger ecology.

An example of the utilization of behavior as a reinforcer to improve reading and other subjects and of the establishment of a program of changing reinforcers is provided in the study by Cohen (1965), previously cited, involving institutionalized juvenile delinquents. The value system, or system of effective reinforcers, it will be recalled, was changed from the initial value system of the lounge (where these students now spend less than 30 minutes of a possible 210) to that of advanced academic subjects. Points were given for academic achievement. The points were reinforcing, since they could be used to gain entry into a lounge, where the students could play pinball machines. At a later stage the points could be used for purchases; at a still later stage, they provided entry into special courses. Among the courses studied was algebra, which turned out to have high prestige value in the institution, and several students who wanted to take it were told that it required learning less advanced mathematics first. They undertook the programs—for which the consequence was algebra. The reinforcing property of algebra derived from the larger social ecology, as do many of those maintaining our own behavior. The critical thing would seem to be to bring the effects of the ecology into the system. In three months the reading level of several of Cohen's subjects rose four years, although no specific remedial reading programs were utilized. Getting points was contingent upon being correct, and being correct was contingent upon reading the material presented; thus reading was maintained and improved.

Behavioral Deficits and Behavioral Curricula

A behavior as complex as reading depends not only upon the current ongoing reinforcers but upon its relation to a complex sequence involving further reinforcers, as well as a history of past behaviors which have been shaped into the current one. Examples of the maintenance of reading behavior by a sequence of later reinforcers that we have discussed have been the use of Moore's classroom, the Staats back-up reinforcer, and Cohen's weekly pay. In actuality, maintenance of a sequence of behaviors by later reinforcers is regularly developed in the laboratory, where it is called "chaining."

Chaining describes many situations in which the organism appears to be working for a future goal. In the laboratory such behavior is established by training the animal on this reinforcer (i.e., goal) at the very beginning. The procedure is best explained through a description of one used to train a white rat, which in succession went through an arch, up a ladder, across a drawbridge, up a staircase, pulled himself along a handcart, went up a spiral staircase, and hit middle C on a piano, which opened a gate blocking a tunnel. He then entered a plastic elevator, where he pulled on a latch which released the elevator to the bottom of the apparatus, where he pressed a lever five times and obtained food. He repeated this last performance four more times, the lights went out, he then went through the arch again and recycled ("Barnaby," in Lundin, 1961). The sequence starts with going through the arch, but the actual training procedure is the reverse. The animal is first trained to work for food. He is then placed in the elevator through which he can see the lever. To get to the lever he must pull the switch on the elevator. He is then placed in front of the tunnel from which he can see the elevator. To get to the elevator, he must open the gate, and so on. The behaviors are acquired in an order which is the reverse of the chronological order by which they run off. They appear to be under the control of a future reinforcer. In chaining, the reinforcer which maintains one behavior (for example, getting to the elevator maintains going through a tunnel) is the discriminative stimulus for the next behavior in this case (the elevator occasions pulling the switch).

Such chains occur throughout education, and may relate curricula to their larger ecology. We like to think that children go to school for the sake of learning, or because they know learning is consequential in our society. If, however, getting an education is irrelevant to what they will be doing later on, the diploma and all the other reinforcers for academic behavior will have little effect. Such irrelevance may produce the gentleman's C for those fortunate few for whom study or lack of study are unrelated to an assuredly rosy future, or dropping out of school for some unfortunates whose study, or lack of it, is unrelated to an assuredly bleak future.

A sequence which differs from the chaining sequence is the systematic sequence exemplified by a curriculum. Here, in order to learn algebra, we must first know multiplication and division. In order to handle multiplication and division, we must first have learned something about numbers. Accordingly, an orderly sequence is set up in which one subject matter must be mastered before the next is attempted.

A well-organized educational system will capitalize on both chaining sequences and systematic sequences. Most architectural curricula work on the systematic sequence. Knowing that calculus is necessary for understanding stresses, and that algebra is necessary for understanding calculus, they start their students out with algebra, then calculus, and so on. In the process they lose many students who would like to be architects. The German Bauhaus used a different procedure. The architectural students were given houses to design immediately upon entering as freshmen. The houses were Polynesian straw huts, but they served the purpose. From these huts, the program moved to slightly more complex houses and finally approached some modern houses, for which knowledge of stress was required. At this point a systematic sequence was introduced, starting with algebra. The morale of the students was quite high, and there were few dropouts.

Programmed instruction makes use of both chained and systematic sequences, and a particular unit may be taught by a chaining procedure; the learning of this unit now makes it possible to build others upon it. The child is supplied with food and attention before he can speak; after a while they become contingent on speech, and speech makes other behaviors possible. Reading involves language, and requires it as a prerequisite. The systematic sequence involves the child's learning to listen, that is, to discriminate between the words his parents make. Such discrimination is related to his behaviors and other consequences that he observes. Verbal behavior is shaped in this setting, with the consequent sounds that such behavior produces being matched against the discriminative repertoire already acquired by the child, as well as being shaped by his audience, which may attach other consequences. In school he is presented with textual material, for which different sounds are reinforced. These sounds may then affect him in the way that the language of his community affects him, and he may now read with understanding. One of the authors recalls coming home from school and reading his first-grade assignment of *Humpty-Dumpty* aloud (this was before the *Go, Dog, Go* readers). His older sister said that she was trying to practice the piano, and asked why he didn't read silently. "But how can I understand what I am reading unless I can hear myself say it?" he asked. His sister then nodded sympathetically and told him that when he developed he would not have to do this. "You mean to say I will read it only with my eyes?" he asked, recalling the way his parents read. In actuality, such reading is not by the eyes alone, since recent research by Edfeldt (1960) tends to support Watson's hypothesis that verbal thinking is subvocal speech. Edfeldt planted microelectrodes in the tongue and larynx of subjects when they read silently, and obtained spikes appropriate to the material they were reading; the more fluent readers produced smaller spikes. By a process possibly analogous to fading, the auditory consequences of reading are faded out, so that eye movements and minute vocal movements replace them. The behavior may become so well established that partial recognition then enters. For example, only the front of a car which projects beyond a house needs to be seen to report an entire car. Parts of a word may suffice to produce the response. Other information extraneous to perception may lead us to respond as though we were perceiving the total stimulus. When your wife tells you that she will pick you up at lunch, the green speck in the distance is "identified" or "recognized" as the car, on the basis not of perceptual information, which is insufficient, but of other information which restricts response alternatives to the appropriate ones (see Goldiamond, 1964a, for discussion of the cocktail party phenomenon in this context). The use of partial presentation, redundancy, and context are involved in rapid reading and scanning, where the reader does not have to process every bit of perceptual information but capitalizes upon response biases and criteria (Goldiamond, 1962b). Thus, rapid and fluent reading will involve the acquisition of a variety of behaviors which can be programmed to produce good reading, as well as programmed to produce faulty reading.

We are reminded of a college student who entered the class late, after the instructor had written his name, Palermo, on the blackboard. She apologized to the instructor privately for having been late. "I'm so glad to meet you, Dr. Panorama," she said. It is quite clear from this comment and from other behaviors that the student had been taught to read through context, rather than phonetically. She was able to get by with this behavior in all cases except those where the context was drastically altered. Indeed, the support of the perceptual behavior or reading by context and other nonperceptual information often masks the deficits so well that neither we nor the person who has the deficit realizes that they exist; this has been related to a behavioral analysis of stupidity (Goldiamond, 1966a). A framework for the analysis of reading behavior in relation to Skinner's (1957) concepts of verbal behavior has been presented by Hively (1966).

Given a behavior which is sustained by so many different variables, the ascription of its disruption to any particular one of them, without considerable evidence, would seem to be hazardous. Thus, it would seem to the authors that there has been a considerable amount of overgeneralizing in medical theory where linguistic deficits follow some injury. The irreversibility of some of these phenomena, or their gradual alteration independent of training attempts, has often been interpreted as indicating anatomical impairment. Be this as it may, rather than stating that certain aphasics cannot rhyme, we might ask what enters into rhyming and see what is necessary to program its reinstatement. Seemingly irreversible changes can be reversed. Riesen (1950), for example, reported drastic visual-behavioral anomalies following deprivation of patterned vision in early infancy; lenses which transmitted only diffused light were placed over the eyes of new-born animals. In his doctoral dissertation Rubin (1965) took such animals, who were unable to fixate for extended periods, inserted a tube in their mouths, and presented spots for fixation. When the animal did fixate (an eye camera was used), milk was presented, and the visual damage was reversed. What might normally have been permanent impairment was permanent only in the absence of the appropriate behavioral technology.

We are currently instrumenting the use of eye cameras which monitor eye movements as well as the field being observed. A television camera is focused on a spot of light projected into each eye, and each spot appears on a television screen in a position corresponding to the fixation of the eye on the field (the field is also on the screen). Convergence produces overlapping spots, and divergence produces differing spots, with the control questions being these: how can we bring the spots together (for strabismus), and how can we have them follow outlines (for tracking and reading)? The analytic questions are these: what variables are involved in such control, and what reinforcers maintain eye movement? We are becoming accustomed to advances in medical technology whereby hitherto inevitable consequences are now being averted. The development of a behavioral technology may have similar effects.

Such medical terms as specific language disability, congenital word blindness, developmental dyslexia, developmental alexia, specific dyslexia, congenital dyslexia, strephosymbolia, and specific reading disability (Cole and Walker, 1964) all refer to behavior deficits related to reading and speech. Many have been assumed to be neurological defects which are genetic. There are no demonstrable, consistently associated neurological stigmata, but one or more of the following behavioral deficits may be associated: delay in motor speech development; failure to develop clearly articulated speech at the expected time, baby talk, sound substitutions, lisps, and persistence of cluttered speech; stuttering or stammering; and specific reading and spelling disability, word blindness, developmental dyslexia, etc. As has been discussed throughout this paper, the behaviors involved in language and reading are highly complex and require both systematic and chain sequences for their establishment and maintenance. Stated otherwise, a deficit anywhere along the sequence may disrupt the complex product, and it would seem that more research is required before such a breakdown can be assigned to a specified link. Among the critical deficits that we have noted throughout this discussion is that produced by an environment which shapes the very deficits it considers causative. If deaf children are conceptually retarded, it may be, as the Hofsteater study suggests, that the social environment, for understandably human reasons, programs itself not to make verbal demands upon the child and thereby retards his language development. This further justifies the special treatment. Mentally retarded children are often behaviorally or socially isolated. Their global statements are treated with "understanding" and are not corrected, whereas those of the normal child are, and become attenuated over time, in contrast to such behavior by many retardates (Goldiamond, 1958). If boys, and particularly left-handed boys, show a higher incidence of specific language disability, we would consider it legitimate to raise the possibility that they are being treated differently from girls and righthanded boys. Whatever speculative status this possibility has is shared by the neurological speculation.

Appropriate programming requires appraisal of the child's current repertoire and the changes that can be made in it. We believe that Bender's (1957) assignment of some reading disorders to a maturational lag, where the home demands are beyond the child's neurological competence to respond, may be interpreted in this manner.

Psychiatric disturbances have often been causally related to reading disorders. Both chaining and systematic sequences may be used to describe the maintenance and development of complex behaviors other than those involved in academic subjects and reading. The behaviors which the psychiatrist deals with may have been learned according to the same principles, and the deficits may be analyzed similarly. The learnings, however, are not academic, but interpersonal. Stated otherwise, the textbook is people rather than words. There are dropouts from interpersonal learning as well as from scholastic learning.

The authors have currently been working with a high school junior who was failing his subjects. He had been an honor student in elementary school and then moved to a new neighborhood and a new school. His parents are professionals, but his interests were restricted to automobile mechanics, and he was not particularly talented in mechanics, either. His typical span of attention in conversation was not over five seconds. This student was apparently "tuning out" his parents, his teachers, and his friends. Inasmuch as reading involves verbal behavior, such tuning out also, it would seem, began to affect his listening to himself, that is, to affect his own thinking. Through psychiatric concentration on interpersonal relations, he was able to sustain conversations for the psychiatric hour, and his general attentiveness, including attentiveness to his own verbal behavior, increased. When the social psychologist (cf. Mead, 1934) infers internalization of the values and the norms of the society, he may be referring to a process similar to the linguistic one we have described; namely, that the subject is affected by his own behavior in the same way in which similar behaviors by members of the community affect him. This presumes a long history of interactions, consequences, and social payoffs to the individual which will maintain such behavior. Accordingly, it is not surprising that symbolic deficits and autistic patterns characterize the verbal behavior of those people whose other behaviors do not tie in with the values of the community. What we characterize as "thinking disorders" may be related to deficits in these social areas.

Thus the deficits which can affect reading may not only be the various behaviors involved, such as orientation from left to right, moving one's eyes, and the like, but the socialization process of the individual, since reading is verbal behavior acquired within this social matrix.

Verbal behavior is a social operant; that is, it is maintained by reinforcers supplied by people, and it supplies the child (and the adult) with considerable control over the human environment. Certain forms of control may be pathological, as in the case of hysterical invalidism; the invalid in the family controls the family. Although the control is considered pathological in that it also produces certain types of consequences which we consider to be undesirable, this does not negate its operant definition as behavior maintained by its consequences. The high school student with whom we were working was exerting a considerable amount of control over his parents by becoming an academic and reading problem. He tuned out in the middle of conversations; his failure in school and his movement toward a mechanic's level disturbed his parents; he had them going in circles. The behaviors were operants (which is not to say that they were planned or thought out), but if not corrected they might result in incompetence in a variety of areas. In this boy's case, correction of the reading disorder involved the direction of attention to other deficits. In other cases, since speech and reading are critical in our relation to people, simple correction of speech and reading deficits may effect a personality change (cf. Goldiamond, 1965).

Clearly, the field is one which requires careful analysis and research, and there would appear to be no pat solution, either through simple prescription of complex personality change or simple discrimination training. However, it must not be assumed that no guidelines exist. Systematic relationships are being discovered and generalizable procedures—as well as some precautions—are being developed. Reading is learned behavior, personality is learned behavior, and algebra is learned behavior. All are amenable to experimental analysis by similar procedures. However, a caveat must be inserted. Each not only has different topographies but may have different sequences, which require special consideration. A simple awareness of such differences may not be sufficient.

For example, we may have a well-thought-out program, developed by the best reading experts in the land, in which each step follows the other appropriately. The behavior, however, is not sustained, and we mutter about complex motivational variables. At the other extreme, we may have developed a beautiful program of reinforcements which will sustain the behaviors that they are made contingent upon. The program, however, is a poor one. It programs one type of discrimination before another in a sequence many of whose stages are in the wrong order. The child's behavior is sustained throughout the program, but he may be learning the wrong things, or learning inefficiently, or developing patterns which will compete with other patterns that will become necessary at a later date. What would clearly seem to be needed is a combination of the two types of skills, an appropriate program and an appropriate procedure for maintaining and guiding behavior through it. And such a fortuitous combination would seem to require an analysis of reading behavior, its development, and its maintenance, as an operant which has effects upon the environment and upon the individual reader, as well as being a complex, special form of behavior which has its own sequences and its own internal logic.

PART II

Teaching Methods and Program Organization

CHAPTER 8

THE ORTON-GILLINGHAM APPROACH

JUNE L. ORTON

I. A History and Synopsis of Orton's Contribution to the Theory and Identification of Reading Disability

In this chapter a historical review is given of the pioneer investigations of the neurologist and psychiatrist, Samuel T. Orton, into the nature of developmental language disorders in children and methods of treatment. He theorized that certain reading difficulties were due to a physiological variation related to the establishment of the normal unilateral dominance in the visual language areas of the brain. Remedial procedures are based upon a combined visual-auditory-kinesthetic training, following a careful appraisal of the child's skills in all language areas. The Orton principles of clinical diagnosis and remediation are discussed, and in Section II of this chapter a summary is presented of the step-by-step methods of instruction developed by Anna Gillingham for teachers and set forth in the comprehensive Gillingham-Stillman manual of remedial training.

BACKGROUND

Orton may well be called "the father of dyslexia" in America. As early as 1925, he had identified the syndrome of developmental reading disability, separated it from mental defect and brain damage, offered a physiological explanation with a favorable prognosis, and fully outlined the principles of remediation by which, in the past forty years, hundreds—thousands, in fact—of disabled readers have been helped to overcome their handicaps.

Orton became interested in reading problems through the study of certain children referred to his pioneer Iowa mobile mental hygiene clinic because of slow learning or behavior disorders. One was a boy of sixteen from a junior high school who could read only first-grade material. Orton's analytical study of this "word-blind" boy was the beginning of many years of work in this field, with many associates and a long procession of young patients.

After presenting his interpretation of developmental reading disability to the American Neurological Association in May, 1925, Orton received a two-year grant from the Rockefeller Foundation which enabled him to organize a full-scale research program at the State University of Iowa, where he was professor of psychiatry and director of the State Psychopathic Hospital. The three-fold program included experimental work in basic cerebral anatomy and physiology, an expansion of the traveling mental hygiene clinic to examine school children throughout the state, and diagnostic and training experiments with children with reading problems. Marion Monroe, then research associate in psychology, investigated the differential errors in oral reading of an experimental group and a control group, and conducted the laboratory school and other remedial programs under Orton's direction (Monroe, 1928). Certain physiological studies of stutterers were carried on with Edward Lee Travis, while an assistant in neuropathology, Lauretta Bender, worked on related research projects in brain physiology in Holland.

In 1928, Orton moved to New York City, where he received a professorship at Columbia University in neurology and neuropathology and was appointed neuropathologist at the New York Neurological Institute. Here, again with aid from the Rockefeller Foundation, he organized another research unit to investigate further developmental language disabilities, particularly spelling, handwriting, word deafness, and developmental apraxia (extreme clumsiness). During the war years he directed other research projects in Connecticut and Pennsylvania and continued to help many parents, teachers, and schools with the problems of their dyslexic pupils.

The Language Research Project of the New York Neurological Institute (1932–1936) was a multidisciplinary research and training unit, with psychiatry, neurology, psychology, speech therapy, and remedial teaching represented on the clinic staff. To Anna Gillingham, formerly psychologist in charge of remedial work at the Ethical Culture Schools, Orton assigned the task of organizing the teaching procedures for the various syndromes. He also encouraged her to explore methods of early identification and prevention. Miss Gillingham later developed a complete remedial program which she called "the alphabetic method." With assistance from her friend, Bessie W. Stillman, a remedial teacher, she prepared and in 1946 privately published the now classic Gillingham-Stillman manual, entitled, *Remedial Training of Children with Specific Disability in Reading, Spelling, and Penmanship,* which has had world-wide circulation and was in its sixth edition, enlarged to 375 pages, at the time of her death in 1964.

Orton espoused the cause of the children with developmental language disabilities in many talks to medical and educational groups, and the Thomas W. Salmon Memorial Award in 1936 gave him the opportunity to present the results of his first ten years of language research in a series of three lectures at the New York Academy of Medicine. These were subsequently published in book form under the title, *Reading, Writing and Speech Problems in Children* (1937) and constitute the most complete exposition of the Orton approach.

Orton's research associates during this period included Earl Chesher in neurology and Paul Dozier and David G. Wright in psychiatry. Katrina De Hirsch was a frequent consultant in speech pathology, and June Orton, who had been associated with the earlier research projects in Iowa as chief psychiatric social worker and coordinator, became her husband's clinical assistant in his private practice in New York. Edwin M. Cole, neurologist, worked for a time with the Language Research Project before organizing the Language Clinic of the Massachusetts General Hospital in Boston, which he has now directed for over twenty-five years. Many others who have since become leaders in the field had contacts with Orton during his twenty years in New York.

After Orton's death in 1948, a group of his close associates informally organized themselves as the Orton Society, to keep in touch with one another and with the continuing developments of their work. The Orton Society has since been incorporated as a nonprofit scientific and educational organization, which meets once a year and publishes an annual professional journal, *The Bulletin of the Orton Society.* Among the early members from the educational field were Peter Gow, Warren Koehler, Harlin Sexton, Page Sharp, Helene Durbrow, and Sally Childs, whom Miss Gillingham appointed to assume the responsibility for the manual after her retirement.

The "Orton genealogy" now has too many branches, too many offshoots, and too many descendants to trace, but there are probably few oldtimers or newcomers in clinical work with dyslexic pupils who have not been influenced by Orton's dedication to these children, his insights into their problems, and his practical methods of diagnosis and retraining. Many of his contributions have now been assimilated into remedial clinic procedures. I have chosen to present the Orton approach in this chapter largely in Orton's original formulations because they impart something of the urgency and the hopefulness, tempered with scientific caution, of his explorations in this field. Many of the same principles are currently being rediscovered and restated in new models and new idioms, but even in the phraseology of an earlier period they are relevant and helpful in understanding the problems of the dyslexic child today.

Conceptual Background

Orton's approach to reading problems derived from his neuropsychiatric background and case-study methodology and included certain basic concepts which were quite different from those of most educators, whose interest in reading was naturally focused on providing uniform classroom instruction for all pupils in the primary grades. Individual differences in rate of learning were sometimes recognized by dividing classes into fast, average, and slow reading groups, in which the less able readers could proceed at a slower pace with easier basal readers. Pupil differences in learning ability or needs for varying instructional methods were rarely considered. Progressive education schools, new at the time, were giving reading instruction only indirectly.

Orton approached reading as one stage of the child's language development, preceded by spoken language (hearing and speaking) and expressed in writing, which includes spelling. He looked upon language as an evolutionary human function associated with the development of a hierarchy of complex integrations in the nervous system and culminating in unilateral control by one of the two brain hemispheres (cerebral dominance). Retardation in acquiring reading suggested to him that there was some interference with this natural process of growth and development. He was impressed with a specific characteristic of reading impairment in the children he studied—the instability in recognition and recall of the orientation of letters and the order of letters in words, which he termed "strephosymbolia," meaning "twisted symbols." This to him indicated an intrinsic difficulty of a special nature in the association process. Further observations disclosed mixed right-and-left laterality in the motor patterns of many retarded readers with these reversal tendencies. Study of the physiology of the brain led to his formulation of the hypothesis of a comparable intermixture of control in the two hemispheres of the brain in those areas which subserve the visual or reading part of the language function and are normally active only in the dominant hemisphere. He postulated that the mirrored (antitropic) images of the two hemispheres might then conflict when the child attempted to build associations between letters and spoken words, producing confusions and orientation errors and a general delay in learning to read. Genetic considerations suggested a probable hereditary explanation of the opposing right-and-left tendencies, which under these conditions might result in a disturbance in the development of the language function:

> The data we have assembled from the study of left handedness and of various language difficulties in the family stock of children who have a specific disability in learning to read and show the strephosymbolia syndrome give what to me is convincing evidence that such children present intergrades between right-sided and left-sided familial tendencies and that the reading disability follows fairly definite hereditary trends. . . . In families with this disturbance there are also more than the expected number of left-handed members and persons with delayed speech, stuttering, reading, writing and spelling disabilities, and abnormal clumsiness (developmental apraxia). In the childhood histories of children who come to attention as presenting reading and spelling problems we not infrequently find indications of developmental deviations in their acquisition of speech and motor patterns (Orton, 1943).

Orton's neurological experience with adults who had suffered language losses through disease or injury to the dominant brain hemisphere, which is usually opposite to the master hand, particularly in right-handed people, also aided him in his investigations of nontraumatic delays in language development in children. Studying not only the reading but also the oral language and the writing skills in his young patients, he found many evidences of both the interrelation and the separation of the various language functions. A poor visual memory for recognizing printed words would result in poor reproduction in recalling them for writing, and thus impair reading and spelling. A poor auditory memory for words would interfere with their reproduction in speech and in writing; hence, word deafness, with poor speech patterns, meager and confused vocabulary, ungrammatical writing, and poor spelling. Poor handwriting or speech would result in poor visual or auditory reinforcement of word patterns, further weakening the circuit.

Another useful neurological concept in the Orton frame of reference was that of the three levels of cortical elaboration of the sensations received by the sense organs, corresponding to anatomically different brain areas and giving rise to: (1) awareness of the external stimulus; (2) recognition of its concrete meaning; and (3) association with abstract or symbolic (language) meaning. Tests showed that in the visual area the children with the specific reading disabilities with whom he was working (1) could see the print clearly and (2) could recognize that they were seeing letters and words and even copy them correctly, but (3) could not identify them as meaningful language symbols, i.e., read them. Similarly, the "word-deaf" cases (1) had adequate hearing and (2) could identify sounds correctly but (3) had difficulty in associating concepts with the spoken words. In discussing these specific language delays, Orton stated that "in the developmental word-blind or word-deaf cases of language disturbances in children, I believe that there is a functional difficulty acting selectively at the Third or Word Level, in the visual or auditory areas of their brains" (1946).

Since it is only at the third, or language, level that these association areas function from the dominant hemisphere, such observations strengthened Orton's opinion that the "dominance" aspect of the physiology of the brain provided the key to language development and its disorders.

Orton's physiological explanation of reading problems of the strephosymbolic type differed sharply not only from the approach of the educators but also from the psychological theories of an exclusively emotional causation of learning difficulties that were current at that time. Orton recognized and delineated the various emotional patterns which the children displayed, but he interpreted them for the most part as reaction to academic frustration and defeat. In many of his cases, the child's personality development seemed to have been entirely normal until the reading difficulty blocked academic progress; moreover, the emotional disturbances generally subsided or disappeared when the specific nature of the disability was established and remedial measures instituted in a direct attack upon the child's educational problem, namely, how to learn to read.

Children with apparent psychiatric disorders were referred to other specialists for study and treatment. Today personality studies by a clinical psychologist often provide helpful insights, and for some children with multiple problems, a two-fold treatment program of psychotherapy in a child guidance center and remedial reading tutoring in a language clinic has proved of value. Orton stressed the importance of including the child himself in the planning and giving him, as well as his parents and his classroom teachers, a direct explanation of the probable physiological nature of his difficulty and the reasons for the recommended treatment procedures. This has a great effect in clearing the air of feelings of guilt—the child's guilt over not being able to learn and that of others over not being able to teach him. Orton described his approach to the children in this way:

> They are usually interested in the story of how only one side of the brain works in the language function and intrigued with the idea that the two halves of their brain may be "squabbling over which is to be the boss" and pleased when it is possible to tell them, as it frequently is on the basis of intelligence tests, that their brains are better than average but not working just right for the particular subject in which they have met trouble. This sort of understanding of how his difficulty may have arisen will often go a long way toward preventing the child from falling back on explanations based on emotional instability, "nervousness," undue fears, or lack of self-confidence which in themselves are not entirely emotionally acceptable and which often seem to operate as a vicious circle. An even more complete explanation to the parents and to the teachers of the specific nature of all of these difficulties is of prime importance in treatment of the child since the school failures have all too often been interpreted as due to some degree of mental defect or to defective attention or to laziness or to poor training and frequently with an implication of blame which may very easily foster an unwarranted feeling of guilt in the child or the parent or both (1937).

Diagnostic Considerations

The Orton approach to developmental language delays is based upon a well-rounded diagnostic case study of the individual child. Orton preferred the term "developmental" because it seemed to cover "both the hereditary tendency and the environmental forces which are brought to play on the individual," whereas he thought the older term "congenital" tended "to overstress the inherent difficulty and to underemphasize the many environmental factors, both specific, such as methods of teaching, and more general, such as emotional and social forces" (1937). Moreover, he had found that the relative part played by each of the three major functions in the language faculty—vision, audition, and kinesthesis—varied markedly in different children, as did the child's emotional reaction to his difficulty. Therefore, he cautioned, the first step toward successful treatment must be careful evaluation of the extrinsic factors—economic, social, educational, etc.—together with an extensive analysis of the status of spoken language, graphic language, motor skills or limitations, and emotional reactions.

In the case study, a full developmental and familial history is obtained, usually prior to the examinations, which provides useful data and also gives an opportunity for the parent to express his anxieties and hopes and, in turn, to be evaluated as a resource in the total treatment program for the child. Outside medical and school data, including examinations of vision and hearing, psychometrics, educational achievement tests, and teachers' impressions, supplement the history. From such reports physical or mental defects or environmental deprivations or disturbances can often be ruled out as of primary significance in the reading problem under consideration, or, if they do seem significant, referral elsewhere for further tests or a different type of therapy can be made. The details of the pupil's school successes and failures in each subject in each grade and his reactions to them will help to gauge the extent and effects of his reading difficulty. A family history characterized by lefthandedness and outcroppings of language disabilities of various types or reports of late development of speech or of handedness in the child will suggest the probability of a "primary" reading disability of the strephosymbolic type.

Direct examination of the child, according to Orton's principles, will include a study of his handedness, eyedness, and footedness through tests and games. Intelligence testing must be done orally and individually to estimate his intellectual development. Achievement tests in oral and silent reading, in dictated spelling and in handwriting speed are administered so that the pupil's attainments in these areas may be compared with the norms for his age, mental age, and grade placement, and also with his performance on arithmetic tests where reading is not involved. It is helpful to enter all of these scores on a graph, or educational profile, which will show whether the language subjects are selectively retarded and a specific reading and spelling disability exists or whether there is some other pattern of achievement or difficulty. Since at least seven items will be plotted—age, grade, mental age, arithmetic, reading, spelling, and handwriting speed—there can be a tremendous number of combinations and individual variations. Some common types of profiles which can be recognized from inspection of the graphs are: (1) a fairly even line across the chart indicating adequate educational development; (2) a drop in mental age and arithmetic with an upward swing in reading and spelling, often associated with the lower IQs; and (3) the typical dip in the language subjects found in the reading cases, with the mental age and arithmetic scores frequently above the age-grade line. The addition of subtest scores under each heading, such as those for speed, vocabulary, and comprehension in silent reading, add to the diagnostic usefulness of the educational survey.

The reading clinician will learn much more from these tests than the quantitative data recorded on the profile. He will experience the feel of the child, noting his reactions to the examiner and to the different parts of the examination, and he will informally evaluate the pupil's speech, vocabulary, and auditory receptiveness to language, particularly any word confusions. He will study the child's oral responses to the test questions and will analyze the errors made in reading and written spelling in terms of auditory, visual, and kinesthetic factors, reversal tendencies, motor skills, etc. The examiner will then proceed to explore the areas of language weakness more specifically.

Orton designed special tests to bring out reversal tendencies and mirror-reading ability and sometimes used lists of nonsense words of increasing difficulty to determine basic reading and spelling confusions in older students. For those who can read only at primary grade levels, the Iota test has proved especially useful. This is a list of fifty-three words prepared by Marion Monroe from the common errors of pupils with reading disabilities in the Iowa project and standardized for grades 1.5 to 5.5 (Monroe, 1928). It is included in her own diagnostic battery of reading tests but may be used separately. In reading these words aloud, the strephosymbolic child will often confuse **b**, **d**, **p**, and **q**, read **form** as **from**, **on** as **no**, perseverate, make phonetic errors, fail to use rhyming clues, or just say, "We haven't had that word." If the pupil has a specific disability, the Iota score is usually his lowest on the initial examination and later is a sensitive indicator of improvement from remedial instruction. Oral reading tests of paragraphs of graded difficulty are also useful.

In all areas of language testing, the examiner keeps in mind the exact nature of the stimulus and of the response required and which of the three "levels" of each modality is chiefly involved. For example, in exploring the auditory capacity of a child suspected of word deafness, there must be an investigation of (1) his actual hearing, (2) his ability to recognize the meaning of sounds, and (3) his oral comprehension of words, but because he may also have some difficulty in speech or verbal expression, he must be given alternate methods of showing whether he has received and understood the various auditory signals. Orton used a conditioned-reflex type of audiometer for testing the hearing of the young children (first level) and special sound recordings of urban and rural noises for checking their recognition of the meaning of familiar sounds (second level), with provision for responses by naming (speech) or pointing to objects or pictures (visual-motor)—or miming, as in the case of one little boy from Mexico, who acted out the milking of a cow when he heard the international moo-ing sounds on the record. The pupil's auditory understanding of spoken words (third level) can then be separately studied through a graded series of oral directions, vocabulary tests, and the like.

Similarly, in evaluating the expressive speech of a child, his hearing and his ability to echo all of the phonemes separately and in sequences of increasing length must be considered, as well as his facility in using meaningful language. At this (third) level his fluency, his sentence length, his grammatical construction, his expressive vocabulary, and any word confusions are all of interest. The alert examiner will be able to appraise the child's development in these various areas in the course of his general testing. For example, he can usually spot a lisp or a defective *r* or *th* by having the child count from one to twenty and can further evaluate the speech maturation by listening carefully to the speech patterns in all of the subject's verbal responses. He can check the auditory element—the child's ability to hear, understand, and use words—as he goes along, and can thus informally cover the various levels and categories as a basis for further testing and the planning of a language training program to meet the child's individual, specific needs.

A breakdown of the child's skills in expressing himself in writing—probably the most complicated of all the language functions—will proceed along similar lines when the examiner or teacher is familiar with this conceptual background. The handwriting facility itself can be easily judged from observation of the child at work and from inspection of the product in different situations during the general testing, such as writing his name on his paper, writing the alphabet to dictation, copying for speed and quality, writing easy-to-harder words on his spelling test, perhaps some blackboard work, and, finally, propositional writing in a composition. The pupil's visual-motor control in handling a pencil for other purposes will be noted: in drawing, in writing numbers, in tracing a maze, in copying designs, on the WISC coding subtest, or in coloring, if the subject is a younger child. Usually, lower level motor difficulties are not present, but if they are, the examiner's observations will lead to a referral for a neurological evaluation. In the strephosymbolic cases the examiner will be on the lookout for right-to-left or bottom-to-top tendencies in forming letters. He may further explore the child's natural abilities by having him write with his eyes closed and, again, with the opposite hand. The pupil's writing on the blackboard with both hands simultaneously while his eyes are closed may disclose confusion in motor leads or dominance patterns.

Slow, effortful, immature, "messy" handwriting may constitute a specific language disability in itself, handicapping a pupil in all of his written work and accounting to a large extent for unsatisfactory examination papers and homework assignments and for the general delaying tactics of many of these students. When combined with a poor auditory-visual memory for spelling, or poor auditory-motor inner speech patterns, or strephosymbolic and spatial orientation difficulties in getting words or numbers down on paper, the problem is compounded, but it can often be clarified sufficiently to start systematic retraining if the examiner keeps in mind the various areas of language and their relationship to one another and to the presenting symptom. Comparisons of the pupil's responses to the same material, such as a vocabulary test, when presented both orally and in printed form, will often be enlightening, as will a differential study of the quality of the pupil's oral and written answers to the same questions.

In his 1937 book, Orton pointed out that the examiner must be careful not to make a diagnosis of a specific reading disability on the basis of finding some of the common correlates of the reading syndrome, such as a delay in the development of speech or handedness or visual-motor skills, or the presence of crossed laterality patterns in the child (right-handedness with lefteyedness, for example), unless the reading process itself is clearly disturbed. Conversely, the diagnosis may be made quite securely in certain cases where the child's development has been normal in all other respects, since, according to the Orton viewpoint, only the reading area in the dominant brain hemisphere (the third level, visual-associative) need be involved to produce the symptoms of specific language difficulty in reading. Again, not all of the children who are found to have a selective retardation in reading with strephosymbolic symptoms will qualify for the diagnosis of specific dyslexia because by definition this designation excludes those with any degree of mental or physical impairment or serious emotional disturbance. These niceties of terminology do not mean that when the reading disability syndrome is found in association with all sorts of complicating problems the children should be deprived of the opportunity for remedial assistance. They are the pupils who will need even more extensive examinations to determine their capacities and the best approach to developing their reading skills. The educational needs of all types of children with unusual difficulty in learning to read and spell present an outstanding challenge in the field of special education today (Karnes, 1965).

Directional confusions and association difficulties which Orton noted primarily in the reading and spelling errors of the children whom he called strephosymbolic have been found by subsequent investigators to have an even wider range. Some dyslexic children have little concept of time and space relationships; they confuse the terms **before** and **after**, or **above** and **below**. Many have difficulty with sequences like the months of the year or the multiplication tables. They may be slow in learning **right** and **left**. Representations of their own body images often are distorted in their drawings. Some show extensive associational errors in their thinking and have symptoms of delayed motor maturation, suggestive of a diagnosis of brain injury or of schizophrenia. Studies of perception and the integration of various patterns in the sensory and motor systems, based largely on the concepts of *gestalt* psychology (De Hirsch, 1963), promise further understanding. It is fortunate that the diagnosis of probable brain injury in children does not now preclude the expectation of learning, as it once did, and that the more exact analysis of their development in all modalities can lead to more precise methods of retraining. New techniques to use in clinical evaluations, like the Illinois Test of Psycholinguistic Abilities (McCarthy and Kirk, 1961), will be of assistance in making more thorough studies of severe reading and prereading developmental language disorders. Tests for screening pupils in the primary grades for specific language problems have already been developed (Slingerland, 1962), and extensive research projects in pediatrics are adding a fund of new information about the growth of the young child in language and other areas, including his acquisition of reading (De Hirsch, 1965).

II. The Method Used by Orton and Gillingham

Orton's Principles of Retraining

Emphasis upon treatment has always characterized the Orton approach to developmental dyslexia. To Orton, the importance of his physiological theory lay first in the fact that it offered hope for dyslexic children through training and, second, that it pointed to a path of attack for such training. "A very considerable degree of prognostic optimism is warranted," he wrote in 1925, "when proper training is instituted early and is conscientiously carried out. The methods of training, however, must be developed in consonance with the neurologic background and tested by carefully controlled experiments." In closing his Salmon Memorial Lectures (1937), he again stated his challenging conviction that "such disorders should respond to specific training if we become sufficiently keen in our diagnosis and if we prove ourselves clever enough to devise the proper training methods to meet the needs of each particular case."

In his instructions to teachers, Orton emphasized the importance of day-by-day observations of the pupil's language difficulties, with flexible procedures to meet individual needs, rather than a fixed formula or method of remedial work. He found two basic principles most useful:

1. Training for simultaneous association of visual, auditory, and kinesthetic language stimuli—in reading cases, tracing and sounding the visually presented word and maintaining consistent direction by following the letters with the fingers during the sound synthesis of syllables and words (Orton, 1928).

2. Finding such units as the child can use without difficulty in the field of his particular disability and directing the training toward developing the process of fusing these smaller units into larger and more complex wholes (Orton, 1937).

Retraining for Reading

Applying these principles, the retraining of a child with a reading disability usually starts with the teaching of the basic language units (individual letters and phonemes), clarifying the visual and the auditory patterns, and strengthening their linkage by introducing the motor elements of speech and writing at the same time. Orton warned, however, that learning the sounds of the letters was of little use in itself and that synthesizing them into a spoken word was of cardinal importance and must be carefully taught, since it was usually the building of sequences in proper order that was most difficult for the strephosymbolic child. By carefully following a step-by-step progression, the pupil is prepared for the longer units, the more complicated letter-sound patterns, sequences of two or more syllables, and words in phrases and sentences. When he has thoroughly mastered these cumulative skills, he will be able to recognize many words almost at sight with full awareness of their meaning—he will, in fact, have learned how to read.

The rationale of the visual-auditory-kinesthetic approach in these retraining procedures was concisely stated as follows:

> Since the majority of the cases of reading disability have shown a normal development of spoken language and could readily understand, when spoken to them, the same words which they could not read, our approach has been an attempt to capitalize upon their auditory competence by teaching them the phonetic equivalents of the printed letters and the process of blending sequences of such equivalents so that they might produce for themselves the spoken form of the word from its graphic counterpart. Since, moreover, in the greater number of strephosymbolics there is not frank disorder in the kinesthetic function, we have made use of movement patterns to aid in eradicating confusions between twin letters and in maintaining consistent dextrad progress in assembling the units of the words (Orton, 1937).

Retraining for Spelling

Faulty spelling always accompanies a specific reading disability and was early envisaged by Orton (1928) as "a failure of a harmonious interplay between visual and auditory material." Auditory and motor factors play an important part; the stimulus is in thinking or hearing the spoken word, and the response is usually in writing. Since spelling patterns are so varied in English, it is necessary for a good speller to have not only a clear-cut auditory pattern of the spoken word and adequate handwriting to reproduce it but also a dependable visual memory of the particular letter symbols and their sequence in its graphic counterpart. Orton wrote in 1937:

> Because of this lack of precision in visual recall, it is important to make use of the auditory patterns by means of phonetic dissection as a guide to spelling and to make sure that careful auditory discrimination between closely similar sounds be well established. . . . In many cases, a campaign for accurate and clear enunciation is indicated. . . . Each linkage of the association process must be checked before it can be trusted. . . . Since the reading disability cases without exception are poor spellers, it has proved advisable to make sure of all of the usable linkages between vision, audition and kinesthesis while the reading retraining is under way.

Training for reading and spelling are closely related in the Orton approach. The associations between the letter units and the phonemes are established in both directions: the teacher presents the letter and the child gives the sound; the teacher gives the sound and the child names and writes the letter. Just as blending the sounds in proper order is taught and practiced for reading, so analyzing the sounds and their order in the spoken word is taught and practiced for spelling. If forming the letters or joining them in writing proves difficult, or **b/d** reversals persist, special training in writing will be given, such as tracing the letter patterns individually and in words. If the child's speech is poor or his pronunciation inaccurate, his written words will often show the same substitutions or omissions; speech training and oral reading practice should be helpful in such cases. In others, an analysis of errors will show a confusion of symbols representing certain voiced and unvoiced speech sounds: **b** for **p**, **d** for **t**, **v** for **f**, **j** for **ch**, and vice versa. More auditory training and direct practice in writing the sounds to dictation with exaggerated differentiation on the part of the child in speaking them may clear up this problem. Students with a good auditory rote memory can sometimes learn to spell words correctly aloud, dividing the longer words rhythmically by syllables and writing them as they say each letter aloud. This simultaneous oral spelling and writing, called the S.O.S. technique, was used extensively by Orton and Gillingham in remedial spelling. They agreed that poor spelling associated with specific disability in reading could never be cured but believed it could be improved to the extent of becoming correct phonetically, and therefore at least intelligible.

Poor spelling may remain as a residual of a dyslexic difficulty after the pupil has learned to read, or it may exist more or less independently in a person whose visual memory for words is sufficient for recognizing the printed word but not strong enough to recall it clearly or reconstruct it in writing. Such students may have trouble in getting other things down on paper, such as arithmetic problems, and often make a low score on tasks like the WISC coding subtest. Poor spellers are prone to have difficulty in learning to write a foreign language unless it is entirely phonetic; Spanish usually proves somewhat easier than French.

Retraining Handwriting

Discussing handwriting problems, Orton and Gillingham (1933) wrote: "The highly individual character of the organizations of skills and disabilities in a given child emphasizes again the need of full analysis of each case and an approach to treatment without fixed methods but rather as an experiment." Before starting any handwriting training with a child, it is obviously important to determine which hand he should use, and this decision involves a thorough study of his laterality patterns through observation and tests as well as through the history of his early development and training in various activities. When there is evidence that most of his dominance patterns are opposite to the hand being used unsuccessfully for writing, and when there is some facility in the opposite hand, it may be advisable to undertake an experiment in training the child to write with that hand. Similarly, the best slant for the individual to use in his writing must be considered through careful study of his spontaneous writing patterns, especially those made when he is writing with his eyes closed or beginning to tire. Short practice exercises with different slants may help to determine his natural patterns.

After the teacher and pupil have agreed upon the hand and slant to be used in the retraining, the pupil may need to be shown a better way to hold his pencil and the proper placement of his paper. For the lefthander, the top of the paper is to the right with the light on that side, exactly opposite to the paper position for the righthanded writer. Certain procedures that may prove helpful to the pupil are: watching the teacher's movements in making a letter and then imitating them; getting the feeling of the letter by letting the teacher move his hand to form the pattern; tracing a model several times, then covering it, writing it from memory, comparing it with the original, and repeating the process until correct; copying from the blackboard without looking at his own hand, or with a shield before his hand on the table; writing words he knows with his eyes closed. The relaxation of muscular tension that usually ensues when the child is not watching his own writing is often striking. Sometimes there is a noticeable improvement in quality, although of course he will need to see what he is doing for spacing and keeping on a line. When working on writing, it is better for teacher and child to sit side by side rather than opposite each other.

The association of the motor patterns with the other components of the writing process can be strengthened by having the child name the letter or give its sound as he writes it but it is not wise to burden him with dictation, which involves spelling, or with propositional writing during the penmanship practice. Well-formed letters, consistency in size and slant, and legibility, rather than speed, are stressed until the desired patterns are well established; then rhythmic exercises and timing devices may be helpful. Although progress is usually slow, and regressions appear with pressure for speed or under physical or emotional stress, inprovement can often be demonstrated by comparing the practice papers from time to time with earlier ones. Occasional timed tests in copying may also show encouraging results in quality and speed.

In working with these handwriting problems, Orton pointed out that "as in all of the special disabilities, the emotional factors are of prime importance in evaluating the severity of the condition and in outlining treatment." It requires a strong and sustained effort on the part of the student to improve his handwriting. There is less recognized need and motivation than for reading and less that the teacher can do directly except to suggest techniques and encourage practice by showing interest and pointing out improvement rather than criticizing defects. In severe cases, or when a shift in the hand for writing is to be tried, it is best not to have the child do any writing outside of the supervised practice period until the new patterns are well established. Since this is often difficult to arrange while the child is attending school, the summer vacation is usually the best time to start a serious remedial handwriting program. Typing sometimes proves useful as an alternative method of communication. As the student's productions improve, he begins to take pride in his accomplishment. He works harder, the quality of his compositions becomes better, and he receives commendation instead of blame from his teacher and gets better marks in related subjects.

Training the Apraxic Child

When the pupil with a handwriting difficulty also has a general apraxia (extreme clumsiness), his retraining needs will extend beyond the language area. Problems in equilibrium and motor disabilities may have a profound effect on the personality development of the child (Bender, 1956) and make it difficult for him to find compensatory satisfactions to offset his academic defeats. He will probably be handicapped in athletics, in which case Orton advised trying to find some one single skill in which he could acquire enough proficiency for successful competition with his schoolmates. The techniques for training such children follow the same general principles used in the other syndromes:

> In such cases, the training which we have found most promising is based upon the analysis of the more complex activity into the simplest component parts. For example, in baseball, you cannot teach a boy how to pitch a ball until you teach him how to stand properly, how to balance his weight, how to get his arm back for a long swing, etc. By separating the patterns which you wish to teach him into units,

> working on each one separately and finally putting them together in a given sequence, I feel that much can be accomplished for these youngsters (Orton, 1946).

Orientation difficulties should also be kept in mind. One college girl could never do turns properly in skiing until a lefthanded instructor happened to demonstrate a pattern opposite from the usual direction, and she found that she could follow it perfectly. A little girl who could not copy her dancing teacher's movements when the teacher was standing facing her found that it was much easier if the teacher stood by her side before a large mirror with the child looking at their reflections in it.

As with the other developmental delays with a physiological background, an explanation of the nature of the difficulty to the child, his parents, and his teachers is often the first step in successful treatment. Learning that general clumsiness is not an indication of mental retardation or inexcusable carelessness or lack of cooperation seems to enable the child to mobilize his own efforts to acquire the desired skills, while encouragement from any small accomplishment which results from his efforts—and the teacher's ingenuity—stimulates the integration of other and more complex patterns.

The Gillingham Alphabetic Method

Anna Gillingham was an outstanding "teacher's teacher." From her own wide school experience, she understood the discouragement and frustration of the classroom teachers over their failures to teach certain pupils to read, particularly when those children appeared to be bright and could do well orally. Repetition after repetition of the classroom drills with word cards and the usual suggestions for word attack prove of little value to these children, even with individual tutoring. If they themselves do not become nervous or disturbing in the classroom, as they often do, the mothers make up for it by communicating their anxiety and directly or indirectly blaming the teacher. But how can they be taught?

Miss Gillingham found both the why and the how answered to her satisfaction in her two-year association with Orton and others in the Language Project of the New York Neurological Institute and she devoted the rest of her life to working with children with specific language disabilities. She taught many pupils herself, but her greatest contribution was in teaching other teachers. Some came to her in Bronxville for the two years of exacting training which she required. Others had the opportunity of in-service training under her supervision in the private schools across the country in which she set up remedial programs and trained selected teachers by personal visits at regular intervals. She continued her contact with the Ethical Culture School in New York and, with Bessie Stillman, spent some time at the Punahou School in Honolulu. She was consultant for many years to the Sidwell-Friends School in Washington, D.C., and the Francis Parker School in Chicago, among others, and was often called upon to help start a new program or to train personnel for Orton-type reading programs in schools or clinics. Teachers whom she trained have in turn taught others: Ruth Slingerland in the northwest, Helene Durbrow in New England, Sally Childs in Texas, and many others throughout the country.

The Manual

To meet the needs of teachers entering this field, Miss Gillingham published her first manual in 1946, with the assistance of Miss Stillman, who died the following year. Ideas and suggestions from other teachers were incorporated in successive editions. The last revision (the green-cover sixth edition) was undertaken to make it accord with the changes in the Merriam-Webster dictionary symbols of pronunication introduced in 1956. Since most readers still preferred the more familiar diacritical markings, the red-cover fifth edition was republished in 1964.[1] Supplementary Gillingham materials included phonics drill cards for reading and spelling, phonetic word cards, a graded series of phonetic stories, and exercises on syllable division and the use of the dictionary. This complete remedial kit was a storehouse of treasures for teachers, schools and parents, especially during the long period when the teaching of phonics was banned in most places and such materials were not published elsewhere.

Although Anna Gillingham was rigid in training teachers, the method itself is peculiarly adaptable to the various types of specific language disabilities and the needs of the individual dyslexic pupil. She fully understood the many variations in the syndrome, and her own approach exemplified the three things which she demanded of her teachers: (1) understanding of what they were doing; (2) unceasing application of the most effective procedures; and (3) deep, unfailing, sympathetic under-

[1] Quotations from Gillingham in what follows are from this work.

standing of the unique plight of the pupil. She also stressed the importance of explaining to the pupil the reasons for the method of retraining not only in terms of his own difficulty but through a review of the history of the development of the English language itself, with the reasons for its inconsistencies in pronunciation and spelling. The advantages of the alphabetic method over pictographs and ideograms were pointed out to the child, and he was told that he was "going to learn the sounds of letters and then build them into words." This material for the teacher is all in the manual, together with definite guides for setting up a remedial program and the requirements upon the school to insure its success: daily forty-five-minute to one-hour lessons for a minimum of two years, in an attractive, well-lighted room, during a period when the pupil would not be deprived of play or art or shop or other activities in which he might find pleasure and success. While building up a new set of habits, precise and definite, he should not be allowed to do any reading, writing, or spelling in the classroom or at home. Parents or others should help him to keep up with the content of his courses by reading aloud to him and should be accepting, sympathetic, and realistic in their demands and ambitions.

Gillingham Technique

The technique (Gillingham and Stillman, 1964) "is based upon the constant use of association of all of the following: how a letter or word looks, how it sounds, how the speech organs or the hand in writing feels when producing it." Gillingham offered the model of an equilateral language triangle with the V (visual), A (auditory), and K (kinesthetic) elements at its points, connected by lines to illustrate the six language linkages. These various linkages are taught in the following manner:

1. *Visual-Auditory-Kinesthetic* (Speech). The pupil is shown the printed letter symbol and repeats its name after the teacher. When this is mastered, the sound is made by the teacher and repeated by the pupil. The child's feel of his own speech organs provides the kinesthetic element. (If there is poor auditory discrimination or a speech defect, this will require special attention.)

2. *Visual-Kinesthetic* (Writing). The pupil watches while the teacher makes the letter and explains its form, orientation, starting point, direction of strokes, etc. He then traces over the teacher's model. (Beginners and pupils with poor manual control may continue tracing for several weeks.) The next step is to copy, then write from memory, finally write with eyes closed or averted.

After these fundamental associations are established, the linkages are strengthened by various stimulus-response drills:

a. Teacher shows phonogram—pupil gives its name.
b. Teacher forms symbols with pupil's hand while he looks away—pupil gives the letter name.
c. Teacher dictates name—pupil writes letter.
d. Teacher gives name—pupil responds with sound orally.

These drills are repeated with substitution of the letter sound for the letter name. The most important linkages in the ordinary reading and spelling case are those which enable the pupil to translate the printed letter into its sound as the basis for reading and to give the letter name or write the letter for a spoken sound as the basis for spelling. The other drills usually can soon be dropped. The inclusiveness and flexibility of the method are indicated in its author's simple statement that "daily observation will enable the teacher to know when other linkages need to be stressed in a special case."

Teaching the Letters. Each phonic unit is presented on a separate card, with consonant letters on white cards and vowel letters on salmon-colored cards. Buff cards are used for the phonemes for spelling. Each phonogram is introduced by a key word, which is always repeated by the pupil before he gives the sound (the initial sound in the key word). This must be produced lightly, with care not to attach the sound of **uh** to the consonant, since this would interfere with blending. The initial sounds are taught for **l** and **r**, as in **lamp** and **rat**, and in the consonant blends (**bl**, **gr**), as in **block** and **grass**.

The letter sounds are taught in groups as rapidly as they can be assimilated, sometimes only one or two at each lesson. The first group should be letters with only one sound and nonreversible forms. Although there is no one right order of presentation, the teacher will usually follow a fairly standard sequence in order to use prepared word lists and stories for each step. The first group of letters suggested for the Gillingham materials is as follows: **a**, **b**, **f**, **h**, **i**, **j**, **k**, **m**, **p**, **t**, with short sounds for the vowels.

Blending. After the pupil has learned the names of these letters, their sounds, and how to write them with all the linkages well established, the process of blending is started. A consonant, a vowel, and another consonant card are laid out on the table and the pupil is taught to give their sounds in succession rapidly and smoothly until he perceives that he is producing a word. The initial consonant is pronounced with the vowel that follows it, e.g., **ba/t**. Blending is the basis for reading.

Spelling. A few days after blending is started, the analysis of words into their component sounds should begin. The teacher pronounces the word very slowly, separating the sounds, and asks the child to repeat each sound in turn, name the letter, place its card on the table, then write it. The cards will soon be dropped out but the child continues to make four responses to the dictated word: (1) he repeats the word: (2) he names the letters; (3) he writes the word, naming each letter as he forms it; and (4) he reads back what he has written. The naming of the letters aloud as each is written (simultaneous oral spelling) has been found a most effective device for establishing visual-auditory-kinesthetic impressions, maintaining the order of the sequences, and, later on, remembering spelling choices or the spelling of nonphonetic words. The teacher and the child together monitor his responses. The right ones are approved, mistakes are corrected immediately, and very often spelling errors can be prevented from occurring if each preliminary step is carefully performed.

Word Cards. Some twenty familiar words can be made up from the first ten letters and others added as each new phonogram is introduced. They are included in packets in the Gillingham materials in a box affectionately named the "jewel case" by children many years ago. Timed drills, graphs, and other devices are suggested to stimulate and reward progress in reading and spelling these phonetic words.

New Phonograms. Additional letter cards and word cards are introduced in accordance with the pupil's rate of learning. Only one sound is used for each at this time. The sequence given in the manual is as follows: **g (go)**, **o**, initial **r**, initial **l**, **n**, **th (this)**, **u**, **ch**, **e**, **s**, **sh**, **d**, **w**, **wh**, **y (yes)**, **v**, **z**. The concept of a one-syllable word and its characteristic pattern, usually a consonant-vowel-consonant sequence, is explained. Spelling Rule 1 is next developed, and the child is taught to remember it exactly: "Words of one syllable ending in **f**, **l**, or **s**, after one vowel usually end in **ff**, **ll**, or **ss**"— like **puff**, **tell**, and **kiss**.

Stories: Group I. After the pupil has been prepared to read and write any three-letter word (four letters with digraphs) which are perfectly phonetic, he can begin to combine them into sentences and stories. Seven little stories are offered, with a few connecting sight words which the teacher supplies at once. The pupil prepares his reading of a sentence silently, asking for help if he needs it. When he is ready, he is expected to read the sentence perfectly, with natural phrasing and inflection, so that it sounds like talking.

These same stories and similar ones can also be used for dictation. Words for which the pupil is not prepared are written for him on a slip of paper, and he traces and writes them several times until he is familiar with them as whole words, not just as separate letters. The teacher then carefully dictates the exercise in meaningful phrases according to the length of the child's auditory memory span. The pupil repeats the first unit, then writes it from memory, softly naming the letters as he forms them. He then reads back what he has written, compares and corrects any doubtful spellings by looking at the original, and discusses with the teacher the phonetic choices or the generalizations which would apply.

Syllables. The concept of syllables is carefully worked out with the pupil before two-syllable phonetic words are introduced for reading and spelling. Later, the rules for syllable division are developed according to the age and maturity of the pupil: Rule 1 provides that when two consonants stand between two vowels the syllable division usually occurs between the two consonants. Later, the pupil is shown how to attack words with one consonant between two vowels, with digraphs, blends, diphthongs, etc.

Next Steps. Consonant blends are next introduced. These can be combined with the short-vowel sounds to make many more words available to the pupil, and he can now read the Group II stories with confidence and success. At this point every teacher would like to change the spelling of the English language, but, with some understanding of its historical development, the student will accept the fact that certain phonograms have more than one possible sound and that certain phonemes can be spelled in more than one way. The **qu (kw)** and **x (ks)** cards are added to his pack, **y** as vowel letter, **ph** for **(f)**, **s** as **(z)**. The rules for the hard and soft sounds of **c** and **g** and the use of **ck** and **tch** are explained. Word forms are changed by adding endings: **ly**, for example, and **ed** with its three pronunciations, with a corresponding increase in the variety of the prepared exercises and stories.

Additional Vowel Sounds. The long sounds of all the vowels are introduced together in the vowel + consonant + e situation on salmon-colored drill cards with a key word for each: **a–e, safe**; **e–e, these**; **i–e, pine**; **o–e, home**; **u–e, mule**. Later, the expectation of the long-vowel sound in such words as **he** or **spider** is explained. The pupil thereafter responds to the vowel-letter cards with both the short and the long sounds accompanying the key words for each and the statement, "A vowel at the end of an accented syllable is long." The special vowel sounds with **r** are studied: **ar, or, er**, with the many variations in spelling to be given to the pupil later as needed. The two-letter vowel phonograms (all called diphthongs) are presented in a new way. Several stories are selected for the child to read from a good basal reading series, and he is prepared in advance for all the new words by practice on groups of such words on tagboard strips along with his drill cards and key words for the new units. The first story given in the manual includes **ay, ow (cow)**; **ou (out)**; **oo (food)**; **ew, ee, ou (soup)**; **oa, oo (book)**; and a list of miscellaneous words. Other units are added as needed on additional strips, as are certain sight words and words in phrases. After he has mastered these lists, the pupil is given the new story to read, first studying it silently to himself and then reading it aloud to the teacher.

Reading. The pupil's reading must be limited to carefully selected and prepared material for some time "to establish the facile application of the alphabetic approach to words." Gillingham points out that this is comparable to the practicing of scales by a musician to perfect his technique. The child will enjoy using his new skills on material with a controlled vocabulary, regardless of the specific content, since it is a part of the teacher's responsibility "to so fit his tasks to his ability that the pupil's effort can result in constant progress and success." When he is ready, he will be encouraged to select books for more independent reading and will be permitted to participate again to some extent in the regular classroom program. He assumes the responsibility for more of his homework, but the amount of required reading should be limited so that he will not be forced to sacrifice accuracy or give up his newly acquired methods of study before they have become dependable habits. Provision should be made for part of his assignments to be read aloud to him as long as it is necessary and for him to dictate his compositions, under certain circumstances, or to take oral instead of written examinations. The pupil with a reading disability is given aid and training in the use of the dictionary almost from the beginning of his remedial work and must expect to depend upon it as a trustworthy friend for many years.

More Advanced Pupils. Many longitudinal studies have demonstrated the need for remedial work in the upper grades for pupils who have had difficulty in learning to read and spell. The strephosymbolic pupil who cannot read at eight years of age will probably have trouble with his spelling in compositions and with foreign languages later. Others with milder degrees of disability may encounter no serious obstacle to their academic progress until they meet the increasing demands upon language skills in high school or college. Still others may always have had some difficulty with spelling in spite of fairly adequate reading ability. Anticipation of possible later difficulties will not create these problems in the older students but rather should point the way to constructive help and to proper guidance in the selection of the courses or their careers.

Anna Gillingham knew these high school students well. In Chapter IV (of the sixth edition) she describes some of their characteristics. They confuse the little words in reading, slide over longer words, or make substitutions. They know nothing about the significance of affixes and pay little attention to endings. They cannot use a dictionary. Their vocabularies are extremely meager. They do not like books and read only what is required. They have little knowledge of the phonetic structure of English words and little power of word attack.

Special programs for the retaining of the older, or more advanced, students are outlined in the manual. The method is similar to that used with the younger pupils, but it proceeds faster and is more comprehensive. The phonograms are presented in somewhat different order; detached syllables and made-up words are substituted in some of the practice exercises for the simple words which would be recognized as sight words; spelling rules are introduced with dictated sentences and paragraphs. Topics which are systematically covered include spelling rules, the simultaneous oral spelling procedure, dictionary technique, the use of diacritical marks, vocabulary building, grammar, paraphrasing, précis work, sentence and paragraph construction, and other subjects merging into a general course in English. The student keeps a well-organized notebook to record this material under various headings, a companion reference book to his indispensable dictionary.

Spelling, Penmanship, Expression in Writing. Detailed procedures for the step-by-step development of these written language skills with their particular visual-auditory-kinesthetic components are presented in the manual as integral parts of the remedial program for both younger and older pupils. The Gillingham approach is two-fold: (1) to establish efficient word attack habits in reading, writing, and spelling through systematic, well-planned sequences of repetitive drills; and (2) to provide the student with thinking patterns to enable him to cope as far as possible with the irregularities of the English language. The teacher will find a wealth of material in the manual from which to select various types of words for illustration or for practice drills in syllable division, spelling choices, or whatever topic the pupil is studying. The statements given for the seventeen spelling rules, summarized on pp. 308–9 of the manual, with illustrative words at different levels of difficulty, are very useful and should be memorized by both teacher and pupil. The amount of supplementary material may seem confusing to the beginning teacher but will prove valuable and time-saving in preparing lessons for individual pupils or classes.

Lists of words grouped according to their spelling of the vowel sounds help the student to make a reasonable choice in spelling according to their relative frequency. After he has learned the various ways of spelling each sound from the pack of buff-colored drill cards, he is shown how to determine the ratio between the numbers of common words with each spelling for those sounds. He then should be easily able to find a word which he does not know how to spell by looking it up in the dictionary under the most usual phonetic representations of its phonemes. Other aids to making the best choices for pronunciation and spelling of variables are given. Some students can memorize short lists of words with unusual spellings by making up nonsense verses or sentences containing them. Many guides for penmanship drills for both right- and lefthanders are also given in the Gillingham-Stillman manual.

Conclusion

Every remedial tutor must experiment to a certain extent with each individual pupil in the application of basic principles of retraining such as those which have been presented in this study of the Orton-Gillingham approach. Experience with many pupils will gradually lead to the development of the teacher's own program of preferred procedures. These in turn will be passed on to others in training and will become the starting point for the development of individual batteries of effective techniques. Several teachers who were associated to some extent with Dr. and Mrs. Orton or with Miss Gillingham have produced teaching materials based upon the Orton-Gillingham approach with adaptations from their own experience. Their common conceptual background can usually be seen in their introduction of the kinesthetic element to reinforce the visual-auditory language associations and to establish left-to-right habits of progression. Their phonetic approach is generally the same: teaching the phonics units in isolation but giving special training in blending; introducing the consonants and the short sounds of the vowels first and building three-letter words with them for reading and spelling; programming the material in easy, orderly, cumulative steps. They also make useful applications of the concept of the interrelationships among the different language areas and the importance of individual diagnostic studies as the basis for differential treatment (Childs and Childs, 1962, 1963; Orton, 1964; Plunkett, 1949; Slingerland, 1962; Spalding, 1957).

As in medical practice, the value of any theory often rests upon the pragmatic, therapeutic test. The many remedial teachers now using the Orton-Gillingham approach would probably agree with Orton's (1946) own conclusions after some twenty years of research and practice in this field:

> Whether or not our theory is right, I do not know, but I do know that the methods of retraining which we have derived from that viewpoint have worked. I do not claim them to be a panacea for reading troubles of all sorts but I do feel that we understand the blockade which occurs so frequently in children with good minds and which results in the characteristic reading of the strephosymbolic type in childhood.

CHAPTER 9

TRACING AND KINESTHETIC TECHNIQUES

MARJORIE SEDDON JOHNSON

Introduction

Difficulty in associating meanings and spoken words with printed words is generally characteristic of the dyslexic child. One approach which has proved successful in helping severely disabled readers to overcome this block to reading, although it is certainly not recommended for general classroom use (Roberts and Coleman, 1958), is the use of tracing and kinesthetic techniques for word learning. Through methods of this type, the child brings to bear on the learning a multiplicity of sensory stimulation (visual-auditory, kinesthetic-tactile). In addition, the highly structured nature of the procedures he learns provides a most advantageous setting for helping him to attend to and concentrate on the task at hand (Johnson, 1963; Morris, 1958). For tracing and kinesthetic techniques to be really effective, they must be used within an experience approach. In this way, the child begins to master printed symbols which represent *his* language, *his* ideas, and *his* interests. He is moving from something which he knows and can handle efficiently to the learning of something new, the association with the printed form.

Having started on their paths to mature reading through tracing words in order to learn them, many nonreaders have moved gradually on to become quite facile, mature readers. In the case of Roger, he was unable to read even the simplest menu before he began with this approach to word learning, although he was of normal intelligence and was nineteen years of age. In fact, he could not recognize all the items on a list of high-frequency words at preprimer level. After two summer sessions and a full school year of special instruction, he was able to get passing grades in college level courses. Wasted years had intervened, however, between his initial failure to learn words and his final success in reading.

This chapter is not intended as a manual for the use of tracing and kinesthetic techniques. Its purpose is to furnish a brief historical review, give an overview of the steps in the procedures, discuss the psychological and linguistic principles on which the techniques are based, and indicate some of the outcomes which can be expected from their use.

Historical Perspectives

Using tracing and kinesthetic techniques as a method for learning is far from new. The history of educational practices abounds with illustrations of the use of tracing for original learning, for reinforcement, and for the correction of errors. In some cases, Greek and Roman writings refer to the teacher's guiding of the child's hand as he traced over forms written for him, and, in other instances, models were made for tracing by carving letter and word forms into wood (Freeman, 1908). Sometimes the child was to move his writing instrument over the copy or through the groove (Haarhoff, 1920). Other recommendations can be found, however, where the importance of direct finger contact appears to have been recognized. Notable among the latter were the Montessori (1912) suggestions.

In recent times, Dr. Grace M. Fernald (Fernald and Keller, 1921; Fernald, 1943) employed a tracing technique with severely disabled readers. Basing her hopes for this learning method on various evidence to support the theory that direct finger contact improved the learning of letters, words, and mazes, she experimented with specific procedures. In her book, *Remedial Techniques in the Basic School Subjects* (Fernald, 1943), she devoted Chapter V to a description of the methods she finally devised. The four stages are those through which, in her experience, children with reading disability passed "as they were developing from inability to recognize the simplest words to normal and superior reading skill" (p. 35).

The specific tracing (VAKT)[1] and kinesthetic (VAK) techniques discussed in this chapter are the results of progressive refinement and modification of the basic steps outlined by Fernald. No change in the fundamental teaching or learning activities has been introduced. Instead, the specific steps to be followed have been clarified and certain

[1] Visual, Auditory, Kinesthetic, Tactile.

modifications made in terms of repeated experience with the technique. For the truly dyslexic child, VAKT is needed at the start. Less severely disabled readers, who are still unable to make and retain associations through primarily visual-auditory experiences, may be able to begin with VAK. Learning usually progresses from the point of needing a teacher-written copy of the word as a model, through the point of needing kinesthetic reinforcement but no teacher-written copy, to the point of normal learning through visual-auditory means. The rate at which a child moves from one stage to the next, of course, varies with the severity and complexity of the factors which have made him a disabled reader.

Overview of Procedures

A detailed, step-by-step description of the teaching and use of VAKT and VAK is not within the province of this chapter. To train a teacher-clinician in the use of these techniques requires that he have a background in the psychology and pedagogy of reading and that he learn the techniques in an educational laboratory course. Furthermore, successful administration of the techniques is really dependent on supervised practice with it. However, a brief overview of the procedures will help to make discussion of VAKT and VAK more meaningful.

In all stages of VAKT and VAK, words are learned as the child needs them in order to express his ideas. At the later stages, he may sometimes learn words he meets in his reading and is unable to handle. At first, however, all the words come from the oral language of the learner as he uses it to attempt to write about his experiences, record his ideas, or label pictures or diagrams he has made. At no point does the child copy words. Rather, he studies the word, in the fashion appropriate to his development, until he is able to write it from memory. As words are traced, studied, or written, they are said as a whole and in syllables. Each reproduction of the word is checked, and the dictionary is always used as a reference for correct syllabication, pronunciation, etc. The child always writes at least two successive correct copies before he uses the word in his story or report. Repeated contact with the word is provided through the directed rereading of a typed copy of his own written materials and a variety of reading experiences with teacher-prepared materials. His retention of the learned words is checked regularly so that need for additional reinforcement and signs of progress in skills can be systematically evaluated.

Introduction of Technique

The purpose of the introductory stage is to have the child get some acquaintance with the procedures to be followed and to gain some confidence in the efficacy of the technique as a learning method for him. If the latter aim is to be accomplished, the most immediate need is for him to experience some success in word learning. The introduction is, above all then, an action procedure. Little reliance should be placed on verbal explanation and a great deal on accomplishment through active participation.

First experiences with the learning procedures may come when the child has an immediate need for a word, or in an introductory session apart from any particular intention to use the word. In either case, the child should come to realize that he can master any word he wants. Free choice of words must be allowed so that he knows that the technique can really meet his needs.

As soon as a word to be learned has been identified, the actual learning procedure begins. The specific steps to be followed would be those of the stage which is being introduced as the most appropriate learning method for the child. For instance, the child whose difficulty with word learning is so severe as to require tracing for word learning would be introduced to the technique as it is carried out in VAKT (Fernald's stage 1). A child needing extra kinesthetic stimulation, but not tactile, would be introduced to the procedures for VAK (stage 2). In either case, the only deviations from those steps used in subsequent work would be the explanations and demonstrations required to help the child find out what he is to do.

VAKT

A word to be learned by VAKT is identified through the child's awareness that he does not know how to write it, or through the clinic teacher's detecting an error in his writing of it. This writing would take place in the setting of the child's putting on record, for a specific purpose, his own ideas and language. The first step in this and the subsequent stages of VAKT-VAK is to make certain that both the teacher and the child are thinking of the same word. This may or may not require overt checking on the pronunciation or intended meaning, depending on the situation in which the need for the word arose. As soon as clarity about the word has been established, the clinician-teacher directs attention to its structure by asking how many parts or syllables it has. Then he checks these details, as well as those of the orthographic and phonetic structure of the word, in the dictionary, reporting the number of syllables to the child.

With these preliminaries completed, the actual learning process begins. The child listens and watches as the clinician writes the word on a large sheet of paper in blackboard size cursive (or manuscript) writing, saying the word as a whole before it is written, saying each syllable on the first stroke of that syllable, and again saying the word as a whole after the writing has been completed. The child then traces his index and middle fingers over the written word, following the same pronunciation routine, until he feels he can reproduce the word without looking at the copy. He puts the learning copy face down and tries writing the word, again with the original routine of whole word and syllable pronunication. If he is successful, he checks his trial copy with the tracing copy and attempts it a second time. When two successive correct copies have been made, the learner is ready to put the word in the place where the need for it arose—his story, report, or whatever he is writing.

From the very start of these steps, the procedure is never allowed to continue if there has been an error. The clinician stops the learner immediately when any kind of error is made—pronunciation, timing, tracing, or writing—or if the process is broken by irrelevant activity.

VAK

Two somewhat different procedures, each providing for more than normal kinesthetic stimulation, fall under this heading. In the first, the clinician writes a learning copy for the child. In the second, the learner studies the form in the dictionary, learning the word directly from print. In both procedures, each studying or writing of the word is done with the saying of the whole word and syllables as it was in VAKT. There is no tracing, of course.

In the first VAK procedure (above) the specific steps are identical with those in VAKT except for certain changes brought about by the absence of tracing. The clinician writes the word in normal-sized script on an index card rather than in larger writing on a tracing slip. The learner studies the word by looking at it, saying it in the regular whole syllable fashion, until he is ready to try writing the word on the back of the card.

In the second VAK procedure (above) an additional change occurs. When the word has been looked up in the dictionary and the orthographic and phonetic structure clarified, the child studies the word as he did in the first procedure, but from the printed form in the dictionary rather than from a teacher-written copy. When he is ready, he makes his trial copies on the file card, checking them with the dictionary. Finally, before going on to use the word, he writes a copy horizontally on the card for filing purposes. In each other stage, the teacher-written word became the file copy.

The Word File

The first word a child learns by VAKT or VAK starts an accumulation which continues as long as he is using the techniques. He files his slips or cards alphabetically, and they become a reference point for him. To some children, the sheer quantity of words learned is a source of pride and confidence. Such an individual sees the file box as a reference point for the number of words learned. As he works with the procedure, he adds more and more words which are now *his*. Simply looking at the box with all its evidence of mastery presents the child with a chance to feel a true sense of accomplishment. The box can also be a reference point for checking on troublesome words. For example, Pat had continuing difficulty with the words **before** and **after**. He decided to illustrate those cards in his file box so that he could always look them up if he met them and had trouble with them. Because he loved horses, he used the evolutionary development of this animal as the source of the meaning of his illustrations. On the card with the word **before**, he drew a horse that was, from an evolutionary standpoint, somewhere between Eohippus and Mesohippus; with **after**, a modern Thoroughbred. Although his pictures might not even vaguely have suggested the right words to someone else, they were very helpful to Pat. When he got stuck on one of these words, he could go back to his file box and find out what the word was.

Another use of the file box is for actual recontact with words learned so that their retention can be constantly reinforced. For this reason, it is a regular part of the procedure for the child to check his file to see if he has the word needed at the moment. If he does, he relearns it from the original card. If he does not have it already, the regular procedure is followed and an entry is added to his file. In either case, he has had the experience of checking his alphabetical file (strengthening his grasp of the alphabetical order and associations between initial sounds and letters) and of seeing again words that he had learned earlier.

The same kind of experience is provided each time he adds a newly learned word to the file.

Each file entry is dated after the word has been learned and then incorporated into the file. The precise moment at which these two acts can best take place depends on the needs of the child. With Francis, retention was an unusually severe problem, even for a dyslexic child. If he learned a word with VAKT and did not meet it again for a whole day, he lost the association completely. Every possible device was used to put the words before him repeatedly in the course of one school day. Dating and filing the word slips offered two opportunities for recontacting the words. Perhaps half an hour after he had finished his writing activity, he might date the slips. Sometimes this was accomplished by the clinic teacher's setting a recognition task for him—"Put the date on **artist** now, Francis." At other times, the recall kind of performance was demanded—"Tell me each word as you date it so I can make a list of the words you learned this morning." Later on, perhaps after many other kinds of activities involving these words, Francis might be directed to file the words, again going over each of them. With all of this reinforcement, he had less difficulty remembering. When retention is not such an abnormally great problem, the dating and filing of the words might not need to be saved for spaced reinforcement of learning, and the whole job might be done within the actual writing period.

The Written Materials

The nature of the material the child writes may, as has already been indicated, be of several types. The important thing is that he should be using his own oral language resources and accomplishing the task of communicating his ideas through the use of the written word. There is no necessity for him to be completing a series of long and highly polished stories or reports. He must, however, be recording ideas that are of importance to him.

When a dyslexic child first begins to use VAKT, it is unlikely that he will be able to write many words without having to learn them as he goes along. Even to record one sentence may require that he learn a great many words. Consequently, he may write very little at one time. In fact, he should not be encouraged to learn and write too many words at one sitting because of the inordinate burden which would be placed on his retentive powers. It would be better for him to learn a few words at a time and find himself able to recognize them when he meets them again. However, regardless of the absolute amount of writing done, it should be well planned and accurately performed so that the child can have some justifiable pride in it when it is returned to him.

In terms of actual procedures for formulating the ideas, working out the way in which they are to be expressed, and getting the actual writing done, there are some definite cautions to be observed. The child should have things well thought out, with the teacher's help, so that when he begins the actual job of writing a word and learning it there is no need for rewriting and changing. To have to rewrite may be more than he can tolerate at first. In most cases, it may be required that the child be given the opportunity to *talk out* his ideas, with the teacher acting as guide and secretary, recording the things in the exact words and phrases in which he wants to write them. In this way, the gist and expression of his ideas will not be lost in the labor of learning and writing words.

No premium should be placed on quantity at the time of planning. In fact, in some cases it is a real task to keep the child from making such big plans that he faces an almost insurmountable barrier when he realizes how much he has to write. To allow him to set his sights too high, so that he immediately faces a sense of real discouragement and frustration, would be working against the very goals of the technique.

As the actual writing is done, each day's accomplishment is added directly to what had already been written until the complete unit has been finished. At the end of the period, if at all possible, the child should have reached the end of a paragraph or sentence or clause, so that what he rereads will be meaningful to him. The material should be typed as it is finished each day, so that there is never a great deal of elapsed time between the word learning and writing and the rereading of the typed copy of the material. With a child like Francis, the materials were typed immediately and returned to him for directed rereading. Periodically throughout the day, other rereadings of the story or report were worked into his school schedule. With other children, a twenty-four-hour lapse between the writing and the rereading of the typed copy would not be too long.

The principles of a good directed reading activity should be followed in the reading of the child's own materials and any clinician-prepared materials which are provided for added experience. None of this reading should be done without definite purpose; silent reading should always precede oral reading; and work on the development of word recognition and on comprehension ability should be integrated with each other.

The additional materials which are prepared for directed or independent reading should be varied, but they must be at a level which the child can handle. The concentration of newly learned words should not be so great as to make the reading beyond the child's grasp. Illustrations should be utilized where they will be helpful in getting the child to succeed in reading the written material. The purpose of illustrative material is to provide the child with as many successful contacts as possible with the words which he has learned, so that they can become a firm part of his immediate recognition vocabulary. He should not be struggling with the recognition of the words or reading them incorrectly, so that a wrong association is made and reinforced.

Psychological and Linguistic Bases

VAKT and VAK as learning techniques for dyslexic children are founded on adherence to sound principles of learning, adherence to the normal development of language and thinking abilities, involvement with systematic use of multisensory stimulation, and provision for development of the child's self-concept. Inherent in VAKT and VAK, as they have been described here, is the necessity for using personal experience as an approach to learning and in the content of systematic instruction. Without this personal framework within which the work takes place, many of the potential psychological and linguistic benefits are lost.

Learning Principles

Learning takes place through purposeful activity. It is an active process. It grows out of reacting to stimuli in a purposeful way. A child using VAKT is participantly involved to a maximum degree. He formulates the ideas to be worked with. They are expressed in his own words. He listens, speaks, writes, and reads to reach his goals. If he fails to involve himself, he suffers the immediate consequences of his lack of involvement in that things do not go well for him—he does not learn what he sets out to learn. Activity and purpose are inextricably bound together in the procedures of VAKT.

Understanding the goals of one's activity, seeing that one's needs are being met, and having opportunities for self-evaluation are essential conditions of good learning and teaching. The dyslexic child knows full well that he has had what appeared to be an insurmountable difficulty in making associations with visual language symbols. He is introduced to VAKT as a method which will enable him to learn words, a need he clearly recognizes. He knows why he is using the procedure and what it is intended to do for him on a long-term basis. However, he does not have to wait for the day when he is an accomplished reader to see that his goals are being reached and his needs met. He gets immediate evidence of success as he uses the learning technique. He needs a word to reach his goal of recording his ideas and language. He learns it—writes it and reads it. Short-term goals are continually being reached; immediate needs are met. He is engaged in a constant process of evaluation of his progress toward both immediate and long-term goals. He checks his efforts as he learns the words; he rereads his own materials and others; he uses his file box as a check point; he even knows how the number of trials he needs to learn a word changes from day to day and how well he can recognize, in subsequent retention checks, the words he has learned. He finds, as his reading vocabulary increases, that he can pick up books and read them—perhaps very easy ones at first, but books, nonetheless. When Francis first found that he could read a particular preprimer which happened to contain no words which he did not know at that point, he was amazed. It had been a long, hard struggle for him to acquire any immediate recognition vocabulary. His reaction showed both his recognition of his difficulty and some hope for the future—an awareness that he could and would progress. He said, "When I get to where I can read a first reader, that will be good enough for me!" By the time he got there, of course, he had changed his mind about his ultimate objectives. The important point is that he had some immediate, objective measures of his progress and, consequently, could see himself moving toward established goals. Further, he was able to put to use each item of his learning in a very practical way; he never had to wait for it to benefit him later on. When he had reached this point, his remedial program could be broadened to include a greater variety of reading activities, as Gates (1947) long since recommended in the total treatment of disability cases so severe as to need tracing.

Proceeding with meaningful wholes, rather than with a process of synthesis of small units, facilitates learning. In VAKT and VAK, the child learns whole words, never in any way breaking them down beyond their syllabic units. These wholes serve his reading and writing needs in practical situations and, at the same time, provide a reservoir of known words which can be analyzed as he is ready to discover certain phonic and syllabic principles. For the dyslexic child, building words from individual graphemes and phonemes appears to present a real obstacle. He has many more separate associations to make and has considerable difficulty in combining these minute elements (Bond, 1935). Thus, the learning in larger, meaningful units—ones in which a direct, three-way association of meaning from experience, oral language, and visual symbol can be made—is particularly necessary for him as a starting point for building a recognition vocabulary.

Learning proceeds from that which is already known; it builds on the foundation of previous knowledge. In VAKT and VAK the child finds a firm support for his new learning in his background of oral language and experience. He knows what he is talking about and has merely to learn how to attach the visual symbol to the already established spoken one. The basic meanings and oral symbols have been mastered and provide the groundwork on which he builds his reading and writing vocabularies. This known-to-unknown sequence leads directly to consideration of certain sound linguistic bases of VAKT and VAK.

Sequence of Language Development

The dyslexic child's disability is an illustration of interruption of the normal, sequential development of language. His experiences, from which his stock of meanings has been derived through a process of organization and reorganization into concepts, have been adequately associated first with aural stimulation, as he acquired a listening vocabulary, and then with his own vocal reproductions, as he acquired a speaking vocabulary. Sequential progress stopped at this point. Whereas the normal child moved on directly to a reading vocabulary, extending these associations to the printed form, the dyslexic child failed to grow in this direction. Enlargement of the oral vocabulary and sentence structure continued. No real reading vocabulary was acquired, and, consequently, no foundation existed for the development of a writing vocabulary.

Use of VAKT and VAK begins with the meaning and oral language background of the child and builds on it to continue the sequential development. The child not only learns the visual symbols for meanings and spoken words he knows, but he also uses his own patterns of speech in terms of the structure of the language he reads and writes. He formulates natural speech sentences and learns to deal with their visual representation. The intonation patterns, as well as the structural patterns, of his speech guide him in his reading activities as he rereads materials which he has written.

This solid foundation in the child's conceptual-oral language background, combined with direct learning through VAKT of the visual symbols to represent its elements, allows him to regain a measure of regularity in language development. He continues on a path of sequential extension of his language abilities. He knows the meanings, has heard the spoken symbols of them, and says what he wants to write. Now he sees the visual symbol, a representation of the spoken symbol (Russell and Fea, 1963), and learns it with the help of visual, auditory, kinesthetic, and tactile stimulation. He reads it, writes it for reinforcement, and reads it again. Gradually, as his blockages to making associations with the visual symbols are circumvented, he comes to the point of extending his reading and writing vocabularies without the need for this routine of using additional stimulation. He rejoins the normal stream of language development.

Multisensory Stimulation

Most children go through the sequence described above with no major difficulty—learning to speak through experimenting with sound-making and sound-combining in imitation of speech sounds they hear. When they meet visual language symbols, they rely primarily on the linking of visual and aural stimulation to associate the spoken word and the written form. Some kinesthetic stimulation is involved, of course, even as they look and speak (Russell and Fea, 1963). However, there is no need for them to have the added kinesthetic stimulation set up in hand and arm muscles by tracing or writing, or the tactile stimulation provided by tracing over the word form with the fingers. Without this enrichment of stimulation, the dyslexic child fails to make and retain the association.

VAKT routinizes the provision of this multisensory stimulation. The child hears, says, and sees the word and feels it with both his proprioceptive and tactile receptors. He does so in a carefully prescribed way. The degree to which dyslexics depend on this multisensory stimulation for retention and recall seems best illustrated by instances from their actual experiences. Judy would resort to "tracing" a word in the air or on her desk when she was having difficulty recalling it. This was long after she needed VAKT for word learning, yet going through this routine seemed always to bring the association back. Bill was taking a spelling test at the end of the term and interrupted, when he finished with a word, to say, "I didn't think I knew that word and when I started to write, it just came out."

How much this multisensory stimulation itself brings results with the dyslexic child is impossible to determine. One can only say that the stimulation, the necessity for complete involvement, the full attention and concentration demanded by the procedures, and the security of the structured learning situation do bring results when they are used in a firm psychological and linguistic framework.

Concept of Self

Many dyslexic children come for clinical help with very low evaluations of their own worth. They see themselves as failures, incapable of doing the things which lead to success, satisfaction, and active participation in the school world. In many instances, they have withdrawn from further effort instead of seeing themselves as sincerely trying and incapable of success. Often this self-doubt has gone beyond the area of learning directly affected by the original disability and has, in fact, pervaded the child's whole life.

From the start of its use, VAKT provides built-in evidence to the child that he is a worthwhile individual. As he is taught the techniques, his clinic teacher's whole attention must be on him. A teacher is not likely to devote himself completely, in a teaching situation, to someone in whom he has no confidence and for whom he has no hope. Therefore, the child soon gets the feeling that he is worth all this time and effort. This very effect, as well as the actual necessity for individual and uninterrupted work with the technique, may well be enough to militate against attempts to use it or modify it for use in the regular classroom situation. Here the child could not possibly be given the teacher's whole attention, and the chances for success would be seriously limited.

The conclusion of each experience with the technique is real learning. There is visible evidence of the child's ability to learn, and he cannot long ignore this. With these regular experiences of success, the child's attitude toward himself begins to change, and he is in a better personal state for further learning.

Outcomes of VAKT and VAK

Certain kinds of progress which are expected from the use of VAKT and VAK have already been indicated. The child gradually acquires an immediate recognition vocabulary and finds less and less need for tracing. He is finally able to learn and retain words even without added kinesthetic stimulation. Ultimately he is able to learn and retain words in the way that others have been doing all along. As he succeeds, his opinion of himself, his self-concept, changes. He no longer sees himself as a failure or as one for whom effort is foolish. He loses his fear of setting goals for himself—goals which involve academic achievement. Conversely, he may lose his need to set obviously impossible goals for himself so that his failure will be foreordained and understandable. He can look at himself realistically.

As the dyslexic child creates his materials for writing, countless opportunities arise for the teacher to guide him toward better thinking, organization of ideas, more mature and wider vocabulary, and variety in sentence and paragraph structure. Consequently, his thinking and his writing skills should certainly be improved. In addition, his constant use of the dictionary under teacher guidance should lead toward mastery and spontaneity in the handling of this valuable object. Using a dictionary will be, for him, a normal part of living, not a last resort to be avoided if possible, as it is to some students.

If VAKT and VAK are used correctly, they are not employed as substitutes for the development of word-form analysis skills (Bond and Tinker, 1957). Only a highly trained and skilled teacher of reading should serve as a clinician administering and supervising the use of VAKT and VAK techniques. As the child develops a readiness for each step in word analysis, he will, with such a teacher, get systematic instruction in the use of every profitable approach to analyzing word forms. Previously mentioned was the sensitivity to initial sounds and letters which should grow from the use of the file box. In like fashion, every analysis skill should be introduced as the child is ready to deal with it and as he has acquired experience with words subject to this type of analysis. VAKT and VAK merely provide a way for the dyslexic child to build a basic sight vocabulary from which to work as he develops these skills.

In summary, it must be said that VAKT and VAK, correctly used, can help the dyslexic child move from failure to success in dealing with visual language symbols. As he does so, he loses the operational characteristics of a dyslexic and develops at least the "outward appearance" of a normal learner. Those facets of his personality which had been shaped by failure may gradually also be reshaped by success. These things are possible only when the techniques are used within the framework herein described. To use them without this framework can lead to an increase in his dyslexic characteristics rather than to an alleviation of them.

CHAPTER 10

THE INITIAL TEACHING ALPHABET (i/t/a)

ALBERT J. MAZURKIEWICZ

Dyslexia, defined as "the inability to read even with adequate teaching" (Money, 1962), while of vast significance to educators at all levels and therefore studied at length by a number of researchers, had not been significantly related to the orthography of the English language prior to 1960. While research on dyslexia has been reported in other countries than English-speaking ones, a difference in the nature of the disability reported upon might be observable. The extent of significant retardation in the English-speaking population suggests some special characteristic of the language as being the cause of this higher incidence. However, it was not until 1962-1963 that evidence was reported to indicate how significant the relationship is between the spelling of English and reading failure. John Downing's early reports (Downing, 1962, 1963) and my subsequent studies (Mazurkiewicz, 1963–65, 1964a, 1965) indicated incontrovertibly that the current system of English spelling accounts for a significant amount of early failure.

In a report to the 29th Educational Records Bureau Conference in October, 1964 (Mazurkiewicz, 1964b), I noted that:

> The first grade child comes to school with the idea that he is going to learn to read and write. The first several weeks go by before he begins any meaningful activity. He leaves school daily not having learned to read or write. When he does begin to learn, the inconsistences in the language for the average child produces a small element of daily failure which cumulatively undermines the child's self-confidence. The result by the end of the first grade year, ego-satisfaction repeatedly denied, is that the child's self-concept, his ego-strength, is damaged and a general negative attitude toward school, learning, and reading, in particular, has been developed. He has learned that the printed page is something he cannot command. It is, therefore, easy to see that the basis for later dropouts and

snowballing reading failure is related to the experience in the first year of formal education.

At this same conference, I postulated, in conducting experimentation with the Initial Teaching Alphabet (i/t/a), that:

> If English were regularly spelled, then the normal curve of learning (which we have seen exist in virtually every facet of the curriculum as a reflection of the normal distribution of learning potential) would undoubtedly also exist in that aspect of reading called word recognition. Therefore, one of the purposes of the evaluation of i/t/a which was undertaken with the Bethlehem population was to determine if this theory would in fact be substantiated. Figure 1 shows that by the ninth month of instruction in i/t/a the normal learning curve in i/t/a is indeed demonstrable and that it contrasts markedly with the skewed distribution of an equivalent population working in the traditional alphabet. We might, therefore, conclude at this early point that if English were regularly spelled or more regularly spelled (not necessarily perfectly encoded) then learning to read and write would be essentially a simple process, that the mean of word recognition ability for a normal population might very well be at a fifth grade or fifth reader level by the end of the first grade, and that it would be a simple process to isolate those children who are having significant learning—not necessarily reading—difficulties, problems of learning related to intellectual potential, emotional or neurological disturbances, etc.
>
> If such an English orthography existed, we might conjecture that the extent of reading disability and the variety of significant reading handicaps existing in the general English-speaking population could be dramatically reduced.

The reference to the inconsistencies in spelling the English language is understandable when it is recognized that English is about 11 per cent phonetic. Assuming as a standard the *American College Dictionary*, the 44 phonemes of English are represented by 251 different spellings; other sources differ. It has been recognized that there are many irregularities in the relationship between sound and symbol in English. Almost every phonic rule that children can be taught, or led to discover, has exceptions. This makes the teaching and learning of English phonics considerably more difficult than it would be if each letter represented just one sound, as is true, or almost true, of several European languages. The recent controversies over look-say versus phonic teaching as the cause for reading retardation are therefore recognized to have

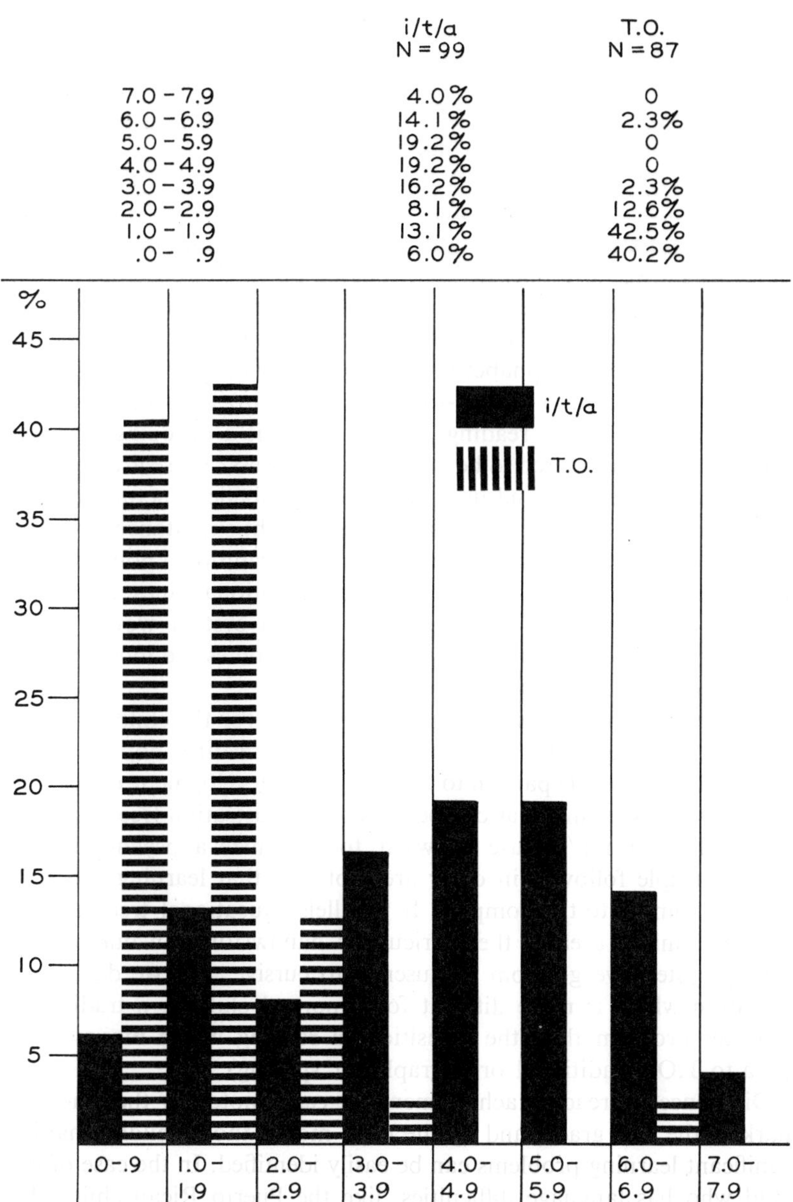

	i/t/a N = 99	T.O. N = 87
7.0 - 7.9	4.0%	0
6.0 - 6.9	14.1%	2.3%
5.0 - 5.9	19.2%	0
4.0 - 4.9	19.2%	0
3.0 - 3.9	16.2%	2.3%
2.0 - 2.9	8.1%	12.6%
1.0 - 1.9	13.1%	42.5%
.0 - .9	6.0%	40.2%

Figure 1. Schonell graded word reading test (translated to grade scores).

been worthless and misleading—particularly so in a language which has not learned to spell yet.

In examining the reading process, we seem to have been looking too long at comprehension as the basis of a definition of reading English; however, comprehension is primarily the goal of the reading activity. Meaning is less important as a clue to word recognition in other language systems; in English, comprehension turns out to be one of the major clues to word recognition. In effect, the definition of reading under which we have operated has focused on the purpose of reading rather than on its nature. We quite naturally stressed meaning, which is the goal of reading, at the expense of the process.

When a phonemic alphabet (or an alphabet which more nearly provides for a one-symbol-to-one-sound relationship) is used, an operational definition of the reading process makes it a decoding process; writing can be considered to be an encoding process. These are opposite faces of the same coin, and in a phonemic alphabetic structure reading and writing can be, and indeed should be, taught simultaneously. The usual clues used when teaching reading from a traditional point of view (language rhythm clues, picture clues, configurational clues, structural analysis clues, meaning clues, etc.) in such a system would be of secondary significance, for the symbol itself becomes the most reliable clue for word recognition.

The design of i/t/a, as a transitional medium for the child to use in beginning reading or for first steps in remedial reading, appears to be a uniquely serviceable pattern to encourage the development of reading skill on what is, as much as can be possible, a frustration-free basis. An examination of i/t/a's use shows it to epitomize a psychologically valid principle followed in other areas of life: that learning proceeds from the simple to the complex. It parallels educational treatment of another familiar area of the curriculum: handwriting. In our present writing system we go from manuscript to cursive, and we demand a transition which is more difficult for a normal child in a traditional alphabet program than the transition in reading which moves from i/t/a to T.O. (traditional orthography or spelling).

Differences in reading achievement are easily noted by the ten-week mark in the first grade, and by the third month those children having significant learning problems can be easily identified. In the case of the child who has language difficulties, like the Puerto Rican child who speaks no English, a program of learning which emphasizes the phonemes of his language, and mastering the phonemes not present in his language, can be structured. It is not uncommon to find that such children by the third and fourth month can read English stories although they have a limited oral English vocabulary. In this case, oral language is acquired from the reading of English.

The mentally slow child, when identified, can also be provided for in the i/t/a classroom. Utilizing prior knowledge, in the manner like that indicated in Johnson's comment (1963) that "slow learners, to a greater degree than normal children, should be provided with an organized and systematic method of word attack" and Fernald's note (1943) that "teaching activities which employ a multi-sensory approach are often successful in teaching reading to children who have primary learning disabilities," a program which emphasizes whole words (the look-say procedure) initially can be structured to include writing simultaneously. Thus tactile and kinesthetic reinforcement is added to learning by auditory-visual methods.

Kirk (1940) advised against any attempt to teach phonic rules to retarded children. He noted that "rules involve generalizations and since mentally retarded children are deficient in the ability to generalize they will have difficulty in learning." He recommended the introduction of phonic training only after the retarded child has learned to read slightly and has acquired a sight vocabulary of fifty to one hundred words. Since Gates (1930) estimated that from forty-five to fifty-five repetitions are necessary for a retarded child to learn a word, while the "normal child needs only from thirty to thirty-five repetitions," a program can be structured which utilizes a high-frequency usage of the same words, and this program would precede analysis and synthesis activities. Such activity, typical in a T.O. program, is found to encourage more rapid learning in i/t/a than is normally possible in the traditional alphabet.

The implications of the above statements are that methodology devised and improved on by numerous individuals need not be modified when utilizing i/t/a as a two-stage process to reading instruction. As implied in its name, the Initial Teaching Alphabet was designed as a simple systematic notation to be used in beginning reading materials and continued until the child or adult has acquired fluency and confidence in the medium. Only then are the inconsistencies of the spelling of our language introduced. The transition from the simple (i/t/a) to the complex (T.O.) is eased in the beginning reader's case by his being surrounded outside the classroom by the world of traditional print.

Pitman's beginning alphabet has forty-four symbols instead of twenty-six (Fig. 2). Twenty-four of the symbols are the traditional ones, while fourteen of the new letters look like two familiar letters

Number	Character	Example	Traditional Spelling
1.	æ	ænjel	angel
2.	b	bell	bell
3.	c	cat	cat
4.	d	dog	dog
5.	ϵϵ	ϵϵgl	eagle
6.	f	fiʃh	fish
7.	g	gœt	goat
8.	h	hors	horse
9.	ie	ies crϵϵm	ice cream
10.	j	jack-o-lanteɹn	jack-o-lantern
11.	k	kϵϵ	key
12.	l	lieon	lion
13.	m	muŋky	monkey
14.	n	nest	nest
15.	œ	bœt	boat
16.	p	pensil	pencil
17.	r	rabbit	rabbit
18.	s	Santa Clauʐ	Santa Claus
19.	t	tæbl	table
20.	ue	uenieted stæts	United States
21.	v	valentien	valentine
22.	w	wagon	wagon
23.	y	yœ-yœ	yo-yo
24.	z	zϵϵbra	zebra
25.	ʐ	siʐʐorʐ	scissors
26.	wh	whisl	whistle
27.	ch	chær	chair
28.	th	thum	thumb
29.	th	fethɹ	feather
30.	ʃh	ʃhꝏ	shoe
31.	ʒ	televiʒon	television
32.	ŋ	riŋ	ring
33.	ɑ	ɑrm	arm
34.	au	automobϵϵl	automobile
35.	a	appl	apple
36.	e	eskimœ	Eskimo
37.	i	indian	Indian
38.	o	ostrich	ostrich
39.	u	sun	sun
40.	ω	bωk	book
41.	ꝏ	spꝏn	spoon
42.	ou	oul	owl
43.	oi	boi	boy
44.	ɹ	giɹl	girl

Figure 2. The Initial Teaching Alphabet (i/t/a).

joined together. The remainder are similar to some form of the traditional. **Q** and X are omitted because they do not have their own sound values.

The characters have their counterparts in manuscript and cursive forms and are not foreign or unusual. The character **ou**, representing the sound **ou** in all words the child sees and hears, is seen to be identical to the ligatured letters in the cursive **out**. Note that the **o** and **u** are joined identically in either the i/t/a or T.O. forms. The difference is in usage: **hou** rather than **how**, **nou** rather than **now**. Similarly, other characters can be traced to their origins in cursive writing.

Lower-case characters only are used, and capitalization is achieved by using a larger version of the lower-case letters. Lower case was chosen because this form provides maximum discrimination in the look-say visual pattern and because it occurs very much more frequently than upper case in traditionally printed books. The paragraphs of Figure 3 indicate how i/t/a simplifies the complex spelling of English.

While various modifications of procedures are utilized to meet the sense modes and rates of learning of the dyslexic child, two approaches, the whole word (or look-say) and the phonic approach, are recognizable as basic. Though the child may be first introduced to whole words and asked to discover relationships between the sounds of his language and the characters used to represent them, teachers very soon add directed instruction on the sound-symbol relationships. In effect, the teacher gives instruction in phonics in this system, where one symbol generally represents one sound, to increase word analysis skill development as rapidly as possible. Other teachers might start with directed instruction on the sound-symbol relationships while at the same time providing activities which develop sight vocabulary.

Whatever the procedure used, the sound that each symbol represents, rather than letter names, is taught. The result is that whenever the child sees a symbol, it is read in its own meaningful way. Once the forty-four symbols are associated with their sounds, and the child develops the concept of blending the sounds into larger structural units, he can read any word. Since words are generally spelled as they sound, the guesswork is taken out of reading.

Since i/t/a is used as a temporary medium, spelling rules designed to promote ease of transition from i/t/a to traditional spelling indicate to the teacher the deliberate inconsistency built into the use of the medium.

The child, however, is not introduced to the inconsistencies until his word analysis skills are well advanced. When inconsistencies are everyŧhiŋ woz redy. it woz tiem for tæk-off but ŧhe skie woz still not cleer.

sam ŧhe spæsman woz sad. "ie hav wæted and wæted for ŧhis big dæ," hee sed tω himself. "nou ie mæ hav tω wæt still loŋger tω flie mie spæs ʃhip around ŧhe erŧh."

Everything was ready. It was time for take-off but the sky was still not clear.

Sam the spaceman was sad. "I have waited and waited for this big day," he said to himself. "Now I may have to wait still longer to fly my space ship around the earth."

Figure 3. A paragraph in i/t/a and its transcription into traditional orthography.[1]

[1] From Book Four, *Early-to-Read i/t/a Program*. Reprinted by permission of i/t/a Publications, Inc., 20 East 46th Street, New York City.

introduced, they signal the beginning of the process referred to technically as a set for diversity, but which is recognizable as the beginning of the introduction to the complex world of traditional spelling.

Since the child knows from the beginning that each symbol stands for its own sound, he recognizes the letter **o** as representing the short sound of the name found in **on, off, not** rather than as in conventional spelling as standing for the various sounds found in such words as: **one, go, do, women**. Individual characters replace the complex combinations of letters used in standard spelling. œ replaces **ough** in **dough**; **ie** replaces **igh** in **light**, etc. Since right-to-left sequence is consistently maintained, the child does not have to move from right to left to decode a word (for example, **lien** rather than **line, tœn** rather than **tone**).

Pitman's aim of providing a simple systematic medium for beginning reading (initial or remedial), without permanent spelling reform, called for a compromise between, on the one hand, the need for simplification and consistency in the beginning reading code and, on the other hand, the need to make i/t/a compatible with conventional orthography, so that transition from i/t/a to standard print should be easy for children when they reach the transfer stage. **C** and **K**, therefore, have both been kept to represent the same single phoneme (sound) to reduce the number of words whose spellings have to be changed at the transfer stage. Similarly, double letters are retained to help preserve the over-all patterns of words, e.g., **rabbit** rather than **rabit**, **letter** rather than **leter**.

Since the design of the Initial Teaching Alphabet is as similar to the traditional alphabet as possible, it is not surprising to note that transition from one to the other is a simple procedure. It should be noted, as well, that reading and writing in a phonemically spelled language is such a simple process that the two activities may be learned simultaneously and that the child can quickly develop the basic concept that written characters are highly dependable symbols for speech sounds. The child's task in reading (in the mechanical sense) is primarily one of determining which sound, or sound cluster, the symbols are intended to represent. In the writing activity he is concerned with encoding sound; i.e., with writing the symbols which represent the sounds he wants to express in writing.

The emphasis in writing activities is always on encouraging the child's creative tendencies. Thus the freedom he enjoys in speech is paralleled by freedom in writing. This emphasis permits him a freedom in spelling in using the Initial Teaching Alphabet which is inhibited only by the criterion of clarity of meaning, both to himself and to his teacher. Even the retarded child is found to be significantly productive in writing under this plan and is found to have a fund of interest information which he gladly communicates. Teachers of such children report surprise at the relative ease with which such children communicate through writing, as well as at the breadth of their interests.

An Illustration of Procedure

A typical example of procedure will illustrate how instruction may proceed with a dyslexic. In this case, the student, a nineteen-year-old male, had been enrolled in a laboratory school after diagnostic testing. He had normal intelligence but was found to have reading skill at a second reader instructional level, in spite of skilled attention over a period of years by psychologists, psychiatrists, and reading clinicians.

Pretesting on letter recognition and the sounds he had learned to associate with the letters indicated that no attention needed to be given to the consonants **b**, **d**, **f**, **h**, **j**, **k**, **l**, **m**, **n**, **p**, **r**, **s**, **t**, **v**, **w**, **y**, and **x**. The consonant **g**, however, was identified as having the soft sound, as in **gentle**. Letter names presented no difficulty. The vowels were, however, consistently confused in sound values.

Instruction on identification of the i/t/a symbols, discrimination between sounds, and association of symbols with sounds was begun after introduction of the new alphabet and its purposes. Experience stories dictated by the young man were recorded by the teacher in i/t/a. Reading of this material was used to help him discover the relationship between his sounds and the symbols used to represent them. Three periods of twenty minutes each served to acquaint him with enough of the symbols to permit his beginning to read simple stories. All of the remaining symbols were then taught (and he learned to write them) by the fifth session. Reading activity progressed to material which included all symbols. Writing activity, moving more slowly, was used as the basis for identification of auditory perceptual problems, and reinforcement instruction was given.

Writing and reading instructional activities in twenty-minute periods were supplemented by encouraging independent reading of i/t/a materials by the third week. Materials increased in readability until commercial materials were exhausted. At this point (the fifth month), transition-type activities were used to show the relationship between the i/t/a symbols and the various ways in which the sounds that they represented were spelled traditionally. Examples: **ae** is written as **a**, **a–e**, **ay**, **ai**; **œ** is written as **o**, **o–e**, **oa**, **ow**.

By the sixth week, some 130 books in i/t/a of various but easy readability levels had been read independently, numerous articles and stories in i/t/a at more difficult levels (sixth and seventh grade) had been read in instructional periods, and writing activities had progressed to two- and three-page stories, which were stimulated in a number of ways but which were written entirely by the student. In the fifth and sixth weeks i/t/a reading continued, along with reading in materials in the traditional alphabet.

Progress in reading materials in the traditional alphabet, as measured at the end of this six-week period by informal means, showed that his instructional level had moved from the second- to the fifth-reader level. The improvement in his confidence in commanding the printed page was pronounced. The relatively marked progress in this instance cannot be expected for all dyslexics, since the high degree of motivation maintained by this young man cannot be achieved in all cases.

Variations on the Basic Procedure

Judith Brown, at the University of Oregon Medical School, working with John B. Isom, Associate Professor of Pediatrics, following consultations with the author found that the group of dyslexic children that she was treating benefited most profoundly by the initial use of experience stories in i/t/a. These stories used the jargon of the teenager ("hou duzthat grab yoo?" is an example from one story) and directed instruction on each of the symbols. This was done despite recognition that previous learning of some sort existed, since it was realized that only a few of the children knew many of the sounds associated with the traditional letters. Their work then included the program of reading instruction as established in the guides, workbooks, and readers of the Early-to-Read i/t/a program. This program begins with experience stories, moves to directed instruction on the recognition and writing of symbols, encourages limited writing skill while reading experience stories, and introduces six readers totaling some nine hundred pages. Modification of procedures to reinforce learning included flash card drill, sand-box tracing of letters and words, and practice in synthesizing words using small symbol cards.

The procedures used here differ little from the basic procedures noted previously, since the teaching pattern for the dyslexic child appears to be, first, to promote confidence in the medium as a new technique which will help the child learn to read, next to capture his interest, then to proceed with directed instruction related to his individual rate and sense mode of learning.

One fact, however, passed over lightly earlier, is significant in the use of i/t/a with the dyslexic reader (and retarded readers generally) and must be further discussed. In various trial tests, as the child developed mastery of the forty-four characters for the forty sounds of his English speech, independence in reading skill was developed. After a child reached this level of independence, he could move rapidly through successively more difficult material until he was reading i/t/a material more commensurate with his grade level, as identified by his number of years in school and/or his chronological age, and therefore nearer his ego satisfaction level. It was later noted with a group of fourteen- to sixteen-year-olds whose reading skill ranged as low as 2.3 on standardized tests that the use of intervening materials, once independence in the use of i/t/a was achieved, proved needless. The student could be moved immediately to materials in i/t/a at his own grade level.

Another group of researchers, led by Dorothy Dietrich of the Uniondale Public Schools, began instruction by teaching the students the sound symbol relationships of i/t/a and followed this with practice work in learning to write the symbols and to recognize them in simple experience stories. As reported by her in *Learning Disorders* (Mazurkiewicz *et al.*, 1965), "Since the attempt was to permit the youngsters to experience something quite different from that which they had been exposed to for years, material at their interest level was transliterated for use, initially at approximately the fourth and fifth reader level. It was found that the students were able to read just as easily the materials which had been written originally for students at their own grade level when it was printed in i/t/a."

Thus these readers were, in a very short time, reading material at eighth- and ninth-grade levels. The implication is that readability, or difficulty, of the material is no longer a significant block to reading at interest levels. The most significant barrier to such reading, the ability to recognize or analyze words, is removed in i/t/a materials.

While students were found to be able to read words at their interest levels, it is axiomatic that they cannot always understand them or fit them meaningfully into context. Thus it becomes necessary for the teacher to build concepts and develop vocabulary skills. "It was also found that students were being asked to use reading and thinking skills which probably had not ever been used before. . . . In most instances [they were] only expected to get the main idea along with sufficient details and to make some general inferences. Now, they were asked to become involved in critical reading skills. However, it was found that with [teacher] help they were quite capable of dealing with such skills."

The transition from i/t/a to T.O. materials in the case of the dyslexic child parallels that of the developmental first-grade reader. It differs only in that the dyslexic child is assumed to have had a significant amount of experience with printed materials in traditional orthography. The transition may be first encouraged by having the child read a T.O. version of a story previously read in i/t/a; it may be made, however, without the use of repetitious reading. The process of transition usually begins, in most cases, with teaching the child about the way sounds are encoded in traditional orthography, as noted earlier. This procedure emphasizes a recognition of spelling patterns rather than utilization of rules and is followed by syllabication and dictionary skill activity for independence in word recognition.

The length of time that the dyslexic reader continues to read i/t/a material after achieving independence in reading is governed primarily by the length of time necessary to develop his confidence in commanding the printed page and his efficiency and effectiveness in oral and silent reading. These seem to develop simultaneously, and readiness to make the transition is signaled by an interest in exploring traditional printed materials, or a preference for reading books in traditional print rather than i/t/a materials. However, the transition has been forced or abruptly begun on occasion. Such a transition may require a return to i/t/a material for security purposes and is governed by the instructor's judgment of the pupil's ability and capacity to tolerate such transfer.

In transition activities, the teacher frequently finds that when a word in T.O. presents unusual difficulty, the child can easily recognize the same word printed in i/t/a and that after several repetitions (writing the word, comparing one pattern with the other, or meeting the T.O. word and then checking the i/t/a word as a phonemic respelling, much like the procedure followed when using a dictionary, and repeating the word) the T.O. word is thereafter recognized in other contexts.

BLENDING

In nearly all cases (either with the retarded reader, the dyslexic, the mentally retarded, the slow child, or the child from a poor socioeconomic environment), the problem area noted in phonics work in T.O.—blending sounds to form words—also occurs in i/t/a work. A variety of procedures is required to aid the development (or catching) of this concept. Some teachers find it desirable to use only the whole word approach for a long period of time and then to isolate a symbol from words fully mastered for directed instruction. Others find that the consonants can be used with different vowels to orient the child to the way in which the speech organs modify the consonant sound to fit the vowel following (**ba**, **bi**, **be**, **bo**, **ab**, **ib**, **eb**, **pi**, **pe**, **pu**, **po**, etc.). Still others use mechanical devices to supply a word at normal speech speed and then at a slower speed to aid in isolating the sounds in a word; then the word is repeated at normal speed. Whatever the procedure used, it is noted that this concept of blending is caught only after numerous repetitions and a variety of activities. It is found to be unrelated either to chronological age or mental age, though normal and bright children most easily develop the concept.

Other Considerations

The emotionally disturbed youngster who is also a dyslexic typically presents an unusually difficult job of remediation. The question of which came first need not concern us here, yet the model of the first-grade child's experience noted earlier is relevant. The disturbed child may be significantly helped by the use of i/t/a for his reading instruction, since it appears to provide an opportunity for success. Reports of a fragmentary nature from institutions using the above procedures have indicated a marked decrease in asocial behavior, a marked improvement in motivation in academic areas, and a more positive self-concept. Students are reported to relate better to adults and to exhibit a more healthy ego structure as seen in projective drawings.

A list of available publications, i/t/a typewriters, and teaching materials is found in the Appendix.

CHAPTER 11

WORDS IN COLOR

I. THE MORPHOLOGICO-ALGEBRAIC APPROACH TO TEACHING READING — CALEB GATTEGNO

II. THE CURRENT STATUS OF WORDS IN COLOR IN THE UNITED STATES — DOROTHEA HINMAN

I. The Morphologico-Algebraic Approach to Teaching Reading
Caleb Gattegno

Teaching reading has taught me many things. Reading the literature has shown me that though there has often been a bright idea at the start of a new scheme, on the whole there has rarely been a study of what reading actually is. Problems in reading exist in phonetic languages, and mistakes are possible even for fluent readers. In English, in particular, people have been mesmerized by the mad spellings of the language and have concentrated on meeting, in one way or another, the challenge thus isolated. It would have taken little trouble to discover that quasi-phonetic languages like Spanish or Italian offer similar problems to teachers of reading. It therefore cannot be the ambiguities (found in so many languages) that are the cause of the troubles known to all educators. In fact, almost all the cultivated minds in most societies have overcome the obstacles that historical development has let creep into written languages.

It is important for the argument that follows that readers keep firmly in mind the fact that they themselves have managed to overcome what seems difficult to some others and that, however phonetically adequate the transcription of sign to sound in some languages, in almost every school in every country there are nonreaders.

It also happens that in deciphering a handwritten or even a printed passage we readers mistake one word for another, or even one single letter for another, and read on until we are unable to make sense of what we were silently uttering and retaining. We then go back to find where we made the error or where an error was made by the writer or printer. This observation tells us two things: (1) that even good, fluent readers may fumble and form images of signs that are not what they should be; and (2) that a check upon correct utterance comes from a sense other than sight or the voice, one that we may call a sense of sense or of meaning.

Emphasis in all current reading research is mistakenly confined to spatial factors. When we see the enormous effort put into reading readiness, and even prereadiness, to ensure that sight is put under the control of the conscious mind and that recognition of concentration, design, alignment, and so forth, have been in turn tested and trained, we cannot escape the conclusion that research has taken on a clear spatial emphasis.

Cases of mirror reading or writing—confusion of letters that only differ by asymmetry with respect to axes or points—have been constantly reported, and either exercises are proposed for correction or such persons are referred to a specialist for examination for indications of brain damage.

It would not take more than a few moments of reflection to realize that when we write we take time to put the signs down and we follow an order which is temporal; and we follow a temporal order again when we scan lines and words to find out what they are supposed to express. Even though the page, once printed, appears as structured space, reading requires temporal reorganization of the sets of signs before there is any hope of bringing to light their hidden meaning. Mankind has developed writing on plane surfaces but has proposed both horizontal and vertical writing, ordered from right to left or left to right and from top to bottom. But whatever their chosen order, all scripts require that the correct temporal sequence be found before reading takes place. Since there is no necessity either for a given spatial arrangement or for any particular signs (which can be Latin, Cyrillic, Sanskrit, Arabic, hieroglyphic, Chinese, etc., all of which are inherited), the question of what it is to read cannot be confined to spatial components or to an understanding of the grapheme-phoneme relationship.

Inner criteria must be generated which reliably relate spatial factors to temporal factors. Since in a two-dimensional space we cannot define an order, and since our inner time is the primitive receptacle of order, generating all the properties of order as studied by mathematicians, it is clear that we must refer to time whenever we study reading. It is, therefore, the orientation of teachers and others toward space rather than toward time that may be one of the sources of difficulty encountered by some learners, who possess a sense of order in their psychological time but cannot find it in space when they are shown a design called a sentence.

There are two people in every teaching situation, one who has overcome the abyss between space and its temporal organization, called reading, and one who may not have understood that he has actually been asked to spread the designs on the page in a certain order—a spatial order—which, in turn, requires a temporal utterance in a definite order.

Any reader who has the opportunity of asking a young child (of two or four to five years) to utter the word "spot," and then asks him to drop the first sound, will find the word "pot" uttered if the question has been understood. But if the child is told, as he looks at the word, "This word is 'pot' " (which he can easily repeat to prove that he can say it), and is then told "put *in front of* it the hissing sound," he is unable to decide that he must say "spot." He may equally well say "pots." This will, I contend, show the difference in the ease with which temporal sequences are recognized as being ordered sequences and the difficulty of deciding what is meant by "in front of" or "at the back of" a word. If he sees that "in front of" stands for *first* and "at the back of" stands for *last*, as they do when the temporal order structure is transferred to the space that is a line, then no errors occur.

Naturally, there is more to it than this, but this experiment may be an eye-opener. Since our vocabulary is heavily biased toward space, and thus our temporal instructions are often given in spatial language, one may be forgiven for being confused until one had adjusted to the bias. At the least, it indicates that as teachers we could be made much more careful by taking this bias into account. We might find that if we expressed ourselves adequately a number of obstacles for our learners would simply vanish. It has been our experience over and over again to discover that we have misled our youngest pupils by expressing a question—making use of a space concept—when, instead, time is the important concept involved.

All this should draw attention to the possibility that mirror reading or writing is not a trouble inherent in some minds but may simply be the outcome of the nonexistence as yet of an adequate criterion for what spatial order of signs represents the time order of the sequence of sound in the same words. Users of Words in Color will never experience this difficulty, or it will disappear quickly, since time is stressed from the beginning.

Inner criteria regarding discrimination of similar letter shapes may also be developed. This confusion over the temporal sequence does not explain the problem of the confusion of similar shapes or the presentation of a sign in a different spatial orientation. For example, **b**, **d**, **p**, and **q** are confused because the shapes differ only by asymmetry, and symmetry usually serves to integrate parts rather than to provide a drastic distinction.

Even intelligent adults who are accustomed to Latin script and are also studying Russian find the use of some of the Latin letters that they know as representing a very different sound (for example, **g** for **d**, **H** for **N**, **P** for **R**) most confusing in the beginning. This confusion disappears when a working adaptation is generated in the learner, one based on the development of additional inner criteria.

So it is with the similar confusions in those learning to read and write English; they are, as a rule, not a consequence of brain injury but of the absence of adequate inner criteria or of sufficiently rapid use of such criteria.

In Words in Color the use of inner criteria is constantly stressed, but there are also some devices used that help. First **p** is introduced and is colored brown when it is a sounded consonant, as in **pop**. When **d** appears, **p** has been thoroughly practiced. To emphasize the distinction wanted, **d** is colored dark green. After **d** has been practiced for some time, **b** appears. However, because this procedure would make one watch only the color and not the shape, we revert to asking learners to watch the orientation of the shape and not the color by making the color of **b** and **d** very close indeed.

Since **q** very rarely appears on its own but is almost always joined with **u** as **qu**, the dangers of confusion are reduced. In fact, in Words in Color **q** is never shown on its own, and **qu** is either one color (gold), as in **liquor**, or two colors (gold and aqua), as in **quickly** (where it represents a double sound).

Before examining the contribution that Words in Color can make to the teaching of reading, let us summarize our discussion. It is useless to provide a strictly spatial organization as the basis of reading and then to be astonished that it creates problems: reading, by its nature, calls upon a temporal element not taken into account in such an organization. Looking at it another way, we can expect that any system that bows to the nature of the task in hand will at once be more successful than others, so long as it does not in turn neglect an essential dimension of reading.

We believe that Words in Color, taken in its entirety, represents progress, since the system consciously moulds itself to what is really required of the learner in the act of reading. Let us add that, when taken as a whole, it does away with a number of preconceived ideas while taking into account more of reality. For instance, in the Words in Color system the number of written words is almost the same as the number of spoken words after approximately six weeks, while with the usual approaches we find the reading vocabulary vastly less than the spoken vocabulary at the same point, or even in a year's time.

Visual Dictation maintains time at the center of the reading process. To explain briefly how the temporal sequence is practiced in the program, we have to introduce the techniques of Visual Dictation, which were developed to meet this challenge.

Having accepted the premise that the task of the learner is to create a codification of his spoken speech, and having recognized that the signs of the written language are arbitrary and that some rules of spatial arrangement are conventional, we may find it convenient to make a conscious distinction between the acquiring of some conventions as habits and the final product of reading from the printed page.

This is done by introducing at first only one sign to represent only one sound. For example, if the sign **a** is associated with the sound it has in **at**, it is clearly possible to write **a** alone. The learner's response to this will be the utterance of the agreed sound. If **a a** is written and the two **a**s are shown in turn, this will elicit the same sound twice, and **a a a** will elicit the same sound three times. The rhythm of pointing can be varied, and, if the pointer's speed is matched by a speed of utterance, **aa** may represent contiguous succession differing only in that respect from **a a**. **aa a** can be shown and uttered as well as **aaa**, but is felt as different. Ultimately, in a few minutes a "sentence" such as **aa a aa aaa a a aa a aaa** could be elicited from learners without any further help. This links the utterance of the sounds to the writing; the spacing shows where pauses are to be made, and the number of signs shows which number of **a**s are uttered in each "word."

This game has provided a number of important conventions that will be used when ordinary reading is the game. In fact, immediate transfer to another sign, say, **i** (as in **it**), can prove that this much mastery has been achieved. In beginning Words in Color, five vowels in this order are chosen, **a, u, i, e, o,** sounded as in **at, up, it, pet, not**. But as soon as more than one sign is used, combinations are possible which show that **au** and **ua** are different because the sounds made are different, and that therefore these signs clearly represent a temporal sequence in which the sound for **a** precedes that of **u** in the first case, but follows it in the second.

During this work the teacher is silent, using a pointer over the five signs put on the board with colored chalks (**a**, white, **u**, pale yellow, **i**, pink, **e**, pale blue, **o**, orange), and the class makes the sounds indicated:

a u i e o

If **oo** is heard, it indicates that the teacher has touched the orange sign twice. But **oi** denotes that the teacher has shown the orange followed at once by the pink, while **ioe a** indicates that pink, orange, and blue were touched in quick succession, followed by a pause, followed by touching the white sign. When the teacher or the pupils write these sequences, they look like what we have seen thus far. Thus this Visual Dictation, by the touching of the signs in various orders with the pointer, ensures that both writing and speech reflect these temporal sequences.

An interesting and most useful variation can now be introduced. If the teacher tells his class that **au** is the reverse of **ua** and conversely, he can now ask for the reversal of any temporal sequence (already shown a number of times in examples with the pointer) which he gives. For **ie** pupils answer **ei**; for **iie** he gets **eii**; for **auio**, **oiua**. Some of the reversals reproduce the same sound: **aa** gives **aa**, **iei** gives **iei**, and so forth. Reversing is a way of meeting the challenge of mirror reading, as we shall show.

In Words in Color consonants are not given a sound of their own, and it is possible to move into reading (as speech has already been met by the learner on his own) with syllables as the smallest unit, many made of a vowel and consonant together, some with just a vowel, but each having only one sound. So when we introduce consonants they are names, as, "the brown one" or "the magenta one," so that we can refer to them. This means that sounds are associated only to combinations like **ap** (or single vowels like **a**) but never to **p** by itself. This is done first by the teacher, who points to **a** and then to **p** in rapid succession:

a u i e o

p

Then when written, it appears as a white **a** followed by the brown one, **ap** (as **au** was written before), and what is uttered indicates how **a** is affected by the proximity of the brown one. The relevant sounds for the similar syllables **up**, **ip**, **ep**, and **op** are to be obtained from the learners by analogy and should not be given by the teacher, so as to ensure transfer and reduce the reliance on pure memory.

Reversing the order of printing produces **pa** (to be given by the teacher first while moving the pointer in the reverse order over the signs as she utters it), and by analogy the rest of these reversed syllables, **pu**, **pi**, **po**, and **pe**, are uttered by learners.

Now comes another exercise that is characteristic of Words in Color, the merging or fusion of syllables to produce one sound instead of two, e.g., **pap** instead of **pa** and **ap**. This exercise usually takes little time, and it establishes the game of fusion of sounds which is available to any throat capable of speech. This is a space-time fusion called Visual Dictation 1. The set of signs on the board is

a u i e o
p t s s
t t ss ss
's 's

(Here one color given to **s ss 's** is green and is associated with the sound in **sat**, and the other color given to the same three signs is purple and corresponds to the sound in **is**.) As the pointer moves from sign to sign, it produces syllables that are spontaneously merged to produce words. For example, **pi it** becomes **pit** because of the speed of the pointer that suggests one sound only, while **it is** is uttered as two sounds because of the pause between the two syllables, which is shown by moving the pointer down and away from the board.

Reversing **pit** in time will provide **tip**, which can then be shown by the learner's moving the pointer rapidly on the three constituent signs: **t**, **i**, **p**. Reversing **it is** yields **is it**, with a change of tone to indicate that a question has replaced an affirmative statement, or the converse, if **is it** precedes **it is**.

To go from **pat is up** to **is pat up** is more complex than reversal, though equally possible. No name has been given to this transformation, although it is immediately met as part of Visual Dictation 1.

A systematic use of reversing as a game from the start will (1) often double the yield in words and sentences; and (2) stress a temporal sequence in the clue to the translation of sound in joined signs, and vice versa. So with these few signs we can form a considerable number of words:

two-letter words: **up, at, it, us, as, is, (ass)**
three-letter words: **pat, pit, pet, pot, pop, pup, pip, pep, top, tip, tap, tat, tit, tot, sat, sit, set, sap, sip, sup, pus, sis, its**

four-letter words: **pass, tess, pitt, putt, pats, pits, pets, pots, pops, pips, peps, taps, tips, tops, tots, sits, sets, saps, sips, sups, stop, spot, step, spit, spat, pest, test, past**
five-letter words: **stops, steps, pests, tests, spots, spits, upset**
six-letter words: **upsets, passes**

Sentences can be produced of varying length and complexity (only some reversals are indicated):

—pop up
—pep up
—it is
—is it
—it is as it is
—is it as it is
—it is up
—is it up
—pep it up pat
—pat it
—tip it up
—tap it
—pat is up
—is pat up
—it is pat
—is it pat
—as is pat
—pat is apt
—pat is as apt as pitt
—pass us
—pass us up pat
—pass it
—pat pass it up
—pass pat
—pat passes pitt
—pat peps it up
—pat tips it up
—it is pus
—pat is past
—it is past
—pop putts

—sit up pat
—pat sat up
—set it up pat
—pat sets it up
—pat sips pop
—pat sips it up
—sit it up pat
—stop it pat
—stop pat stop
—pat stops at steps
—step up pat
—step it up
—pat steps it up
—it stops it up
—spit it up
—sis spits up
—pat spat
—pat spat at pitt
—it's pat
—pat sits at its top
—pat's pets
—pat's pop's up
—pat pets spot
—pat's pet is spot
—pat is pop's pet
—pop spots pat's pet, spot
—pat's pest spits
—test it
—test pat
—pop tests pests
—pat tests pitt
—tess tests pitt's pups

It is now obvious that the learners have been doing some intellectual exercises far more difficult than reading a page, and as they succeed at once with it, it becomes clear that the willingness to introduce Visual Dictation before the words have been presented in the traditional way has paid handsome dividends. In fact, any teacher using Words in Color who can master the presentation of these beginning lessons will know with certainty that his pupils will learn to read a page in a much shorter time than is usually required to read a page with full understanding.

Since Visual Dictation 1 is the hardest of all the exercises, we can expect that when we introduce the wall charts it will be, in general, no surprise to the students that the words they formed in their minds are now found as patterns in which the colored signs are linked by proximity. The convention of translating sounds into signs has been so frequently practiced that, though the charts may not have been seen until now, they are accepted in a moment as familiar objects.

On Wall Chart 2 (Fig. 1) we can practice:

1. recognition of reversals, such as **pot** and **top** or **sap** and **pass**, etc;
2. recognition of passage from one pattern to another, such as **at** to **pat**, or **top** to **stop**, which we call addition;
3. recognition of the passage from **pot** to **pit**, which we call substitution; and
4. recognition that **pat** becomes **past** and **pet** becomes **pest**, by what we call insertion.

We call this kind of playing the game of transformation, which may then combine the simpler transformations recognized above. For example, from **it** to **steps** can be seen as the succession:

$$\mathbf{it}\xrightarrow{a}\mathbf{pit}\xrightarrow{s}\mathbf{pet}\xrightarrow{a}\mathbf{pets}\xrightarrow{r}\mathbf{step}\xrightarrow{a}\mathbf{steps}$$

where *a*, *s*, and *r* stand for addition, substitution, and reversal. There are alternative routes of transformation between **it** and **steps**, or any other two words, and thus the game becomes most stimulating.

With the same wall chart (Fig. 1) we can also play the game of Visual Dictation 2. Though it is easier than the Visual Dictation 1, it is equally useful to our goal of maintaining time at the center of the reading process. Visual Dictation 2 and the game of transformation maintain time as our focus and so provide for full comprehension. By pointing at varying speed to words that are known, we get:

Figure 1. Wall chart 2.

pat pit pet

pot at it up

tap tip top

pep pup pop tot

as us is

sat sit set

stop step pass

stops steps past

sap sips test pest

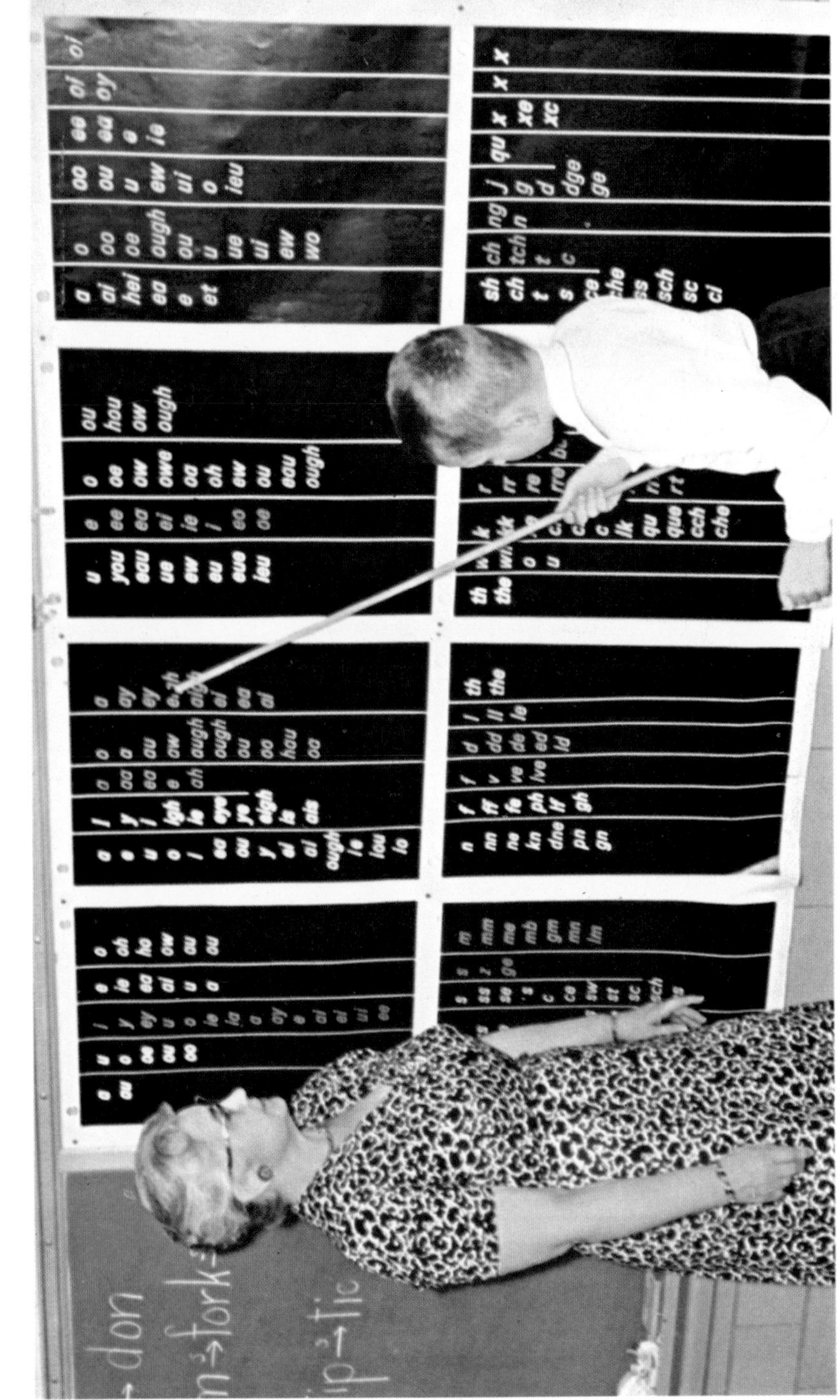

Figure 2. Word-building chart.

pat is up,

or

pat is up,
pat is up,

said without chopping and at the speed of normal speech.

Because it is spoken speech which brings with it comprehension, as soon as words and sentences have been met at the speed of speech in the two types of Visual Dictation, we cannot help but see how reading is always to be understood. It is uttering, as if they were to be spoken, what is stored in the temporal patterns indicated to us by the successions of spatial patterns on the page.

In the Words in Color system there is no reading that is not natural. A number of techniques have been devised toward this end which are explained in the teacher's guide and in other notes for teachers. Here we shall limit ourselves to emphasizing that we find meaning in the flow of spoken speech, and so we use meaning to help reading to be as natural as speaking. In Words in Color at no moment is there separation of reading and comprehension, yet no picture is ever used to give a clue to the meaning in a sequence of words.

The role of the two Visual Dictations is to bring time to the center of activities, and it is this act that is of paramount importance—the more so because we have been able to do it from the very beginning.

But Words in Color does not consist only of what has just been described. The game of transformation is one of a number of games that keep the learner's mind on the peculiarities of the written patterns and their sounds. Awareness is developed of sounds in words, of sets of spellings for each sound, of the structure of sentences, and of what constitutes free and creative composition. As is seen in the work sheets that are part of the program, as soon as the main obstacles of making sense of the conventions which transcribe sounds into signs, and signs into sounds, are surmounted, we shift the emphasis toward the acquisition of deeper and deeper insights into one's language.

1. Phonetic awareness is exalted mainly through the color clues found both in the wall charts and in the colored Phonic Code (a different version of which, in black and white, forms the Word Building Book).[1]

[1] It is our belief that what i/t/a is offering teachers is similar to the contribution which could be given by our Phonic Code if proposed alone. The advantage of Words in Color is that it requires no distortion of traditional spellings. But Words in Color is far more than this. It is, in addition, a battery of materials and techniques which meet the central challenges of extending linguistic power to reading, writing, spelling, and creative writing as a unity.

2. Spellings are met by a graded encounter through all the materials and exercises, culminating in the classification shown in Figures 2 and 3. The Phonic Code (and Chart 16 of the Word Building Book) gives in forty-eight columns all the vowels and consonants. This means that meeting the complete reality of written English in all its complexity is made into an achievable goal task through this program.

3. Sentence structure and the rules of English writing are laid open to every learner, who thus becomes aware that although spoken speech—because it is in time—has a structure that is most difficult to perceive, written speech presents advantages of permanence that can be put to good use.

4. Composition is encouraged from the beginning, first as the provision of an alternative for one statement, then as the coordination of a number of statements, still later, in the form of alternatives or additions to endings in stories, and finally, as free composition using words found in one's reading or specially selected to express what is wanted.

5. There is no limit set on vocabulary—no limit to the number and length of the words to be presented to the learners, nor to the complexity of their meanings, nor any limitation on what learners do with words.

Experimentation and further development are in process. We all need to appreciate fully the impact upon learners of these particular pedagogical attitudes, whether in their positive or negative effects. The attempt in Words in Color is to be as flexible as is required by the reality of the situation of persons learning to acquire and use written speech. If it is used properly, it can lead only to its improvement and development, for no one inventor can encompass the whole of reality. Since flexibility is a requirement of this encounter with what is, the system would be the poorer for its loss.

This brief description of what Words in Color brings to teachers of reading would perhaps be more useful if the contribution of actual pupils could be added; however, this is left to other writers and users of the approach.

Published teaching materials for Words in Color are listed in the consolidated bibliography under my name and that of Sister N. Leonore. Additional information may be obtained from the Encyclopedia Britannica Press, Chicago.

a	u	i	e	o	a	I	a	o	a	u	e	o	ou	a	o	oo	ee	oi	oi
au	o	y	ie	oh	e	y	aa	a	ay	you	ee	oe	hou	ai	oo	ou	ea	oy	
ai	oe	ey	ea	ho	u	i	ea	au	ey	eau	ea	ow	ow	hei	oe	u	e		
	ou	u	ai	ow	o	igh	e	aw	eigh	ue	ei	owe	ough	ea	ough	o	ie		
	oo	o	u	au	i	ie	ah	augh	aigh	ew	ie	oa		e	ou		ei		o
	a	ie	a	ou	ea	eye		ough	ei	eu	i	oh			u				
		ia	ay	a	ou	ye		ou	ea	eue	eo	ew			ue				
		a			y	eigh		oo	ai	ieu	oe	ou			ui				
		ay			ei	is		hau	et		ay	eau			ew				
		e			ai	ais		oa			ey	ough			wo				
		ai			ough										ieu				
		ei			ie														
		ui			iou														
		ee			io														

p	t	s	s	s	m	n	f	f	d	l	th	th	w	k	r	b	h	g	sh	ch	ng	j	qu	x	x	x
pp	tt	ss	ss	z	mm	nn	ff	v	dd	ll	the	the	wh	kk	rr	bb	wh	gg	ch	tch	n	g		xe		
pe	te	se	se	ge	me	ne	fe	ve	de	le			o	ke	re	be		gu	t	t		d		xc		
ph	ed	z	's		mb	kn	ph	lve	ed				u	ck	rre	bu		gh	s	c		dge		cc		
	cht	zz	c		gm	dne	lf		ld					ch	wr			gue	ce			ge				
	ct	si	ce		mn	pn	gh							c	rh				che			gg				
	bt	thes	sw		lm	gn								lk	lo				ss			dj				
	pt	x	st											qu	rrh				sch							
	tte	's	sc											que	rt				sc							
	th		sch											cc					ci							
			ps											che												

Figure 3. Black-and-white reproduction of phonic code charts 1 to 8.

II. *The Current Status of Words in Color in the United States*

Dorothea Hinman

In 1957, while working for UNESCO in Ethiopia, Dr. Gattegno accepted the challenge of finding a new approach to bringing to the local population literacy in Amharic. Through this attempt he was led to discover an approach to the teaching of reading and writing (the English version is called Words in Color) which demonstrates that it takes only a few hours to teach a person to read and write his language if he can speak it—no matter what the language. World literacy is now something we can realistically contemplate, since the approach has already been applied successfully to nine languages with widely varying alphabets and scripts, both phonetic and nonphonetic.

Dr. Gattegno's experimentation with English came first in 1958 in Texas with kindergarten children and later in California. In August, 1961, he returned to California to work out the approach fully with nonreading children from migrant families, ranging in age from six to eleven years. His results were published simultaneously in the United States and the United Kingdom in early 1963. Since that time I have been Dr. Gattegno's principal assistant in introducing Words in Color to the United States, having helped him in 1961 with the production of the materials and having experimented with them myself in the classroom and in teacher education.

When I began to train teachers in this approach, it had just been published, and only a handful of teachers, supervisors, administrators, and college professors were aware of its existence. Today, only two and a half years later, it is an approach widely talked about and experimented with in hundreds of classrooms. It has already found its place in the new National Education Association leaflet on current approaches to reading. In the summer of 1965 I gave several one-week workshops in the method at colleges and universities. A number of schools and school systems have now tested it sufficiently to choose to continue and extend its use in their first-grade classes, in remedial classes, or in both, and also in special education classes. Many of these schools have initiated, either on their own or with our assistance, in-service training programs. It has already been adopted in the State of New Mexico. Since Dr. Gattegno's demonstration at the United States Office of Education in May, 1964, where he showed that, using his method, illiterate English-speaking adults could be taught to read the newspaper with ease in less than nine hours (*Time*, June 12, 1964), it has been in use throughout the country in programs under the antipoverty and manpower development acts, as well as in literacy programs supported by local, state, and foundation funds—the most notable among them being the one initiated by PACE (Program for Action by Citizens in Education) in Cleveland, Ohio, last spring, involving over three hundred adults.

Many experienced teachers are enthusiastic about this new approach: it seems to them to be based on what they have always thought important—rapid recognition of whole configurations is compatible with a simultaneous phonic and linguistic sense of how sound components are represented, so that word-attack skill may be astonishingly swift and accurate. Since there is, from the start, no reading without comprehension, written material is always meaningful in terms of the student's activities and experiences in life.

Beginning teachers are also pleased with the new method. Many are relieved to be freed of the necessity of putting their pupils into a basal series or phonetic program, which is a heavy burden on the child's memory and which often bores him. Without using these more traditional approaches, they find that their pupils can read and write whatever they can communicate in talking— in the case of some first graders and kindergarteners, even what may be considered fifth- and sixth-grade material.

Because of the de-emphasis of rote memorization and drill, special education classes and classes made up of slow or immature learners are having outstanding success. Teachers report that enthusiasm on the part of some pupils is often unquenchable.

Dr. John I. Goodlad, professor of education at the University of California in Los Angeles, put it this way to me, when he had an opportunity to see Words in Color in action in February, 1964: "What it appears Gattegno has done is to remediate a process. If this is so, it means that we should not have to diagnose and remediate students' learning problems in reading; and it also means that remedial problems should not be created for beginners. As learners participate, they apparently either should avoid problems or correct the problems they already have. This has profound implications for the profession of teaching reading. Words in Color is a significant approach which deserves testing in practice and careful research."

To me, this was a perceptive analysis of the contribution of Words in Color. What Dr. Gattegno has done is to allow the linguistic learning process in reading to become a whole one, as it is during the period when children teach themselves to talk. In sharp contrast is the atomized program in most schools, where one isolates the teaching of reading, spelling, writing, and comprehension. The beginners (whether they are six or sixty years old) who experience Words in Color retain the full responsibility for their learning. Those who have done poorly under other approaches re-establish themselves, and by participation in the process generated by Words in Color they are able to remediate their own difficulties. One may expect the following results: (1) reversals disappear; (2) those who have not seen the sounds in those configurations which they have memorized now become aware of these sounds in all words, not just in those they have met; (3) those who have read words and not understood them now find the meaning of their own speech in what they read; (4) those who have read but have misspelled now find that they possess the criteria for accurate spelling when they try to communicate through writing; and (5) even those who have had fusion problems now find decided improvement from the total impact of the approach upon the eye and the mind—especially the impact of the technique of Visual Dictation.

Yet these results do not depend upon the teacher's work upon a particular difficulty. Difficulties take care of themselves as the student participates in the process opened to him by a teacher who allows him once again to take continuous responsibility for his own learning at every point, as he did when he was learning to speak. Rapid and accurate reading, writing, and spelling come easily—but come as byproducts of a linguistic learning process whose integrity is continually guarded.

CHAPTER 12

THE COLOR PHONICS SYSTEM

ALEX D. BANNATYNE

The Color Phonics System is a set of individual letters and letter combinations printed on small cards, the letters being color coded in such a way that once the principle of the coding has been learned the child can immediately identify each sound. A key word and illustrated object are printed on the reverse side of the cards to provide additional cues. The theory behind the system is that most dyslexic children suffer from an inability to remember constantly changing patterns of sound-symbol associations and that therefore the simultaneous manual, auditory, and visual sequencing of phonemes and letters is the essential element in learning to read. The letters of the system are used for systematic word and sentence building, for syllabication practice, for the analysis and synthesis of successive sounds, and for various activities and word games. The five stages of a teaching program for dyslexic children are outlined, and the importance of motivation, pupil activity, and creative writing are stressed.

The Color Phonics System, which is a new technique for teaching dyslexic children, evolved out of my interest in the ingenious Letter Case devised by Edith Norrie. It is essential that any book collecting the various available methods of treating dyslexics, if it is to be complete, must include an account of what is popularly known as the Danish method. The following account comes from my own visit to the Ordblinde Institut in Copenhagen and from Edith Norrie's paper (1960), in which she describes her use of the Letter Case in practice.

Although originally constructed for use in Denmark, there is also an English version of the Edith Norrie Letter Case, or Composing Box. It is arranged phonetically because her method embraces speech training (Miss Norrie was a speech therapist) as well as exercises in spelling and reading. A small mirror is supplied with the box which enables the pupil to see his lips and tongue. This helps him to understand how the sound for which he seeks the appropriate letter is produced; as a consequence, he can decide where to look for that letter in the box. The vowels, which are printed in red, are arranged in compartments along the lower edge of the box, and the pupil learns that there must never be a word or syllable without a red letter (the letter **y** has a red band because it can be used as a vowel). The large upper section of the box contains the consonants and is divided into three areas, the lip sounds or labials being the "family" contained in one area, the front tongue sounds or palatals in another, and the throat sounds or gutturals in the third. A further classification is the division of the consonants into those which are voiced and those which are unvoiced, the former being printed in green and the latter in black.

If the child suffers from severe dyslexia, the teacher usually begins with the phonetically regular words and short sentences. The pupil spells out the sentence from the box and is allowed as much time as he requires to sort out the words he finds difficult. He then reads through, searching for possible mistakes, and, if any remain, the teacher will supply more and more clues to help him to find and correct them, for example, "Say that word again and look at your lips in the mirror," or "How many syllables are there in that word and how many red letters have you got?" When the sentence is correct, including the capital letters and punctuation, it is copied into an exercise book, and since the pupil no longer has to worry about the spelling, more attention can be paid to the forming of the letters. The next stage is that the sentence is covered up, and the pupil has to write it from memory. The more advanced pupil will write the dictation directly into his exercise book, using the letters from the composing case only when he is not sure how to spell a word.

Miss Norrie herself depended a great deal on graded dictation, and this technique is still widely used both at the Ordblinde Institut in Copenhagen and at the Word Blind Centre for Dyslexic Children in London. In her paper, Miss Norrie points out that the letters should be selected and the words built up in the correct sequence from left to right and that words should be used in a sentence and not learned out of context. She also stresses the great importance of praising the child for his successful efforts, particularly as they involve a tremendous output of energy.

Of course, the whole lesson need not be made up of dictation from the Letter Box and reading practice. The child may be taught grammar, given auditory exercises, directional training, tracing, or any other method in use with dyslexic children.

It is interesting to note that Miss Norrie was herself severely word blind, and her Letter Box is an extension of the method she devised to teach herself to read and to spell when she was in her twenties. She went on to found the Ordblinde Institut in 1936, years before any other country had specialized teaching for dyslexics, and she was its principal until a few years before her death in 1960.

The above is a very brief account of Edith Norrie's technique, and it would be most unfair to her or the Ordblinde Institut to suggest that it is at all complete. I heartily recommend that any teacher of dyslexic children visit Copenhagen to see for himself the various excellent teaching methods in use there.

For some time, in my work with dyslexic children, I had felt that none of the available systems provided for all the essential mechanisms through which dyslexic children appear to learn. So I began by setting down the various criteria which an ideal technique would satisfy. As one reads through the list, it will be apparent that I have a particular viewpoint about the nature of dyslexia.

I would classify all dyslexic children into two main genus groups. The first is composed of pure dyslexics whose disability is essentially an inherited lack of ability to use language fluently. It is the tail end of a normal ability continuum in the community as a whole. The cause of the difficulty appears to be an inability to sequence associated sounds in phase with visual symbols, even though there is no sensory problem of hearing or vision as such. This auditory-sequencing genus of dyslexics is not neurologically abnormal in any way and is relatively homogeneous, although overlays of secondary emotional symptoms may blur the pattern.

The second genus of dyslexic children includes many species which can be collectively labeled neurologically abnormal, although the causes may be many and varied; e.g., anoxia at birth, disease, congential abnormalities, etc. Within this second genus the species of dyslexias are formed more by clusterings of individual children with similar neurological and/or sensory deficits than by a common etiology. This is because several distinct original causes may damage a particular brain area in some children while apparently identical causes (e.g., anoxia) may result in quite different types of injuries in other children.

The Color Phonics method is intended for use with almost every type of dyslexic child, although in a few cases, such as children suffering from neurologically caused visuospatial difficulties, specific training in visuospatial concepts will be necessary. Color Phonics is not good for the color blind, nor in cases of brain injury with color agnosia.

The various criteria on which the ideal technique should be founded are as follows:

1. It has been demonstrated by many workers in the field over the last thirty years that the only successful techniques for teaching dyslexics are those firmly founded on a phonetic basis. The logical phonetic structure of English, even if it is not perfect, seems to provide the dyslexic child with a memory reference basis which is more economical than the multitude of arbitrary sound-symbol associations used in nonphonetic methods of teaching reading.

2. The individual letters of the alphabet must be discrete units so that they can be arranged and rearranged in given order again and again; that is, each letter must be printed on a tiny, individual card or plaque so that words can be spelled in sequence.

3. The somewhat irregular orthography of the English language must be further systematized so that the child is always able to identify a particular letter or combination of letters by referring to a logical cue. Replacing the irregular phonetic structure of the language with a regular one requires the child to transfer to the traditional orthography at a later date. As the dyslexic child finds it extremely difficult to memorize a set of sound-symbol associations, an additional set of symbols for the same sounds is scarcely likely to solve his problems.

4. The technique must allow the child to overlearn sound-symbol association through a variety of stimuli and sensory pathways.

5. The technique should allow the child to work equally well when moving either from the printed to the sounded word or from the sounded to the printed word. Therefore, the letters with their logical cues will help the child both to spell words which he hears and to identify the phonetic structure of words which he sees in print.

6. The system should be usable in conjunction with any other technique which uses the traditional orthography as its basis.

7. It should be pupil-oriented rather than teacher-oriented. It should involve the pupil in active, manual, multisensory participation, rather than relying solely on the passive, visual approach which occurs in so much remedial reading and which has had so little success with dyslexic children.

8. Most of the systems for teaching dyslexic children rely on a formal, open-ended phonetics approach; because of their lack of finite definition in space, a practical goal cannot be presented to the children. The best system will enable the child to appreciate, understand, and accept the extent of the practical nature of the complete task ahead.

9. The technique should permit a feeling of increasing mastery, in

the sense that the child must not only know from the outset his ultimate goal in terms of that material but must know also that each new step mastered brings the goal nearer by a well-defined amount.

10. The central idea of the technique must be equally applicable to the learning situation in all its steps. Whether the pupil be a seven-year-old dyslexic who is beginning to read or a poor speller at the university, the method should be of value to each in a variety of ways.

11. The child must become involved with and enjoy the materials with which he is working. Apart from this interest in the material for its own sake, the material itself should be sufficiently flexible and adaptable to allow for a variety of interesting approaches in each lesson.

The simplest way to describe the Color Phonics System is perhaps to work through each of the above criteria systematically and in each case to explain how the system translates them into concrete form. It is self-evident from the title that the Color Phonics System has a phonetic basis. By using the system from day to day, the child should be able to memorize rapidly the sound-to-symbol associations because the color coding system facilitates that learning process. Thus the child is provided with a phonetic means of word attack which, in common with any phonics technique, frees him from a purely *gestalt* recognition of words and phrases. This latter method, commonly called look-and-say, may be effective with those two thirds of first- and second-grade pupils who are sufficiently gifted in the realm of language to be able to learn to read quickly. I believe that these verbally capable children rapidly teach themselves to analyze words phonetically in spite of a deliberate nonphonetic approach on the part of the teacher. That this is so can easily be tested by asking children who have learned to read well using the look-and-say method to sound out difficult words; this they usually do quite competently. Incidentally, because these capable children learn their phonics anyway, all beginner classes might as well learn through a phonetic technique from the outset. While the rapid learners may gain only a little, there is no doubt that the less competent could be saved a lot of prolonged difficulty and perhaps much unhappiness.

In compliance with the second criterion, the Color Phonics System consists of discrete letters or letter combinations which can be separately arranged and rearranged over and over in any particular order. The letters are printed on tiny cards or plaques, and each plaque is printed in color to provide cues to help the child identify the sound or letter. These cues will be described in the next paragraph in some detail; for the moment I wish to stress the fundamental importance of sequencing.

I personally believe that the fundamental neuropsychological deficit of the pure dyslexic child is the inability to sequence correctly. While this may not apply to a proportion of that group of dyslexic children who suffer from a minimal brain impairment, it certainly does apply to all those pure dyslexics whose disability is presumed inherited. Furthermore, I believe that the sequencing problem is essentially an auditory one and that any deficit in lateralized visual or ocular-motor sequencing is secondary to the auditory one. At the Word Blind Centre I have found that most dyslexics would appear to have an average or better than average visual acuity and an excellent appreciation of three-dimensional space. This should not be confused with directional confusion, which I believe to be primarily a verbal associative problem, not a pure spatial one. The statement that the essential disability of the dyslexic is one of auditory sequencing obviously requires a great deal of supporting evidence and close argument, but it is neither feasible nor appropriate to present such material in a book on remedial methods. I hope to put forward my views on dyslexia in detail elsewhere. In terms of teaching techniques, the need to reinforce the child's auditory sequencing processes means that child and teacher, particularly the child, must vocalize constantly. This applies not only to the careful sounding of the successive phonemes which make up a particular word, but also to the conversation which should proceed almost continuously between child and teacher. The pupil should be encouraged to think aloud at all times. It is surprising how many teachers and educational authorities who are concerned with verbal processes forget that language is almost entirely an auditory sequencing process, and I would go so far as to say that a specific language disability could be redefined as a specific auditory sequencing disability. This at a still deeper level is essentially a malfunctioning of auditory memory.

Perhaps it is necessary to re-emphasize that the Color Phonics System has been developed for teaching children suffering from specific developmental dyslexia in whom visuospatial and motor functions are at least average in terms of their peers. This does not mean that the system cannot be used with those neurologically impaired children who do have minimal spatial and/or motor dysfunctions, but it is not necessarily recommended as the best method to use with such children. However, we have used it successfully with them, probably because the technique contains a considerable spatial element in the positioning of letters in lines.

The color coding of the letters in the Color Phonics System is intended to systematize logically the irregular orthography of the English language. The color coding enables the child to identify the sound in a direct way, circumventing the variety of spellings that any particular sound may have. Conversely, by linking the color to one specific, regular spelling of the sound of a phoneme, the child is enabled to hazard an informed guess at vowels printed in black and white. At this point it is necessary to give specific instances of color-letter-sound combinations in order to clarify the situation.

All the consonants and the two consonant combinations **ph** and **qu** are printed in white on charcoal gray, while all the vowels, including diphthongs, are printed in color on a white ground. A thin line runs along the lower edge of all the plaques to indicate the top and bottom of the letter, and these join to make a continuous line under the word. On the back of all the consonants and colored vowels is a picture of some object or situation which represents the key word printed underneath. Each key word contains the appropriate phoneme in one of its particular spellings. The consonants are alphabetically arranged in the box, which is divided into compartments, while the vowels are arranged to keep similar sounds and similar colors as widely separated as possible. In the consonant section, the problem of coping with two letters which have the same sound (for example, **s** and **c**, which may both be sounded as **s**) was overcome by printing them without a colored stripe (see Fig. 1). Those particular **c**s are then kept in the **s** compartment. In a similar fashion, the **c**s which sound like **k**s have a common stripe of another color running through the middle of the white, and they are all kept in the **k** compartment. Therefore, there is no separate compartment for **c**. In like fashion, **f** and **ph** have a common color-stripe code, as have soft **g** and **j**. The remaining consonants are not color coded because we have found from experience that it is not often the consonants which present difficulty to the dyslexic child. Vowels are the main offenders, and the color coding reduces the many possible spellings of one particular phoneme to a single color identification process. Other systems of color-coded books and charts are available, but the Color Phonics System is, I think, unique in that the letters can be sequenced and that each phoneme can be identified from the name of the color itself. For example, the phoneme **ee**, as sounded in **green**, is printed in a green color, and the phoneme **ow**, as sounded in **brown,** is printed in brown, and so on. In the **ee** phoneme compartment are separate cards with each of the spellings of that phoneme, namely, **ee**, **e**, **y**, **ea**, **ei**, **ie**, and **i**. The key words and pictures on the backs, most of which I have tried to associate with the color green, are as follows:

a daub of green color with the key word **green**, a green man with the key word **he**, a monkey surrounded by green foliage with the key word **monkey**, a green leaf with key word **leaf**, a **receipt** printed in green, and a **field** and **fatigue** printed in green. There is no point in elaborating the description for each of the other vowel phonemes, as they are all worked out on the same principle.

One very simple way of using the system is for the teacher to set out a sentence composed of the letters, which the child will then be able to read by sequencing the phonemes, the vowels of which he is able to identify by means of the color name. All consonants, it will be remembered, are white on charcoal gray. For example, in British usage, the phrase **Colour Phonics System** (Fig. 1) would begin with a **C** having a red stripe through the white letter with a charcoal gray ground (**k**), the **o** being rust, the **l** white on charcoal, the **ou** pink on gray, and the **r** white on charcoal gray (according to British pronunciation). The **Ph** which begins the word **Phonics** will have a green stripe through white on charcoal gray, denoting that it is pronounced **f**, the **o** is orange, the **n** is white on charcoal gray, the **i** is pink, the **c** is red-striped white on gray (**k**), and the **s** has a purple stripe through the white letter on charcoal gray. The initial **S** of **System** is an unstriped white on charcoal gray, the **y** is colored pink (as the **y** in **body**), the **s** as before, the **t** is white on charcoal gray, the **e** as in yellow, and the **m** white on charcoal gray.

The colored vowels will need to be used only as long as the child is finding difficulty with a particular phoneme or difficulty in spelling a particular word. Much of the time the child who is reasonably familiar with the system would only be wasting time if he were to lay out words in color which are already well known. Therefore the vowels **a**, **e**, **i**, **o**, **u**, and **y** have been printed in black on white (the white denotes them to be vowels), and as there are many duplicates of each of these vowels, they can be used in place of the colored ones for setting out familiar words and long sentences.

Two more sets of vowels—**a**, **e**, **i**, **o**, **u**, and **y**—are available, the first of these sets representing the silent vowels; these are printed with a broken outline which encloses the solid letter, so to speak, on a white ground. Obviously, these will be used only whenever a particular vowel sound is not sounded in the word. The second set of letters represents the neutral vowels. These are printed in pink on a light gray background, and they can be used in all those words where a vowel is so clipped in sound as to sound like a very short **i**—hence the color, **pink**. In theory, the neutral pink-on-gray **i** and the pink **i** on white are interchangeable, although in practice, of course, if the phoneme **i** is a short **i**, occurring in the most accented syllables, one should use the pink **i** on white. For example, in the word **initial** the first two **i**s will be pink on white, and the last **i** will be a neutral **i**, pink on gray. One further aid is a small plaque on which is printed the word **silent**, and this can be used for indicating silent consonants by being placed immediately above them; for example, in the word **ghost** the **h** plaque would have the word **silent** in tiny print above it.

A verbal description of the Color Phonics System such as that given above may, in the absence of the actual letters, sound rather complicated, but in practice the system is easy for a child to master, particularly when the different sets of letters are introduced at the correct stage of the learning program. The reduction of the work of six months to a few paragraphs without the ability to demonstrate the system makes a simple operation seem unduly complex.

The key words and their associated pictures, which are printed on the back of the cards, are intended as additional cues to reinforce the color-phoneme association. In a way, the key word and the picture lead to an overlearning situation, and overlearning, as Marianne Frostig (1965) continually emphasizes, is obviously essential if the dyslexic child is to learn to read and spell with any permanence. Three separate associations, namely, color, key word, and picture, are together more effective than any one of these by itself. Quite apart from this, the pictures can be used for a variety of games which an ingenious teacher can invent for herself, although in due course I hope to publish some suggestions for games to be played.

In keeping with the fourth criterion in my list, the Color Phonics System does allow the child to work from print to sounded word or from sound to printed word. I have used the word "print" because eventually the child must be introduced to reading books, but, in practice, one would prefer to say the "written" word, which of course emphasizes the importance of pupil participation, inasmuch as he will initially be reading his own writing. It is almost axiomatic with dyslexic children that they will not be able to read a selected passage of printed material until they have had a great deal of varied experience centered around an analysis of both the component phonemes and their visual symbols in the vocabulary of the printed matter in question. Children who learn to read normally do so rapidly and almost automatically, and so educators tend to disregard the vital importance of the individual phoneme-symbol associations which must eventually be synthesized into words. Verbally competent children will only take a few weeks to

Figure 1. The illustration shows how the colored letters or phonemes are sequentially arranged to form a sentence. An alternative spelling of the word "colour" or another pronunciation for it could easily be substituted because the system is very flexible—it can cope with most accents. The lowest line is composed of a selection of the pictures and key words which enable the child to identify the phoneme on the reverse side.

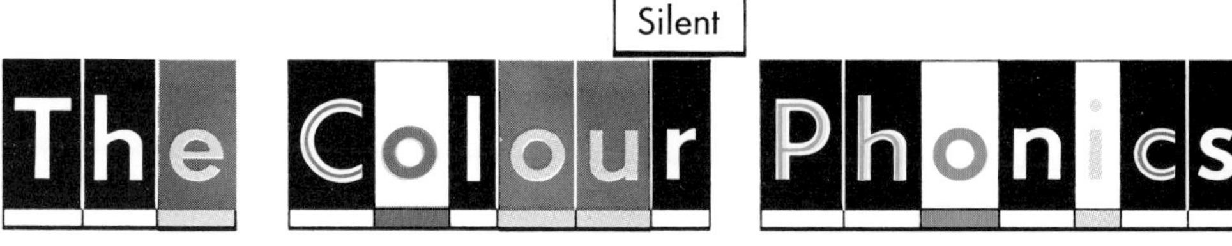
Silent
The Colour Phonics

System helps you to

learn to read well.

cork

skirt

whale

jewel

SUSAN
row

leaf

learn which of the (auditory) phonemes that they have possessed from infancy are associated with which particular letter symbols, even if they are not taught on a phonetic basis.

Before going on with the main theme, I feel that I must point out here something which too many people of the whole word school seem to disregard completely, namely, that English *is* a sound-symbol-associated language, that the letters *do* actually stand for sounds and *not* for the object itself. The phoneme-letter components (a standard set) are arranged and rearranged in an unlimited number of sequences called words, and it is only one sequence of phonemes which symbolizes the object, but within any such sequence the letters symbolize the phonemes. In Chinese, Japanese, and divers ancient languages this is not true, the printed symbol being a pictograph or hieroglyphic symbol of the object itself. None of these picture-words have any bearing on, or logical association with, the spoken sounds which aurally and vocally symbolize the visual symbol-object association. I sometimes think that the dyslexic child would have much less difficulty with a pictograph system of writing than he has with a phonetic one, primarily because his problem, I maintain, is an auditory one. Of course, the pictographs must not be so stylized that the visual symbol-object association is no longer obvious.

To return to my main theme, it is necessary that in the case of the dyslexic child this preliminary learning of the sound-symbol associations and their sequential combinations in everyday words be very much prolonged, and the implication for the Color Phonics System is that initially the pupil will spend a great deal of time reading the words and sentences which he has composed with a great deal of help from the teacher. The child has to learn the color cues by rote, which is not a very difficult task. As he progresses through the first few weeks, the responsibility for composing words is gradually shifted from teacher to child. Therefore, although I have said that the system should allow the child to work equally well when moving either way between phoneme and symbol, the temporal order of the learning process demands that initially the direction must be from the letters to the sound, that is, it must be a process of recognition, not of recall. Obviously, once the child can quickly recognize or identify the sound-symbol associations from the available cues, he is ready to begin to cope with more and more unprompted recall. Ultimately, the child should be able to reproduce dictated material very competently, at which point the educative process becomes mainly one of correcting errors as they occur. I would go much further than Edith Norrie does in terms of mistakes, for I would prevent the child from putting the wrong letter into a word he was composing. The moment I saw he was about to choose a wrong letter I would try to circumvent its placement. Remedial teachers should cultivate vigilance, so that during the period before the child's fingers actually put down the letter they can halt the process and suggest that perhaps some other (undefined) letter might be more appropriate, offering more detailed guidance only if necessary. The essential point I wish to make is that the first few times the child sees the whole word it should have the correct *gestalt* of color and form.

During the foregoing development, the dyslexic child will be required to copy all the corrected work with the letters into his workbook, and, in keeping with my fifth point, many other techniques may also be used as appropriate. I see no reason why, for example, the Fernald system, with its high interest factor and its emphasis on kinesthetic tracing and vocabulary building, should not be thoroughly integrated with the Color Phonics System. They are in no way incompatible; in fact, the kinesthetic channel associations of sound and symbol are doubly strengthened because the child handles one set of printed letters and traces another set of cursive letters. The purpose of getting the child to copy composed words, sentences, and the story he creates into a workbook is two-fold: it reinforces the whole learning process in several obvious ways, particularly if he vocalizes, and it provides him with a permanent record of his work, which maintains his interest in learning in general. If it is felt to be helpful, the written work can be typed and inserted into a folder, as Grace Fernald (1943) suggests. During the later stages of the initial course with the Color Phonics System, the child will make copious use of the black-on-white vowels, and it is then that he is ready to begin reading suitably graded books for a small part of the lesson.

The Color Phonics System is quite compatible with the gradual introduction of particular phonemes and phonographs, as suggested in the Gillingham method (Gillingham and Stillman, 1960). In fact, I would even go so far as to say that any teacher who had been trained along Gillingham's lines could quite easily use the Color Phonics System to replace partially or to supplement the written work the child is required to do. I would retain the black-on-white flash cards, as they would be an excellent screening method to discover which of the color-sound-symbol associations were causing the most difficulty. Still another teaching aid which could be successfully used to give variety alongside the Color Phonics System is Stott's Programmed Reading Kit of Phonic Games (1962). These are particularly useful for very small groups of children and provide them with practice on an experiential level. As they do not require the immediate presence of the teacher, she can be giving individual tuition to another child. Stott's apparatus, although not color coded, is largely self-correcting. It provides an excellent opportunity for the children to test out their acquired color-coded knowledge independently. Consideration should be given, as well, to the Royal Road Readers (Daniels and Diack, 1958) or any other phonetically oriented series, to which the child should be introduced when he has worked through the initial stages of the Color Phonics System.

The seventh point on the list of criteria hardly needs more elaboration, as it should be apparent from what has been said above that the Color Phonics System involves the pupil in a great deal of active, manual, multisensory participation. Quite apart from the continual handling of the letters, the color coding itself involves the child in yet another kind of concrete handling, as it were, since it stimulates a visual activity which would otherwise be lacking. Our experience has shown that this visually coded presentation of sounds gives the child an awareness of the great variety of phonemes and phonographs in the English language, as well as an insight into the conventions of English spelling. This is very important, because pure dyslexics tend to rely on vision and visual imagery in learning, and the color coding of phonemes lends to what would be a pure auditory process a systematic visual reality. One could go even further and say that the systematic color coding provides a permanent physical reference point, for the dyslexic child, for what would otherwise merely be transitory, unmemorized sounds. This is an important point which needs to be stressed. Auditory types of people find it quite easy to memorize and to subsequently recall a particular sound or sequence of sounds at will, and this they can do as easily as they recall visual images, but the dyslexic child, along with other nonauditory types of people, does not have this facility, and therefore he requires the help of systematically organized visual prompts.

One of the main advantages of the Color Phonics System is that it can be presented to the child as an attainable, practical technique which is contained in one box, the contents of which, once mastered, transform him into a competent reader. Most phonetic systems for teaching dyslexic children are open-ended, in that the child's goal is seen by him as one of almost unattainable adult complexity. The very insecurity of knowing the limitless nature of written language in all its manifestations can arouse a great deal of worry in an intelligent child who is unable to read because of a specific disability. The box of colored letters is reassuringly finite in the eyes of the dyslexic child. He feels he can grapple with it physically and visually, and the very fact that it is all there in one small box takes his mind from the oppressing thought of having to master an indefinite number of books of increasing complexity. This is not to present the child with a false situation because, as he finds that he does learn to read reasonably well, his self-confidence is boosted at every step, and he is enabled to accept the challenge of a widening range of literature.

Although essentially the system is not broken up into an extended series of separate exercises, nevertheless, at any stage in his learning of the system, the pupil is aware of both the amount he knows and the amount he has still to learn. Whenever the child feels that he knows how to spell a particular word, he will use the black-on-white vowels, and the more frequently he uses these, the more extensive his vocabulary must be. Even so, it does not follow that the child should look on the use of the black-on-white vowels as his only ambition—this would be quite wrong. It is not a question of prestige but rather a matter of appreciating where he stands along the road; otherwise, he will attempt to use the black-on-white vowels before he is ready to do so.

Dyslexic children who learn by the Color Phonics System will for many years probably see the words they read in ordinary books in patterns of color. Thus the system has the advantage of providing the child with a store of background information which, like a set of arithmetical tables, is always there whenever needed, no matter what stage of reading ability he has reached.

Another great advantage of working with separate colored letters is that they are maturationally neutral, in terms of the age groups of the students who may use them. Many reading systems which depend a great deal on organized verbal content are too childish for most adolescents to accept. A technique which requires the student to provide his own content, which of course would automatically appeal to him, has the advantage of being adaptable to the needs of dyslexic people whether they are six-year-olds, adolescents, or adults. Even quite long technical words can be read when color coded.

Perhaps the most important point of all is that the child must become involved with and enjoy the materials with which he works. A system which can operate independently of books enables one to by-pass the initial negative attitudes of the many dyslexic children who have experienced repeated failure with countless classroom readers. The sight of still another book being opened during the first few remedial lessons gives many of these children a sinking feeling, which originates in the thought of beginning yet another long, uphill, and perhaps fruitless struggle towards literacy. A colorful method which, while disassociated from books, is still associated with pleasant activity, with enjoyable games, with creative writing, and with reliable self-help cues is eminently desirable. Suitable books can be later introduced, once the teacher feels that the child has regained sufficient self-confidence to tackle suitable reading material. I find that dyslexic boys prefer short books with a high adventure or humorous content.

The Royal Road Readers (Daniels and Diack, 1958) are suitable for younger children. Reader's Digest Services, Inc., now has several series of remarkably inexpensive books which, though not systematically phonic, are very useful for older pupils and adults. The ones to which I refer are the Series of Adult Readers for Adult Illiterates (published in 1964 and 1965), the English as a Second Language Series (Kitchen, 1964; Kitchen and Allen, 1965; Allen and Kitchen, 1965; Croft, 1965), and the Reading Skill Builders and Advanced Reading Skill Builders (1965). Another very effective series of seven New Practice Readers (Stone, 1960) was published in a paperback edition by Webster Publishing Company and is now handled by McGraw-Hill Book Company, Inc. There is a great opportunity for authors and publishers to build up similar series which are phonically regular in their presentation.

A corollary of providing pupils with sustained interest in a continuous learning process is the flexibility and adaptability of the material. Not only should it be usable to present many different facets of the reading process, it should also be employable in other types of lessons altogether—for example, to introduce spelling rules, English grammar, and the host of language concepts which we collectively label linguistics. Supplied with the Color Phonics System is a box full of prefixes and suffixes and other common word elements, which can be used for various purposes. This eliminates much of the gadgetry, such as word wheels and the like, which remedial teachers are frequently advised to make but which they rarely do. By laying out the essential core of several words, the series can be made up, adding and subtracting the appropriate prefixes and suffixes. For example, if **tract** is set out on the table as root or core word, it can be turned into other words by laying on either side of it in columns the appropriate extras, thus:

dis		**able**
con	**tract**	**or**
ex		**ed**
sub		**ing**

These prefixes and suffixes are printed in black on gray so that they will not become confused with all the other letters of the system.

The very flexibility of the Color Phonics System and the fact that it is a practical, largely self-teaching system means that a rigid program administered by the teacher is neither necessary nor desirable. Rather, it calls forth from the teacher the ability to guide the pupil along that particular path which is most suited to his needs, and this can only be done by a day-to-day appreciation and anticipation of what those needs will be.

Nevertheless, broad developmental stages are discernible when using the Color Phonics System, and the general approach for each stage is suggested here, even though it is not desirable to present a detailed program within each stage. I am assuming that the child is almost completely illiterate and certainly has no knowledge of phonics. If the child does not know the shapes of the letters, obviously he will have to be taught them, and the best way to do this is to sort out the alphabet from the box. In the case of the vowels, one should select the single letters which have the largest number of single-sound associations in language usage. These will be an azure **a**, a yellow **e**, a pink **i**, an orange **o**, and a rust **u**. The child will have to copy the letters many times, perhaps using very simple words, until he becomes familiar with them, and if he does not know the names of the letters, the above vowel sounds should be the ones associated with them.

Obviously, most children who do know their alphabet will be introduced to the system at the beginning of stage 2. Even if they should find this rather easy, it is preferable that, rather than skip it, they should progress rapidly through this early stage because it not only enables the teacher diagnostically to check reading deficits, but also acquaints the child with the mechanics and principles of the Color Phonics System.

Therefore, once the child knows the shapes of the letters of the alphabet, he can begin the second stage, namely, building up a knowledge of simple phonics by a process of gradual introduction to the sounds of both consonants and vowels. There are several recognized systematic procedures for the successive introduction of phonemes, of which the

Gillingham method is one (Gillingham and Stillman, 1960). Most of them start with a few frequently occurring sounds, which are built into simple little words and sentences, using the common vowels mentioned above. The less frequent consonants and more complex vowel phonemes are introduced at appropriate intervals. It is necessary at this stage that the child have every opportunity to overlearn the color coding for each vowel phoneme as it is introduced. From the outset the child rapidly comes to realize that there are several ways of spelling each phoneme, but, of course, only a very few of the ways of spelling any particular sound are selected for use at this point. Throughout the procedure, the initial introduction of the sounds and phonically regular simple words should be made by the teacher who presents the finished word to the pupil, as this ensures that the child will first see how to spell a word in its correct form, and all such words should be copied into a workbook in black and white. From experience, I have found that children find it easier to write neatly if they use a cursive system of writing. Certainly the encouragement of cursive writing prevents the pupil from feeling he is still at an immature infant level of printing. This second stage is essentially one of bringing the child to the point where he understands, in terms of a few important letters and sounds, how the system works, and it should not be unduly prolonged—two or three weeks, at the most, should be sufficient, except in the most difficult cases. The immediate object is not to acquaint the child with all the possible phonemes, their colors and combinations—that goal belongs to stage 3.

The purpose of stage 3, then, is to extend the range of color-sound associations and to build up rapidly a reasonable vocabulary using those associations. Since the pupil by now will understand the color coding principle on which the system works, he should be encouraged to experiment freely even to the use of quite long words, but throughout this stage the teacher must ensure, through constant help and vigilance, that the first impressions made are the correct ones. The boy can begin building a story centered round his own interests, keep vocabulary cards, and, above all, practise spelling the words he is overlearning by using them in many different contexts. At all times, with the help of the teacher, words will be broken up into syllables whenever the individual letters are used, but of course syllabication is not necessary when the child is copying them into a word list, writing a story, or tracing. One technique which helps the child with breaking a word into syllables, memorizing colors, and spelling generally is the use of rhymes and rhyming. If teacher and pupil make up little verses, preferably humorous, with accurate scansion, the child will be helped to appreciate the part played by rhythm in sound-symbol association. He will also come to appreciate that rhyming words which are spelled differently are still the same color, and thus their auditory similarity is reinforced visually.

Another problem frequently encountered during stages 2 and 3 is that of blending phonemes. Frequently, the inability to blend is a direct result of faulty teaching, inasmuch as the pupil has learned to voice unvoiced consonants by adding unwanted vowels. In other words, the individual phonemes are not being correctly pronounced by the child, so a correct blending is impossible. The word **lit** cannot be blended if the **l** is pronounced **luh**. More often than not, this inability to synthesize sounds into meaningful speech is an aspect of the primary inability of the dyslexic to sequence auditory material in the absence of auditory prompts, whether these be in the form of environmental stimuli (e.g., heard words, color cues) or neurological engrams, that is, permanent thought-word associations available on demand. I know of only two methods for facilitating blending. The first is to tell the child to form his mouth in preparation for saying the initial consonant of a syllable but then to say the following vowel instead. This technique is useful when the initial consonants are unvoiced ones anyway. The second technique I learned from Dr. Samuel Kirk, and it is used in his own published method of teaching reading (Hegge, Kirk, and Kirk, 1940). The process is first taught by always demonstrating a single syllable in two parts, namely, the initial consonant and the remainder of the syllable as a whole. Thus cat is taught not as **c a t** but as, **c at**, the number of "breakdown units" being kept to a manageable minimum. At the same time, the word **cat**, as a *gestalt*, is presented in both its written and spoken forms, and these are simultaneously analyzed into their component letters and phonemes. If this intensive analytic-synthetic simultaneous approach is thoroughly taught during the first few weeks and months, the dyslexic child will be prevented from forming many of the poor blending habits that such children so often acquire. The individual letters of the Color Phonics System are eminently suited to this analytic-synthetic method of teaching blending because they can very easily be physically separated or drawn together. Before leaving the problem of blending, it is worth re-emphasizing the importance of teaching the phonemes correctly in the first place. Probably more damage is done to dyslexic children by slovenly teaching of phonics than by any other cause, and all courses for remedial teachers should contain a large amount of precise speech training.

At some time toward the end of the third stage, or even perhaps earlier, the child should be introduced to the twenty or so spelling rules one by one, which he can then use as mnemonics. He should be given plenty of practice in applying the rules, and although this should take up no more than a few minutes at a time, during the remainder of the lesson he should constantly be reminded when he contravenes any rule he has learned. In the long run, it is easiest for a dyslexic, with his weak verbal memory, to remember a few set principles than thousands of those arbitrary letter-sound sequences called (printed) words. The learning of the spelling rules can continue right through stage 4.

It will be appreciated that this third stage comprises the major part of the whole remediation process through which the dyslexic child must work. It takes him from the point where he vaguely realizes what reading is technically all about to the point where he has attained a recall vocabulary of one hundred to two hundred words and an immediate recognition vocabulary of three hundred to five hundred words. By this time the more frequent sound-symbol-color associations will have been overlearned, and he should be able to blend well-known phonically regular words by sight reading from the teacher's or his own handwriting without being dependent on color. In addition, the pupil should have learned most of the common phonetically irregular words which are linguistically necessary for structuring the language. These irregularly spelled words, which are the bane of the dyslexic child's life, are much less of a problem when he learns them initially by using the color coding cues.

Once all these skills have been acquired, he is ready to move on to stage 4, and it is only at this point that he should be introduced to the set of black-on-white vowels included in the Color Phonics box of letters. As mentioned previously, the black vowels replace the colored ones when both pupil and teacher are certain that the child knows how to spell the word in question. As the child becomes more competent, the initial spelling out of every word and sentence in syllables, using the colored letters, can be gradually decreased until the child reaches a point, much later on at the end of stage 4, where he is using the letters only for those words which either are new or present a personal spelling problem. In other words, much of his story writing, reading, and English study will not require using any of the letters but will be carried out in the orthodox way, using normal writing. Throughout stage 4, his word-list building, occasional tracing, and story writing will of course continue. It is important to stress here that during stages 2, 3, and 4 it is usually necessary to ensure that he pronounce clearly and in an overly precise way each phoneme in every word he speaks or writes. It may even be necessary to train the child to speak clearly, and in such a case a speech therapist should be called in and briefed. The teacher herself must be careful to avoid sloppy or rapid speech, and at all times she must realize that clear vocalization and auditory sequencing of words are the most important requisites for successful remediation.

It is only by iterated sound-symbol association (with the emphasis on sound) that the dyslexic child obtains that intuitive appreciation of language skills and usage which provides the basis for an automatic, instantaneous recognition or recall of the written word, and it is the acquisition of this associative fluency which is the objective of the fifth stage.

The pure dyslexics, particularly the more intelligent ones, should by this time be able to read at least up to the level of a normal eight- or nine-year-old child, and they should now be launched into an interest in the English language for its own sake, not so much for its literary value as for its structure and usage. This opens up a whole field of study for those intelligent dyslexics for whom the main problem now becomes one of vocabulary building and correct spelling. This interest should develop naturally from having learned the spelling rules during stages 3 and 4, and the enlightened teacher can make the study of English come alive by keeping away from formal grammar, stressing instead the early origins of all language and how present-day English is the end result of several interwoven linguistic strands. Several specific techniques come to mind (e.g., Bodmer, 1949). The child can classify groups of words according to the language of origin, and the conventions of spelling peculiar to those languages can be abstracted. Prefixes and suffixes can be categorized according to their language of origin and can be used with different roots in the way indicated earlier in this chapter. This can be further developed by pointing out that quite often the Latin prefix determines which particle follows the word in question, for example, "com" or "con" (from the Latin *cum*, "with") as a prefix to a word usually indicates that that word will be followed by "with." Furthermore, the child may be delighted to learn, in order to correct his elders, that one complies with, and not to, regulations, or that one thing is different from, not to or than, another. On a more general level, some of the brighter pupils may like to make a family tree of languages, starting with the earliest of the hypothetical Indo-European languages and tracing the branches to our present-day diversity. Other possible topics of investigation include a study of local dialects, word magic, ritual language, slang, technical language, place names, personal names, shifts of meaning through usage—all these topics and many others can provide motivation for the child not only to learn spelling but also to learn to write for the sake of the content and not simply to acquire a skill. Once this objective has been achieved, the task of the remedial teacher is complete. One can never hope to eradicate the poor spelling of a dyslexic person completely, but if one has managed to develop in him a reasonable accuracy, a love of language, and a willingness to consult the dictionary, he should be able to carry on without other help.

It can be seen from what has been said that I do not consider the dyslexic child to have overcome his disabilities because he has achieved a reading age of say, nine years, and this is all the more true if the child in question is above average in intelligence. The emphasis all the way through the system on auditory processes, on spelling, and on writing for content facilitates a degree of creative growth which is as essential to a dyslexic child as is a hearing aid to the partially deaf. To leave a dyslexic child at the stage where he has the skill but never the desire to read a simple novel is depriving him of his right to read spontaneously for knowledge, enjoyment, and pleasure. The Color Phonics System is almost unique in that throughout its five stages the child does not just passively sit and struggle to read. He can make use of the system in the active, creative process first of writing and later of reading, however simple the content may be. The actual letters are used to construct words during the learning process. There is a sound psychological reason for placing a primary emphasis on writing and spelling during the initial stages, and I am not referring here to the obvious emotional need for a high motivation. Rather, it is that the acquisition of permanent reading skills by dyslexic children demands overlearning, and in turn overlearning requires at every point complete recall without prompts; prompts are the printed word in reading books, and the dyslexic child of whom the only memorization demanded is that of merely recognizing printed words (prompts) will learn to read only slowly, if at all. The point which it is always necessary to re-emphasize is that, when memorizing material, it is more economically overlearned by using recall than recognition processes. Obviously, the child must be acquainted with the word and its letter-phoneme associations before recall can commence, and the reader is referred back to stages 1 and 2 for a clarification of this point.

Of course, other systems of teaching children to read do not prevent children from writing, but in most of them the actual learning process is not primarily based on writing, as the stimulus material is in the form of reading books, and any writing which may occur is usually presented as exercises or stories which are the secondary consequences of the reading. The Color Phonics System, because it is an active, creative, pupil-oriented technique, does make considerable demands on the teacher's ingenuity, and although the manual published with it will provide many ideas and games, it is not our intention to produce workbooks for the children. Of course, as has been indicated above, children are encouraged to read more and more as their competence increases, but it should be realized that as a part of the technique this reading is always secondary and should never take up more than approximately one third of any lesson, and then only during the later stages. On the other hand, I personally always encourage my pupils to read interesting books at bedtime, and I suggest to mothers that even for a growing child the sacrifice of a little sleep is well compensated for by the gain in reading skills.

The Color Phonics System will be available to the public shortly, published by Educators Publishing Service, 301 Vassar Street, Cambridge, Massachusetts 01239, to which inquiries should be directed. The system will be published with its own manual, and in time it is hoped that this will be supplemented by extra material which will give guidance to teachers and suggest activities for pupils. I would be very grateful if those who use the system would let me have their suggestions for improvements and suitable additional material.

CHAPTER 13

THE PROGRESSIVE CHOICE READING METHOD

THOMAS J. EDWARDS

The Progressive Choice Reading Method is the direct outgrowth of a learning theory based on a study entitled "The Effect of Varying the Number of Choices in the Identification of Very Similar Stimuli," by Dr. Myron Woolman. This research has formed the broad base of a variety of teaching methods, ranging from the training of pilots and guided missile operators to the teaching of basic concepts of electricity to unskilled workers at the Bell Telephone Laboratories.

The Progressive Choice Reading Method is essentially a technique for presenting the multitudinous aspects of the learning to read process in an orderly, systematic manner designed to result in maximum rate and efficiency in learning, practically assured success, and minimum confusion. The author, Dr. Woolman, was cognizant of the immense complexity of the reading process as a highly involved, multifaceted psychological activity, and he therefore brought to bear his training and experience as an experimental psychologist in his careful analysis of the diverse aspects of the total reading process.

It would be difficult to classify the Progressive Choice Reading Method within any of the traditional systems, although it combines certain aspects of programmed instruction with the so-called linguistics approach to reading. Yet its unique aspects bear careful examination as they incorporate and interrelate a variety of learning principles related to the acquisition of language skill, involving, among a number of other problems, the inconsistencies of English orthography or sound-symbol relationships.

A Language Arts Program

The basic aim of the Progressive Choice Reading Method is to provide the learner with facility in handling sound-symbol relationships in reading. However, Woolman was fully cognizant of the fact that perceptual learning of printed symbols proceeds more effectively if it is combined with other aspects of language. For this reason, Woolman has integrated the learning to read process within a broader matrix of language factors. This matrix includes: the careful introduction of meaning at the spoken level; auditory discrimination of speech sounds; correct oral reproduction and use of spoken language; the reinforcement of perceptual learnings through written reproduction with its implications for spelling; the visual discrimination of carefully contrasted letter elements in preparation for eventual letter discrimination, also a part of his total approach; auditory and vocomotor associations with the functions of letters and graphemes; and the utilization of word forms that the learner has mastered within contexts which stimulate comprehension of sentences and longer selections, enhance precision in knowledge of word meanings, and reinforce perceptual learning of word forms.

A Description of the Method

Readiness

Few, if any, assumptions are made in the Progressive Choice Reading Method regarding the readiness of the learner for beginning reading instruction. For this reason, Woolman introduces meaning, together with auditory and visual discrimination, prior to the introduction of words and their structural and functional components. This he does in recognition of the fact that these aspects of readiness are often problems of the beginning reader and militate against his subsequent attempts to perceive and recognize word forms.

Structural Elements versus Whole Word Forms in Beginning Reading

Basic to Woolman's Progressive Choice theory is the contention that complexity in a learning situation tends to be confusing to the learner and thereby decreases efficiency. The whole word approach to the teaching of beginning reading involves the introduction of a variety of forms in terms of length, configuration, and phonetic elements. It is this diversity which Woolman feels to be the source of complexity and confusion for many beginning readers. He contends that perceptual familiarity with the elements that comprise a given word form facilitates its easy grasp and recognition and that "the whole-word approach tends to de-emphasize structural components and to produce perceptual uncertainties which lead to poor spelling and confusion between similar pattern configurations" (Woolman, 1962a).

Woolman's point of view is consistent with that of Brown (1958), who makes the following statement: "while the general shape of a word has some cue value, the clear view of letters is a more important factor in word identification . . . the adult reader is able to identify words at a glance but it may be that this ability is best developed out of letter-by-letter reading."

Cycle I: Beginning Reading Instruction

In his attempts to simplify the beginning reading experience, Woolman selects a "target word" for the beginner to learn. The selection of this word is not random but rather is based on two criteria: (a) the word should be common to the vocabularies of most learners; and (b) the word is made up of letters that have rather simple linear and curvilinear components. Also, the letters comprising the target word must contrast maximally for greater ease of discrimination. The actual word learning proceeds as follows:

1. The first step in the learning of the target word is to discuss its meaning or variations in meaning. This is done orally in informal discussion at what Woolman refers to as the audial meaning level. At this level, not only is there a clarification of the meaning of the target word, but also a requirement that the learner hear and pronounce the word correctly.

2. The second step in the word-learning process is referred to by Woolman as the discrimination level. Here the learner must first differentiate among the linear and curvilinear components which compose the letters of the target word. This involves rather simple discrimination or matching exercises. Afterwards, these components are combined into individual letters, and again matching exercises are provided so that the learner can demonstrate his ability to discriminate between a given letter and other geometric forms that are similar to it.

When discrimination of the letter has been learned, the student is required to reproduce it in writing for the purpose of reinforcing his perceptual learning of the letter form. He first traces the letter in its completely printed form. Then the letter is presented in partially dotted form, which the learner still traces. The solid lines diminish and the dots increase until only a dotted outline is presented, which the learner still traces, but with increasingly less help from the printed form itself.

Finally, without any help at all, he is required to reproduce the letter form himself several times.

3. When this discrimination level has been mastered in accordance with the steps described above, the learner moves to the third phase, which is the identification level. Here he learns the sound that is most commonly associated with the letter he has been working on visually.

There is considerable controversy among phoneticians and reading specialists regarding the sounding or vocalizing of consonants. The point of this controversy is simply that consonants represent various positions of the mouth either before or after the uttering of a vowel sound. The letter G, for example, has no sound of its own, and if one were to ascribe a sound to it the results would be a **guh**. Woolman conceded the truth of this point but challenges the arguments against the temporary attaching of a vowel sound to consonants. He feels that this is a necessary crutch which the beginning reader needs in order to "feel" the function of a consonant. And he has demonstrated the validity of his contention by showing that learners quickly dispense with the artificial vowel crutch, retain the "feeling" of the consonant's function, and can readily synthesize a given consonant with any vowel.

At this identification level, therefore, the learner does make sounds which he associates with consonants and with vowels. Beyond this, he is required to make two specific responses: (a) he must utter the sound when he sees the printed form of the letter, and (b) he must write the letter when he hears it pronounced for him. Thus, the sound-symbol relationship is established.

4. The next step in Woolman's method is the compounding level. This involves the compounding of combinations of vowels and consonants into single sounds. Here again Woolman violates one of the "sacred tenets" of current thought in the teaching of reading by giving the learner meaningless graphemes to read. His contention is that the precise mastery of phoneme-grapheme relationships demands that the reader be able to decode printed symbols even though they may have no meaning for him. This, he asserts, is a reality which every reader faces: unfamiliar (and therefore meaningless) word forms are encountered even by sophisticated readers and must be deciphered. Furthermore, this reduces considerably some of the guessing which is practiced by readers who rely very heavily on configuration, picture, or context clues.

At this compounding level, as was true at the identification level, the reader is faced with two response requirements: (a) he must pronounce the letter combination correctly (although it may be meaningless in some instances) when he sees it in printed form, and (b) he must write the letters in correct sequence when the combination of letters or phoneme is heard by him. By this means he acquires both a reading and a writing mastery of a given phoneme.

5. The fifth and final step in this initial word-learning procedure is the visual meaning level. Here the learner demonstrates his ability now to read and write the "target word" which previously had only been a part of his listening and speaking vocabulary.

Several additional observations should be made regarding this technique for teaching beginning reading. First of all, Woolman divides his programs into three cycles, and the steps described above are characteristic primarily of Cycle I. His major aim in Cycle I is to teach the consistent or regular sound-symbol relationships of all the letters and letter combinations of the English writing system except for the letter Q, since it never functions independently of the letter U. And, as was mentioned previously, the learner is required both to read and write them. The irregularities of the English system of orthography are postponed for subsequent cycles. This is consistent with Woolman's contention that a learning task should not be complicated, lest efficiency diminish and frustration result for the learner.

Another aspect of Woolman's initial reading instruction is the introduction of only capital letters during the first cycle. His rationale for this is that only simple linear and curvilinear forms should be presented for perceptual learning and for reproduction because lower-case letters are considerably more complicated. Proponents of the whole word method for initial reading instruction would argue with this position of Woolman's and contend that the extensions above and below the line of lower-case letters, often referred to as "determining tendencies," add richness and uniqueness to a given word form and thereby facilitate learning and recognition of a given printed form. This latter view is unquestionably valid for a method which relies much more heavily upon the perceptual learning initially of total configurations than upon mastery of structural components.

Another consideration to which Woolman has given much attention regarding the initial stages of perceptual learning is maximum discriminability. The learning tasks which are presented are sequenced in such a way as to produce maximum contrast among the stimuli to be perceived, and this, in turn, lessens the likelihood of perceptual confusion and error. Again, this is an attempt to ensure success in the learning situation.

Woolman has also placed a very high premium on successful progression through his entire program. This requires a clear demonstration of mastery of a given learning task before a student proceeds to progressively more difficult challenges. This contrasts somewhat sharply with systems for teaching reading that ignore learning difficulties, permit cumulative failure to develop, and frequently subject students to intensive frustration by requiring them to work in materials which they cannot handle.

Woolman's constant insistence upon a variety of types of response requirement is another somewhat unique feature of his learning system. Students are required to respond orally to printed stimuli and in writing to spoken stimuli. This provides a reciprocal type of reinforcement in the establishment of sound-symbol relationships. It is also this requirement to respond constantly that yields evidence of learning mastery or of learning difficulties and thus provides for constant diagnosis en route.

A somewhat incidental but very important by-product of motor reinforcement to perceptual learning is the fact that improved spelling and formation of letters results.

It should also be pointed out that letter naming is delayed throughout the entire first cycle. If letter naming is required in the initial stages of learning to read, the student is likely to become confused, since he will have to make two essentially different responses to a given printed stimulus, the sound of the letter's name and the sound that a letter symbolizes. And these two sounds are frequently at variance with each other.

Cycle II: Systematic Expansion of Decoding Skills

When a student has successfully completed Cycle I, he will be thoroughly familiar with the upper-case forms and the most common single sounds of all of the letters of the alphabet except Q. Because of the gradual and systematic manner in which letters are introduced, the number of words that can be constructed from them is rather limited in the beginning of the program. However, as rapidly as possible, an increasing number of graphemes is introduced, along with a larger number and variety of words and sentences. By the end of Cycle I many reading selections and vocabulary exercises have been introduced.

Cycle II introduces the lower-case forms of all the letters, single-sound values of selected compounds, the letter Q with its functional dependence upon the letter U, the final E's effect upon medial vowels, the distinction between long and short vowel sounds, and punctuation.

As was true throughout Cycle I, the learner is constantly required to make responses in Cycle II both for practice and as an indication of mastery at a given level necessary to move forward to more advanced levels.

Because of the increased proficiency in word-recognition and word analysis ability developed in Cycle II, together with the requirement of comprehension of materials of increasingly more difficult levels, more complex selections are presented to the student. In addition, vocabulary is developed in functional and meaningful contexts with adequate provision made for overlearning.

The following is an excerpt from Cycle II of Reading in High Gear, one of Woolman's reading programs designed for adolescent and adult underachievers (Woolman, 1965a):

> The three men think not of gold but of the important discovery of landing on the moon. It is, indeed, a bold plan and as Barbicant, Nicol and Ardan wait on the ship for blast-off, the three count down the seconds.
>
> In the midst of the countdown Ardan shouts, "Hold on," and in a red flash, the three men leave for the moon. As it left this planet with a burst of speed, the ship got nearer the moon and it got very cold.
>
> Barbicant comments, "I felt nothing. Did we blast off?" "We did, and I see the moon getting nearer and nearer," comments Ardan. "How can we be this far away this soon?" asks Nicol. "The speed of the ship is carrying us very fast and the moon is very near," explains Ardan. "He is correct, she is, she is!" shout Nicol and Barbicant as the men peer out of the glass opening of the rocket ship.

Cycle III: Handling of Variant or Inconsistent Sound-Symbol Relationships

As was noted previously, Woolman contends that consistent sound-symbol relationships should be thoroughly mastered and stabilized before the inconsistencies of the English writing system are presented. The basic problem is essentially two-fold in nature: First, a given sound in the English language may be represented in various ways when it is written. Likewise, a given letter or combination of letters may represent various sounds, depending upon the word in which it appears. If these shifts in sound-symbol relationships are presented randomly to the learner, confusion develops in the process of translating printed symbols into sound or sounds into printed symbols (i.e., spelling). And Woolman's basic thesis is that *a given learning situation should create an absolute minimum of confusion if learning is to proceed in an orderly, efficient, nonfrustrating, and success-ensuring manner.*

Thus, having focused upon the consistent sound-symbol relationships during Cycles I and II, he feels that the learner is better able now in Cycle III to recognize and come to grips with the deviations from consistency that English orthography presents to the reader, frequently causing him grief, confusion, and failure.

The major psychological problem which Woolman has attacked, then, is one involving a single stimulus to which two or more responses may be made and which is, therefore, one of sensitizing the learner to make the appropriate response choice from among multiple alternatives.

It is not merely Woolman's recognition of this problem but his program design for handling this problem systematically which strengthens his approach and would tend, therefore, to alleviate a large number of reading problems caused by learners' confusion regarding the appropriate response to make to a given stimulus, spoken or written.

By the end of Cycle III, word recognition, vocabulary expansion, functional grammar, and reading comprehension have progressed to a point that permits the reader to handle the following type of selection (Woolman, 1965a):

> The form of the Huron trembled in every fibre as he looked at Cora clinging to a tree. His intention was to kill the young girl and he raised his arm but dropped it again with a bewildered air, like one who shunned the idea of killing. Once more he struggled with himself and lifted the keen weapon, but just then a piercing cry was yelled above them. Magua recoiled a step and a young Huron, profiting by the chance, joyfully sheathed his own blade into the bosom of Cora and dropped it with a clang on the rocks. Magua sprang like a tiger on his offending and already retreating countryman, but the falling form of Uncas separated the unnatural combatants. Maddened by the murder he had just witnessed, Magua buried his weapon in the back of Uncas, uttering an unearthly shout as he committed the dastardly deed.

In addition to the systematic presentation of the variant forms of letters or letter combinations in Cycle III, Woolman also introduces additional compounds and words made from these compounds, dictionary usage, syllabication techniques, and cursive writing.

Built-In Motivational Devices

The Progressive Choice Reading Method has been developed on the premise that there should be intrinsic interest inherent in instructional materials themselves. This, Woolman feels, keeps the learner actively and independently involved in the learning task, diminishes tendencies toward boredom, and relieves the teacher of much of the task of reinforcing motivation within a heterogeneous group when individualized attention is required. To achieve this end, Woolman has consciously engineered techniques for providing this essential motivation.

Learning Addiction

The fundamental principle underlying Woolman's concept of learning addiction is this (Woolman, 1962b): a learner generally faces a normally unthreatening learning task in a state of emotional equilibrium or calm. The introduction of a learning task disturbs this equilibrium and generates tension. And the *rapid* restoration of equilibrium and calm reduces tension. If the learning task is only challenging but not frustrating, and if the disturbance in equilibrium or the tension involved is not prolonged, then pleasure results from this total experience—disruption and then restoration of tranquillity (Woolman, 1965b).

If this process is repeated many times within the learning situation—a pulsation of disruption-restoration-disruption-restoration—then a kind of learning addiction sets in whereby, according to Woolman, the learner is reluctant to leave the situation. (The writer has seen this phenomenon actually in operation both among first graders with learning disabilities and among so-called pre-dropouts at the junior high school level.)

Active Involvement through Response Requirements

In the preceding descriptions of each of the three cycles, mention was made of the fact that learners employing the Progressive Choice Reading Method were constantly required to make responses. This requirement to respond demands activity rather than passivity in the learning situation and thereby maximizes learner involvement. In addition, responding is an important factor in the creation of learning addiction discussed above. Further, the overt responses made by the learner yield knowledge of results—success or failure—which rewards or challenges the student and also permits constant diagnosis en route on the part of the teacher.

Built-In Provision for Success

Because of the sequential arrangement of the learning increments in the Progressive Choice Reading Method, a student is required to give concrete evidence of mastery at every level prior to his moving to a higher, more difficult level. In any number of programs, students are "pushed along" within a social promotion philosophy and move into materials of increasing difficulty until they are overcome by frustrations in the learning to read situation. This failure, in turn, "spills over" into other areas of subject matter and thereby becomes generalized, increases academic disability, and may lead to the psychological "drop-out syndrome."

Success is also provided for in Woolman's program through a technique of "remodeling" the foundation of a student's reading ability. Very often a learner who has progressed uneasily and unevenly until he achieves, say, a score of 5.0 on a standardized test of reading has innumerable gaps at levels far below that which his test score would indicate. Many diagnostic instruments are based on the assumption that students have moved through a generally agreed upon, traditional, and somewhat standard sequence of skill development. They therefore identify skills which should have been learned at a given grade level. Further, there is considerable agreement among reading specialists that standardized reading tests tend rather consistently to overestimate the achievement level of students: a student is generally frustrated by materials at the level indicated by the standardized test, should receive instruction at a somewhat lower level, and is able to read independently at still an even lower level than his instructional level. Hence, at best, standardized tests tend generally to be gross screening devices which may well mask specific weaknesses that hamper growth toward the highly sophisticated levels of mature reading ability.

In the Progressive Choice Reading Method, the learner is required to go back to the beginning reading stage and move through a considerably different sequence in the development of a foundation of word meaning related to the processes of auditory and visual discrimination, word analysis, comprehension, and language structure mastery. According to Woolman, both the systematic sequencing and the novelty of the approach are factors which result in a significant renovation of the reading foundation.

Social Status Derived from Achievement

As students progress successfully through the Progressive Choice reading program, their achievement is rewarded also by peer recognition. Having completed Cycle I successfully, a learner receives the title of Student Helper. This permits him to assist other learners who are still in Cycle I. Again, successful completion of Cycle II earns for the student the title of Assistant Student Instructor, and he may assist students in either Cycle I or II. The uppermost designation along this achievement status ladder is Student Instructor, and this, of course, permits him to assist learners in all of the cycles.

Woolman has indicated that assistance should be given by students only when they have reached a convenient stopping place in their own work and that such assistance should not exceed approximately fifteen minutes a day. Also, he limits very specifically the type of help that an assistant may give, indicating that such help is never a substitute for the teacher's important functions, since she must administer and check all "checkout tests" and be aware at all times of the learners' progress.

Underachievers in reading frequently secure peer recognition through various types of antisocial behavior within the classroom which militates against academic success. Woolman contends that by ensuring success and then providing rewards through positive peer recognition and status achievement, motivation and progress are enhanced.

Multisensory Modalities Employed

Both empirical and experimental evidence strongly indicates that a multisensory approach to learning tends to be generally superior to a unisensory approach. As related more specifically to perceptual learning involving printed symbols, the employment of auditory, visual, and vocomotor stimulation in a meaningful word-learning situation reduces the number of contacts that a learner requires for word learning to take place successfully (Edwards, 1956). In addition, educators frequently suggest the involvement of kinesthetic and tactile sensory modalities as adjuncts to successful word perception (Fernald, 1943).

This multisensory approach is crucial in Woolman's Progressive Choice Reading Method. As was indicated previously, a given target word is handled at the audial meaning level before it becomes the object of perceptual learning. This, of course, involves not only meaning but also clear auditory perception prior to the presentation of its components. Visual perception enters into the clear perception of letter elements, letter wholes, and finally whole word forms.

Vocomotor stimulation (i.e., reinforcement through articulation) occurs not only at the audial meaning level but also when sounds are related to individual letters, to letter compounds, and the whole word when its printed form is presented for visual perception.

Kinesthetic stimulation, through tracing and unaided reproduction, is required of the learner throughout the entire program. It enters into the learning of letter elements, letters themselves, compounds, and whole words, as was true of vocomotor stimulation discussed above.

This multisensory approach is seen by Woolman as crucial not only as an aid to the perceptual learning act itself but also to maximize the active involvement of the student in the learning task.

Classroom Administration of the Program

Reading programs based on the Progressive Choice method have been organized in such a way as to provide maximum assistance to the teacher or to an untrained instructor. The manuals that accompany the students' workbooks give first of all an overview of the entire program, including a description of the format, the basic principles underlying the program, and general instructions regarding the use of the materials.

For each segment of each cycle, every step involved in the administration of the program is detailed and falls into four categories: learner objectives, indicating specifically what ultimately the student is to learn; basic instructor procedures, specifying what is required of the teacher; required learner responses, describing what the student is to do for the successful completion of a given learning task; and suggestions for instruction, advising the teacher how to proceed in the event that the learner is not successful.

It might well be argued that too much is "spelled out" for the teacher in the Progressive Choice reading program and that therefore there is too little left to the teacher's imagination or creativity. Woolman's posture is, however, that it is a boon to the teacher who has large classes to have specific guidelines regarding the use of the method. In addition, this specificity in direction lessens the liklihood of any significant deviations in procedure that could do violence to the psychological principles upon which the program rests. Woolman further contends that once a teacher thoroughly understands the method it is quite possible and, indeed, desirable that she develop activities and materials that are compatible with the method.

In an attempt to assist the teacher in developing a thorough awareness of the rationale undergirding the Progressive Choice Reading Method, Woolman has appended a special section in the instructor's manuals which is a programmed, self-administering course that teaches the principles of the method.

Concluding Comment

The Progressive Choice Reading Method falls within the ranks of several very recent methods that have been developed in response to a clamor during the past decade or more for new and improved techniques for reading instruction. Two criteria stand out as essential for the effective evaluation of these several methods: the soundness of the psychological principles that underlie each of them and, more important, objective data regarding their effectiveness. Because of the newness of most of these recent methods, time will be required to determine the ultimate validity of each or to identify the specialized segment of the beginning reading population for which a given method may be most appropriate.

At the time of this writing two programs have been developed by Woolman based on his Progressive Choice Reading Method. The first one, Lift Off to Reading (Woolman, 1966) was originally designed to meet the needs of both educable and trainable mental retardates. However, the prepublication tryouts strongly suggest that it will also be appropriate for use with a much wider variety of special learning disabilities. It is anticipated that these will include the culturally disadvantaged, the emotionally disturbed, bilinguals, dyslexics, and possibly other groups with special learning problems.

A second program developed by Woolman (1965a), Reading in High Gear, is designed to meet the special needs of older, underachieving, culturally disadvantaged readers at the adolescent level or beyond. A special attempt is made in this program to provide for much more mature story content and simultaneously to renovate the presumably shaky foundation of their reading abilities. A unique feature of Reading in High Gear is Woolman's attempt systematically to program attitudes of potentially antisocial older learners in the direction of a more positive social orientation.

Quite clearly, Woolman's movement from an initial conceptualization of a theoretical framework, to a careful detailing of specific cogent principles, to the actual production of a program represents a kind of operational paradigm for future program developers as the increasingly stronger and healthy competition continues for the creation of improved materials and classroom practices.

CHAPTER 14

MATURE CONTENT FOR IMMATURE SKILLS

GILBERT SCHIFFMAN

SUGGESTIONS FOR REWRITING MATERIALS

Many teachers are becoming increasingly aware of the lack of materials with high interest content and low readability level for the older retarded reader. The author reported, in the 1963 International Reading Association Conference Proceedings, instructional reading levels of retarded readers and readability levels of assigned texts used in the classroom (Schiffman, 1963), summarized below.

Elementary Level:

1. The grade level of the standardized tests averaged 0.41 grade level over the readability level of the assigned texts.
2. Readability level of the assigned texts averaged 1.15 grade levels over the instructional levels as determined by informal evaluations.

Secondary Level:

1. The readability level of the assigned texts averaged 1.35 grade levels over the grade level of the standardized tests.
2. The readability of the assigned texts averaged 2.24 grade levels over the instructional levels as determined by informal evaluations.
3. The average readability level of content texts (history, science, social studies) averaged 3.24 grade levels over the instructional level as determined by informal evaluations.

Data supporting an inconsistency among the standardized tests, book-level scores, and informal evaluations are not new. Botel (1957) stated: "Seven to ten million pupils in our schools are reading books which are too difficult for them." Until the time arrives when publishers will recognize this problem, teachers must look elsewhere for assistance. This chapter will serve as a guide for teachers who themselves wish to rewrite material for lower level readability.

The level of readability of a selection depends to a large degree upon its structure. Teachers who rewrite materials on lower readability levels must be constantly mindful of vocabulary load, sentence construction, and paragraph length. The following suggestions will give them pertinent help in making adaptations.

Use as Many Basic Words as Possible

When a learner is confronted with materials that have a readability that is beyond his grasp, he is likely to be frustrated in his learning activities. Too difficult vocabulary is one cause of frustration. The reader should be able to pronounce ninety-five out of one hundred words at his proper instructional level. In rewriting materials, the teacher should use as many basic words as possible from one of the many published word lists. For example, Dale's 3,000 Familiar Words (Dale and Chall, 1948) contains words that are known in reading by at least 80 per cent of the children in fourth grade. If most of the words in the rewritten selection are on this list, the vocabulary of the selection is probably close to the fourth-grade readability level.

Make the Sentence as Short as Possible

This suggestion is self-explanatory. A short sentence is easier to read than a long sentence. For example (Namowitz and Stone, 1960):

> At the surface, the earth is covered by a very thin crust of comparatively lightweight rocks like granite and basalt. This crust is between twenty and forty miles thick under the continents, but only three to ten miles thick under the oceans. Below the crust is an eighteen hundred mile thick mantle or intermediate zone, consisting of rocks much heavier than those in the crust and probably containing much iron. This brings us nearly halfway to the earth's center. Next comes the dense outer core, nearly fourteen hundred miles thick, believed to be iron and nickel in a hot plastic condition just short of the molten or liquid state, and from 9.5 to 12 times as heavy as water. (Average sentence length: 23.4 words.)

This could be written:

> If we could go down into our earth, we would find that our earth has four parts. The part of the earth we live on is called the crust.

It is about 3 to 40 miles thick. Most of the crust is made of rocks called granite and basalt. Most of our land rocks are granite. Rocks under the ocean are basalt. Below the crust is a layer of heavy rocks. This part is about 1,800 miles thick. It is called the mantle. The mantle is made of heavier rocks. We think these rocks have a lot of iron in them. (Average sentence length: 9.2 words.)

Sentence length is considered an important factor in every available readability formula. Table 1 shows the average sentence length per hundred-word selection of six basal readers used in Baltimore County.

Table 1. Sentence length and grade level

	Grade Level of Basal Reader					
	2^1	2^2	3^1	3^2	4	5
Average Sentence Length	8.7	9	10	11	12	14.9

Try To Start Each Sentence with the Subject

The sentence may lose some of its literary style, but it will be easier to read. Simple sentences with subject and verb in that order are easier to read than compound and complex sentences or sentences in inverted order. For example:

To promote the development of a wholesome, outgoing, cooperative, and emotionally well-balanced personality, the teacher must guide the pupil in setting up achievable goals.

This could be written:

The teacher must guide the pupil in setting up achievable goals. The teacher should promote the development of a wholesome, outgoing, cooperative, and emotionally well-balanced personality.

It Is Best to Introduce Only One New Word Per Sentence

The reader may be able to figure out the meaning of the new word from context clues. This is especially true if adequate background and concepts have been developed. If only one new word is introduced per sentence, it is often possible to figure out the meaning of the unknown word. For example, the reader may identify the word "covers" from the context of this sentence: "Bill began to pull the covers off the bed." By reading the rest of the sentence and coming back to the unknown word, the student learns to infer the meaning.

Use Picture Clues Wherever Possible

The words on a page can be called the verbal context, and the illustrations can be called the nonverbal context. Illustrations, pictures, and other nonverbal materials are included to make the books attractive, to stimulate interest, and to facilitate comprehension. Since these pictorial aids further understanding, they also contribute to word recognition. Picture clues are one type of context clue. In all learning situations, pictorial aids should be used to ensure adequate working concepts.

The following excerpt from a science selection demonstrates how valuable an illustration (Fig. 1) can be in clarifying a difficult concept or word.

> There are two small gears and two large gears. The two small gears are connected to the propeller and shaft. They move the large gears

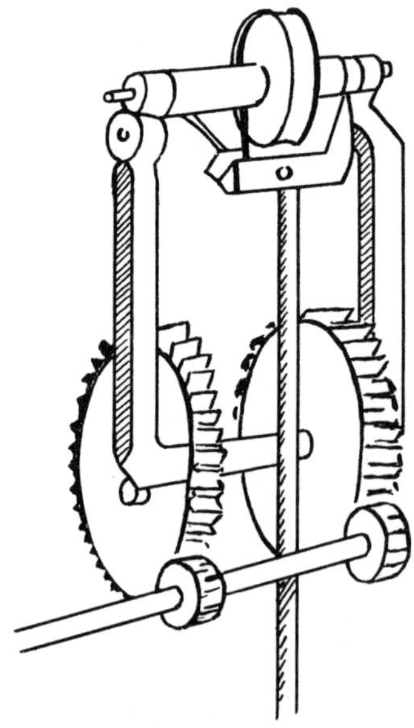

Figure 1. Gears.

as they turn. Two pins stick out like a handle from the large gears. The pins are placed a few inches from the center forming an *eccentric*. Eccentric means off center.

Be Sure That Every Pronoun Has an Unmistakable Antecedent

The ability to recognize the word or words to which a selected pronoun refers is a critical reading skill. For example, this sentence might be difficult for the retarded reader:

> Millions of workers dragged stone blocks for the outside walls and packed basket after basket of earth between *them*.

This could be written:

> Millions of workers dragged stone blocks for the outside walls and packed basket after basket of earth between the blocks.

Avoid Figurative or Symbolic Language

Stay at the level of the oral language development. Here is a self-explanatory example: "The herd thundered across the prairie." This could be written: "The herd galloped so hard that the hoofs striking the ground made a noise like thunder."

Watch the Difficulty Level of the Concepts

Frequently, complex concepts cannot be developed in sentences and must be developed in paragraphs. Since words in themselves have limited meaning, the approach to language growth is through the development of concepts. At first, simple concepts of "over" and "under," "big" and "little," and the like, are organized. The pupil learns to classify categories such as "dogs" and "animals," "days" and "weeks," "pennies" and "money," and so on. Activities which lead the pupil to relate a specific term to a general term prepare him to deal with other concepts in reading.

As the child develops skills of listening, speaking, and reading, his concept development continues. He learns that sometimes the same word designates different things. He puts on his "coat." He puts a "coat" of paint on the toy. He learns about different kinds of "elevators," "farms," and "cities." He begins to develop concepts of "afraid," "proud," "brave," "faraway," and other higher-level abstractions. He learns the meaning of figures of speech, such as "the country mouse looked down his nose at the city mouse." As concepts become more abstract and generalized, the learner must spend more time in making this a working "concept."

Use as Few Polysyllabic Words as Possible

Evidence indicates that the number of syllables per hundred words influences the readability level of the writing. Table 2 summarizes the results of a study of six basal readers used in Baltimore County. When a difficult concept is being developed, it is sometimes advisable to repeat a polysyllabic word several times to ensure mastery of the word and understanding of the concept.

Table 2. Polysyllables and grade level

	Grade Level of Basal Reader					
	2^1	2^2	3^1	3^2	4	5
No. of Syllables per 100 Words	116	121	125	128	130	133

Applying Readability Formulas

Today there is no composite method that can be used to measure all aspects of readability. A readability formula can be used to get a rough approximation of the difficulty of a piece of writing. However, readability formulas have at least three fundamental weaknesses: they do not evaluate the difficulty of the concepts; they do not measure the abstractness of the subject matter; and they do not consider the way in which the text is organized. These formulas measure only one aspect of readability, namely, structural difficulty. Only such factors as vocabulary load, number of syllables, and sentence structure are evaluated. Results from formulas should, therefore, be interpreted cautiously. One must be flexible in interpretations of the formula's grade measurement. One must consider separately the aspects of format, organization, interest, and content and then make a judgment as to the suitability of a particular article or book for a particular group. The pamphlet, *Readability*, edited by Edgar Dale (1949), presents an excellent evaluation and summary of the numerous readability formulas.

Illustrative Lesson

An example of how one can employ rewriting techniques to advanced content material can be demonstrated with the following selections. The original material, "Famous Volcanoes" (Brown *et al.*, 1958), has a readability designed for secondary school pupils who have effective secondary reading skills. The rewritten selection, "The Eruption of Mt. Pelee," contains much of the former's content but has a readability level geared for upper elementary reading skills. The retarded secondary pupil using the latter material may then acquire some knowledge about volcanoes through the use of printed verbal material.

Famous Volcanoes

Volcanic disasters have reaped a tremendous toll of human lives and property. You may wish to consult various geological references and read about some of the most famous and vicious volcanic eruptions such as Mt. Somma (Vesuvius), 79 A.D.; Krakatao, 1883; and Mt. Pelee, 1902.

An account of the eruption of Mt. Pelee, as related by Professors Brown, Monnett, and Stovall, follows:

Mt. Pelee, overlooking the thriving city of Saint Pierre, on the West Indian Island of Martinique, had been dormant for fifty years. In April, 1902, steam was seen to rise from its summit, and during the following two weeks there were ejections of dust and cinders, slight earthquakes, sulfurous vapors, and torrents of mud.

Extremely viscous lava rose in the crater of Mt. Pelee, and hardened to form a solid plug sealing over the surface of the crater. Pent up forces within the volcano then began expelling material through lateral cracks in the walls, beneath the plug. On the eighth of May a tremendous explosion tore a gash in the south wall of the crater. Through this opening there issued a dark cloud consisting of extremely hot steam and other gases, filled with hot dust and other solid fragments up to many feet in diameter. This cloud raced down the side of the mountain at a speed estimated to be a mile a minute, straight toward the town of Saint Pierre. With the violence of a tornado it knocked down buildings, hurled statues weighing several tons about, and uprooted trees. In a few seconds the ruins of the town were in flames, and all its 30,000 inhabitants, with four exceptions, were dead. The cloud continued its course into the sea, where it destroyed all except one or two of the considerable number of ships lying off-shore.

Three of the four survivors died within a short time after their rescue. The only one to escape unscathed from Saint Pierre was, ironically enough, a Negro murderer under sentence of death, who owed his deliverance to incarceration in an underground dungeon with very poor ventilation.

The Eruption of Mt. Pelee

You have just learned that some volcanoes are dormant. These "sleeping" volcanoes are most dangerous. People who live close forget that they can erupt at any time.

There is an island in the West Indies called Martinique. In 1902, the capital was Saint Pierre. Over 30,000 people lived in this city.

Three miles from Saint Pierre stood Mt. Pelee, a dormant volcano. The people were not afraid of this volcano. It had not erupted since 1851.

In April, 1902, Mt. Pelee began to throw out steam, dust, and poisonous gases. This went on for two weeks. Still, no one was afraid.

Then lava began to rise in the volcano's crater. It cooled very fast, forming a plug of solid rock. This plug held back lava and gases that were forming inside Mt. Pelee.

On May 8th a giant explosion tore away the south side of Mt. Pelee. A great cloud of hot, poisonous gases raced down the side of Mt. Pelee at a speed of more than a mile a minute. The cloud raced through Saint Pierre.

Within seconds the city was in flames. All but 4 of the 30,000 people were killed. Three of the 4 people died soon after. The only one to escape was a murderer under sentence of death. He had been kept in a dungeon deep in the ground.

Even today there are sleeping volcanoes which may erupt at any time. Do you know where they are?

Checking Comprehension

The difficulty of a piece of writing depends to a great degree upon what the author expects the reader to get out of the material. The pupil's purposes, interests, and background must be considered. If difficult questions are asked on a given piece of content, even if the passage has a low readability level, the reader may not be able to comprehend the questions or handle the level of abstractions. However, it is most important to determine the amount of comprehension derived from the rewritten material. Whenever possible, the reader should have a minimum comprehension score of at least 75 per cent, based on both factual and critical questions. A mere recall of facts provides an index to the accuracy of comprehension. However, it is also desirable to ask critical questions to appraise the quality and depth of comprehension.

The following selection, written at about a fourth-grade readability level, demonstrates the many types of critical question that can be developed in a reading activity.

Critical Reading Selection

Strong Bow rode into the valley. The sun, directly overhead, beat down with increasing fury. The Black Toe chief was very tired. The raid had not been successful. One third of his men had been killed. Six mounted braves trailed close behind their chief. Small puffs of dust arose from the horses' hoofs, and their manes lay motionless against their wet sides.

The chief was very sad. He was returning to his village in disgrace. He had no booty; he had no scalps. Slowly the small band headed home towards the mountains. As the sun sank behind the mountain range, they were still far from their loved ones. The chief decided to stop for the night. The men and horses needed rest.

In fact, this would be the final resting place for some of the unlucky warriors.

Critical Comprehension Exercise

1. The sentence which uses the word *range* just as it is used in the story is
   1. The band of Indians *ranged* over the country.
   2. The cook made the breakfast on the *range.*
   3. The gunners adjust the *range* of the cannon.
   4. The climbers reached the top of the highest *range.*
   5. The boys went to the shooting *range.*
2. The main important idea in the story is that
   1. Strong Bow was very tired.
   2. The Indians were returning home after an unsuccessful raid.
   3. The Indians had no booty or scalps.
   4. One third of the Indians had been killed.
   5. The Indians were still far from their families at the end of the day.

3. From the story we should *not* believe that *all* of the Indians
    1. rode horses.
    2. returned home safely.
    3. were tired.
    4. returned home in disgrace.
    5. were Black Toes.
4. The row with ideas from the story that belong together is
    1. Strong Bow, chief, dust
    2. booty, scalps, sun
    3. manes, hoof, sides
    4. home, families, hoofs
    5. puffs, dust, manes
5. The word *their* in the sentence, "As the sun sank behind the mountain range they were still far from *their* loved ones," stands for
    1. horses
    2. Strong Bow
    3. Indian
    4. Black Toe tribe
    5. Indians
6. Strong Bow is to the Black Toe tribe as ______ is to the United States of America.
7. Following the story, the first sentence out of sequence is
    1. The Indians rode into the valley.
    2. The chief decided to stop for the night.
    3. The noon sun beat down with increasing fury.
    4. Small puffs of dust arose from the horses' hoofs.
    5. The band of Indians headed towards the mountain.
8. The idea not found in the story is that
    1. The raiders needed rest.
    2. Three of the horses had been killed.
    3. The Indians were far away from their homes.
    4. The Indians were traveling towards the mountains.
    5. The band of Indians would lose some more men before they returned home.
9. What time of the day was it when the Indians rode into the valley?
10. Was it a wet or dry country? How do you know?
11. Was it a calm or windy day? How do you know?
12. How many Indians started out on the raid?
13. In what direction was the band headed?

Comprehension Answer Key

1. (4)
2. (2)
3. (5)
4. (3)
5. (5)
6. Lyndon Johnson
7. (2)
8. (2)
9. Noon (sun directly overhead)
10. Dry (small puffs of dust)
11. Calm (manes lay motionless)
12. Ten (nine braves plus the chief)
13. West (band headed towards the mountains; sun sank behind the mountain range)

In the above selection, the following critical reading comprehension skills are tested:

1. Multiple meaning of vocabulary—tests the reader's ability to identify a similar usage of a given word from the selection.

2. Main idea—tests the ability to identify the key or most important idea in the story.

3. Generalization—tests the ability to form a general conclusion or principle applicable to an entire class of data on the basis of a limited number of specific instances stated in a selection.

4. Association of ideas—tests the ability to see the relationships among ideas in a series.

5. Antecedence—tests the ability to recognize the word or words to which a selected pronoun refers.

6. Analogy—tests the ability to perceive relationships between two pairs of ideas.

7. Sequence—tests the ability to determine a time sequence.

8. Extraneous ideas—tests the ability to determine relevancy of ideas to a selection.

9–13. Inference—tests the ability to draw a specific conclusion from facts explicitly stated.

The development of this type of comprehension, of course, is not only in the hands of the reading teacher or the elementary classroom teacher. All content teachers have a responsibility to evaluate the reader's understanding of the material and to develop critical thinking skills. Of course, this is just a small sampling of the different kinds of critical comprehension that can be developed. If one takes all these factors into consideration, one realizes the tremendous responsibility that is placed upon the conscientious teacher. Not only must he select material with the appropriate readability level, not only must he develop good effective word recognition and comprehension skills in the proper proportion, but he must also keep in mind the different types of comprehension, and before him he must see the ultimate goal—that the pupil should read for meaning, for enjoyment, and for learning.

CHAPTER 15

PROGRAM ADMINISTRATION WITHIN A SCHOOL SYSTEM

GILBERT SCHIFFMAN

A total school reading program is three-fold: developmental, corrective, and remedial. In addition to the routine program of developmental reading instruction, the Board of Education of Baltimore County has, for a number of years, provided for retarded readers two special programs, corrective and remedial. The corrective program is typical of the supplementary reading programs throughout the country; experienced reading teachers offer additional reading instruction to pupils in small groups, utilizing basically the same techniques employed in the regular program. The remedial program is clinically oriented, applying special techniques to severely retarded readers individually, in classes composed of no more than ten selected pupils. The purpose of this chapter is to present the basic organization of the developmental, corrective, and remedial reading programs in the Baltimore County schools.

Salient Features of the Program for Developmental Reading Instruction in the Baltimore County Schools

The developmental program involves systematic instruction at all school levels and in all content areas for those who are developing language abilities commensurate with their general capacity levels. This developmental program is the responsibility of every teacher, affects all the pupils, is provided for in the regular curriculum, and is a continuous, ongoing process. A balanced program includes instruction in the basal, curricular, and recreational reading skills.

Basal readers are the major means used to develop those skills common to most reading material. They are used to teach many of the comprehension skills that enable the reader to interpret, organize, and react critically to the printed page. They are used to develop word meanings and word recognition techniques leading to independent reading.

Several series of readers are supplied to the schools. The principal, coordinator, and teachers plan the series to be used by each class of each grade. This arrangement makes it possible for the teacher to choose a series that will best meet the needs of those children who are reading below grade level, those who are reading on grade level, and those above grade level.

Fast readers use the more difficult series, those with more new words per page and with greater difficulties in language structure. The average pupils use the books in which the story is told more simply. A set of readers with a quantity of supplementary material is provided for pupils below grade level. Some primary teachers, in an attempt to find a more effective method of meeting individual needs and differences, have introduced a total language experience approach in the first grade. In this method the child's oral language facility is utilized. The experience-story technique promotes increased skill in reading and spelling because the concepts and words are a part of the pupil's speaking-meaning vocabulary before they become a part of his reading-writing vocabulary. With this approach, the child has an opportunity to read his own experiences in his own words before being introduced to the printed material of others.

Curricular reading provides instruction in the basic skills using social studies and science textbooks and supplementary curriculum material, including newspapers and magazines. Additional skills are developed that are peculiar to each area of the curriculum. The obtaining of information from maps, graphs, or tables is taught most effectively with social living or arithmetic materials.

Recreational reading is reading that a child does for his own pleasure. Here those skills are emphasized which enable the reader to enjoy reading. He begins with his own interests and broadens into acquaintance with a rich and varied reading for leisure, including the finer types of literary writing.

In addition to instructing the class as a whole, the teacher utilizes many ways of grouping children to meet their basic needs. At all times groups are kept flexible, since children differ in their interests, ability, and rate of mastery of the basic requirements.

There is no formal developmental reading program at the secondary level. However, English teachers and teachers of special subjects are expected to replicate, reinforce, and continue to develop certain reading habits and skills that need particular attention at the high school level.

By the time the pupil has completed the sixth grade he has often attained a fairly rapid rate of reading and a high degree of comprehension. Also, his ability to read orally may be adequate to serve his present needs. The task then becomes one of adjusting his rate for various types of reading and of refining his comprehension skills to meet a variety of new demands. Abilities and skills that often require further refinement or development include:

1. Developing comprehension
   a. Following directions and finding information
   b. Finding answers to personal and social problems
   c. Reading a story for various purposes
   d. Understanding words and increasing one's personal vocabulary
2. Reading to remember
   a. Remembering important ideas
   b. Remembering significant details
3. Associating ideas and materials
   a. Finding proof
   b. Finding information relevant to particular problems
   c. Examining basic assumptions
   d. Studying the adequacy of presentations
4. Organizing ideas and materials
   a. Arranging events in sequence and making outlines
   b. Summarizing
5. Increasing speed of silent reading
6. Improving oral reading
7. Reading for the content, with wide application of reading skills

Functional Concepts of Corrective and Remedial Reading in the Baltimore County Schools

Unfortunately, some educators, many of whom are interested in reading disabilities, have a severe communication problem because of their own semantic difficulties. The writer decided that it would be beneficial to the reader's understanding of this chapter to present a detailed description of the corrective and remedial programs.

Definition of Corrective Reading

The corrective phase of reading must deal with those pupils who are able to comprehend the assigned material, but only after undue and laborious effort. Many difficulties involved are those common to all pupils in reading, but are found in a greatly exaggerated form here.

Fernald (1943) refers to such children as "cases of partial disability." She feels that these children usually develop normal reading skills when they are given the opportunity to learn by ordinary methods after the faulty conditions (poor vision or hearing, illness, emotional instability, or lack of adequate schooling) have been removed. Vernon (1957) classifies this group as "backward readers" or "semi-illiterates." Johnson (1957) states that a corrective case is "a case of reading retardation not complicated by neurological difficulties, deficiencies in associative learning, and so on." She feels that these cases may result from "lack of readiness when initial experiences with reading were provided, continued instruction above the proper level, lack of adequate stimulation in instruction, inadequate background of experience or oral language facility, and so on." The important thing is that these students do not usually require clinical instruction unless the retardation is compounded by prolonged inattention to correction and its attendant emotional complications.

Definition of Remedial Reading

The procedure known as remedial reading, as contrasted with corrective reading, applies to a small clinical group showing severe symptoms of reading retardation. Children in this group differ from those in the corrective group by the degree of their deficiency. The cases are frequently characterized by associative learning disability, inadequacies in memory span, deficiencies in concept formation, and neurological or emotional complications. Pupils with these problems demand individual and small group instruction on a clinical basis by specially trained personnel. It is often in this last group that reading difficulty may result in extended damage to the personality. A child who cannot read or who cannot read as well as his age group is marked before all as a failure. He is reminded of being a failure many times a day and every day. Even a skilled classroom or corrective reading teacher often cannot restore his confidence in himself, since his classmates and worried parents often magnify his deficiency.

Vernon (1957) labels these pupils "illiterates" and defines them as "those who for some reason or other are unable to master even the simpler mechanics of reading." Fernald (1943) calls them "total or extreme disabilities." She defines these disabled readers as "those individuals who fail to learn to read under the most careful instruction by methods that are successful with the average child."

Other educators classify this group as word blind or alexic or dyslexic. Many medical researchers conclude that this type of reading disability is organic in nature, and in some early papers lesions in specific areas of the brain were suggested. More recently, investigators have reasserted the claim of heredity as causal factor of primary reading disability. Members of the Orton Society diagnose these cases as having a specific reading disability of the strephosymbolic type. Dr. Orton (1926) pointed out some of the following characteristics:

1. They show no overt evidence of any significant impairment of vision or hearing, brain damage, or primary personality deviations, nor do they have any history thereof.
2. They show great difficulty in remembering whole word patterns and do not learn easily by the "sight method."
3. They are poor oral readers and fundamentally poor spellers.
4. They usually come from families in which there is lefthandedness or language disorder, or both.
5. In their early attempts at reading and writing, they show marked confusions in remembering the orientation of letters (**b**, **d**, **p**, **q**) and the order of letters in words or numbers in sequences (**was–saw**, **on–no**, **felt–left**, **12–21**). They are sometimes called mirror-minded or mirror readers.
6. They usually show some evidence of delayed or incomplete establishment of one-sided motor preferences (unilateral cerebral dominance). They tend to be lefthanded, ambidextrous, or mixed in their motor choices, e.g., righthanded and lefteyed, or they may have been slow in the establishment of their handedness.
7. They often show delays or defects in more than one language area. In addition to poor reading, they may have delayed or imperfect speech; a poor ear for words; a poor oral vocabulary; or clumsiness in handwriting or in other motor acts.

Gallagher (1960) summarizes the Orton philosophy as follows: specific language disability has also been termed specific reading disability, congenital dyslexia, congenital word blindness, etc., and is one of the many causes of scholastic failure. When present, it is a handicap to a pupil, even though failure may not result. Its basic cause, though still unknown, would seem to be a neurological disorder of a kind which does not lend itself easily to treatment, such as those from intellectual and sensory deficits and from learning problems primarily due to emotional disturbances.

The Program for Corrective Reading Instruction

Corrective instruction is the responsibility of all teachers in their daily class activities. In some school systems, as in Baltimore County, a special reading teacher also provides systematic instruction in small groups. If a school system is fortunate enough to have special teachers to work with the corrective cases, one of the three following approaches is usually taken.

One type of corrective instruction is demonstrated by the St. Louis public schools. Pupils are assigned to the clinics two or three (occasionally four or five) times a week for forty-five to sixty-minute instructional periods, depending upon individual needs. Pupils pay their own carfare to and from the clinic. Most pupils are given individual instruction when they first enter the clinic, but they may work in very small groups after they become independent in word perception skills. Pupils are usually given clinic instruction until they can perform independently with books in their home classrooms.

In the second type of corrective program the pupil does not travel to a special clinic but is transferred from his own school to the nearest school having a reading center. There he is placed in a classroom on his grade level for all work but reading. For one period a day he goes to the reading center for instruction in reading at his instructional level. The Baltimore City public schools offer this type of service.

In a third type of program, each school is staffed by a corrective teacher. The teacher is an experienced classroom teacher who has had additional training in reading and works with these retarded readers in small groups at their proper instructional level without worrying about the course of study. The students come out of their regular classroom and meet with the reading teacher for half an hour to an hour a day, three to five times a week. Usually there are five main planks in this corrective program: parent education, teacher education, individual small group instruction, individual small group testing, and research. The corrective reading teacher takes part in these five areas, depending upon the needs of the local school. Modifications of this type of program are presently being conducted in such systems as Baltimore County and Prince Georges County, Maryland; the Philadelphia and Mt. Lebanon, Pennsylvania, public schools; and the public schools of Sarasota, Florida.

Corrective reading in the Baltimore County schools is designed to supplement and support the basal reading program rather than to take the place of it. The basic purpose of this program is to give additional help to those pupils whose reading achievement is not commensurate with their ability. Corrective reading emphasizes the sequential development of word attack skills and comprehension skills. These are the same goals in the basal or developmental reading program carried on by the classroom teacher. The differences in the two programs lie in the use of special techniques and materials that concentrate on a particular reading deficiency until the pupil develops a reasonable degree of mastery over it. The goal of the corrective reading teacher is to increase the pupil's competence to the point where he can function successfully in the usual reading situation.

The operation of the corrective reading program is explained in the answers to the following questions:

Q. 1: Who is a retarded reader?

A.: A child whose level of performance is not commensurate with his general capacity as indicated by other achievements. Performance may be evaluated by teacher judgment or by tests, including (1) Lee-Clark Reading Readiness Test; (2) Iowa Tests of Basic Skills; (3) Gates Basic Reading Tests; and (4) informal teacher-made tests.

Mental capacity may be estimated by teacher judgment, though preferably measured by standardized tests such as (1) SRA (Science Research Associates) Primary Mental Abilities Test (PMA); (2) California Test of Mental Maturity (CTMM); (3) Revised Stanford-Binet Intelligence Scale; (4) Pintner-Cunningham Primary Test; and (5) Wechsler Intelligence Scale for Children (WISC).

Q. 2: What is meant by instructional reading level?

A.: The highest reading level at which the child (a) recognizes ninety-five out of one hundred running words, i.e., needs help with no more than one out of twenty running words; and (b) understands most of the ideas of a story in a basal reader when he is reading silently, reading orally, or listening to a selection being read aloud.

Q. 3: Who is eligible for admission to the corrective reading program?

A.: Children reading below grade level who can profit most as determined by the classroom teacher, principal and coordinator. Preference should be given to pupils in the primary grades.

Q. 4: What are the objectives of the corrective reading program?

A.: To identify the needs of retarded readers; to meet these needs in order that the pupil may function effectively in the classroom reading program; and to stimulate a desire to read.

Q. 5: What is emphasized in the corrective reading program?
A.: Improvement of comprehension skills; improvement of word attack skills; and improvement of oral reading skills.

Q. 6: What materials are used in the corrective reading program?
A.: A Baltimore County curriculum guide, entitled *A Guide for the Reading Program*, with sections on comprehension, word attack, and oral reading skills; basal readers and other readers assigned to the school as part of the regular curriculum; and supplementary commercially published material furnished by the corrective reading office.

Q. 7: What factors must be considered in planning a schedule for corrective reading classes?
A.: Children in the corrective reading program should be scheduled for corrective reading classes in addition to reading classes in the regular classroom. Class size should be six to eight pupils; there should be eight thirty-minute teaching periods daily. The remainder of the school day should be utilized by the corrective reading teacher for performing his other responsibilities such as parent conferences, individual testing, or other activities (see Question 8, below). Particular situations may require modifications of the above.

Q. 8: What are the major responsibilities of the corrective reading teacher?
A.: (1) To administer diagnostic tests to pupils who have been referred for admission to the corrective reading program; (2) to consult with the classroom teacher, principal, and coordinator to determine the children to be admitted to special reading classes; (3) to work toward all of the objectives of the corrective reading program (see question 4); (4) to keep appropriate records; (5) to evaluate continually the progress of each pupil who is in the corrective reading program; (6) to consult with the classroom teacher to determine the marking of the report card for each child in the corrective reading class (instead of a mark in reading on the report card, the code *CR* [Corrective Reading] should be recorded, and in the section entitled "Achievement in Relation to Grade Standards," the check should always indicate below-average achievement in reading), while a mimeographed form indicating the reading progress of the child is to be completed by the corrective reading teacher and the classroom teacher and signed by the principal; (7) to cooperate with the classroom teacher in scheduled parent con-

ferences; (8) to consult with the classroom teacher, principal, and coordinator to determine when children are to be discharged from the special reading classes; and (9) to demonstrate for classroom teachers developmental reading techniques (consistent with those in *A Guide for the Reading Program*).

Q. 9: How do we determine when pupils should be discharged from the program?

A.: When the child reads within one-half level of his grade placement. If, within a two-year period, the child has not progressed to within 50 per cent of the level of his grade, a conference should be held by the following personnel to evaluate and make further recommendations: classroom teacher, corrective reading teacher, coordinator, and principal.

The Program for Remedial Reading Instruction

A few years ago, psychologists in Baltimore County were disturbed by the fact that many of our most severely retarded readers apparently could not benefit from the developmental or corrective programs in the local schools. At that time, a group of educators, including psychologists, assistant superintendents, general supervisors, and reading teachers, came together and formed a committee to develop a third type of special reading program.

This remedial reading program is a clinic-type program designed for the retarded reader with a slightly below average, average, or superior intelligence who cannot profit from the pedagogical techniques that are used in the regular developmental or corrective programs.

Basic Criteria Which Are Observed in Selecting Pupils for the Program. The following criteria and procedures have been developed. Who should be referred? First, students who have average, above average, or slightly below average intelligence and who exhibit difficulty with some or many phases of reading. These children have an average or a high capacity level but a low achievement level. In other words, if orally read to, they are able to comprehend and answer questions about information beyond the level at which they themselves read independently with understanding. Second, students who seem to be intelligent enough to read at a much higher level than they do, even though their intelligence tests scores are significantly below average.

This latter is a very important point. The present author made a study of the relationship between the California Test of Mental Maturity and the WISC for retarded readers. It was found that low scores obtained by children who have reading difficulties frequently reflect their degree of reading retardation rather than their basic capacity to learn. An examination of a sample of seventy clinically referred pupils diagnosed as remedial readers revealed a mean IQ score of 79 when measured by the CTMM. The same sample of pupils yielded a mean IQ of 95 when measured by the WISC, indicating a mean IQ difference of 16 points. There is no question that when group intelligence tests are used the IQs of children who have severe reading disabilities present an erroneous picture of the learning capacity of these children.

Who should not be referred? The mentally retarded or very slow-to-learn students who are reading as well as such students can be expected to read should not be included. Students with average or superior intelligence who are not reading quite so well as they might, but whose difference in achievement and capacity is not significant enough to require outside help, should not be referred, nor should students who have learning problems other than reading, or students who are disciplinary problems because of factors other than deficiencies in reading.

Procedures in Identifying and Selecting Pupils. Any member of the professional staff who feels that a specific pupil needs special reading help should consult the teacher responsible for instruction in the developmental reading program.

In the elementary schools, in the initial screening, the teacher responsible for the developmental reading instruction should make the referral to the principal. In the secondary schools, the referrals should be made to the principal or other authorized person. In some secondary schools the referrals are made directly to the reading teacher. After this initial screening, the student is sent to the corrective reading teacher, who determines the type and nature of the reading disability.

The corrective reading teacher meets with the teacher who referred the pupil to discuss recommendations for placement. If the pupil is not sufficiently retarded for small-group instruction, the corrective teacher discusses with the classroom teacher how to meet the needs of the pupil in the developmental program. However, if the pupil is found to be in need of corrective aid, the reading teacher plans an appropriate program. If the corrective teacher feels that the pupil is a candidate for the remedial reading program, he makes a referral to the remedial reading diagnostician.

The reading diagnostician determines the needs of the pupil and with the assistance of the psychologist and visiting teacher makes one of the following recommendations: the pupil may be assigned to the

Remedial Clinic, where an individual program will be planned by the remedial clinician; if the pupil is not found to be in need of remedial assistance, he will be returned to either the corrective or developmental program; or if it is found that the pupil's problem is not primarily one of reading, he should be referred to the proper service.

When it is determined that a child should be placed in the remedial reading program, the visiting teacher should contact his parents to explain the nature of this service and to secure permission for placement. It must be understood that parents are responsible for transporting the pupil to and from the clinic for instruction. Clinic instruction usually continues for at least a year, often longer. A pupil should be discharged from the remedial clinic when the reading specialist feels that the pupil is ready to progress in either the corrective or the developmental program.

To determine the actual factors contributing to the inability to achieve in reading and to plan an adequate therapeutic program requires thorough diagnosis of the case. Diagnostic procedure will be described here briefly.

Capacity tests. The general intelligence level is the yardstick against which adequacy of achievement is measured. Therefore, an individual test of mental capacity is necessary. In order to detect the degree to which verbal functioning is depressed, the test should allow for comparison of ability to handle verbal materials. Markedly uneven achievement on varying types of items within the test may be indicative of problems of a neurological or emotional nature. This uneven performance may be revealed in failure on easy items coupled with success on difficult items, or in a generally disparate performance on separate subtests.

The individual intelligence test, such as the Wechsler or the Binet, should be given, rather than a standardized paper-pencil test which is dependent on reading ability. It should be pointed out that some pupils might have difficulty in concentrating or performing on the sections of the test which are similar to academic situations. For this reason, the performance score might be a higher and more accurate indication of true potential than the verbal score.

Altus (1956), Kallos, Grabow, and Guarino (1961), and others indicate that an analysis of the individual WISC pattern may have diagnostic value for predicting reading disability. Many researchers feel that a statistically low coding and arithmetic subtest score correlates highly with severe reading disabilities. The writer's experience with over four hundred clinically referred remedial readers seems to support this hypothesis.

Achievement tests. For both measurement of the present status and recommendation for remedial measures, a complete picture of current achievement is necessary. Ability to recognize words presented in isolation and in context, to think adequately with the stimulation of the materials to be read, and to interpret the material through oral reading should be appraised. Since reading is a kindred process to listening, speaking, and writing, performance in these areas must also be measured. Comparison of achievement in reading with that in manipulation of numbers also is instructive.

Two informal measures that have particular diagnostic value are the Word Recognition Test and the Informal Reading Inventory. The Word Recognition Test is made up of word lists consisting of fifteen to twenty-five words at each level—pre-primer through tenth grade. The words themselves are taken from word counts of books commonly used in grades one through ten.

The test is designed to determine the student's word recognition ability at various grade levels and to diagnose specific word perception needs. The test has two parts, the flash section, which enables one to find the sight vocabulary of the pupil, and the untimed section, which reveals the pupil's ability to employ word attack skills. In administering the test, each word is presented for approximately one second. If the word is pronounced correctly, the teacher continues down the list. If a word is mispronounced, it is exposed again for as long as the student may require. This untimed exposure will reveal his word attack skills. Comprehension cannot be tested by this device. In true remedial cases, children will probably have considerable difficulty with this test; some corrective cases may also have difficulty, though in the corrective cases there may be only comprehension problems.

The Informal Reading Inventory is the principal instrument for discovering the specific reading needs of the reader. It consists of two selections from each graded basal reader—pre-primer through grade nine. Usually, the Informal Inventory is started one grade below the level at which the first error is made on the Word Recognition flash test. In administering this test, the teacher first has the student set up a purpose for reading a particular selection. The student then reads orally and the teacher asks questions (factual, vocabulary, and critical) concerning the material. These steps are then repeated as the student reads silently. As a result, the teacher gets information about the student's reading levels and his needs.

Associative learning tests. Special capacities such as associative learning ability and memory span have already been pointed out as important. Tests which will reveal ability in these areas should be employed. These tests measure the span for various types of materials, verbal and nonverbal, presented both visually and orally, as well as the ability to associate meaning with word-like and non-word-like figures with varying modes of presentation. Even the effect of the introduction of kinesthetic clues on the associative or retentive process may be measured.

Emotional status evaluation. Projective tests and clinical observation offer the best possibilities for evaluation of the emotional status of the individual and its part in the reading disability. Factors which may be basic to the maladjustment are frequently revealed. In addition, the degree of disturbance of intellectual functioning can be appraised through the individual's responses. Need for therapeutic measures directed toward the solution of basic emotional problems can be judged in terms of the results. In some cases, the true extent of the emotional involvement may not be clear until the child is observed over a period of time in a learning situation with his peers.

Summary of diagnostic test findings. Some of the obvious findings that help to diagnose a remedial retarded reader are as follows: (1) low frustration level in word recognition abilities, with a sight vocabulary inadequate at a low level and very few word-analysis skills evident at any level; (2) no improvement in oral re-reading; (3) in the capacity measures, nonverbal test scores higher than verbal test scores, as well as limited performance in subtests involving memory association, organization, and persistence; and (4) in the associative learning tests visual-auditory abilities higher than visual-visual abilities and geometric superior to word-like pattern learning.

Generally speaking, developmental and mild corrective cases can learn to read mainly through visual and auditory stimulation. Severe corrective and remedial cases need kinesthetic and tactile stimulation as well. Many factors may be involved in the need for these specialized techniques. Although clinical diagnosis is necessary for full understanding of the cases and planning of their remedial programs, the classroom teacher has responsibilities for the detection of possible cases of this type.

Organization of the Remedial Reading Program. Each clinic is staffed by a remedial clinician, a consulting psychologist, and a visiting teacher. Twenty remedial retarded readers are serviced by each clinic program. The program is so geared that one reading center covers a wide area, and only a small percentage of the candidates can be accepted. (The remedial group is variously estimated to comprise from 1 to 9 per cent of the school population.) If the child is accepted, the parents are notified of their responsibilities to the program. They must provide transportation to the reading clinic each day and attend P.T.A. (Parent-Teacher Association) and Parent Life Discussion Group meetings. The elementary school child reports to the building at 9 each morning and is picked up at 11:40 A.M. to be returned to the regular school for the afternoon session. The parent of the secondary school child must also provide transportation. The student should be picked up at his regular school each day and transported to the clinic by 12:45 P.M. Classes are dismissed at 3:30 P.M., and parents make arrangements to call for their child at that time.

Seven P.T.A. meetings are scheduled during the school year. Three meetings are conducted by the reading clinician, who conducts a highly structured P.T.A. meeting. The other four meetings are headed by a visiting teacher trained in family life discussions. The parents have an opportunity to discuss some of the things, either old or new, that have been bothering them. Here the parents see that they are not alone: other parents have similar problems; other children share personality changes. In many cases parents can help each other to solve some of these pressing issues. The whole program is conducted in a nondirective, relaxed fashion and acts as a type of catharsis. The psychologist and reading clinician are there as observers, and only join in as consultants when requested by the parents. The group discusses such practical problems as "How do I make my child do his homework?" and "How should I handle my child now that he is so aggressive?" The philosophy of the family life meetings is based on the assumption that all children who need the remedial reading program are emotionally disturbed to some degree. Therefore, it is felt that therapy for the children and discussion groups for the parents should be an integral part of the program. The aim is to develop and increase parental understanding of the emotional growth and emotional needs of the children.

Instructional Procedures in the Remedial Reading Program. As stated above, elementary school students attend in the morning, secondary school students in the afternoon. Whenever possible, the programs are so structured in the local school that the youngsters attend classes and participate in activities requiring limited reading and writing skills. This, of course, is much easier to do in the secondary program. However, it has been found in the fourth, fifth, and sixth grades, where reading is conducted in the morning, that the pupils can meet success in the afternoon in some subjects that do not bear directly on the reading area of the language arts program. Ideally, the reading specialist will work with about seven to ten youngsters in both the morning and the afternoon session. Grouping so far as instruction is concerned is very fluid. It varies with the immediate needs of the individual. The tracing or VAKT (Visual, Auditory, Kinesthetic, Tactile) techniques are used instead of the VA alone, as used in the developmental and corrective programs.

Three pedagogical techniques are considered in the remediation of these severely retarded readers: the basal and the language experience approach, using V and A; the Fernald approach, using VAKT in analytical breakdown; and the Gillingham approach, using VAKT in a synthesis attack. It is desirable for the selection of the particular pedagogical procedure not to depend on the training of the clinician and the bias of the diagnostic center. It is not desirable to expose every remedial pupil to the same technique. Educators embrace the philosophy of individual differences, but all too often accept the "one right way" of teaching reading to all retarded readers. Pupils and teachers alike are forced to adjust to the one procedure instead of the teacher and the technique adjusting to the needs of the child. Too often teachers have followed one policy blindly because some authority has said, "This is the way." Experience has demonstrated the fact that there is no magic panacea for all children. Severely retarded readers have one consistent syndrome, besides their retardation, and that is inconsistency. The clinician must select the appropriate technique through diagnostic teaching and must use all sensory pathways to reinforce the weak memory patterns. The method or combination of methods that helps the child is the right method.

The program should be so geared that the youngsters have a wide variety of high-interest, low-reading-level material, supplemented by such kits and gadgets as tape recorders, filmstrips, slide projectors, hand and eye coordinators, primer typewriters, and SRA (Science Research Associates) material.

During the day, a certain number of youngsters will visit the psychologist for individual and group therapy. There is no apparent direct relationship between the psychologist and the reading teacher. Neither ever invades the other's domain. The children soon realize that they cannot play one against the other. They soon realize that there is no stigma in being in the program: everyone in the clinic has a reading problem: everyone has an opportunity to meet success at his proper instructional level.

The afternoon program is structured in almost the same way. However, these youngsters in the afternoon program, being somewhat more mature, have individual therapy sessions instead of the group therapy given the elementary pupils. They also work more independently than the morning youngsters.

The actual value of therapy with remedial assistance is still under question. Research findings are quite controversial and varied. Arthur (1940) gave a number of examples of children with severe reading problems who were helped with psychiatric treatment, which enabled them to improve their reading levels. Axline (1947) and Lecky (1945) have postulated that poor reading may result from inconsistencies in the attitudinal system of a child, or from difficulty in resolving a conflict between a concept of self as a poor reader and a concept of self as a good reader. A study by Bills (1950), using nondirective play therapy with a group of retarded readers, suggests that significant gains in reading may be accomplished by therapy alone. In extensive studies conducted in Baltimore County, an attempt has been made to evaluate the effectiveness of remedial reading with psychotherapy in the public school system. Unfortunately, it has been impossible effectively to control the variables for large groups of children and psychologists. The objective evidence at this time is still inconclusive. Nevertheless, many teachers are of the opinion that some therapy or assistance must be given to all severely retarded readers.

The writer believes that many retarded readers, particularly secondary pupils, have such a low self-value system, such a negative level of aspiration, and such a poor sense of self-worth so far as academic achievement is concerned that they cannot succeed in school. Even if we are successful in teaching them their basic elementary reading skills, their value system is so warped they cannot utilize or maintain these skills. To test this hypothesis, a group of 84 functional slow-learners who had been placed in seventh grade junior high school classes for children with "low" (below 90 on a group IQ test) capacity and achievement (below third-grade reading level) were studied. Parents and former elementary teachers were also consulted. The 252 people involved were asked to check the point on the continuum of a rating scale at which they felt the pupil was located as far as his or her capacity to achieve in school was concerned. The scale is reproduced below.

Capacity Evaluation Scale

Mentally Defective	Borderline	Dull	Average	Bright Normal	Superior	Very Superior

The results are summarized in Table 1.

Table 1. Percentage distribution of capacity evaluation according to WISC IQs and ratings by parents, self, and teachers

	WISC			Rating		
Intelligence Classification	Verbal Scale	Performance Scale	Full Scale	Parent	Self	Teacher
Mentally Defective	0	4	4	4	14	32
Borderline	29	4	7	25	4	24
Dull	46	14	50	57	68	37
Average	25	54	32	14	14	7
Bright Normal	0	10	7	0	0	0
Superior	0	14	0	0	0	0
Very Superior	0	0	0	0	0	0

The findings which pertain to capacity evaluation are as follows: over 78 per cent of the retarded readers had either a verbal or performance Wechsler IQ that indicated normal potential; 39 per cent of the full-scale IQs indicate average or better ability; only 7 per cent of the pupils had average ability, according to the estimates of the elementary school teachers; and only 14 per cent of the pupils had average ability, according to the self-ratings of both children and parents.

The reading teachers in the Baltimore program have regular conferences, either by telephone, letter, or in person, with the classroom teacher to integrate the remedial and the general classroom programs. The reading teachers also meet with the psychologists to discuss how the youngsters are progressing. Once a month the entire staff meets in an evaluation conference. Whenever the student is academically and psychologically prepared, he is returned to the corrective or the developmental program. If he is not meeting with any success, he may be returned to the local school for further specialty referral, study, and recommendations.

Financing of the Remedial Reading Program. A remedial clinic program, with its small class size, use of trained reading specialists, and supplementary services of psychologists and visiting teachers, is, of course, very expensive. Very few school systems can afford to finance such a program with local funds. Fortunately, several state departments of education have passed special regulations for the handicapped that afford some financial assistance to the local school systems. In May, 1959, the Maryland State Department of Education adopted a code of "Standards, Rules and Regulations governing the Provision of Special Programs for Handicapped Children of School Age Who Are Residents of Maryland."

Section Four of the code offers financial aid for children with varying types of specific learning disorders, as follows:

1. The local department of education may provide a special program within the public system for any child whose specific learning disorder results in such impairment or dysfunction of the intellectual process that he cannot benefit from the instructional program usually found appropriate for most children. Specific learning disorders include, for example, problems in reception, formulation, and expression of language; problems in visual perception and integration; and specific reading disability, such as strephosymbolia.
2. Wherever seven of these children who have similar learning disorders can be found, a special class may be formed and a qualified teacher may be employed.

Conclusions

A great many studies have been made and books written about the problem of the seriously retarded reader. Unfortunately, a survey of the literature indicates that there is considerable lack of agreement among the interested professionals as to etiology and appropriate pedagogical procedures. However, there appears to be general agreement that 10 to 15 per cent of school children are seriously retarded in reading. Even if this figure is slightly exaggerated, the number of handicapped children in our growing school population is reaching an alarming figure.

This writer does not believe that the schools will ever solve or even contain this serious problem by the addition of large numbers of reading specialists or diagnostic clinics. This is not to say that skilled reading clinicians are not helpful to a total reading program. Baltimore County's commitment of over seventy special teachers to the corrective-remedial programs is a denial of this statement. However, as the educational staff becomes more sophisticated in identifying children with learning disabilities, waiting lists grow in size and the reading personnel are unable to keep pace with the overwhelming demands for their services. Corrective reading classes scheduled outside the regular classroom are often too large to provide effective individual remediation. Also, heavy tutorial loads cause some children to be scheduled for reading during times when classroom activities are the most interesting. Overloaded remedial classes prevent the use of reading specialists as effective resource personnel in helping teachers develop the necessary techniques and attitudes and in assisting in the planning of effective programs for children with special reading problems.

The answer lies in developing a strong preventive, developmental, and corrective reading program in the local classroom. If this be true, administrators must make sure that they are providing the regular classroom teacher with every advantage, skill, and opportunity to do his job. Teachers must be assigned classes that are small enough to meet individual differences and techniques, so that the pedagogical procedures may be adjusted to the needs of the child, not the child to the procedures. Of course, this is easier said than done. With our swelling school population, lack of plant space and facilities, and large numbers of inexperienced teachers, the task seems almost insurmountable. If school authorities recognize the need for small classes, especially in the primary grades, they may be able to alleviate the problem with annexes and/or trailers.

The problem of inadequately trained teachers is most pressing because it involves a serious difference of opinion among educators in teacher-training institutions. The argument about whether to emphasize subject matter courses or professional techniques courses has been going on for some time. The subject matter proponents appear to be in the ascendancy. Local universities offer a very minimal training in the approaches to the teaching of reading. In fact, a secondary school teacher of English or language arts can be graduated from most teacher-training schools in the country without ever having had a course in the teaching of reading. The average primary school teacher may be required to take one course in the teaching of reading or language arts. If educators cannot change the requirements and philosophies of the teacher-training institutions, then the local school systems must provide an ongoing program of in-service education and curriculum development. In other words, schools will have to teach not only children but also teachers.

PART III

Illustrative Examples

CHAPTER 16

CASE 1: SPACE-FORM DEFICIT

JOHN MONEY

CASE REPORT

Name and Number:	Malcolm ________. 105 67 39
Date of Birth:	August 17, 1952
Date First Seen:	March 8, 1963
Chronological Age:	10 yr. 7 mo.
Follow-up:	Continuous

Introduction

This case, reported in extensive detail, represents an unusually complete, though still insufficient, workup, combining the findings of several specialists, with follow-up for both statural growth and reading achievement. It offers an example of how much time must be spent in individual case study if there is to be any hope of elucidating the baffling problems of the disabled reader. Phenomenologically, there is a basic deficit in space-form and directional-sense perception, and in finger localization, with a related basic deficit in phonemic-graphemic matching.

Reason for Referral

The patient was referred by Dr. Dennis Whitehouse for psychologic evaluation related to a complaint of nervousness and a prolonged history of poor academic achievement and reading retardation.

Medical-Chart Excerpts, 1963–65

In the initial physical examination, the only finding of significance was short stature. The pediatric endocrinologist, Dr. Robert Blizzard, found the bone age and the height age to be two years below the chronological age, without evident signs of glandular disorder. The diagnostic impression was of delayed growth and short stature of the so-called constitutional type. Puberty began slowly in the thirteenth year, with height and bone age still two years in arrears.

There was a lifetime history of spontaneous, rhythmic, side-to-side rocking movements in sleep. They lasted three to five minutes and occurred at intervals of approximately two hours during the night. The school physician once reported that the boy would rock back and forth in his chair when frustrated and that he constantly played with all kinds of objects. He was always hyperkinetic at home. "I've always said he runs all day and rocks all night," the mother said. Nonetheless, no gross signs of neurological anomaly were evinced in any of the physical examinations. An electroencephalogram taken in 1963, however, was read by Dr. Hugo Ruiz thus: "This is a mildly abnormal tracing because of the diffuse, disorganized, slow activity seen during the resting stage."

Dr. Herman K. Goldberg did the ophthalmological examination and found no evidence of ocular disease. A slight degree of astigmatism was considered unimportant, not requiring glasses. Muscle balance was normal, and stereopsis and fusion were excellent.

According to the scanty evidence obtained, the family psychodynamics did not appear to be of contributory significance, except that the father could not relate closely to people, including his own children, though he was close to his wife. The marriage was one of mixed religious background, Jewish (father) and Protestant, entailing complex intrafamilial adjustments. The domestic climate was not turbulent. At home, the boy was generally easy to get along with. His bickering with his younger sister occasionally caused an emotional crisis. He compared himself adversely with this sister half his age.

Schooling

The boy entered first grade a month after his sixth birthday. He repeated the first grade. He had corrective reading lessons for half an hour four days a week in second through fifth grades. All his grades were poor, not only those in reading. His self-opinion was low, but there were no gross problems of misbehavior. He believed himself stupid and was embarrassed at not being able to read and spell. He was placed in an extramural remedial reading program, two hours once a week, for a semester. In the sixth grade, he spent an hour and a half of each school day in a remedial reading clinic (three pupils per teacher) and has continued there until the present (he is now in seventh grade). He still manifests great difficulty with learning and is ranked at about third-grade level in both reading and arithmetic achievement at the age of thirteen.

Psychologic Tests and Procedures,[1] *First Series, March 8, 1963: Dr. Ernesto Pollitt and Dr. John Money*

Wechsler Intelligence Scale for Children
Human Figure Drawing (Draw-A-Person)
Bender Visual-Motor Gestalt Test
Benton Visual Retention Test
Auditory Attention Span for Related Syllables
Two-Finger Discrimination
Right-Left Discrimination
Road-map Test
Informal Graded Dictation and Spelling
Informal Graded Reading
Interview with the Mother
Interview with the Patient

Wechsler Intelligence Scale for Children

IQ Scores:

Verbal	106	(101, prorated for Digit Span)
Nonverbal	86	
Full Scale	96	(93, prorated for Digit Span)

Scaled Subtest Scores:

Verbal		Nonverbal	
Information	13	Picture Completion	9
Comprehension	11	Picture Arrangement	9
Arithmetic	9	Block Design	6
Similarities	12	Object Assembly	6
Vocabulary	10	Coding	10
Digit Span	6		

The verbal IQ of 101 and the full-scale IQ of 93 were obtained after the verbal scale was prorated with the optional Digit Span subtest included.

An IQ between 90 and 109 ranks at Wechsler's Average level of

[1] There is a bibliography of tests at the end of this volume.

intelligence classification and places a person between the 25th and 75th percentiles. An IQ between 80 and 89 ranks at the Dull Normal level and places a person between the 9th and 25th percentiles.

There is a significant twenty-point difference between the verbal and nonverbal IQs. With the exception of the low Digit Span score, which brought down the verbal and full-scale IQs after prorating, the range of the verbal subtest scores is not significantly widespread.

In the nonverbal scale the Block Design and Object Assembly subtests, the lowest subtests of the whole protocol, brought down the nonverbal (performance) IQ. Both of these subtests are considered tests for perceptual organization.

On the Block Design subtest, the patient was able to solve only the first three items. These three items are the only ones for which the examiner gives a demonstration. In the subsequent items the boy was completely unable to solve the problems; even though he was allowed to work beyond the time limit, he gave up trying after he proved his inability. In Item 4 he tried to reproduce the stimulus using nine blocks instead of the four required; he said he thought that in order to reproduce the original stimulus he needed nine blocks. In that same item he also tried to place the corner of one block erroneously at an angle with the straight side of another.

In the Object Assembly subtest the patient obtained most of his points following a trial-and-error method of problem solving. There were times when he tried to push one part of the puzzle to another without considering the relationship of the shapes of the parts to the whole. His method of problem solving in the Block Design and Object Assembly subtests and the comments he made, with noticeable anxiety, when he was unable to solve an item suggested a visuospatial impairment that prevented him from organizing visual elements in space. It brought down the performance IQ and with it the full-scale IQ.

Only when the patient met the items requiring visuospatial organization did he show noticeable anxiety. At these times he held his right hand to his head, and tears appeared in his eyes. He said, more than once, "Why can't I do it?" Otherwise, he was interested in the different items of the test, with friendly and cooperative behavior. He then impressed me, the examiner, as a calm boy, easily able to relate with me.

In view of the satisfactory conditions under which this test was taken, it is my impression that the results of today's testing are an accurate representation of the patient's present intellectual functioning.

Human Figure Drawing. The few component elements of the man drawn by the patient show marked lack of proportion (Fig. 1). The nose and the hands are too big in relation to the rest of the body. The head is almost the size of the trunk, and the legs are thin and tiny.

The drawings of children four to five years old show characteristics similar to those of the man that this boy drew. At age ten, it earned a rating low in the first percentile, according to the Goodenough-Harris norms.

In this test the patient showed no signs of lack of motor coordination. Besides his obvious lack of drawing skill for human figures, his drawing apparently indicates an impairment of his ability to recall assimilated perception into meaningful shapes. In the lack of proportion of the

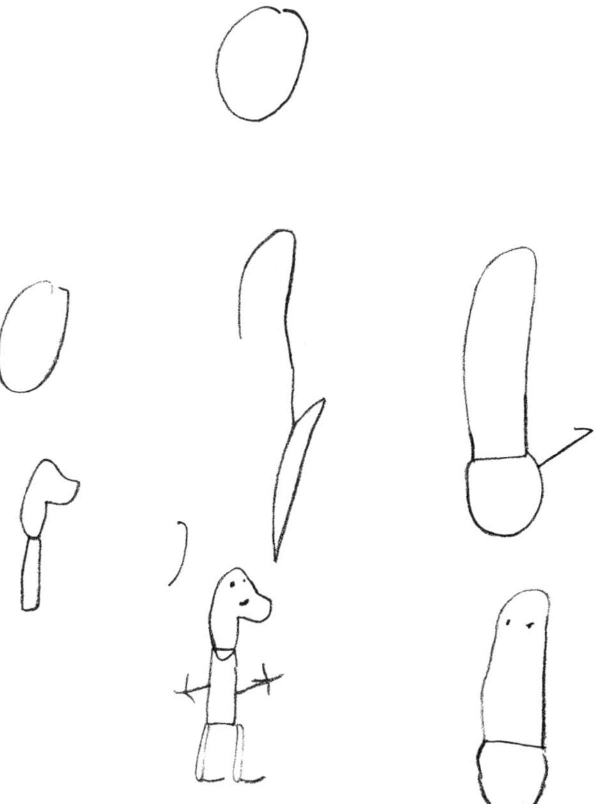

Figure 1. Human figure drawing, Case 1.

figures in the drawings, it also appears that the patient has some impairment of his ability to organize elements in space visually.

Bender Visual-Motor Gestalt Test. In the reproduction of the Bender drawings (Fig. 2) especially in copies A, 7, and 8, there was severe difficulty in reproducing some shapes, maintaining proportions, and also closing boundaries. The patient was aware that his drawings were different from the stimuli, and although he repeatedly tried to do them correctly, finally he had to give up and say he was unable to reproduce the copies as desired. He became very frustrated.

These Bender reproductions confirm the impression of the Human Figure Drawing Test, namely, immaturity of ability and difficulty in ordering visual perceptions in graphic representations.

Benton Visual Retention Test. Forms C and D, Administrations C and D, respectively, were used. On the former, in which the stimulus is not removed, there was a total of six errors (distortions) on four of the ten cards.

On Form D, in which the examinee has to copy by memory different combined geometrical figures, the patient showed major and significant difficulties. He was unable to do eight out of the ten cards because he could not remember the shapes of the stimuli. On card six he started to cry and, with an expression of severe frustration, said, "Why, why can't I do these?" There were thirteen errors—eight distortions and five omissions.

The inference possible from the test results is that the patient has a specific impairment of his visual memory for organized and combined shapes.

Auditory Attention Span for Related Syllables. In this informal test the examinee is asked to repeat in the same order different sentences that add one more word from sentence to sentence. The patient was able to repeat, without mistakes, sentences that had nineteen words. With more than nineteen words, he started to make errors such as omissions, replacements, or changes in order.

The test results were satisfactory. His auditory memory and attention span were quite adequate. The results of this test differ from the Digit Span subtest of the Wechsler, where the patient obtained a low score. The Digit Span subtest supposedly tests attention span and auditory memory, but without coherence of meaning, as in sentence or phrase repetition.

Two-Finger Discrimination. The patient was able to discriminate properly which pairs of fingers had been stimulated on his hand.

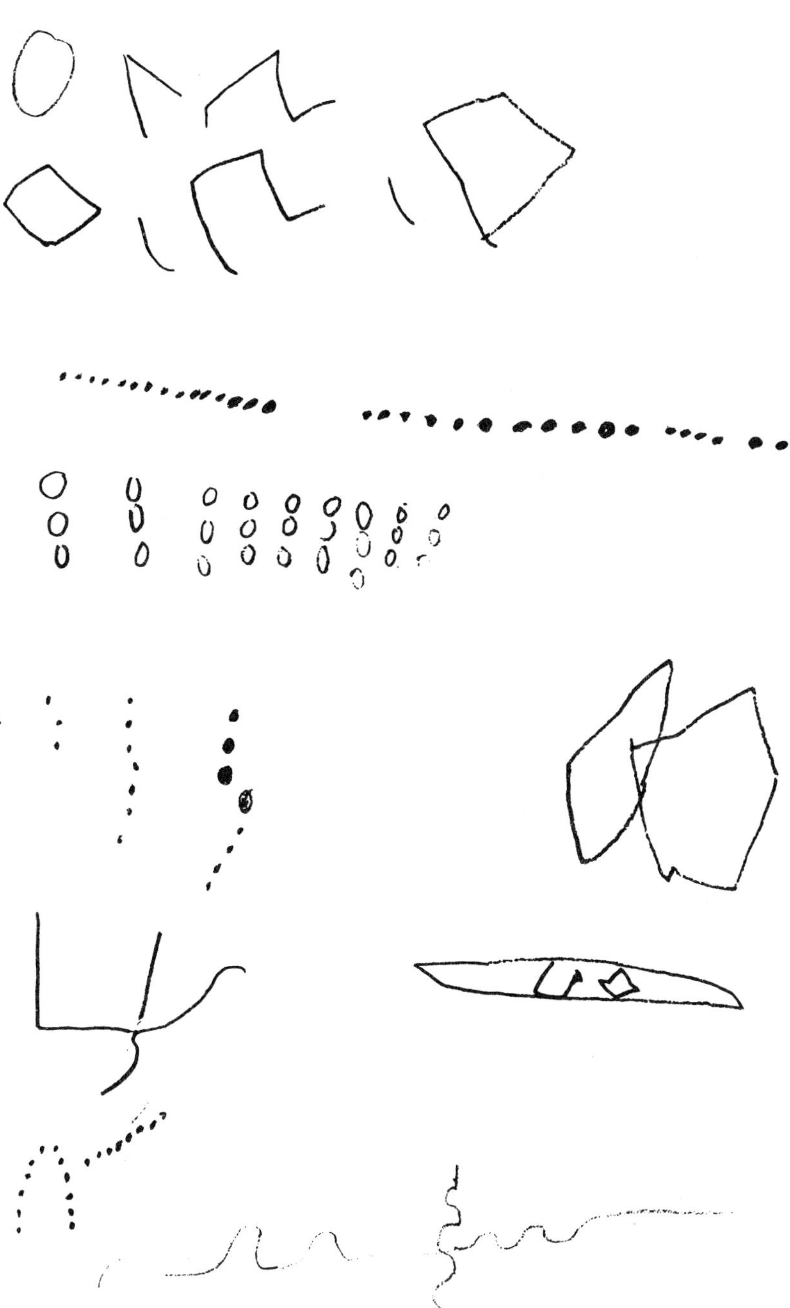

Figure 2. Bender design reproductions, Case 1.

Right-Left Discrimination. The patient made no errors in discriminating his right from his left limbs. A problem appeared when he was asked to point to right and left organs on the examiner's body when I was standing in front of him; here he made some mistakes. When I explained to him, however, how to discriminate right from left in another person's body, he no longer made mistakes.

Informal Graded Dictation and Spelling. Without errors and difficulty, the patient wrote and recognized the letters of the alphabet. On the dictated sentences and words given him, he made many mistakes unexpected in a ten-year-old boy. Even though the boy is in the fourth grade, he misspelled words that belong to the second- and third-grade level.

Some of the errors the patient made could be considered essentially phonetic. For example, he spelled **kee** instead of **key**, and **deer** instead of **dear**. The boy has had three years of phonic instruction in remedial reading. His spelling errors indicate that he has some grasp of how to translate auditory into visual symbols but also show that he is unable to cope with the arbitrary nature of English even at its phonetic best. He cannot recall what a word looks like. Thus, for example, his version of the word **remember** was phonetically half correct but graphemically totally wrong: **reymyny**.

Informal Graded Reading. In the informal reading test, the patient read without mistakes exercises of the second-grade level. Exercises from the third-grade level, however, affected the boy's reading speed, and he started to make significant mistakes. He made reading errors that are often seen in children considered retarded readers. For example, he changed the word: **as**, for **where**; **there**, for **then**; and **did**, for **dad**. When I asked him to spell and pronounce syllable by syllable a word that he was initially unable to read, he was sometimes able to assemble the sounds satisfactorily, sometimes not. Thus, he had some word-analysis skills.

Interview with the Mother. The patient's mother was an attractive, friendly woman in her thirties. She was able to give me a clear statement of her son's reading problem. Malcolm, she said, is a boy who is now in the fourth grade but not in reading ability. Although he has had corrective reading for the past three years, he has been a retarded reader since the very beginning of his school life.

The mother reported her son had been clumsy until he was about six years old. For example, he could scarcely throw a basketball. He avoided games in which he had to use his hands and seldom used the chalk and blackboard that he had available at home. She reported that Malcolm was in the third grade before he was able to handle his pencil correctly.

Interview with the Patient. Malcolm was a cooperative, friendly child, who with patience and perseverance took the different psychologic tests administered him. It is unusual to find a ten-year-old boy who will work for about five hours, with only a one-hour break, without making any complaints.

The patient was a short fellow for his age but gave the impression of an older boy because of his fancy teenage hair style. Generally, his behavior in the office was calm and controlled, and only when he met some specific problems that he was completely unable to solve did he show intense feelings of frustration. Twice he cried and, with expressions of anxiety, uncombed his hair with his right hand. When he was encouraged, however, he came back under control in a short period of time.

Malcolm told me that his reading problem was difficult to explain. He said that he just feels unable to read, and that it is not because of laziness because he tries hard. His difficulty started when he started to read. The patient also reported that sometimes when he is reading he jumps from the line he is reading to another, as if unable to read in a straight line.

Malcolm did not report any untoward facts about his social adaptation. He claimed plenty of friends, though without conviction, and he thinks that his classmates like him. At the present time he is still involved in juvenile kinds of games, and he feels that "girl stuff" is for older boys.

Impression. The patient exhibited today a marked impairment in his reading and spelling skill. In both reading and spelling he made phonetic errors of similar nature. He confused the sound of a word or syllable with that of another word or syllable when he came to read or write it, although he understood and recognized the word when presented orally.

In the psychologic tests administered, the boy presented a specific impairment of ability to memorize visually combined shapes and to organize visual elements in space.

Considering the type of mistakes found in the informal reading and spelling tests and those found in the tests for perceptual organization, it is possible to infer that this boy has an impairment in the process of translating phonetic sounds into visual symbols and visual symbols into phonetic sounds—that is, he has a problem of intersensory transfer, or synesthesia.

Recommendation. Referrals for reading evaluation, eye examination, EEG, and neurological evaluation.

Psychologic Tests and Procedures, Second Series, May 11, 1964: Mr. Duane Alexander and Dr. John Money

Right-Left Discrimination
Finger Differentiation (Kinsbourne and Warrington)
Informal Writing
Spelling (Wide Range Achievement Test)
Reading (Gilmore Oral Reading Test)
Lateral Dominance (Harris)
Room Floor Plan
Draw-A-Person
Mazes (Wechsler Intelligence Scale for Children)
Benton Visual Retention Test
Rorschach Test (Dr. Pollitt; Dr. Money)

Right-Left Discrimination. Malcolm was able to identify right and left parts of his own body perfectly, but when asked by me to do the same as I faced him, he systematically reversed my right and left sides. According to Benton, such behavior is typically found in a seven- or eight-year-old.

The patient made eighteen errors on the thirty-two turns of the Road-map Test. Most of the time he alternated right and left responses, a trait outgrown by seven to nine years old. This performance suggests that the patient has not yet developed a sense of right and left orientation in space, apart from his own body.

Finger Differentiation. The patient was consistently able to tell whether one or two fingers were being touched, but only about half the time was he able to say correctly how many fingers were between those touched. According to Kinsbourne and Warrington, most children can do both tasks accurately by age seven. His performance suggests that he is able to localize fingers but has not yet developed the ability to order them in terms of their spatial arrangement.

Informal Writing. The patient's handwriting is legible, but only with difficulty. He writes rapidly but unevenly. He has only slight difficulty in copying, but when writing dictated words his spelling and his letter formation are poor.

Spelling. The patient made a Grade Equivalent Score of 3.5 on the Wide Range Achievement Spelling Test. Many types of errors were made, with a tendency toward phonetic spelling: for example, **egs**, for **edge**, **sheir**, for **chair**, and **rizit**, for **result**.

Reading. The patient's upper limit of reading ability, estimated by the Gilmore Oral Reading Test, was between the third and fourth grades. Despite his stumbling over words, his comprehension was adequate at this level, and he quickly and accurately answered questions about what he had read. His comprehension level thus seems to be considerably above his reading accuracy level.

Lateral Dominance. Test results indicate that the patient is right-handed, rightfooted, and lefteyed.

Room Floor Plan. The patient got off to a good start on this, but when he turned the paper sideways to do the wall on his left, he reversed the order of all the objects on that side of the room.

Draw-A-Person. With much complaining that he could not draw well, the patient drew a childish little stick figure. Asked if he would draw something different if he drew himself, he said, "Yes," and on the third try produced an armless, form-lacking side view of a boy with prominent buttons. When asked what he could draw well, he said, "cars," and, turning the paper sideways, he drew a primitive picture of a "sports coupe."

WISC Mazes. Malcolm seemed to enjoy doing these mazes but had some difficulty with them, receiving a scaled score of 7 on the test instead of the expected 10.

Benton Visual Retention Test. The attempt to remember and copy these designs seemed to be a very trying and frustrating task for the boy. There were several outbursts of "I just can't do it," "I can't remember," "I can't write," "I can remember it but I can't write it." He drew only three designs correctly on the two forms combined and made more errors than would be expected even from someone whose general intelligence was defective. Most of his errors were of the omission and distortion type. His over-all performance on this test strongly indicates a specific disability in visual memory/visuomotor function.

Impression. Malcolm's development seems to be retarded in many ways, in addition to his short stature. His performance was defective on every test given, and suggests for these tasks the maturity of an eight- to nine-year-old rather than that of a boy of almost twelve.

Comparison of the patient's performance at this time with that of last year shows little progress. His right-left discrimination, finger localization, and handwriting have not improved measurably. His reading level may be a little higher but is still retarded. His spelling still shows the characteristic phonetic errors. His figure in the Draw-A-Person test has advanced to the stage of having a head and legs but is still infantile. His performance on the Benton Visual Retention test shows no improvement, remaining defective.

The patient appeared to be very easily frustrated, particularly when he had to write or draw. The fact that his reading comprehension is well above his reading accuracy further supports the possibility that some specific cognitional difficulty is responsible for this boy's reading problems.

It is my opinion that only if further steps are taken to try to overcome this defect will the patient have a chance to make progress in school beyond his present level. Otherwise, his behavior will probably become troublesome and disorderly.

Recommendation. Placement in remedial reading clinic, if a vacancy can be found within the school system.

Rorschach Test. There were fourteen responses to the ten cards, with good form and a varied use of color and shading. Nine responses were to the whole blot (W) and the others to large details (D). In the W responses, parts were organized into a whole with some skill, but the conceptual content departed from mundane realism in six instances, becoming fanciful. For example, Card 6: "looks like a sphinx—those great big things standing on a mountain and on the mountain there is a stream." The further explanation was added: "You see them in the museum—from far away. That little whiteness [midline] gives you the impression of clear water."

In five of these fanciful responses, and in one other card, the conceptual content touched on the gruesome. In Card 1 a bug was said to be lying on "polluted water." In Card 3 "two twilight zone bugs (the usual little men) are holding up somebody's ribs." The butterfly in Card 5 "has its wings torn up." Card 8 "looks like somebody's insides . . . real bright . . . people's insides are bright." Card 9 "looks like somebody's insides too," and Card 10 "looks like a cut that is bleeding—and germs over it—looks like my cut."

Responses of this type suggest a somewhat untrammeled imagery for a boy of twelve, in which the poetic easily becomes decay and destruction. The relationship of this type of visually evoked imagery to the defects of visual perception and memory observed in other tests is problematical. If there is a causal relation between them, the issue of which is cause and which effect cannot, at the present time, be settled.

Addendum, November 16, 1965: Dr. Money

Wepman Auditory Discrimination Test Form II
Informal Graded Arithmetic
Draw-A-Person
Interview with Patient

Wepman Auditory Discrimination Test Form II. The final score was perfect. To begin with, however, the patient gained apparent error scores as a result of his unusual conceptual transposition of the instruction to identify the pairs of words that sounded either the same or different. He developed two categories of response, "same sound" versus "different sound," and "same word." All his "same word" responses were correct. But his "same sound" responses referred only to the vowel sound, disregarding the different consonants, so that he made thirteen errors. All of these errors were corrected on a second trial, when the items were repeated with the instruction, "Tell me if they are the same word."

The scoring of the first trial gave a false-positive index of hearing loss. The scoring actually indicated an error of conceptual transposition (analogous to the rotation phenomenon) of the type classically associated with dyslexia.

Informal Graded Arithmetic. There were no errors at the first- and second-grade levels. Thereafter, there were two slips of addition, but mostly he was fluent in the + and × tables. The remarkable feature of many of his errors was that they were examples of transposition or rotation of digits and/or procedural steps; for example, in multiplication, the boy said "28" but erroneously wrote down 2 and carried 8. When subtracting 1 from 6, he said, "6 from 1." In long division, he wrote numbers to the right of the row which should have been placed under it. These errors are analogous to the difficulties he showed on other tests (above) in spatial orientation and sequence.

Draw-A-Person. The result was essentially unchanged from last year. The boy was mortified at having to draw, as he was at doing arithmetic, and wanted to avoid it.

Interview with Patient. The boy once again envisaged himself as a total and irredeemable failure if unable to go to college. He was unrealistically unable to allow any alternative future as worth while for himself.

Conclusion

Neither the question of etiology nor of prognosis of the boy's academic disability can be resolved at the present stage of his career. Etiologically, there is some possibility of an unknown familial trait, for he has three cousins in two maternal line families who have been examined for severe academic underachievement. Two of the cousins are siblings successfully under treatment for congenital hypothyroidism. The other is presented in Chapter 19.

There was no evidence of sensory deficit. If neurological deficit or brain damage, even minimal, is present, it must be covert.

There was ample evidence of retarded maturation, for it appears in his retarded statural growth, in his all-round academic development, and in various test performances of cognitional functions and skills. Yet his space-form, or visuoconstructional, disability goes beyond simple immaturity, since the amount of progress upon retest was disappointing. Likewise, the amount of his academic progress is disappointing—to himself as well as others.

A next investigative step, in an attempt to decipher the source of present academic faltering, might be a trial period of psychotherapy, preferably family therapy. In this way it may be possible to alleviate some of the demoralizing effects of cumulative failure, which tends to freeze further learning. Additionally, it may disclose new clues as to the nature of the basic blockage of academic progress.

The possibility of further experimentation in teaching technique might be considered. The boy has already tried using his own tape recorder at home in order to maximize the auditory input of material to be learned. He soon got discouraged with his slow progress and lost interest.

Phenomenologically, this boy's learning problem seems to be related specifically to space-form (visuoconstructional) perceptual disability, to a disability in right-left orientation in space, and to a disability of body sense, namely, in finger localization. It includes a problem of keeping symbols properly positioned instead of being rotated and transposed. It includes also failure to recognize a visual representation (grapheme) as being the correct rendition of a phoneme in a given word, even though the boy has some skill in matching phonemes and graphemes.

The case is complicated and made all the more confusing by inconsistencies in the pattern of pubertal maturation and statural immaturity, and by a pattern of general psychologic growth characterized not only by immaturity but also by a suggestion of regressive deterioration.

CHAPTER 17

CASE 2: DIRECTIONAL ROTATION AND POOR FINGER LOCALIZATION

JOHN MONEY

CASE REPORT

Name and Number:	Gordon _______. 102 80 90
Date of Birth:	September 24, 1952
Date First Seen:	April 17, 1962
Chronological Age:	9 yr. 7 mo.
Follow-up:	Yearly

Introduction

It is a byword of contemporary psychiatry, and of much of medicine also, that one treats not a symptom but the whole patient who manifests that symptom. In the patient as a whole person, one may discover much to augment or explain one's understanding of the symptom. Beyond the patient, one finds another, larger entity to which the symptom belongs, namely, the social entity of family and/or community. It is a basic premise of public health that in this entity, also, one may discover much of explanatory value. This present case report illustrates the complementarity of relationship between the patient's symptom and the events of his home life. It also illustrates the inordinate amount of time and attention that must be expended on some disabled readers in order to identify the problem and the diagnosis precisely. It is a mistake to think that one can ever make a rapid or abbreviated evaluation of reading disability. There are no shortcuts. It is particularly necessary for one person to take the responsibility of coordinating and evaluating the findings of all the specialty reports. Reading disorder is still so poorly understood that such coordination is essential for the proper identification of its etiology and treatment. In the present instance, problems of directional orientation were uppermost, together with the very severe pathology of the family relationships.

Reason for Referral

The patient was referred by the pediatric neurologist, Dr. John Menkes, to whom he had come for "evaluation of school difficulties." Four months earlier, he had been recognized at school as needing psychologic testing because of an inability to learn to read or remember the sounds of letters. The testing had not yet been done.

Medical-Chart Excerpts

The neurological examination was essentially unremarkable, except for higher mental functions, particularly reading and spelling. It was noted, among other things, that the boy had a history of various allergies. Between two and twelve months of age he had eczema. Since the age of four he had had fairly severe intermittent attacks of asthma. At three he fell, struck his head, and was unconscious for a short period of time. Of two siblings, sisters, one adult and one teenage, the younger was said to have had a mild problem with schooling and to have been slow in reading.

The neurologist's impression was that this boy had three major deficits: a severe dyslexia, severe left-right discrimination problems, and also some difficulty with calculating, especially doing sums mentally. He felt that in other spheres Gordon's intelligence was about average.

Dr. Curtis Marshall read the EEG and said that it exhibited a very small increase in slow activity over what is considered average for his age, though certainly this activity did not consitute a gross abnormality and had no focus. The skull x-ray was read by Dr. Fein as negative. Dr. Herman Goldberg did the ophthalmological examination, and his findings were negative. A sex chromatin test was done and read by Dr. Peter Bowen as chromatin negative (normal for a male), thus indicating no disorder of heredity of the type that can be recognized in an abnormal number of the sex (XY) chromosomes.

Schooling

In April, 1962, at the time of referral, the patient was in the third grade at school but was failing to make adequate progress in reading. His independent reading level was rated by his teacher as pre-primer.

Spelling was equally bad, arithmetic somewhat less so. Handwriting, often untidy, sometimes was of good quality. His second-grade report card showed four marks of D, two marks of C, and a mark of Average for music, art, and physical education.

Following the evaluation at Johns Hopkins, it was difficult to place the boy within his school system. At the start of the 1962–63 school year, he entered a special class for severe learning disabilities. Neither he nor his mother adjusted well to this class, which, he claimed, was for the mentally retarded. His mother attributed a behavior change at home to the school issue. Instead of being calm and agreeable, he became rebellious and destructive. After six months there was a major emotional crisis in which the boy refused to return to his school. Following evaluation by the school psychologist, he was relocated with another specific learning disability group and another teacher, to his own and his family's satisfaction.

Meantime, in the six months since January, 1963, he had been enrolled in a Saturday program of remedial reading, two hours a week, which he enjoyed. He developed a good relationship with his instructor, which met with his mother's approval. He continued with weekly remedial reading instruction during the summer. Whatever the gains that may have been made in reading, however, they were not subsequently sustained.

By December, 1963, storm warnings were up again. The boy was still attending the special class. The mother reported the teacher as saying he was fidgety, nervous, and procrastinating in school and was a possible candidate for medication that had benefited other hyperactive children in the classroom. Partly in the expectation that there were other issues involved, I recommended that the medication issue be settled by a psychiatrist experienced in treating minimal brain damage. The appointment was made but not kept.

In the summer of 1964 the boy failed to re-enroll in his summer school remedial reading course, for reasons not well explained. The reading evaluation (see below) done at the end of the summer showed him to be deficient at even the first-grade level. At this time, laboring under a peak load of her own psychiatric pressures, the mother cast around for a general panacea. She considered selling her home and moving the boy to a new school district, but elected instead to remove him from special education and return him to a regular classroom, where he would not be branded as abnormal. At the end of 1964, shortly before this change was effected, the boy's father died suddenly of "a massive brain tumor." On long-distance follow-up in the winter of 1965, the boy, now adolescent, was in junior high school, reportedly being passed ahead on an age basis. He still received special reading instruction and was said to be functioning at around the second-grade level.

First Impression

At age nine and a half, Gordon was an attractive, pleasant schoolboy with a diffident, engaging manner when it came to being tested. Some of his failures were mortifying to him, and he needed reassurance so as not to feel exposed as a freak. Otherwise, he was cooperative and willing, with no evidence of antagonism.

Psychologic Tests and Procedures, First Series, April 17, 1962: Dr. Ernesto Pollitt and Dr. John Money

Wechsler Intelligence Scale for Children
Draw-A-Person
Bender Visual-Motor Gestalt Test
Informal Graded Reading
Informal Graded Transcription
Informal Graded Dictation
Informal Right-Left Discrimination Tests
Forehead Writing
Arithmetic Worksheet

Wechsler Intelligence Scale for Children

IQ Scores:

Verbal	101	(97, prorated for Digit Span)
Nonverbal	106	
Full Scale	104	(101, prorated for Digit Span)

Scaled Subtest Scores:

Verbal		Nonverbal	
Information	11	Picture Completion	12
Comprehension	13	Picture Arrangement	12
Arithmetic	5	Block Design	9
Similarities	9	Object Assembly	12
Vocabulary	13	Coding	9
Digit Span	6		

An IQ between 90 and 109 ranks at the Average level, between the 25th and 75th percentiles. The difference of ten points in favor of the (prorated) nonverbal IQ is significant in view of the patient's known reading difficulty and in view of its inconsistency with the high scaled scores on some of the verbal subtests, particularly Vocabulary. The lowering of the verbal IQ can actually be accounted for by the lowness of the subtests Arithmetic (5) and Digit Span (6), both of them dealing with a numerical or calculation factor. The scores for subtests dealing with visual-perceptual organization are not discrepantly low. On the verbal items, especially, the boy frequently said, "I don't know," then, with further encouragement, gave a good answer. Otherwise, the sequence of successes and failures was reasonably orderly.

The findings appear to be representative of the boy's present intellectual functioning. It is not possible to conjecture whether the IQ has been or will remain constant in a case of this type.

Draw-A-Person. The drawings were primitive and schematic, in the manner of a much younger child. They earn a low rating on the Harris norms, between the 10th and 20th percentiles. The male was drawn first, which is typical for a boy, and then replicated, but in a much smaller version and without the disproportionately long legs of the first drawing. The female was differentiated only by the addition of hair and the superimposition of a skirt onto the basic male figure. Her arms are gesturing, in the position that a traffic officer uses to mean "Stop." All the figures are faceless, including the small boy and girl side by side of a third drawing. Only the first two males drawn have feet.

These drawings are of poor quality relative to the Bender geometrical reproductions. They suggest a special problem with human beings.

Bender Visual-Motor Gestalt Test. The reproductions of these geometric forms were adequate for his age, except in Cards 2 and 3. On Card 2 the small open circles were made as dots, and the row curves vertically to the right instead of remaining horizontal. The dotted chevron of Card 3 was rotated 90° from the vertical to the horizontal position, and could be corrected only on the fourth trial.

Informal Graded Reading. The patient was supposed to read, within forty seconds, and with four mistakes as a maximum, the first-grade selection: "A little boy had a cat. She ran away. She said: 'I want some milk.' "

He read only six words in five minutes and therefore was unable to achieve the first-grade level of reading. After he had been trying for some time to read the words, he showed his anxiety by constantly rubbing his hands together and becoming unsteady in the chair.

In the six words he read the patient made two mistakes. First, he changed one word when he said, **A little dog** instead of **A little boy.** Second, he changed one letter, when he said, **had e cat** instead of **had a cat**. After he made this last mistake, he asked: "Is this an e or an a?"

Naming letters: when the boy was asked to name the following letters, six, in parentheses, were wrong:

b	m	w	c	n	r	t	f	l	q	p	u	d
		(n)			**(b)**			**(d)**	**(d)**	**(q)**		**(b)**

Note the classical rotations made in the substitutions for **q, p,** and **d.**

Informal Graded Transcription. Copying sentence: the boy copied the first-grade exercise of the reading test, running it clockwise around the page (Fig. 1). He could not explain this rotation. The letters were copied as a series of unrelated items.

Informal Graded Dictation. The same sentence as in Exercise 1 was dictated. The child made an almost unintelligible reproduction (Fig. 2). When I dictated, "She ran away," the boy asked, "Away is before or after ran?" Without answering the question, I repeated the dictated words, and again he asked about the position of the word, "away."

In Figure 2, note **doy** instead of **boy**, the mirrored **s**, the transposition of **t** and **a** in **want**, the substitution of **n** for **m** in **some**, the omission of **e** in **little**, the deleted substitution for **away**, and the nonsense spelling of **milk**.

Informal Right-Left Discrimination Tests. When asked to show his right, then his left arm, the boy showed extraordinary difficulty in deciding. The more trials, the more his confusion. He put a marker on his left hand but ten minutes later could not remember whether it was supposed to be his left or right that was marked. There was similar insecurity in choosing the right and left of a person facing him, and in choosing which way to walk when following left and right turn instructions.

Forehead Writing. He was not able to write with ease on a card held to his own forehead—a position which makes mirror writing easy for some people. He read the resultant unrecognizable scrawl as "F.M.Q.," which he then expanded as "F" for "Gordon," "M" for "Wilson," and "Q" for "Edward." He was confused and could offer no further explanation for the garbling of his own initials (here offered only as disguised equivalents) in this way and the gratuitous addition of a third one.

A little boy had: she ran away: she said "I want some milk."

A l

A LITTLE BOY HAD A CAT.

SHE RAN AWAY.

SHE SAID, "I WANT SOME MILK."

Figure 1. Sentence copied with spontaneous rotation, Case 2.

A LITTLE BOY HAD A CAT.
SHE RAN AWAY.
SHE SAID, "I WANT SOME MILK."

Figure 2. Sentence written from dictation, showing rotation, dysgraphia, and confusion over the letter **b**, Case 2.

Arithmetic Worksheet. Figure 3 shows a sample of school work that the boy brought to the hospital. Note the mirror rotation of **5**, and the high number of errors, the general spatial layout being neat.

Impression. This is a case of academic retardation, most severe in reading, in a boy of average IQ. There is considerable evidence of a problem in right-left discrimination, with errors of reading and writing rotation. Visuospatial perception appears to be intact. There are no problems of praxis, nor of heard or spoken speech. There is no evidence of so-called crossed lateral dominance, since the boy showed a right lateral preference in the use of hand, foot, and eye. The special senses are not implicated. There is a possible familial trait, since the younger sister (second child) was reported to have been a slow reader, and the father's brother, still illiterate, is believed to have been "just like Gordon."

The case may be regarded as one of specific developmental dyslexia, with some lesser involvement of dyscalculia. The etiology is not established. Specific developmental dyslexia is not necessarily a curable condition, nor necessarily a hopeless one. Affected children may make significant academic gains from oral and auditory learning. With special teaching in selected classes for dyslexics, they can usually make some progress in reading and writing the language.

Recommendation. A strenuous effort should be made to have this boy placed in a program of special instruction for dyslexic children. Return for follow-up.

Interval Notes: Partial Reading Analysis, May 22, 1962

Dr. Schiffman briefly recorded this procedure as substantiating the previous findings of a severe dyslexia.

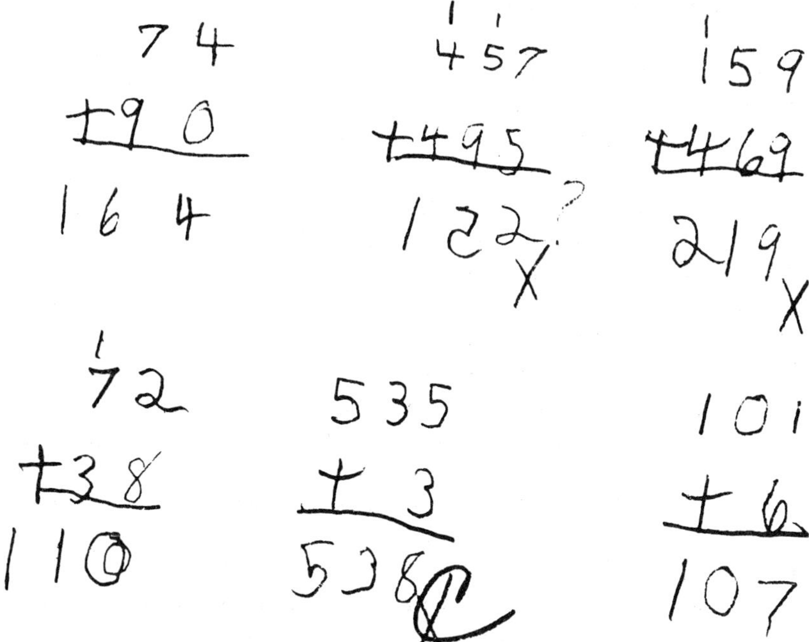

Figure 3. Sample from a school paper, showing rotation of the figure **5**, Case 2.

Mirror Reading Investigation, December 11, 1962: Dr. John Money

Two pre-primer 1 selections were used and presented in the following sequence of rotations:

1. Near-far mirror reversal,
2. Right-left mirror reversal,
3. Upside down,
4. Right side up.

The patient did not decipher them in rotations (1) and (2), but he was as fluent (two errors in the second selection) in the upside-down position as he was subsequently in the right-side-up position. On a second trial, after a brief distraction, the pieces were again presented, and he was equally fluent in all rotations. He said it was because he could remember what he had read before.

These findings indicate no special skill in or proneness to mirror rotation, but they do suggest a facility in short-term memory not matched by long-term retention in the learning of reading.

Finger Gnosis Investigation, December 11, 1962: Dr. John Money

A finger on the left hand and one on the right hand were touched simultaneously. Out of nine trials, both fingers were correctly identified in only four instances. On one trial the response for each hand was erroneous; on four trials the response for one hand only was erroneous.

An object (the examiner's finger) was placed in one of the interdigital spaces of the subject's hand and allowed sometimes to touch only one finger to the side, sometimes both. The answers were correct except for the first one, when the boy thought only his left fourth finger, instead of left fourth and fifth fingers, was touched. After a brief pause, he was asked: "Which was that again?" His response was very odd—"Four, left—and four right"—which suggests a perseveration from the preceding procedure, which required a left and a right finger to be identified.

Two-point discrimination was tested on the back of the forearm and hand. Two successive touches were correctly identified as such. When the two spots were touched simultaneously, he made one mistake in each of five trials per hand, saying that three spots had been touched. In these cases, the actual paired touches had been four and six inches apart, respectively.

These various findings suggest a poorly developed body schema and body image and poor ability to focus attention on body sensations. There could be a relationship between these findings and his poor ability to discriminate right and left on himself.

Report of Projective Testing, April 1, 1963

In connection with the boy's refusal to go to school, a series of projective tests was administered at another clinic. They showed a preoccupation with the school and reading issue. The injury and destruction entailed in the content of some Rorschach responses contrasted with his friendly, juvenile manner of responding. There was a precocious and unexpected amount of narrative material on boy-girl themes, rivalry, and dating, with grandparents rather than parents interfering.

In private discussion with a woman examiner, the mother revealed some highly charged material about earlier mother-in-law problems.

Partial Reading Analysis, September 11, 1965: Dr. Gilbert Schiffman

Individual Word Recognition

Level	Flash	Untimed
Pre-primer	82%	88%
Primer	45%	50%
First-grade	20%	20%

Informal Reading Inventory. Pre-primer and primer instructional level.
Informal Spelling Inventory. 40 per cent of first-grade level.

Handwriting Speed (Ayres). Below second-grade level.

Stanford Achievement Test (Reading and Arithmetic). In reading, performance was so poor that no score was obtained. In arithmetical computation, grade level 3.0 was achieved.

Impression. This is probably one of the worst cases of specific language disability seen in a youngster of this age and IQ. In informal evaluation the boy makes classical reversals, which occur also in his handwriting. He has learned the initial consonant sounds but still has much difficulty with vowel letter formation and sounds. It is difficult to evaluate comprehension because of the over-all severity of the word recognition problem.
Recommendation. Continued special education in remedial reading. The prognosis is guarded because of the age and severity of disability.

Psychologic Tests and Procedures, Second Series, September 11, 1964: Mr. Duane Alexander, Dr. John Money

Road-map Test of Direction Sense
WISC Mazes
Orientation Battery (modified from Detroit Learning Aptitude Test)
Benton and Kemble's Right-Left Discrimination Battery
Kinsbourne and Warrington's Finger Differentiation Examination
Benton Visual Retention Test
Draw-A-Person
SRA Primary Mental Abilities
Room Floor Plan

Interview with Patient
Thematic Apperception Test
Informal Graded Reading

Road-map Test. The patient made eight errors on the test, a performance ranking him at the 35th percentile. He seemed to possess the ability to orient himself for right and left simultaneously with coming nearer and going away in space. Seven of the eight errors were made on the route back, coming toward oneself, in which right and left on the map are reversed relative to one's own right and left. The result shows that the boy's right-left discrimination in map reading is below what is expected at his age.

WISC Mazes. The patient received a scaled score of 10, which is average and indicates no difficulty in spatial orientation.

Orientation Battery (Detroit, modification). The patient performed all five tasks correctly, again showing no difficulty with spatial orientation, including turning his body to the right correctly in each of the three trials requiring right-left discrimination.

Benton and Kemble's Right-Left Discrimination Battery. In twenty-four trials, the patient made five errors in identifying right and left on his own body, four of the errors being of the crossed-lateral type, e.g., "Touch your left ear with your right hand," and one error in four trials of doing the same on a person facing him, e.g., "Put your left hand on the man's left (or right) eye." There are no age norms for this test. The result shows that the boy still has difficulty handling the concepts of left and right simultaneously, even on his own body. Usually one assumes that a twelve-year-old will have no such trouble.

Kinsbourne and Warrington's Finger Differentiation Examination. The patient made errors on four of eight items in the "fingers-in-between" subtest but none on the other subtests. There are no age norms for this test, but one generally expects finger gnosis to be completely developed at about the age of twelve, and no later than fourteen.

Benton Visual Retention Test. On form C the patient reproduced six designs correctly and on Form D, eight. Reproducing eight designs correctly at age twelve corresponds to a Superior general intelligence level, and six designs, to an Average level. With an IQ of 101, the boy is expected to reproduce seven designs correctly, so his performance is as good as or better than expected, and there is no evidence for a perceptual or visuomotor deficit.

Draw-A-Person. The sex of the person drawn was male, which is expected in a boy with a masculine psychosexual identity. The drawing, though juvenile, is not bizarre. On the Harris norms, it is rated in the 10th percentile. The drawing of a female was not asked for. The self and best friend drawings are slapdash and much inferior to the drawing of a person. Both figures are without hands or feet. The self drawing is smaller, more asymmetrical, and has only three dots for facial features. In the friend drawing the eyes, nose, and mouth are more clear, but the lateral lines of the figure are overdrawn for no apparent reason. The patient could not spell his friend's name at all, and he made two errors in his own name. The first **o** was produced as **a** and was followed by a telescoped **o** and **r**. These drawings suggest a defect in self-concept and in establishment of friendship.

When asked to draw anything he wanted to, the boy drew "a piece of paper with square holes in it," because that "was easy," and a poorly executed jacket shirt. He also drew very poor sketches of his rather grand plans for a backyard patio and a hotrod he wants to build.

SRA Primary Mental Abilities. The patient's subtest percentile scores were as follows: Verbal meaning, 1; Number, 2; Space, 42; Word-fluency, 16; and Reasoning, 14. For the Word-fluency subtest, the words were written by the examiner as the patient gave them, since the latter could not spell them. The fact that the Space subtest score is relatively high further suggests that the boy has little or no problem in space-form perception. The low Number score suggests difficulty with this skill as well as with reading.

Room Floor Plan. The patient succeeded in drawing a floor plan of the office he was in, with only a small table located incorrectly.

Interview with Patient. The boy was not explicitly aware that the scheduling of this visit was precipitated by a recent minor incident in which he had gotten mixed up with too poorly disciplined local boys, brothers. His interview was conducted after the mother had herself been through two three-hour interview sessions, in which she disclosed dramatic, highly charged, and confidential material which she had been bottling up for seventeen years or more. In brief, it appeared that the emotional relationship in the marriage had been a severely abrasive one, in which the couple had adjusted themselves to mutual feuding and household guerrilla tactics. Very conventional in matters of sex, the wife interpreted her husband's approach to the marital relationship as perverse. She worried that the son might grow up to be "marked" like his father.

As is routine in any social system, the role of each participant partly determines the role of every other participant. In the social system of this family, the lead roles dictated that the father and son be maximally separated socially and emotionally, whereas the mother and son were overinvested in one another.

Though the mother believed that she had hidden the true state of affairs from the boy by refraining from mentioning it, it was abundantly evident, in his own interview, that he was acutely aware of the parental struggle and was attempting to hide it from the rest of the world. He was very alert to his father's neglect of him and wanted the situation to be otherwise. To an inquiry about schooling, he said: "Um, I get worried over—when they had their fights and everything. And it bothers me when I'm trying to do my schoolwork."

Thematic Apperception Test. Ten TAT cards were presented after the preceding interview. The stories, all short, were thematically carried over from the interview. Breakup and divorce were mentioned in three stories, unhappiness in one, and "a man just killed his wife" in another. The wife was never held responsible. The husband once was identified as lazy and as not supporting the family; once as a murderer who experienced unhappiness and guilt but whom the cops didn't get because "It's one of these murder rings"; once as listening to lies that lead to divorce; and once with a mind "all mixed up . . . It just ends up in confusion."

The possibility of a happy resolution appeared with an abrupt change of theme on the blank card (No. 16) (italics represent the examiner's voice):

> Gosh, I'd say everything was wrong here. I'd say—it was a clean life, and no troubles. (*How did it start?*) With the husband acting the right way and the wife acting the right way. (*And is there an ending to it?*) Um, yes, and it might end up in happiness. Just ended up in happiness for both of them.

For the first picture, that of the boy with the violin, the patient made a possible commentary on his own position in reading: "The boy didn't like the violin. . . . He just didn't practice the violin—he's stubborn."

It was two and a half months after the production of this material that the boy had to face his father's sudden death from a brain tumor, as mentioned above.

Informal Graded Reading. Following the TAT, a sample of the boy's reading of the first-grade selection was recorded on tape. In the transcription the dots represent pauses and the italics, the examiner's voice:

> A little boy had a . . . kitten . . . a cat. . . . . .She . . . ran . . . away. She . . . said I am . . . . . . (*want*) want . . . his . . . some . . . . . (*some?*) a . . . eleven . . . eleven . . . make . . . (*What do you think a kitten would want?*) Milk. (*Now read it to me.*) A little boy had a kitten. Was . . . she ran away. She said I want a . . . I want . . . some milk.

The second-grade selection reads: "A man took me to see his large barn. There was a horse in the yard. Its tail was black." The boy began: "A . . . man lived . . . " Then he paused, staring at the examiner's watch, in a long pause, until reminded that he couldn't read something without looking at it. He began again:

> A man lived . . . (*Look, that word begins with t.*) took him . . . to his . . . to see his . . . (*large*) large . . . (*barn*) . . . That was a . . . (*horse*) horse in the . . . (*yard*) . . . It . . . his . . . it . . . (*tail*) tail was . . . (*black*) black.

Clearly, there was a problem of attentiveness and effort involved here, but it cannot be decided *a priori* whether the poor reading was a function of distractibility and inattentiveness, or vice versa.

Impression. As compared with two and a half years ago, this boy shows development of skill in right-left discrimination, though he still has not reached the fluent accuracy one expects of most twelve-year-olds. The cause of the impediment in directional-sense maturation is not known. His space-form conceptualization is not highly developed for his age, but it is superior to his directional sense and right-left conceptualization. Numerical conceptualization is also not up to the proper level. There is no clear evidence that maturational improvement in right-left conceptualization is being matched by improvement in reading. One is not too surprised, however, that the blockage in reading assumes, at this advanced age, a relative autonomy, since there is so much overlay of frustration and belief that failure is foredoomed. The difficult thing to explain is what induced the blockage, what sustains it, and what role, primary or secondary, may be attributed to disturbance in home life as it affects the learning of reading.

Recommendations. 1. Continue special reading instruction with particular attention to visual learning, as perhaps in a color method. Meanwhile, other lessons can be approached aurally, for the most part. 2. Look into the practical feasibility and availability of psychotherapy and the chance of its being acceptable to the patient and his family.

Follow-up. Follow-up has been by long-distance telephone, as the mother felt that it would be better not to have the boy's disability emphasized by return hospital visits.

Conclusion

This case illustrates the very troublesome problems one encounters in trying to conceptualize the cause of failure to learn, and it raises the unsolved issue of a primary functional deficit versus a so-called psychogenic or secondary one. The case was presented in the referral as one of reading disability or dyslexia. The language of mathematics (arithmetic) as well as of written speech was found to be somewhat affected. The case was then shown to be one of maturational lag in the conceptualization of left and right and finger localization. Next, the case was found to be one involving a severe family-relationship problem by which the boy was clearly affected, according to his own evidence. Might it be possible that the links of a causal chain led from the familial problem to the school one?

Such a hypothesis seemed attractive, insofar as the mother took very decisive action in regard to schooling on the basis of what she herself believed to serve his best interests. Moreover, from time to time she gave overt clues to the effect that the longer a child stayed young and innocent, the better—that children become sophisticated too soon these days. There was also a lurking fear that he would grow up to be "marked" psychosexually, as his father was misunderstood to be.

Looking at the boy himself, one can construe further evidence in favor of this home-school hypothesis, for it is possible to interpret his reading failure as the end product of a lifetime of inattention to and neglect of the printed or written word. The process of such neglect would be pathologically similar to the dissociation found in hysterical blindness, deafness, anesthesia, paralysis, and the like.

In order to maintain the home-school hypothesis, it is necessary, however, to maintain another hypothesis, antecedent in the chain, namely, that of a connection between the family problem and the interruption of maturation in right-left and finger-sense localization. This hypothesis is much harder to accept. There is no plausible evidence of how the parental problem might have led to retarded maturation of these two aspects of the body schema or body image, and to them only.

It is more logical to assume that the boy's situation with regard to body schema and hence to reading is analogous to that of, say, a child born with hydrocephalus, or of a baby who develops infectious meningitis and is rendered mentally deficient. Confronted with such a tragedy, some families cope. Other parents, however, deal with the trauma in terms of their own personal, perhaps neurotic, motivations. For example, when the personal and sexual relationship between the parents is poor, the mother may snatch at the opportunity to devote herself in neurotic martyrdom to the defective child, as a legitimate way of absenting herself from involvement in a relationship with her husband. By analogy, one may see a parallel in the case of a family with a child who has the basis (irrespective of its source in heredity or in any other agent) of what could become a learning difficulty. In consequence, the deleterious effect of what might have been only a minor handicap is maximized. Such an interpretation seems the most likely one in the present case.

Therefore, the next investigative and therapeutic step, if it could possibly be arranged, would be to have the mother and son enter into psychotherapy jointly with the siblings, in an attempt to ascertain whether or not it is too late for the boy's habits of family relationship and learning to be revised, so that he may utilize effectively whatever ability he has—which he is certainly not doing at present.

CHAPTER 18

CASE 3: CONCEPTUAL IDIOSYNCRASY

JOHN MONEY

Case Report

Name and Number:	Brenda _______. 114 22 74
Date of Birth:	August 8, 1954
Date First Seen:	January 13, 1965
Chronological Age:	10 yr. 5 mo.
Follow-up:	Upon Request

Introduction

This case presented a difficult diagnostic problem, with a question of an aphasic-like disorder versus an autistic-like one. It required the cooperation of specialty consultants in neurology, electroencephalography, hearing and speech, psychology, and psychiatry. The case also demonstrates the need to select the psychologic test battery in terms of the time available. The basic problem appears to be one of idiosyncrasies of imagery and concept formation.

Reason for Referral

A psychiatrist in the home town thought that the child might have an aphasic type of defect rather than some other type of learning and personality disturbance. The child was accordingly referred to Dr. William G. Hardy's Hearing and Speech Clinic at Johns Hopkins for a diagnostic workup.

Medical-Chart Synopsis

The neurological evaluation, by Dr. William T. McLean, Jr., included a complete physical examination and was found to be unremarkable. Dr. McLean's impression was as follows: "I would guess that this girl has a minimal organic cerebral dysfunction with, among other things, some mild limitation of intellectual function. This may be somewhat complicated by a mild, intermittent, conductive hearing loss associated with ear infections. Her speech surely seems to be up to the rest of her intelligence and I think we would be hard-pressed to refer to her as being aphasic. On the other hand, she does seem to have a rather marked dyslexia and, although there may be an organic basis for some reading problem, I think a very large part of her own problem must be psychiatrically determined. We have no basis on which to guess an etiology."

The electroencephalogram was read by Dr. Curtis Marshall, with the interpretation as follows: "This tracing shows a mild disorganization for age during the awake resting stage, but there are no seizure patterns present. This tracing then does suggest that we are dealing with some diffuse damage."

The audiological findings were interpreted by Dr. William G. Hardy: "These findings indicate a mild conductive impairment for pure tones and speech-hearing, only slightly below the margins of normal hearing. The patient has recently had a head cold. Without doubt, there has been hearing fluctuation in past years, with some instability in communication as a result. The girl does not now have a significant auditory impairment. One may be fairly sure that her variable attention gets confused with lack of hearing. Her status in terms of reading has nothing to do directly with the past problems with hearing."

Psychiatric Synopsis

At the age of seven, the possibility of a diagnosis of autism was entertained. The girl began two years of individual psychotherapy once a week at a university clinic in her home state. During the second year, the mother attended weekly group therapy, and the father had intermittent sessions with a social worker. After two years the patient was transferred to a psychiatrist in private practice, through whom she was referred to Johns Hopkins, with a question of an aphasic type of language deficit. Her psychiatric evaluation at this hospital was made on March 16, 1965, by Dr. Leon Eisenberg, assisted by Dr. Sarah E. Howell. The impression was that the child was trying somewhat histrionically to make the most of her assets and to de-emphasize her difficulty with reading, with resultant patterns representing an emotionally immature personality. One suggestion was that the parents look into the possibility of instruction by the Responsive Environment technique developed by Dr. O. K. Moore (see Chapter 7 by Goldiamond).

First Impression

One's first impression was of a sociable, attractive little girl who was immediately confident and at ease in the situation of being tested. Left to her own devices, she initiated chatter or trivial activity rather constantly. She responded to inquiry and test instructions, but often with her own idiosyncratic version of what was entailed. It was easier to collect information as she shed it, so to speak, than to follow a systematic course of inquiry to obtain the information wanted. Sometimes she made tangential digressions or changed the subject, so that the train of her associations had to be guessed at.

Psychologic Tests and Procedures, January 13, 1965: Dr. John Money

Interview with Mother
Interview with Father
Draw-A-Person
Informal Graded Transcription
Informal Graded Dictation and Spelling
Bender Visual-Motor Gestalt Test
Road-map Test of Direction Sense
Arithmetic (own choice)
Wepman Auditory Discrimination Test
Benton and Kemble's Right-Left Discrimination Battery
Detroit Orientation Test (modified)
Kinsbourne and Warrington's Finger Differentiation Examination
Harris Lateral Dominance Examination
Informal Graded Reading
Wechsler Intelligence Scale for Children

Interview with Parents. One item, among others, reported by the mother illustrates an idiosyncrasy of thought process under which the child labors. Last summer she returned from camp a completely changed person. She was afraid of everything, as she had never been before. She would say, reiteratively, "I think I'm going to die; I'm going to die." She had a hand-washing compulsion. It transpired that she had been involved in sex play, including genital kissing, with two girls of her own age. She spoke of bursting open to get a baby. Her erroneous ideas and fears expanded to include new propositions from her talks with her mother, so that she had a ritual, every time she saw a strange man, of persistently asking her mother in a stage whisper: "Did I just have intercourse with him?" Or, "Am I going to have intercourse with him?" She knew of the mechanics of intercourse, but did not seem to understand. Such questions ceased about two months ago. Another ritual remains. Every night, after her mother puts her to bed and is about to leave the room, the child calls out: "I think I'm going to die. Am I going to die?" If the mother hesitates, the girl repeats the inquiry, a little more urgently. The mother's response that she is not going to die is ritualistically reassuring and leaves the girl able to go to sleep easily, but she always concludes the little interchange with, "And don't forget to tell Daddy."

After repeating the first grade in public school, in September, 1962, the girl changed to private education in a special school for problem learners. The enrollment includes children with cerebral palsy. Sometimes at home Brenda exhibits the peculiar movements and behavior characteristic of some of these children. She has asked whether she is brain-injured and whether she cannot read for that reason. The reading problem, a complete block, has existed from the beginning of school. Arithmetic is better, but still at only first-grade level, and she does it in a strange way: she gives answers demonstratively with her fingers and then, very slowly, counts to give the answer in words.

The child was adopted at two and a half days of age, little being known of her parents. They were high school graduates. She has always known of herself as adopted, as in her prayers she has from the beginning said: "Thank you, God, for adopting me," and has talked about it with her psychiatrist. There is no known incidence of mental illness in the geneology. The religion of birth is Christian; the adoptive religion is Jewish.

The reason for adoption was childlessness. Subsequently, there have been two siblings, not adopted, Fred, aged eight and a half, and Ernie, aged three and a half. Both are considered normal developers, though Fred was a slow starter academically, whereas Ernie is already trying to read. Brenda "fights and loves" Fred. She gets along better with Ernie. She has an equal share of her parents' affection.

Both parents are high school graduates and probably above average in intelligence. The mother is highly literate in writing of her child's history and condition. She is interested in the theater. The father is a businessman.

Draw-A-Person. The first figure is of a girl with "a pocket on her shirt and hair ribbons." To draw one's own sex first usually indicates no incompatibility between psychosexual identity and assigned sex. Qualitatively, the drawings are passable for age, but not at a high level. They rank at around the 25th percentile, according to the Harris norms. When completed, and upon request, the first drawing was identified: "It's a robot and her name is Brenda." The reference was later explained as belonging to "George Judson TV Guide." Upon further request, the name Brenda was written (in cursive script). The girl could not write the remainder of the title, after attempting the word, "It's. . . ." She made instead a peculiar symbol which is an undotted cursive i, with horizontal cross-bars near the top and bottom, as if in a twice-crossed t, thus: ŧ. This symbol was, without apparent purpose, put onto drawings 2 (boy) and 3 (self and best friend). It seems to be as much an indication of eccentricity and obsessive repetition as of dysgraphic confusion or memory failure.

By the patient's own choice, drawing 4 was a map depicting her trip south. The four compass points were indicated, but two of the signs were rotated, the **W** to become an **M** (fore-aft rotation), and the **SS**, for the south, rotated as left-right mirror reversals, **ƧƧ**.

Two oddities appeared in the commentary that the patient made while drawing. One occurred on drawing 2, when, completely without context, a sentence was interpolated: "Cat and the rocks." The reference, I could infer, was to a small assemblage of antiques on my desk which included two rock fragments and a small brass oriental temple lion.

The second oddity occurred in the chatter to drawing 5, Santa Claus, with two Menorahs, Stars of David, and "little star people." She added "I'm the only architect in my room, but I don't think I'm very good sometimes." (*What's an architect?*) "It means you're good at art," she said.

Graded Reading and Writing. Reading was imperfect at the first-grade level. When the stimulus, **He had a big dog,** was given, she read, **Huh-ee can a big dog.** Copying was clear at the first- but not the third-grade level. All writing and spelling was severely defective. The only recognizable forms were (1) her own name (without a capital for the surname); (2) **goy** for **boy**; (3) **He**; (4) and **a cat Bong book** (a free choice selection; the fourth word was erased after the sentence was read as, **can a cat bowl**? Then the word **book** was added adjacent to the erasure, and the reading changed to **can a cat book**? No further explanation could be elicited). A special instance of rotation occurred on the word **was**. The girl began to sound it out phonically with **s**. Then she wrote, **sery**!

Bender Visual-Motor Gestalt Test. The designs are in part well done, for her age, and in part haphazard. The haphazard approach was quite evident in the way the girl looked only at the stimulus cards, apparently paying no visual attention to what her hand and pencil were doing on the worksheet. She proceeded very rapidly.
Arithmetic. During an interruption for a phone call the girl produced, with pride, a sample of her skill in arithmetic, a school subject which she likes. The sample was completely made up of two-line, paired digit additions, but all with two zeros in them, either vertically or horizontally, so that no carrying was necessary.
Tests of Directional Sense and Orientation in Space. The various tests employed showed that the girl (1) has reached the stage of always knowing her own left and right; (2) consistently and wrongly identified left and right of a person facing her as being the same as her own, and is old enough not to make the error; (3) is not mature enough, but still within limits for her age, to orient herself in space from verbal or mapped instructions; (4) does not have finger gnosis problems; and (5) shows a right-sided lateral dominance, the only exception noted being a preference to hop on the left foot.
Wepman Auditory Discrimination Test. On trial 2, this test was done correctly. On trial 1, the responses were haphazard and often wrong up to Item 32, at which time the girl suddenly seemed to achieve the appropriate mental set for the test.

Wechsler Intelligence Scale for Children: Mrs. Florence C. Clarke

IQ Scores:

Verbal	77
Nonverbal	96
Full Scale	85

Scaled Subtest Scores:

Verbal		Nonverbal	
Information	5	Picture Completion	10
Comprehension	8	Picture Arrangement	8
Arithmetic	5	Block Design	9
Similarities	8	Object Assembly	11
Vocabulary	6	Coding	9

An IQ between 80 and 89 is Dull Normal and places a person in the top range of the lowest 25 per cent of the population; 96 is Average, placing a person among the middle 50 per cent of the population; and 77 is Borderline, with a percentile placement among the lowest 9 per cent.

There is sufficient idiosyncrasy of response that it is not possible to be sure that this testing is representative of what the girl may be able to do from one day to the next. On some items it seemed that the child would surely have the correct answer, but she did not produce it. Because the testing may not be representative, the resultant IQ need not necessarily remain constant from test to retest.

Idiosyncrasy of response is illustrated in the case of two easy items of vocabulary, a concept ("banging") from one response inappropriately contaminating the following one, with a resultant failure.

Item 7, Nail: "When you are building a house or put a picture up, you use a nail."

Item 8, Donkey: "If you are outside and they are inside and you start banging, the donkey will take his feet and clobber you and the wood will break."

Again, in Arithmetic, another eccentricity can be found in question 4 ("If I cut an apple in half, how many pieces will I have?"). The answer was: "Two halves from a quarter. What apple is called a quarter?"

Impression and Conclusions

On the basis of the foregoing findings, it is confirmed that the girl has severe reading retardation which is part of a more generalized academic retardation, more severe than can be explained on the basis of IQ alone. From the point of view of the reading problem, it is relevant that the development of right-left directional orientation is in arrears. In reading and writing themselves, there are many examples of directional problems in the form of rotations, as well as of phonic and visual recognition problems of the type that one finds in beginning readers. One concludes, therefore, in the present case, that the girl has scarcely progressed beyond the prereader stage of development. The reason for this academic developmental arrest is another question, and an extremely difficult one.

There is no demonstrated involvement of the special senses. There is also no demonstrated specificity of dysfunction such as in color blindness, word blindness, or space-form blindness occurring alone. The total pattern of cognitional functioning appears to be involved.

I am inclined to seek the answer to the academic problem in terms of the child's communicational idiosyncrasies. Perhaps one can understand her learning dilemma by likening it to the dilemma of the newcomer in a foreign-language country who is trying to communicate: he and the natives start out their interaction on the basis of different assumptions about competence in the use of the language. This girl does not seem to operate on the same communication standards as the rest of us do, nor in the same universe of semantics and logic. She operates more from the world of her own imagination, and she has frequent, periodic difficulty emerging from that world to be attentive to the rules and expectations of the world of school or psychologic testing. Herein lies her basic handicap.

Where this handicap originated is, I think, a riddle that science and medicine are not yet ready to answer. There may or may not be a hereditary component, or an effect of an adverse event, either in intrauterine life or at the time of birth. There is no known illness, infection, or accident after birth that may have insulted the central nervous system. The timing, amount, and quality of social exposure and interaction are known to affect the functional development of neural and psychologic development in infancy and childhood. In the present instance, in the one day of contact with the child and her parents, I did not become aware of a possible etiology in complementary pathodynamics within the family. By contrast, it seemed to me that, given another rearing and another family—the consanguineous one, perhaps—the girl might very well have become more handicapped, more withdrawn, autistic, and shut-in. As it is, for all her difficulties, she presented a pleasant and engaging sociability to the various people who met her in the hospital.

Recommendations

1. Continued special education with tuition tailored to individual need and capacity to respond.

2. Psychotherapy geared to indications for its need arising in school or family life, or relative to special emergencies, such as the one arising from camp last summer.

CHAPTER 19

CASE 4: PHONEMIC-GRAPHEMIC MATCHING DEFECT

JOHN MONEY

CASE REPORT

Name and Number:	Ronald _______. 116 17 63
Date of Birth:	February 12, 1950
Date First Seen:	June 14, 1965
Chronological Age:	15 yr. 4 mo.
Follow-up:	Anticipated

Introduction

This case came directly for psychologic evaluation on the recommendation of relatives who had been evaluated. One cousin had a history of dyslexic underachievement (Case 1). Two other cousins, a brother and sister, had a history of congenital, treated hypothyroidism with episodes of severe underachievement at school. The patient's health history and preliminary pediatric consultation contraindicated a general medical workup. Only the psychologic workup is therefore presented here.

Reason for Referral

The ostensible problem was school failure in both the boy and his younger sister, along with the possibility that they might be like their cousins. Actually, the problem was a much broader one of behavioral difficulties in the two children and in the home. The boy was on probation for vandalism—wanton vandalism of a school during a holiday. Also, an issue had arisen about his school placement as he entered eighth grade.

Schooling

He had repeated the fourth and the seventh grades, the latter in an opportunity class, in the hope that, with individual tuition, he would be able to make up for some of his academic lag. Academic achievement remained always poor. The school authorities made plans for a vocational school placement in the eighth grade, in the hope of improving the boy's morale and self-respect through achievement. The mother instead took refuge in the hope that her son would somehow manage to pick up and become normal if placed in a normal, graded classroom. Consequently, he entered a low section of the eighth grade with plans for special reading instruction.

Psychologic Tests and Procedures, First Series, June 4, 1965: Dr. John Money

Interview with Patient, one and one-half hours
Interview with Mother, one and one-half hours
Informal Graded Reading
Informal Graded Transcription
Informal Graded Dictation and Spelling
Bender Visual-Motor Gestalt Test
Draw-A-Person
Road-map Test of Direction Sense

The above are reported in the sequence actually followed. The sequence is slightly rearranged below.

Informal Graded Reading. The third-grade selection was adequately read with only two self-corrected stumblings over singular and plural endings. The fourth-grade selection required one hundred seconds instead of fifty, and he made twelve errors, including the following renderings:

Stimulus	*Response*
the big black	**the dog blacked**
grasses	**grass**
farthest	**farest**
under	**underneath**
heap	**hoop**
beneath	**bannerth**
the	(omitted)

These errors were self-corrected, but the selection was misread as being about a **snake**, not a **skunk**. In testing the limits, it appeared that the boy had no phonic analysis skills. He attempted to rectify his error with "skunk" as follows:

	Stimulus	*Oral Response*
(aural)	**s---k,**	**makes me think of snake**
(visual)	**kunk**	**nook**
(visual)	**s - kunk**	**snook**
(visual)	**k**	**k** (sounded)
(visual)	**sk**	**sk** (sounded)—**skunk**

The original reading was so stumbling and disjointed that the boy jumbled major propositions in its meaning, even when able to look at the selection while answering comprehension questions.

Informal Graded Transcription. The copying was correct at the fourth-grade level except for two occurrences of an uncrossed t. The first effort, at second-grade level, was copied without being read for meaning, and at the fourth-grade level meaning was obtained from only the first line. Handwriting was quite well formed and legible.

Informal Graded Dictation and Spelling. The third- and fourth-grade samples were used, with errors in both, as: **If you lived were are snow storms you would be gleed you can pick orges fron the trees,** and **Notterlo** (nocturnal) **amanies hunt at night they acturwly see better in the darkness then in the bright light of day.**

Bender Visual-Motor Gestalt Test. The designs were reproduced with adequate accuracy for age. There were signs of slapdash lack of thought as when the row of dots in Figure 1 was first reproduced as a line of dashes—because it was quicker. Figure 7 could not be completed without overlapping Figure 5, and Figure 4 had its curve overdrawn four times in an attempt to make it symmetrical.

Draw-A-Person. The male was done first, which is typical for boys. It had to be started twice, as the head was begun too big the first time. The girl is a clumsy-looking creature subsequently identified as a teenage sister. No breasts are shown—"I just didn't think about it."

On the Harris Quality Scale, the male drawing rates at the 61st percentile and the female at the 71st percentile. Thus the boy's drawing is competent and within the average range for age.

Road-map Test of Direction Sense. There were four errors in thirty-two turns, all at the end of the route—which suggests finish-line carelessness. Children in age group fifteen to eighteen should be able to do the test perfectly, and four errors earns a low rank, the 15th percentile.

Interview with Mother. In addition to being on probation for vandalism, the boy had also recently taken to staying out all night. The first time was because he played hooky from school, lied about it, and then left home when his mother threatened to check with the school. His stepfather reportedly threatened him with a whipping. The mother thereupon took on the discipline, protecting the boy from his stepfather, since she believed that her husband (whom she invariably referred to formally as "Mr.") would carry out his threat, and she did not like to see a child beaten.

It was rather transparently clear that the mother, only imperfectly aware of her own motivation, was entangling the relationship with the children, this boy included, with the chronic feuding relationship existing between her and her husband (her third after two divorces). She had also the rationalization that her husband had recently had a heart attack and could not risk getting violent with his stepson. According to the boy, the stepfather never speaks to his stepson. The present crisis of behavior problems appears to date from two years ago, when the boy entered junior high school and began playing hooky.

It was difficult to talk with the mother; she had much to talk about but was confusing, unsystematic, and often edited out, glossed over, or reconstituted information that was essential to an accurate picture of what was going on. This is the kind of person whose memory slightly changes a story or quotation in the retelling so that it is more suitable to the immediate context or purpose.

Interview with Patient. The boy was interviewed first. He neglected to disclose anything about being on probation because of vandalism. He did mention broken windows, however, in trying to recall a single example of behavior that in his opinion set his stepfather against him; but then he saved face, prevaricating, and said that one time he had been hitting rocks with a baseball bat and had broken a window. The result was to make his stepfather seem utterly unreasonable.

He saved face by neglecting also to mention something that occurred with respect to school achievement. I pressed him hard before being given the information that he had been in the lowest seventh-grade section, and he never did reveal that it was the opportunity class. He also did not disclose that he had repeated the fourth as well as the seventh grade. He managed to be not in the least obnoxious while being noncommittal. It appeared rather that he was not quite comprehending.

In reply to my initial query, he defined his problem as: "My eyes—they get blurred." He said that this happened when he tried to read but that it could also happen when he went bowling. The pins got blurred after fifteen to twenty minutes, he said. I remained unconvinced and gave the example of poor vision and good school achievement, then asked what he thought "the real trouble" was. His reply was: "My brain. I'm not interested in reading. It's something I don't like to do." He could not explain his lack of interest or its origins.

Because he had been unable to spell his stepfather's first name and did not know what work he did, I turned the inquiry to family relationships. It is a large family made up of half-siblings from four different marriages of the two parents, the oldest ones of whom are away and married. The patient appeared to have an accurate recognition of the facts of who treats whom well or badly, but at no time did he pass judgment, nor did he indicate that he held anyone, himself included, morally responsible, either to himself or to someone else.

In his version of the unyielding mutual antagonism that goes on between him and his stepfather, he saw the stepfather as the only one who should change, and yet he did not expect that he would change. Nor did he blame the stepfather for not changing. He believed it would be useless to initiate a truce, himself, even with the assistance of his stepbrother, who gets on well with his father. The other stepbrother at age twenty got fed up with his father's demands on one occasion and left home then and there, never to return.

All in all, this boy gave the impression of conceptualizing no relationship between motivation and goal achieved. He is one of the "buy now, pay later" people. His concept of personal responsibility seemed to be: do it now and take what's coming to you if you have to. He was quite congenial and goodnatured, provided that one didn't raise an issue with him about what he was doing now. Then he hung his head and had little to say. He seemed to have no plans for the future, except to wait for the day when he would be off probation. He would attend summer school for remedial reading because he had been given no choice. He did not want to consider seeing a psychiatrist, for then everyone would think he had something wrong with his mind.

Psychologic Tests and Procedures, Second Series, April 19, 1965: Miss Anke Ehrhardt, Dr. John Money

Wechsler Intelligence Scale for Children
Harris Lateral Dominance Examination
Gilmore Oral Reading Test
Benton Visual Retention Test

Wechsler Intelligence Scale for Children

IQ Scores:

Verbal	85
Nonverbal	94
Full Scale	88

Scaled Subtest Scores:

Verbal		Nonverbal	
Information	7	Picture Completion	9
Comprehension	7	Picture Arrangement	8
Arithmetic	7	Block Design	10
Similarities	6	Object Assembly	11
Vocabulary	8	Coding	8
Digit Span	10		

An IQ between 80 and 89 is Dull Normal and ranks between the 9th and 25th percentiles. An IQ between 90 and 109 is Average, ranking between the 25th and 75th percentiles. The difference of nine points between the verbal and nonverbal IQ is not particularly unusual. The scatter of the scaled scores, 6 to 11 with a range of 5, approaches significance and indicates good perceptual organization (Block Design, 10; Object Assembly, 11) according to the criteria of Cohen's (1957, 1959) factor analysis. The verbal factor (Information, 7; Comprehension, 7; Similarities, 6; Vocabulary, 8) is, by comparison, low, and the numerical factor (Arithmetic, 7; Digit Span, 10) lies in between.

Item analysis showed some unexpected failures on easy items and half-credit answers in the verbal subtests. For example, in the Comprehension subtest, Question 8, "Why should women and children be saved first in a shipwreck?" the answer given was, "They might not be able to swim." In the Similarities subtest, Question 6, "In what way are a cat and mouse alike?" the response was, "Cat chases a mouse." In addition, there were some poorly conceptualized responses, for example, in the Comprehension subtest, Question 7, "Why should criminals be locked up?" the answer was, "To stop the bad stuff." When asked, "Can you explain that more?" he said, "To punish them."

Throughout all verbal subtests the patient seemed to be little interested and rather inert. He quickly gave up if he did not know the answer at once. However, if asked again, he often gave the right response. Lack of persistence might have detracted from his verbal IQ.

In Block Design and Object Assembly, the patient showed more ambition. His performance in those subtests can be described as skilled trial-and-error learning. He turned and changed the position of the different pieces all the time, until he was successful in copying the model.

In my opinion, the test results of today are representative of the patient's present level of mental functioning. However, I feel unsure of making a statement on IQ constancy, since a change of the boy's motivation toward achievement might influence test results in the future.

Harris Lateral Dominance Examination. The patient was righthanded, righteyed, and rightfooted on the various test items.

Gilmore Oral Reading Test. The accuracy score was 42. This result corresponds to an equivalent grade of 4.7. The comprehension score was 44. A raw score of 44 corresponds to a grade equivalent of 9.8. According to Gilmore, this result is above average for a student in the seventh grade. The rate in words per minute was 90. A rate score of 90 is below average for a seventh-grade student. The patient was extremely slow throughout the whole test.

Benton Visual Retention Test. Seven of ten geometric forms were correctly reproduced, which corresponds to a category of low or dull average intelligence and a Wechsler IQ of 80 to 94.

Impression. This is a boy whose school achievement is reported as severely substandard in all subjects relative to his IQ and who required special placement last year in an opportunity class in an attempt to have him catch up. On the WISC, his IQ tested at the Dull Normal level. It could edge over into the Normal range at some subsequent testing. Improved literacy could easily upgrade the verbal scores by a few points.

His reading achievement level tested at the third- to fourth-grade level. He is beyond the stage of making errors of right-left rotation of letters, though he had some difficulty, unusual for a boy of his age, with right-left direction sense on the Road-map Test.

His spelling shows that he cannot spell some quite simple words. By contrast, he had success with other more difficult ones for which he has achieved correct visual recall. His inventory of correct-recall words was, however, inadequate. He could not compensate by applying the principles of syllabication and phonetic analysis. It is here that his primary weakness lies, namely, in deficient conceptual grasp of how to translate the acoustic into the visual elements of language. On various tests of accuracy of geometric form perception and of conceptualizing shape relationships, he was average or slightly above average for his age. Thus, there were no space-form difficulties to impede his reading. His handwriting reflected his ability in this direction. It was legible, and the letters were well formed.

At his present age, the boy is mature enough in reading skills to avoid the classical beginner's errors of the dyslexic. He is now a slow reader and is underachieved, rather than dyslexic—which is, perhaps, one outcome of an early reading disability partially overcome.

Recommendation. Plans for this boy depend partly on water that has already flowed under the bridge, as well as on facilities available. I recommended that the mother consider the elasticity of the family budget with a view to hiring a private tutor in remedial reading. Through Dr. Schiffman, she could locate a tutor with whom the boy might well be able to build up a strong and constructive relationship. At the time of making this recommendation, I believed it would be possible for the boy to go to a vocational school, where achievement in shop classes would be good for his morale and self-respect. However, I have since learned that he will have to be re-enrolled on a waiting list for the vocational school, having lost one opportunity to accept a vacancy. In the meantime, he must return to school in the fall to an eighth-grade classroom with special provision for extra reading instruction.

Partial Reading Analysis, June 22, 1965: Dr. Gilbert Schiffman

Individual Word Recognition

Grade Level	Flash	Untimed
Third	90%	100%
Fourth	65%	80%
Fifth	65%	75%
Sixth	45%	50%

Stanford Reading Achievement. Word meaning, grade level 3.9.

Word Opposites

Fourth grade	80%
Fifth grade	20%
Sixth grade	10%

Phonovisual Spelling. Eight words correct out of seventeen.
Informal Reading Inventory. Fourth-grade instructional level.

These tests indicate clearly that this boy has a severe reading disability. He has a limited sight vocabulary at the intermediate grades and does not have sufficient control of his basic word-analysis techniques to unlock these unknown words. He is not sure of the basic vowels, short vowel sounds, and syllabication principles.

Throughout the testing, he gave a spotty, irregular, dips-and-peaks type of performance. For instance, he recognized words like "imaginary" but missed words like "cub." In spelling, he got right only eight words out of seventeen. Every child at the completion of the third grade should be able to spell all seventeen of these words correctly. He spelled **prize** as **prise, thrown** as **thron, mule** as **mual,** and so forth. Since the boy has adequate intelligence, there is no question that he should get some reading help immediately. He needs help in developing satisfactory sight vocabulary and word-analysis techniques, and also some help in comprehension and spelling. The latter two areas are definitely important, but I think at the present time some emphasis must be made immediately in the area of word recognition.

I suggested that, if possible, the boy be referred to the special reading program in the city schools and that, if the schools agree, I could offer him some help through the college practice program in the fall.

Conclusion

The boy's primary problem at school has been one of not being able to apply himself and achieve at a level commensurate with his IQ. It is always a problem in a case such as this one to know the origin of the difficulty—which is the cart and which the horse? It could be that he has a primary difficulty in firmly establishing the aural-visual bonds of language, in order to hear what he sees and see what he hears and remember both. It could also be that this difficulty is secondary, though now chronic and fixed, to earlier disturbances associated with family and home life and the emotional upset he experienced in adjusting to the role of stepson. The role of the underachiever is itself a difficult one and is well known to be associated with the role of delinquency, which provides some sort of achievement and renown. Whether the delinquency is primary to underachievement or whether it is derivative and compensatory is another cart-and-horse issue without a final answer. Either way, the boy fits the classical mold of underachievement associated with delinquency. The prognosis in such a case is guarded.

CHAPTER 20

CASE 5: ARRESTED LITERACY

PHILIP W. DRASH

Case Report

Name and Number:	James _______. 116 45 88
Date of Birth:	March 31, 1956
Date First Seen:	June 12, 1965
Chronological Age:	9 yrs. 2 mos.
Follow-up:	Long Distance

Introduction

This case of arrested literacy represents an unusual example of educational disability associated with lack of academic instruction and complicated by social and emotional factors. Unlike other cases presented elsewhere in this volume, specific perceptual, sensory, and intellectual deficits could not be demonstrated among the contributing factors in reading failure. The case offers a particularly instructive example of the way in which a series of complex factors, relatively benign in isolation, may in combination interact to produce reading failure and generalized lack of academic achievement. It further illustrates the difficulty of isolating specific etiological factors in reading disability. Phenomenologically, the case demonstrates a lack of word-analysis skills, deficiency of basic sight vocabulary, and deficient knowledge of vowel sounds.

Reason for Referral

The child, who had been elsewhere diagnosed as partially dyslexic, was referred for further psychologic evaluation and recommendation for treatment by an aunt with whom the child was residing. The parents lived too far away to be seen. The child has a lifelong history of academic difficulty and reading retardation, and, although he should have been entering the fourth grade, he was essentially a nonreader. Since the child was referred directly for psychologic evaluation, no medical history is here reported, the child being under medical supervision elsewhere.

First Impression

This handsome but somewhat asthenic child immediately impressed me with his amicability and quickly established a friendly working relationship with me. He was quite at ease when left alone by his aunt and displayed no visible signs of either anxiety or negativism.

On the other hand, the boy, while very alert, was by contrast quite lacking in verbal spontaneity. Though he readily answered my queries, he seldom initiated the conversation. It was my initial impression that the child was somewhat introverted and lacking in self-confidence. Otherwise, his appearance and conduct were normal.

Schooling

The boy initially entered first grade in a private school and shortly transferred to a parochial school which his siblings attended. The change was somewhat upsetting and ostensibly induced a school phobia. During the first two grades the child continued to attend parochial school. However, his attendance at school was sporadic, as a result of the interaction of several factors. First, his second oldest brother, who was six years his senior, was also having scholastic difficulty, with frequent absenteeism. Second, the father developed an acute illness during this period with chronic sequelae which necessitated prolonged hospitalization and consequent disruption of the family routine. Third, the mother developed an incapacitating reaction to the seriousness of the father's illness and was limited in her ability to care for the children. A result was that frequently the youngsters were not sent to school.

Before entering the third grade, the boy and his family moved to a new community. The third-grade placement was made on the basis of age, not achievement level. The child was at an academic loss in the new school, frequently cried in school, and often left to return home. A psychiatrist was consulted, who was reported to have recommended that the child be removed from school and brought up to grade level by a private tutor. Before this recommendation could be fully implemented, the family moved to another community, where the boy was again irregular in his school attendance.

During the summer prior to what would normally have been the child's fourth school year, the present evaluation was made, and special school placement for the child was recommended. The child was at the time living with an aunt who was interested in rehabilitating him educationally. However, before a program of remedial education could be undertaken, the child was recalled by his parents. He was placed by them in a special school where, on follow-up, it was ascertained that his school attendance continues to be sporadic.

Psychologic Tests and Procedures, June 12 and 22, 1965: Dr. Philip Drash

Wechsler Intelligence Scale for Children
Bender Visual-Motor Gestalt Test
Draw-A-Person
Self-and-Friend Drawing
Gilmore Oral Reading Test
Informal Graded Reading
Informal Graded Spelling
Informal Graded Transcription
Wide Range Achievement Test (Arithmetic)
Embedded Geometric Figures
Harris Lateral Dominance Examination
Road-map Test of Direction Sense
Interview with Aunt
Interview with Tutor
Interview with Patient
Planning conference

Wechsler Intelligence Scale for Children

IQ Scores:

Verbal	110
Performance	93
Full Scale	102

Scaled Subtest Scores:

Verbal		Performance	
Information	13	Picture Completion	12
Comprehension	13	Picture Arrangement	10
Arithmetic	5	Block Design	9
Similarities	11	Object Assembly	9
Vocabulary	16	Coding	5
Digit Span	10		

A full-scale IQ of 102 is Average and falls between the 25th and 75th percentiles. An IQ of 110 is Bright Normal and falls between the 76th and the 91st percentiles. The seventeen-point difference between the verbal and the performance IQs is significant and is commented on below. There is also a significant range of verbal scaled scores.

The superiority of the verbal over the performance IQ reveals that the patient, at least on the skills herein tested, is more proficient in verbal skills than in visuoconstructional skills, and that he tends not to hold up well when working under a time limit at school-type tasks such as arithmetic and coding. In the timed Coding subtest, he made three sequence errors (for example, following the code sign for 6 by that for 7 instead of 3, as required) and by making one 90° rotation. This type of error might be expected at age five or six, though not at nine. By contrast, there were no similar evidences of verbal immaturity.

On item analysis of the verbal subtests, only two peculiar answers were given. One was an error in the naming and sequence of the seasons (winter, summer, Christmas, school season) accompanied by visible signs of blocking and confusion. The other was a successful 1-point answer on the question of why it is better to give to an organized charity than to a street beggar, made after failure on the two preceding questions and 1-point answers on the two preceding them. There is thus a possibility that the result of this testing might be improved upon at a subsequent retesting, since the boy did not do full justice to himself on some of the easier items. According to the aunt, the child had obtained an IQ of 128 on a test administered one year ago. While I do not see evidence of a score quite that high, when the verbal tests are prorated without Arithmetic and Digit Span, a verbal IQ of 120 or Superior is obtained. Such a score is somewhat more representative of the verbal intelligence of this child.

Bender Visual-Motor Gestalt Test. The Bender figures were well organized, and no gross distortions, rotations, or fragmentations were present. A few signs of developmental immaturity were present, but these were not marked. They included drawing of circles rather than dots and a somewhat below average performance on Figures 7 and 8. In general, however, the Bender is within normal limits for a child of nine years and does not suggest the presence of gross disability.

Draw-A-Person. The male figure was drawn first and the female second, this being the normal order for males. The male figure received a Harris quality scale score of 2, for a standard score of 68, and a percentile rank of 2. The drawing is almost completely devoid of detail. Both the arms and the legs are represented by straight lines. The face is a circle with rudimentary eyes, nose, and mouth. Neither ears nor hair are present. Such a drawing would be below average in quality for a five-year-old child and is thus grossly immature for a nine-year-old. The drawing of the female received a Harris quality scale score of 3 for a standard score of 78 and a percentile rank of 7. It is hardly recognizable as a human figure. Such a drawing would be average or below average for a child of six. The drawing of such grossly immature human figures is inconsistent with a child who is of average intelligence and who also has relatively adequate visuoconstructional skill as demonstrated by the Bender drawings. It is inconsistent even with the performance IQ on the WISC which, though inferior to the verbal IQ, is, nonetheless, Average. This type of inconsistency may simply represent poor graphic memory skill (the Bender is a copying test), or it may represent the interference of disrupting emotional factors. Qualitatively, the appearance of the drawings, especially that of the woman, is consistent with the latter interpretation.

Self-and-Friend Drawing. The figure drawings for this test, which was devised by the author, were of the same immature, ghostly quality (Fig. 1) as those drawn for the Draw-A-Person. The patient drew himself first and his friend second. His best friend is a boy in the fifth grade, a year older than the patient. He said he also has at least four other friends, two of whom are in the fourth grade, one in the fifth, and one in the sixth. While the patient seemed to have an average number of friends and selected them from his own age group or slightly older, he did not go into detail in describing his friends and their activities, as is normal for a nine-year-old. For example, when asked why he chose Mike as a best friend, he said, "I met him first." Most nine-year-old children give a more detailed response indicating why the friend is preferred to other children who might have been chosen.

Gilmore Oral Reading Test. On the Gilmore, the patient scored below first-grade level. He was unable to read such words as "boy," "has," "is," "here," "in," and "girl." An analysis of his mistakes revealed that the child was excessively slow, appeared to have no word-attack skills, and guessed at the meanings of words from a picture even though the words were completely irrelevant, such as the substitution of **cat** for **girl**. Because of his extreme reading retardation he was administered a number of additional reading and spelling tests, including a reading analysis by Dr. Gilbert Schiffman (see below).

Informal Graded Reading. The first-grade sentence is: **A little boy had a cat. She ran away.** The boy read: **I little boy had a cand. Is run will . . .** At the second-grade level, the sentence is: **A man took me to see his large barn.** The boy read: **A man did took me to see him lurk bree.**

The reading time for both first- and second-grade sentences was excessive. Although the child is below the first-grade level, and although he shows a lack of phonics and word-attack skills, it is encouraging to note that he did not show a large number of reversal mistakes in the identification of letters such as **b**, **d**, and **p**. It appears that the primary problem here is one which involves lack of the fundamental skills which may possibly be learned through instruction.

Informal Graded Spelling. At the one-year level, the patient was able to spell correctly only four of ten words. He spelled correctly "go," "he," "it," and "on." His spelling for the remaining words was:

Word	*Spelling*
mother	**machno**
was	**wx . . wz**
in	**on**
do	**dou**
can	**cn**
with	**whth**

As may be seen from the foregoing examples, this patient is below the most basic level in spelling.

Informal Graded Transcription. On the graded transcription test, the patient was able to transcribe correctly simple sentences at the first- and second-grade levels which were placed before him. Neither reversals nor mirror writing were present. It is notable, however, that he was only able to print, and his printing was at about the first-grade level.

Wide Range Achievement Test. Only the arithmetic section of the Wide Range Achievement Test was administered. The boy was able to add correctly single-digit numbers but did not know how to attack addition with two columns of numbers even though no carrying was

Figure 1. Self and friend drawing, Case 5.

involved. He was able to subtract a single-digit number from another single-digit number but was unable to subtract a single-digit number from a two-digit number, for example, 14 minus 8. He did not know any multiplication. His over-all arithmetic score was at the 2.5 grade level, but this may be an overestimate of his arithmetic ability, as he was slow on those problems to which he did respond correctly.

Embedded Geometric Figures. The boy responded correctly to four of six of the embedded figures. Though there are no norms for this test, such a response is adequate, in a child of nine years, to indicate no severe problems in identification of geometric figures—and, to the degree that this test can be generalized, in the physical differentiation of letters.

Harris Lateral Dominance Examination. This test indicated that the patient has a slight degree of mixed lateral dominance. He used his right hand for writing, drawing, and tapping, but used his left eye for sighting and his left foot for kicking.

Road-map Test of Direction Sense. This technique, designed to test for confusion in right-left orientation on the part of the subject, indicated that the patient is at least average for a nine-year-old, according to the norms for his age group.

Interview with Aunt. The important facts of family and school history have been given under Schooling. The rationale that the aunt had for being interested in the boy's needs is that she had helped to care for him during the prolonged illness of the child's father. With no children of their own at home, the aunt and uncle volunteered to care for the child and provide for his educational needs.

There are various parts of the aunt's statement that are of necessity confidential. As far as could be ascertained, her report was reliable. Although it is the usual policy of our research unit to obtain information from several members of the family, it was not possible in the present case.

Interview with Tutor. The tutor, a distant relative of the child, was a qualified public school teacher and had known the child all his life. She had examined the boy prior to our interview and agreed that he had a severe reading disability. She had a very good relationship with him, and it was her impression that the child had both the ability and the necessary interest to benefit from tutoring.

Interview with Patient. In reviewing his scholastic difficulties, the child said that, although he had never been physically punished in school, his teachers frequently shouted at him, took his papers away, and told him to do his work again. His major concern about entering a new school was whether the teachers and the prinicipal would be nice or mean. During the course of the interview I gained the impression that the child is extremely sensitive to criticism and emotional outbursts directed at him.

The child appeared willing to remain with his aunt and uncle and expressed interest in being placed in a school in which he could be given the special instruction which he needs at this time. I was impressed, however, by the child's passive compliance, which at times bordered on apathy. He seemed equally acquiescent to remaining with his aunt and uncle or returning home to his parents. Indeed, the child's only expression of personal involvement in the efforts being taken to rehabilitate him educationally was a rather bland, passive agreement to attend special remedial classes and cooperate with a private tutor.

The child's expression of emotional affect was relatively appropriate, but his expressions were in attenuated form. He smiled on occasion, but seldom laughed. Furthermore, he showed none of the spontaneous, sparkling outbursts of humor or disappointment which so many children characteristically display.

During the inquiry directed at vivid or eidetic imagery, the child reported seeing on occasion ghost-like forms which had a nightmarish and frightening quality. These images usually occurred when he was in bed, though not asleep.

It was my over-all impression that the child had definite emotional problems, but their etiology and precise role in his reading disability are, at this point, difficult to ascertain.

Impression. On the basis of the foregoing, it seems to me that this boy's reading disability is not an example of specific developmental dyslexia but is part of a general academic underachievement, including a weakness in arithmetic. The poverty of academic instruction reflects the fact that he has not been obliged to go to school and has, for his own part, shown an extreme lack of initiative. There are factors in the social history that make this state of affairs understandable, though only incompletely so. The boy has definite primary emotional problems. Some of these stem from his constant failure experiences in school, which have produced a degree of anxiety associated with academic learning, but others appear to be antecedent to school failure and directly related to the home situation. The case appears, therefore, to be one of immaturity of reading skill which is part of a general academic retardation. Insufficient schooling is one of the major etiological factors, and personality difficulties, complex in etiology, are another.

Recommendations. The prognosis in the case of a child who has reached nine years of age without mastering the basic first-grade skills must be somewhat guarded. However, if the boy is to make progress, it is essential that remedial steps be taken immediately. Progress for this child may be both slow and difficult. The following recommendations are considered the minimum essentials for successful remedial treatment of this boy.

1. The child should be in a home setting which is stable and one from which he will be supervised and required to attend school regularly and without interruption.
2. The child should immediately begin a program of remedial tutoring which will place stress on pre-primer and first-grade skills.
3. In the fall the child should be placed in a school which is designed to meet the needs of children with special learning and emotional difficulties. The ideal remedial program for this boy will stress both his educational and emotional needs.
4. In the event that the child's emotional problems become exacerbated, a psychiatric referral may be indicated.

Partial Reading Analysis, June 22, 1965: Dr. Gilbert Schiffman

Individual Word Recognition

Level	Flash	Untimed
Preprimer	55%	60%
Primer	10%	30%

Informal Reading Inventory. The instructional level is at the reading-readiness and pre-primer stage.

This child has a severe reading disability. His sight vocabulary and word-analysis skills are inadequate at the pre-primer level. He has some understanding of initial consonants but does not know the long or short vowel sounds effectively. Therefore, with such a limited sight vocabulary and so few word-analysis skills to analyze the unknown words, he is paralyzed severely in the comprehension area.

He has a great number of misconceptions about some of the basic vowel sounds and vowel rules, which hinder his word-analysis techniques. However, on an informal word learning test, he indicates that he can learn new words on the fifth or sixth trial. The expected average rate for first-grade children is on the fifteenth or sixteenth trial.

I could not, with the limited testing I did, classify this youngster as a dyslexic child, although academically he gives this appearance. I feel that he has been exposed to insufficient pedagogical procedures in his two to three years of schooling. It is suggested that the boy get a strong systematic sequence of word analysis, starting with a visual, kinesthetic, and tactile approach, using the synthesis techniques.

We will discuss possible summer school placement for the child with his tutor, and it might be effective to have him attend a special summer remedial reading program. If he is able to do this, it will be very important to give him a follow-up partial analysis in September to see what effect the summer tutoring has brought about and to make further recommendations for the fall program. It seems to me that the prognosis in this case, as far as educational growth is concerned, is good if we can employ the proper program with the proper tutor and prevent the emotional and social complications from getting out of hand.

Planning Conference

Following the psychologic evaluation and the reading analysis, a planning conference with the aunt and uncle was held by Dr. Money, Dr. Schiffman, and me. We discussed the child's need for uninterrupted instruction and recommended that he continue his individual tuition until the fall. If the boy were to remain with them, the aunt and uncle fully agreed to enroll him in a private school which offered both remedial educational programs and programs for children with emotional problems. We also recommended that the child be enrolled in a summer remedial reading clinic being conducted by Dr. Schiffman.

The child could not, because of long-distance transportation problems, attend the remedial reading clinic. However, the recommendation for individual tuition was implemented and plans were initiated to place the child in a private school in the fall. Before the latter could take place, the child was, as already indicated, recalled by his parents.

Conclusion

Does the present case represent a failure to achieve simply through a lack of systematic academic instruction in reading, spelling, and arithmetic? One possible answer is yes. It seems more likely, however, that something from within the child himself has been in collusion with the paucity of instruction. One does not know what this something might be—it might range all the way from a genetic trait to the emotional aftermath of experience in the social environment at home or school.

It is also possible that there is a critical period for the development of efficient reading. If, for any of a number of reasons, socioenvironmental ones included, a child passes through this critical stage in his development without mastering the basic skills of reading, his ability to acquire them may be greatly impaired despite average to superior intelligence and subsequent instruction. In retrospect, determination of the etiology in this case is not possible.

Even when the question of etiology can be successfully answered, the answer does not necessarily indicate the course of remedial therapy or the prognosis in a particular case. The role of the family as a catalytic and sustaining agent in cases of improvement in reading appears to be very important. Thus, if the boy achieves a stable and well-structured living environment, his reading deficiency may not deteriorate into an irretrievable academic disability.

In the present case, the prognosis for the child, if given remedial reading, initially appeared rather optimistic. This optimism was not put to a real test. The problems of the home circumstances won out, and the child continued to be an absentee pupil. Thus remediation of reading disabilities is frequently a pragmatic undertaking which may be relatively independent of both the diagnosis and etiology of the deficiency.

CHAPTER 21

THE DEVELOPMENTAL GERSTMANN SYNDROME

MARCEL KINSBOURNE AND
ELIZABETH K. WARRINGTON

The Gerstmann syndrome (Gerstmann, 1924) (finger agnosia, right-left disorientation, dysgraphia, and dyscalculia) has long been recognized as indicative of disease of the parietal lobe of the dominant hemisphere and appears to be due to impairment of a basic physiological function involving sequential ordering (Kinsbourne and Warrington, 1962; Kinsbourne and Warrington, 1964). The question arises as to whether this syndrome may appear in children on a developmental basis, and if so, what effect it has on their acquisition of educational skills. It therefore becomes important to establish diagnostic criteria for the syndrome in children. The problem revolves around the definition of finger agnosia in childhood.

Finger agnosia, as conventionally elicited (Gerstmann, 1924), is difficult to diagnose in childhood. Normal children are not necessarily able to name their fingers, and failure on an unstandardized task involving the names of the fingers is of doubtful significance. As the presence of finger agnosia is essential to the diagnosis of the Gerstmann syndrome, this diagnosis cannot at present be reliably made in a child. This does not imply that the Gerstmann syndrome does not occur in children, but that the conventional means of detecting finger agnosia as used in adults (which demand a knowledge of the names of the fingers) are unsuitable for use with children. Recent clinical studies have shown that deficits resembling those which constitute the Gerstmann syndrome in adults are, in fact, not uncommon in children with apparently selective reading retardation (Hermann and Norrie, 1958; Hermann, 1959). It therefore becomes all the more important to introduce into clinical practice tests for finger agnosia which, by proper standardization, have been shown to be suitable for use with children, and which are of clear-cut significance.

Empirical test batteries for finger localization (Benton, 1959), though standardized on children, are of doubtful relevance, as there is no evidence that they test a function corresponding to the one lost by the adult with finger agnosia. However, Kinsbourne and Warrington (1962) introduced a series of tests of "finger differentiation and order," failure on which was highly correlated with failure on conventional tests for finger agnosia. Three of these tests were then standardized on a group of normal children, and it was shown that by the age of seven and a half years criterion was met by more than 95 per cent of the children (Kinsbourne and Warrington, 1963). It was concluded that, unlike finger naming, the test of finger differentiation and order are suitable for use with children, and that failure to reach criterion on these tests at above the age of eight years is of pathological significance and indicates the presence of finger agnosia.

Below are reported seven cases of children with finger agnosia. In every instance, two or more of the other elements of the Gerstmann syndrome were also present, so that it became possible to regard these cases as examples of the Gerstmann syndrome as it occurs in childhood.

Case 1

The patient, aged nine, was admitted under the care of Dr. W. Gooddy because of supposed mental backwardness. There was a strong family history of nervous disorder but none of specific educational disability or generalized mental retardation. Pregnancy was uneventful and delivery occurred spontaneously at term. The patient was born in good condition, weighing 6 pounds, 12 ounces (3,063 grams). However, she was difficult to feed and had trouble in sucking. She sat up at eight months and walked only at the age of two years and three months. Her speech development was normal. Although she appeared to be of above normal intelligence, she failed to make the expected rapid progress at school. She had some difficulty in learning to read and write and very marked trouble in drawing, associated with considerable clumsiness of her hands. She had difficulty in feeding herself and in doing up buttons. Her gait was clumsy, and she was unable to run efficiently. After starting school, she became increasingly restless and hyperkinetic, tense, excitable, and talkative. She repeatedly and compulsively asked the same question and appeared to find it difficult to attend to any one task more than momentarily. She was tearful and demanding of attention. She had been to many schools and still more doctors.

On examination, she was obviously emotionally disturbed, and her co-operation was difficult to enlist. She showed evidence of considerable anxiety, and this was mirrored in the attitude of her parents. Her speech was rapid and staccato but not otherwise abnormal. There was no abnormality of skull or spine. She was righthanded and rightfooted, though lefteyed. There was no focal abnormality in the nervous system, nor any abnormality on general examination. However, there was a non-specific clumsiness of fine movements of the hands, and this was also evident in her gait.

Radiological examination of the skull and cervical spine was unremarkable. The cerebrospinal fluid was of normal constitution and under normal pressure. The Wassermann reaction in cerebrospinal fluid was negative. The electroencephalogram was within normal limits, but lumbar airencephalography revealed gross symmetrical enlargement of the lateral ventricles.

Summary

A girl, aged nine years, was the product of normal pregnancy and delivery, with nonspecific clumsiness, educational difficulties, and emotional disorder, but with no focal neurological abnormality. Airencephlography revealed bilateral dilatation of the lateral ventricles, consistent with a developmental cerebral defect.

Case 2

The patient, aged eight and a half, was admitted under the care of Dr. W. Gooddy on account of difficulty in learning to read and write. No one in the family had experienced a comparable difficulty, and there was no relevant family history of neurological disease. Her mother and three of her mother's siblings were lefthanded. The patient was the product of a fulltime normal pregnancy and normal delivery, weighing 6 pounds, 3 ounces (2,832 grams) at birth. There was physiological jaundice and an entirely uneventful neonatal period. She was breastfed from the start. However, at the age of three weeks she developed a breast abscess, which was incised and drained, followed less than a week later by gastroenteritis, streptococcal pneumonia, and then septicemia. She was in the hospital until the age of six months, during which time an empyema was drained through a thoracotomy incision.

After this she was found to be developing slowly, in that she did not walk until the third year of life. However, her speech development was within normal limits. When she reached school age, she could not learn to read and write and also had difficulty in learning to calculate. Nevertheless, those who knew her thought her to be of normal intelligence, with good memory and verbal fluency. She appeared to be an active and sociable child and gave no evidence of emotional disorder.

On examination she was lefthanded, leftfooted, and lefteyed. Her speech was somewhat explosive but normal in content. There was no abnormality of skull or spine, and the neurological examination was entirely negative. The blood pressure was 100/70, and there was no abnormality on general examination. The blood cell count, sedimentation rate, and analysis of cerebrospinal fluid were within normal limits. The Wassermann reaction in blood and cerebrospinal fluid was negative. X-ray of the skull showed no abnormality other than a slight diminution in size of the right half of the posterior fossa. Chest X-ray was normal. The electroencephalogram showed mixed fast, theta, and slow activity occurring synchronously in all areas but predominating over the parietotemporal areas, especially on the right. Lumbar airencephalogram revealed a normal ventricular system. Neuro-otological examination revealed no abnormality of cochlear function. However, there was bilateral reduction of the caloric responses.

Summary

A girl aged eight and a half years had sustained damage to the cerebral hemispheres, and perhaps also to the brain stem, either on a developmental basis or, possibly, in relation to severe illnesses in early infancy.

Case 3

The patient, aged ten years, was admitted under the care of Dr. W. Gooddy for investigation of difficulties in learning to read and write. There was no comparable abnormality in the family. His twin brother was lefthanded and his father ambidextrous. He was the product of twin birth at term, and after a difficult labor he was born weighing 6 pounds, 12 ounces (3,063 grams). He required three weeks of nursing in an incubator. After this, however, he passed his early milestones normally, in that he sat up at five months, walked at a year, and acquired speech at the normal rate. When he reached school age, it became apparent that he was experiencing difficulty in learning to read and spell out of proportion to any generalized intellectual defect. He also had difficulty in doing up his shoelaces and in using knife and fork skillfully.

Jerking movements of his eyes had been present since early infancy.

On examination he was righthanded, rightfooted, and righteyed. His speech was normal, and there was no abnormality of skull or spine. He had a left convergent strabismus of about 20° and a visual acuity of no more than Jaeger 18 in the left eye, but Jaeger 1 in the right. There was nystagmus of the ocular type on central fixation, and this was more marked when he fixated with the left eye alone, or looked to the left. The optic fundi were normal, and there were no other abnormalities in the cranial nerves. The motor and sensory systems were also normal. The blood pressure was 110/70, and there was no abnormality on general examination.

Blood cell count, sedimentation rate, and analysis of cerebrospinal fluid were normal, as were skull and chest X-rays. The Wassermann reaction in blood and cerebrospinal fluid was negative. An electroencephalogram revealed a generalized abnormality, with excessive theta and slow activity over both cerebral hemispheres. Neuro-otological examination revealed second degree vestibular nystagmus to the left with the head in the erect position, and directional preponderance to the left of optokinetic nystagmus. Cochlear function was normal. Lumbar airencephalogram showed generalized enlargement of the right lateral ventricle with focal enlargement of the trigone, proximal part of the temporal horn and of the occipital horn.

Summary

A ten-year-old boy had sustained damage both to cerebral hemispheres and brain stem as a result of perinatal trauma, which had resulted in the abnormalities of his eyes, as well as in educational retardation.

Case 4

The patient, aged nine years, was admitted under the care of Dr. J. St. C. Elkington because of difficulty in writing. Her father also had trouble in learning to write, but there was no other family history of educational or neurological disabilities. She was an only child, born at term after a pregnancy characterized by toxemia from the seventh month onward. The labor was difficult, with delay in the second stage, and she was delivered by forceps. Her parents did not see her till the next day, when she was jaundiced. However, no exchange transfusion was carried out. She was not an energetic feeder and was slow to gain weight. Her motor milestones were moderately delayed, in that she was standing at the age of eighteen months and walking independently at the age of two years. On the other hand, her speech development was normal. However, even at the age of two years she was unusually clumsy and tended to knock things over. And when she reached school age, although she learned to read without conspicuous difficulty, she had great difficulty in learning to write, and this difficulty persisted in spite of three years of child guidance. She had similar difficulty in drawing and copying drawings and in such maneuvers as sewing, knitting, and fastening buttons and laces.

On examination she was righthanded and rightfooted but lefteyed. There was no abnormality of speech, and her skull was normal in shape and 22 inches in circumference. There was no abnormality of the spine. All cranial nerves were within normal limits. However, although power was normal in the limbs, there was some fluctuation of tone, and mild athetoid movements were present in all four limbs, especially in the arms, with corresponding lack of coordination of movements. There were no other motor abnormalities, and sensory testing was entirely negative. Her blood pressure was 110/80. There were no abnormalities on general examination. The electroencephalogram showed a consistent asymmetry with slow activity predominantly over the right posterior temporal region.

Summary

A nine-year-old girl was the subject of mild generalized athetosis following a trumatic delivery with neonatal jaundice. There was also electroencephalographic evidence of cerebral cortical damage.

Case 5

The patient, aged fifteen, was admitted under the care of Dr. J. St. C. Elkington because of epilepsy. There was no relevant family history of epilepsy or other neurological or educational disabilities. Her father was lefthanded, while her mother and brother were both righthanded.

On examination she was lefthanded, leftfooted, and lefteyed, and spoke normally. The skull was of normal circumference, but there was some hemiatrophy on the right side of the body. Her visual acuity on the right was 6/12 and on the left 6/18, and there was a right homonymous hemianopia complete in the inferior quadrant. There was a mild spastic hemiparesis on the right but no abnormalities of sensation. Blood pressure was 120/80, and there were no abnormal findings on general examination.

Blood cell count, sedimentation rate, and analysis of cerebrospinal fluid were normal, and the Wassermann reaction in blood and cerebrospinal fluid was negative. Electroencephalograms showed a severe degree of diffuse abnormality with a suppression of activity over the left hemisphere and frequent paroxysmal features. Skull X-rays were normal, but lumbar airencephalography revealed bilateral enlargement of the lateral ventricles more marked on the left, indicative of a degree of left hemiatrophy.

Summary

A fifteen-year-old girl had sustained perinatal damage to the cerebral hemisphere, particularly the left, in association with prematurity, which was now manifesting itself in the form of epilepsy and educational retardation.

Case 6

The patient, aged eleven and a half, came under the care of Dr. P. H. Sandifer at the age of four because of clumsiness of the hands and inability to walk without assistance. None of his relatives was similarly affected. He was the product of a normal pregnancy which ended in spontaneous delivery by breech, ten weeks before the expected date. At birth he weighed 3 pounds (1,361 grams). After being nursed in an incubator for six weeks, he was breastfed and gained weight in the normal way. However, he could not sit up till he was eighteen months old. He crawled at two years and even at four years could not yet stand without support. On the other hand, he began to speak before he was a year old and was forming short sentences at the age of eighteen months. He was lefthanded; there was no other lefthandedness in the family.

When seen at the age of four he was found to have an asymmetrical skull with left frontal recession. There was a convergent concomitant strabismus, but no other abnormality in the cranial nerves. Fine movements of both arms were clumsy, and there was a tendency to mirror movements, but no paresis. There was a spastic diplegia of moderate severity, more marked on the right, with bilateral extensor plantar responses. He could walk holding onto a helping hand for support.

The strabismus was corrected by right internal rectus recession when he was five years old. His equinus deformity was corrected by bilateral soleus neurectomy when he was seven.

At the age of four and a half he was tested on the Stanford-Binet scale (by Norah Gibbs) and achieved an IQ of 102, scored mainly on the verbal items. Three and a half years later his revised Stanford-Binet IQ was 113, again almost entirely scored on verbal items, and this was futher brought out by testing on the Wechsler scale at age nine years and three months, when his verbal IQ was 121 and his performance IQ was 51. On Object Assembly and Block Design he failed to score at all. By this time it had become apparent that he was having severe educational difficulties, and he was still completely unable to read or write. At ten years and three months his manipulation was still clumsy, especially on the right, as tested by placing of pegs in holes and threading of beads, and he still required the aid of two sticks in walking. He had now begun to read a little (Holborn reading age, six and a half years). He remained a nonstarter in spelling and also experienced great difficulty with arithmetic and drawing.

At age eleven and a half his physical disabilities were unchanged. He was noticed to show right-left confusion. His reading age on the Holborn scale was now seven years and nine months, and his spelling age (Schonell and Schonell, 1956) was eight years and one month. His arithmetic was impaired by confusion of the rank of the digits.

Summary

A boy aged eleven and a half had a spastic diplegia and educational disabilities as sequelae of perinatal damage due to prematurity.

Case 7

The patient, aged twelve years, was admitted under the care of Dr. W. Gooddy for investigation of epileptic seizures and educational disability. There was no history of epilepsy or of neurological or educational disability in the family, and apart from her mother's sister, all close relatives were righthanded. Following a normal pregnancy, which went to term, she was delivered by forceps after prolonged labor, and weighed 6 pounds, 7 ounces (2,921 grams) at birth. Her speech development was normal, as was her motor development, and she was able to walk before she was a year old. However, at the age of three months she had the first of her epileptic fits, which were of an infantile spasm type. At the age of seven months she had two generalized convulsions. Since then she has continued to have attacks in which, following a visual aura, she tends to bend forward, while her arms straighten. She may talk nonsense during an attack but never remembers this, and after about thirty minutes she continues with her normal activities. These attacks occur between three and seven times a week. In other respects she remains well, though rather clumsy, particularly in tasks requiring fine finger movements. She has some difficulty in learning to read, write, and calculate.

On examination, she was righthanded and rightfooted but lefteyed. Her speech was normal, as were her skull and spine, and there were no abnormalities in the cranial nerves or motor and sensory systems. Her blood pressure was 110/70, and no abnormalities were found on general examination. Blood cell count, sedimentation rate, and analysis of cerebrospinal fluid were within normal limits. Skull X-ray was normal, and lumbar airencephalography showed no abnormality of the ventricular system. The electoencephalogram revealed bilateral widespread theta activity, which at times became rhythmic and appeared in short paroxysms, predominantly over the right temporal area.

Summary

A girl aged twelve and a half had sustained cerebral hemisphere damage at the time of her birth, which had left her with temporal lobe epilepsy and which was also responsible for the educational disabilities which later became apparent.

The salient features of the seven cases are presented in Table 1.

Test Results

General Intelligence

The seven patients in this series were tested on the Wechsler Intelligence Scale for Children (WISC). This intelligence scale is in two parts, containing verbal and performance tests, respectively, so that verbal and performance IQs can be separately calculated. All patients in this series obtained a verbal IQ at least twenty points higher than

Table 1. Summary of age, sex, and clinical and neurological findings

	1	2	3	4	5	6	7
Sex	F	F	M	F	F	M	F
Age	9.5	8.5	10.3	9.6	14.6	11.7	12.1
Dominance:							
Hand	R	L	R	R	L	L	R
Foot	R	L	L	R	L	L	R
Eye	L	R	R	L	L	L	L
Family History of:							
Reading or writing retardation	None	None	None	Father	None	None	None
Lefthandedness	None	Yes	Yes	None	Yes	None	Yes
Birth injury	None	None	Yes	Yes	Yes	Yes	Yes
Motor development	Delayed	Delayed	Normal	Normal	Normal	Delayed	Normal
Speech development	Normal	Normal	Normal	Normal	Delayed	Normal	Normal
Neurological abnormality	Concomitant strabismus	None	Nystagmus, visual defect left eye	Athetosis	Rt. homonymous hemianopia, rt. spastic hemiparesis	Spastic diplegia	None
Lumbar airencephalogram	Enlarged lateral ventricles	Normal	Right cerebral atrophy	Not done	Left cerebral atrophy	Not done	Normal
Electroencephalogram	Normal	Diffuse abnormality	Diffuse dysrhythmia	R > L abnormality	Left temporal	Diffuse dysrhythmia	Diffuse dysrhythmia
Audiometry	Normal	Normal	Normal	Not done	Not done	Not done	Not done
Other abnormalities	Nonspecific clumsiness			Not done*	Not done*	Not done*	Not done*
	Emotional disorder		Nonspecific clumsiness		Epilepsy		Epilepsy

*Clinically normal.

the performance IQ. The verbal IQ scores ranged from 81 in Case 3 to 128 in Case 4. Three of the patients had a verbal IQ in the dull average range, the other four were average or above. The scores on the performance tests were in all cases lower than the verbal scores; the discrepancy ranged from 20 points in Case 4 to 35 in Case 2. All the performance IQs were within the mental defective range, except Cases 4 and 6, which were average. The pattern of individual test scores within the performance scale was similar in all the patients. Scores were considerably higher on the two tests involving picture interpretation than on the two spatial or constructional tests. If the scores on the latter two tests are compared with verbal ability, then the discrepancy noted above becomes even more marked. These findings are summarized in Table 2.

Table 2. Summary of intellectual and educational test findings

	1	2	3	4	5	6	7
Chronological age	9-5	8-5	10-3	9-6	14-6	11-7	12-1
Verbal IQ	89	97	81	128	84	116	86
Performance IQ	64	62	58	108	53	93	58
Subtest scores:							
Information	4	10	6	16	5	12	7
Arithmetic	4	5	8	12	8	12	4
Similarities	13	11	7	16	10	13	10
Vocabulary	14	13	7	15	5	13	6
Digit Span	—	—	5	13	10	—	7
Picture Completion	10	5	5	15	10	10	9
Picture Arrangement	3	6	5	14	3	8	2
Block Design	4	3	6	10	5	9	5
Object Assembly	2	4	0	6	0	—	0
Reading age	7	6	6	12	8	8	11
Spelling age	8	5	6	9	7	8	9
Arithmetic age	6	6	8-6	10-6	11	7-9	7-9

Language Functions

Apart from the WISC assessment of verbal intelligence, all patients were subjected to clinical assessment of language impairment. The tasks consisted of naming objects and pictures and carrying out simple and multiple instructions. Choice of words in conversation and clarity of speech were noted. Verbal learning was tested by sentence and digit repetition (digit span +1). No children in this series had any difficulty with these tasks.

Constructional Abilities

The constructional tests used were joining two points with a straight line, copying a series of simple figures (line, angle, diamond, star, cube), and spontaneous drawings.

Two of the patients had a gross constructional disability (Cases 1 and 2). They were unable to join two points or to copy a circle or a square recognizably. Four patients had a moderately severe disability—they could copy very simple drawings such as a line or an angle, but they could not copy a diamond or any more complex figure. One patient (Case 5) has a fairly mild disability; she was able to copy a diamond and other simple drawings but completely failed to draw a cube or a star. The diamonds drawn by these patients are illustrated in Figure 1.

Finger Differentiation and Order

These three tests are described in detail by Kinsbourne and Warrington (1963) (see Figure 1, Chapter 4).

In test 1, two points on the fingers are touched simultaneously. These may both be on the same finger or on two adjacent fingers. The patient is required to say whether one or two fingers are being touched.

In test 2, two fingers are touched simultaneously, and the patient is required to say how many fingers there are between the ones being touched.

In test 3, four wooden blocks, shaped as shown in the illustration, are placed in front of the patient. While his eyes are closed, the subject's fingers are molded around one of four corresponding blocks. He is then asked to open his eyes and, without looking at the block in his hand, to pick out the corresponding one on the table.

Six patients in this series failed all these finger tests, and the other patient (Case 4) failed two of them. The patients were tested repeatedly and were considered to have failed if they made persistent errors (Table 3).

Right-Left Orientation

The patients were asked to indicate their right and left hands. They were asked to carry out instructions involving right and left on their own person. They were required to point to the examiner's right and left. Four patients (Cases 1, 2, 6, and 7) made errors of right-left orientation on their own persons and three patients made errors only

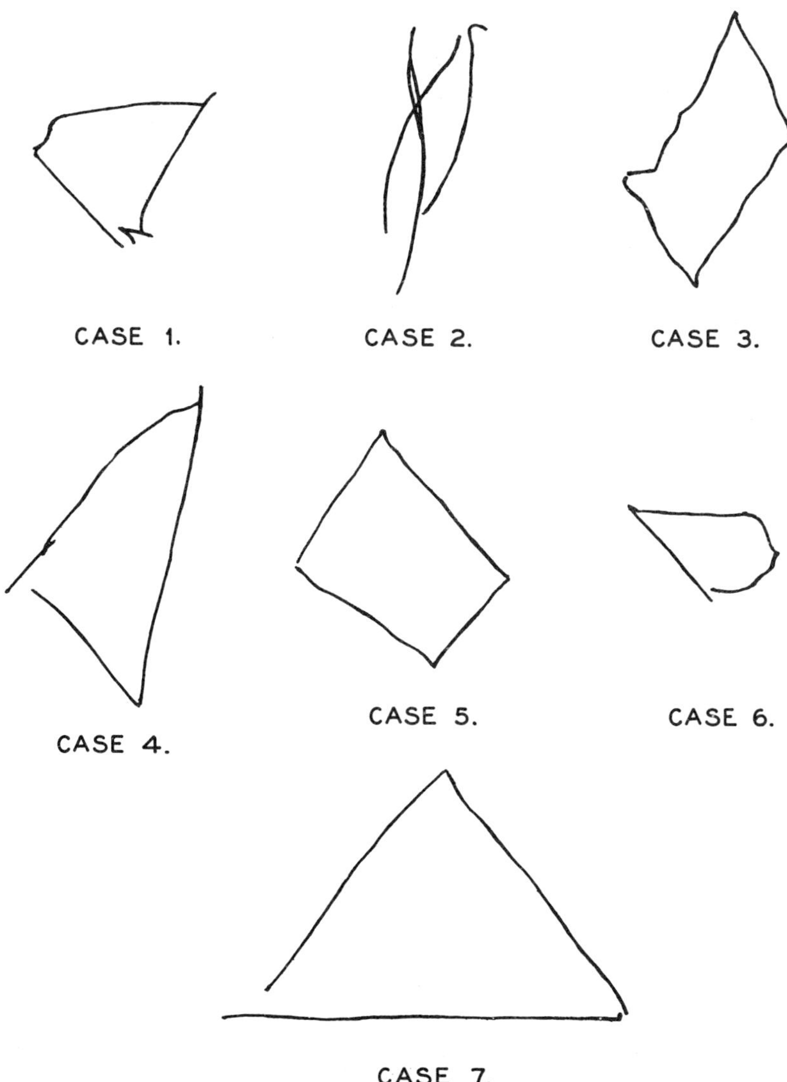

Figure 1. Copies of a diamond, Cases 1–7.

with extrapersonal tasks involving right and left (see Table 3).

Arithmetic

Arithmetical ability was assessed by the WISC subtest of oral arithmetical problems, and the score was converted into a mental age. The patients were also asked to do simple subtraction and addition

Table 3. Summary of clinical psychological test findings

	1	2	3	4	5	6	7
Speech:							
Expressive	—	—	—	—	—	—	—
Receptive	—	—	—	—	—	—	—
Constructional ability	+*	+	+	+	+	+	+
Writing:							
Script	+	+	—	+	—	+	—
Spelling	+	+	+	+	+	+	+
Calculation:							
Addition and subtraction	+	+	+	+	+	+	+
Problems	+	+	—	—	—	—	+
Left-right orientation:							
On self	+	+	—	—	—	+	+
On examiner	+	+	+	+	+	+	+
Finger order tests:							
Finger differentiation test	+	+	+	—	+	+	+
In between test	+	+	+	+	+	+	+
Finger block test	+	+	+	+	+	+	+

* + denotes abnormality.

on paper, with the exception of Cases 1 and 2, who were unable to write legibly and were tested orally.

Three patients (Cases 1, 2, and 7) were very retarded in their ability to do mental arithmetic problems. Four patients were able to do mental arithmetic problems at a level consistent with their general intellectual level but showed a definite disability when required to perform addition and subtraction on paper. The greatest difficulty was encountered with subtraction or when the problem involved two columns of figures (Table 3).

Spelling

All patients in this series were tested with a standard word list (Schonell and Schonell, 1956). The attainment levels ranged from five to nine years. In all patients except Case 4, spelling ability was retarded. The difference between chronological and spelling age ranged from one and a half to seven years (Table 2). A characteristic type of spelling error was made by all these patients (including Case 4). Letter substitutions were less common than errors in letter order; thus letters in the word might be reversed or jumbled. Omissions and letter duplications were also common. When the patients were asked to spell words by the use of solid letters, it was observed that the letters were often picked out in the wrong order, but after repeated corrections, the right order was sometimes achieved.

Script

All patients were asked to write their name, short simple sentences from dictation, and words from a graded spelling test. They were also required to copy letters and short words. One patient (Case 2) was totally unable to write her name or to copy single letters. This patient also had the most severe disability on constructional tasks. Cases 1, 4, and 6 had a moderate degree of impairment of script. They were able to copy letters and short words so that they were recognizable, though ill formed. The degree of impairment of script correlated well with the severity of defect in copying drawings (see Fig. 1). The remaining patients, 1, 5, and 7, had no specific defect of script (see Table 3).

Reading

Reading age was assessed by means of a graded word list (Schonell and Schonell, 1956). Five of the patients were retarded in their reading by two or more years. Cases 4 and 7 were not significantly retarded in reading. The patients in this series had, on the whole, more difficulty with spelling than with reading (Table 2).

Comment

The present cases showed the features of the Gerstmann syndrome.

Finger Agnosia

The children all had difficulty in naming their fingers. This alone does not justify the diagnosis of finger agnosia, as a proportion of normal children aged nine to fifteen have comparable difficulties (Hermann and Norrie, 1958). However, tests of finger differentiation and order were applied and were inadequately performed in every case. This result was outside the range of normal variation (Kinsbourne and Warrington, 1963). Failure on these tests has been consistent in cases of the Gerstmann syndrome but not in control cases (Kinsbourne and Warrington, 1962), and it was therefore believed that the children were exhibiting finger agnosia, a disability which, in these cases with developmental lesions, was regarded as failure to acquire the relevant function (of finger differentiation) in the normal way in the course of maturation.

Right-Left Disorientation

The children failed to achieve the expected level of efficiency in tasks involving right-left orientation. Here again, the relevant ability appeared not to have been acquired at the expected time in the course of development.

Systematic reversals (Benton, 1958) were not found.

Dysgraphia

There was difficulty both in spelling (oral, written, and by arrangement of letters) and in script (spontaneous and copied). Spelling achievement, as measured in terms of spelling age (Schonell and Schonell, 1956), fell short of the chronological age by more than three years in five of the seven cases. The spelling difficulty was characteristic. Letter choice was, on the whole, correct. Letter substitutions were less common than errors in letter order, with reversals of letter pairs and quite often complete word jumbles that resulted in an anagram of the word. Omissions of letters were common. This type of spelling difficulty was prominent in oral as well as written spelling. It was particularly evident in the use of solid letters, when it was observed how often the letters were picked out in a totally wrong order.

This type of misspelling, which has been previously reported in similar cases (Gooddy and Reinhold, 1961; Hermann, 1959; Orton, 1937), is not common among the errors of normal school children of comparable age. It forms only a small percentage of the errors of aphasics (Weisenburg and McBride, 1935). We have rarely found it in children with reading and writing backwardness of types other than the Gerstmann. On the other hand, letter reversals and omissions are notably common in the spelling of much younger children (Hildreth, 1932). Again, in regard to spelling, children with the Gerstmann syndrome are seen to have failed to acquire an ability normally gained at a younger age.

The typical order errors in spelling become manifest where the test word is, in other respects, within the patient's reach. When the word is far too difficult, the misspelling will be nonspecific. When spelling is tested with the help of a word list of graded difficulty, the results fall into three groups: the simplest words, spelled correctly; the ones next in difficulty, distorted by order errors; the still more difficult ones, nonspecifically misspelled. This will remain true whatever the actual level of spelling achievement (which depends on the interaction of many factors). Even the two children whose spelling age approached their chronological age produced the characteristic word jumbles when they began to make errors.

Four children also had impaired script; the written letters were often crude and misshapen. There was difficulty both with the orientation of letters and letter parts and with their correct formation. The difficulty in forming and copying letters was matched by comparable difficulty in tasks of drawing and copying drawings and of spatial arrangement.

Both in their spelling and their script, these children showed abnormalities closely comparable to those found in adults with the Gerstmann syndrome (see Chapter 5).

Dyscalculia

The arithmetical difficulties exhibited by the present cases were striking and profound. Even the simplest additions were beyond the scope of Cases 1, 2, and 7. The concept of number was, however, understood by all the patients. The difficulty was best brought out by tasks requiring a knowledge of the significance bestowed upon numbers by their relative positions.

Constructional Apraxia

This is almost invariable in adults with the Gerstmann syndrome (Ajuriaguerra and Hécaen, 1960; Critchley, 1953; Stengel, 1944). In the developmental variant here described, it is represented by a marked specific disability in certain spatial tasks. This is well brought out by the results of testing on the WISC (Table 2).

In every case, the nonverbal IQ is less than the verbal IQ—a remarkable finding in children with reading and writing retardation. If the tests with the highest spatial loading (Block Design and Object Assembly) are compared with tests of high verbal loading (Vocabulary and Digit Span) (Maxwell, 1959), the discrepancy becomes still more obvious (Table 2). In every case, language abilities are normal and spatial abilities relatively depressed. Correspondingly, the children all had undue difficulty in copying line drawings and match stick patterns.

Dyslexia

Reading retardation of varying degrees was present in all but one of the cases, though it was characteristically somewhat less severe than the retardation in spelling. The presence of this additional feature in the developmental syndrome requires explanation.

It has become apparent that the elements of the Gerstmann syndrome have in common a difficulty in the correct differentiation or arrangement of parts that constitute a whole—the fingers as they are arranged on the hand, right and left in relation to the self, the arrangement of the letters with a word, the significance that numbers acquire by virtue of their relative positions, and the correct arrangement of the parts of a spatial pattern. Does reading involve such an ordering function?

The adult reads most words as a whole (Erdmann and Dodge, 1898). The word is not necessarily built up from its elements. This process, once established, is unimpaired in the Gerstmann syndrome. This is not true, however, of children who are learning to read. Unless they are taught by an uncompromisingly visual method, which is rare in this country, they learn words letter by letter. Correct order is essential. Where there is ordering difficulty, as in the present cases, some reading retardation is to be expected, and its presence is consistent with knowledge of the basic mechanism of the Gerstmann syndrome.

The developmental Gerstmann syndrome reveals its fullest expression in a child who, backward in reading and still more so in spelling, fails tests of finger differentiation and order, confuses right and left, makes errors of letter sequence in spelling and of rank of digits in calculation, and, since he is poor in spatial and constructional tasks, performs significantly less well on the performance than on the verbal scale of the WISC.

The seven cases here reported for purposes of illustration fulfill all or most of these criteria, but one might expect occasionally to encounter the syndrome in a less complete form, particularly if the child is examined during a transitional period, in which a delay in cerebral cortical development is finally being overcome. The typical educational deficits may then outlast the underlying disorder of physiological function. Conversely, expert teaching methods applied to an intelligent child may occasionally permit the acquisition of good reading and writing ability in spite of the presence of the developmental Gerstmann syndrome (e.g., Case 4), but at the limits of performance, the tell-tale order errors in spelling appear. The discrepancy between verbal and performance scores on the WISC is characteristic of, but not limited to, the developmental Gerstmann syndrome. A similar situation may arise due to the presence of simple clumsiness (Walton, Ellis, and Court, 1962), a motor defect of a lower level than that which typically impairs performance in the Gerstmann syndrome.

The developmental Gerstmann syndrome is probably not rare. The present cases are in many respects similar to those of Hermann and Norrie (1958). The adult reported by Spillane (1942) may also fit into this category, although his low general intelligence and history of late speech development leave this hypothesis uncertain. Critchley (1942) mentioned an adult with a notable difficulty in the ordering of letters, numbers, and the elements of the Morse code, which he regarded as a partial Gerstmann syndrome of developmental origin.

Identification of the developmental Gerstmann syndrome with congenital word blindness (Hermann and Norrie, 1958) produces difficulties of definition. If congenital word blindness is regarded as "pure," in the sense that it affects recognition and recall of symbols exclusively (Orton, 1937), then it is patently not identical with the Gerstmann syndrome, which represents a more general disorder of function. However, it may be doubted whether Orton's cases would have been regarded as "pure" by him had he considered them in the light of the Gerstmann syndrome and performed the relevant investigations.

Hermann and Norrie's attribution of the Gerstmann syndrome to a group of children with reading disability finds support in the present results, which, in comparable cases, add the ingredient of finger agnosia to the manifestations which they described. It does not follow that this condition is the only organic cause of reading backwardness. Retardation in the language sphere may also cause reading retardation (Ingram, 1959; McCready, 1910), but the resulting appearances are quite different from those described in the present study as characteristic of the developmental Gerstmann syndrome. It therefore seems unjustified to identify one variety of organically determined reading retardation, that due to the developmental Gerstmann syndrome, with the supposed entity of congenital word blindness. It seems sufficient to state that, among the many causes of reading and writing retardation, the developmental Gerstmann syndrome is one. Nor does it necessarily cause retardation of the utmost severity. Insofar as it may represent a developmental lag rather than an absolute deficit, the accompanying difficulty in learning to read and write may be only temporary. It may, however, be turned into a permanent deficit by the intervention of a secondary emotional disorder which blocks attempts at making up lost ground even at a time when the features of the Gerstmann syndrome are no longer in evidence. Conversely, an enduring organic disability may, as far as its practical consequences are concerned, be overcome by skillful teaching of an intelligent and emotionally stable child. The interaction of organic and environmental factors against the changing background of a maturing nervous system can give rise to infinitely varied clinical appearances. Among the causes of reading retardation, the developmental Gerstmann syndrome does not necessarily give rise to the most severe or enduring disability (Case 4). As with any other disease, its severity varies from case to case, and both the technique of the teacher and the attitude of the parents must be expected to affect the outcome materially.

The developmental Gerstmann syndrome may occur in a setting of perinatal trauma (Cases 3 to 7). In the absence of the latter, it may be presumed to be due to some developmental defect (Cases 1 and 2). A strong familial tendency, as reported by Hermann (1959), was not a feature of the present series, nor was there any regularity of hand, foot, and eye dominance. All but Case 5 had normal speech development and all had normal hearing, but motor development was delayed in Cases 1, 2, and 6. Cases 3 to 6 also showed other neurological abnormalities, and Cases 5 and 7 had epilepsy. In Cases 1, 3, and 5, cerebral atrophy on one or both sides was demonstrated by airencephalography. This relatively high incidence of demonstrable neurological abnormality may be a consequence of the method of selection, which was from among cases initially referred for a neurological opinion, and is not expected to arise should other methods of selection be used. Particularly among Scandinavian populations, and even among children in remedial reading classes in this country, a stronger familial trend and fewer associated abnormalities are to be expected. Whatever the cause of the underlying cerebral deficit—whether perinatal trauma or developmental error—it, and its consequences, is not to be regarded as necessarily permanent. There may be a lag rather than a complete arrest of maturation of the relevant cerebral areas, the situation here outlined may resolve spontaneously in due course, and the Gerstmann syndrome may disappear, leaving behind a residue of educational retardation. Such retardation should then respond to straightforward teaching methods.

The localizing significance of the congenital Gerstmann syndrome is not yet known. The present cases do not include autopsy material and cannot be used as indicators of localization. Were autopsy material available, we would not necessarily expect it to reveal gross structural damage of the left parietal lobe, as in most adult case of the Gerstmann syndrome.

Summary

Seven cases are reported of the developmental Gerstmann syndrome diagnosed in childhood. The presence of finger agnosia was established by the use of tests of finger differentiation and order, and two or more of the other elements of the syndrome were present in all cases. The developmental Gerstmann syndrome may arise on a constitutional or traumatic basis, and it may exist in isolation or in a setting of other neurological disorder. It may cause reading and writing retardation of a characteristic type.

PART IV

Conclusion

CHAPTER 22

TEACHING READING: A CRITIQUE

THOMAS J. EDWARDS

We are in a dilemma. Only a few decades ago very little thought was given to the teaching of reading. It was simply taught. Some children learned easily and quickly; others did not. Those who experienced cumulative failure in their mastery of reading and the other language arts were likely to quit school and get a job, and there was little concern about the "dropout problem." Further, it was tacitly assumed that students who failed to learn by traditional methods were simply incapable of learning and were therefore relegated to the plow.

Now, however, very serious questions are being raised regarding reading failures: is a certain amount of reading disability inevitable? Are our methods inadequate? Do we need a variety of types of approach to correspond with a possible variety of learning styles within the school population? Reading has now become a "field of study," and a variety of disciplines is impinging upon this field with vigor. A significant hypothesis upon which these newly directed efforts are based is this: many students fail to learn reading and other language skills because we have not been clever enough to devise techniques for coming to grips with their problems. The nature of the reading process has not been thoroughly analyzed. The interrelatedness existing among the various aspects of language development has not been clearly understood, and a multitude of other psychological phenomena that interact with or are prerequisite to language learning have too frequently been ignored.

As a result of this new attention to reading and related behaviors, there has come into existence a variety of theories, schools of thought (often verging on cultism), specific approaches to the teaching of reading and the other language arts, and instructional materials for the implementation of these divergent points of view.

The harassed educational community is asking which is the best method? Which of the dramatic claims for this or that approach am I to believe? How can I go about selecting instructional materials? A careful reading of the chapters preceding this one is likely to increase the anxiety level of educators, since the rationales of many methods are rather clearly structured and therefore still leave the reader frustrated at a number of important points.

It is the firm belief of this writer that our basic dilemma is one of logic; that is, we are caught in the bind of asking ourselves which is the right method. We are groping for absolutes and are therefore thinking in either/or terms. Might we not better ask which method is the best for a specific type of problem or for a special segment of the learner population? We might also consider the teacher: what has been her background of experience and training? Is she more comfortable with one approach than another? What about her creative ability and her temperament? How much structure or flexibility does she require?

We are indeed "people in quandaries" and should heed Wendell Johnson's admonition, proffered some twenty years ago, that we not look at problems in absolute either/or terms but rather that we consider a variety of possible alternatives, each of which might have some merit and some validity.

The purpose of this final chapter is not to recapitulate the points of view discussed in the foregoing sections. The authors have done a quite adequate descriptive job. Rather, it is to structure certain considerations that might prove helpful or at least provocative to the educator, who must, in the end, either join one of the several schools of thought or become eclectic in approaching the problem of teaching reading and the other language arts. It is also the purpose of this chapter to point out a number of the unsolved riddles at which we must take a hard look in the development of hypotheses, experimental designs, curricula, and instructional materials.

The English Language: Orthographic Chaos

The relationship between the sounds of the English language and the way that these sounds are represented in writing is one of great inconsistency. It is amazing, therefore, that a much greater segment of our school population is not plagued by severe reading retardation. This problem of sound-symbol inconsistency may be divided into two major subproblems. The first subproblem is the fact that a given spoken sound or phoneme may be represented by a number of written symbols. Hence, the long **a** sound, for example, may be represented variously by **ay**, **eigh**, **ai**, and a medial **a** can be made long by a final **e** or by the letter **a** itself at the end of an open syllable, as in **caper**.

A second subproblem related to this sound-symbol inconsistency involves the fact that a given combination of letters or graphemes might shift its function so that it represents a different sound, dependent upon the word in which it appears. Hence, one might compare the pronunciation of the single grapheme **ough** as it appears in **plough**, **ought**, **rough**, **though**, **cough**, or **through**.

This problem of orthographic irregularity remains a central, basic and persistently bothersome challenge, particularly to those who are attempting to develop improved methods and materials for the teaching of beginning reading and writing skills. At later stages, after the reader has amassed word analysis skills and has had sufficient contact with an extensive array of reading materials, he is quite likely to glide along the printed page, no longer aware of the peculiarities of our writing system, since he reacts almost completely to whole word forms and is propelled by meaning in his rapid and accurate perception of printed material.

It is extremely interesting to note that two essentially different approaches have been taken in an attempt to handle the problem of sound-symbol inconsistency, and the distinction between these two approaches is worthy of careful consideration.

One attack on this problem centers upon the teaching medium; that is, the emphasis is placed upon somehow modifying the physical properties of word forms. The fundamental contention underlying this approach might be stated as follows: There is not a one-to-one relationship between the sounds and symbols of the English language. Therefore, something must be done to the printed stimuli themselves so that they will conform consistently to our speech-sound system. We will transform our writing system—temporarily at least—so that this consistency will obtain, and the beginning reader will not be plagued by the vagaries of our language and risk failure.

Sir James Pitman's Augmented Roman Alphabet, sometimes referred to as the Initial Teaching Alphabet (i/t/a), is a good example of the modification of printed stimuli in order to ease the task confronting the beginning reader. He simply changed the alphabet for the purpose of teaching beginning reading so that there would be consistent sound-symbol relationships. His artificial alphabet gives the child an opportunity to enjoy comfort and success from the very beginning of his reading and writing experience and postpones his confrontation with the irregularities of English orthography until symbol manipulation has become commonplace, habitual, and rewarding. Pitman was careful, in the modifications that he did make in his Initial Teaching Alphabet, to retain a fairly close similarity with the regular alphabet in order to facilitate later transfer to the printed stimuli that the learner will ultimately have to master.

In contrast with Pitman's approach is the color-coding method with its several variations. Here again it is the printed stimuli that become the point of focus and are modified. However, whereas Pitman changed the actual forms of letters and ascribed consistent sound values to each one, the color-coding people superimposed consistency upon letters as they actually exist by merely assigning a given color to a letter or a compound of letters if the phonetic or sound value of the letters was the same. It was indicated here previously that the sound of the long **a** may be represented in a variety of ways in printed form. However, in accordance with the color-coding approach, letters representing this sound would all be colored in the same way. It might be mentioned here that some color-coding programs involve the imposition of color on both vowels and consonants. On the other hand, there are those who feel that this requires too many color discriminations (sometimes as many as forty!). In addition, this latter group feels that it is the vowel sounds which cause the greatest amount of difficulty, and therefore they color only those letters or letter groups that represent the various sounds of the vowels.

Still another approach to the problem of sound-symbol inconsistency in the English language is the so-called linguistics approach. The central rationale of this approach for the teaching of beginning reading is this: the inconsistencies of the English writing system should be delayed, therefore, and at the beginning stage of the teaching of reading only letter combinations or graphemes that represent regular or consistent relationships between sounds and printed symbols should be introduced. Only after the decoding of these consistent elements of the language has been mastered reasonably well are their regularities presented gradually and systematically. It should be pointed out here that primary emphasis during the earliest stages of the beginning-to-read process is upon decoding. Materials developed in accordance with this approach are made as meaningful as possible. However, the systematic sequence in which various sounds are introduced limits the richness of the syntactical patterns that can be introduced until considerable progress has been made in the accumulation of a variety of sound symbols.

Rapprochement: Critique and Dilemmas

In the preceding section we have given three major systems that have been developed for attacking the beginning reader's problem of trying to handle the baffling irregularities inherent in the English writing system. The i/t/a approach says, "Just change the alphabet initially so that it will provide the beginning reader with consistent sound-symbol relationships." The color-coding proponents disagree. They say, "No, leave the forms of letters intact, since these are the stimuli that the learner must perceive. Rather, superimpose consistency upon the existing alphabet by ascribing a single color to letters representing a given sound, regardless of how this sound is represented."

These two methods—i/t/a and color coding—both direct attention to the printed stimuli themselves, with the former making structural changes in these stimuli and the latter making chromatic changes.

By contrast, the several techniques based on the linguistics approach direct their attention away from the printed medium and toward method or sequence of presentation. Hence, they say, "Initially, we will avoid the confusing inconsistencies of English orthography. Instead, we will feed the beginning reader an uncomplicated and consistent diet of sound-symbol relationships until he has them clearly fixed. Only very gradually will we introduce the irregularities and this at a time when his perceptual skills and decoding expertise will lessen the trauma of contradiction or inconsistency."

On the face of it, the rationales underlying each of these approaches have validity and obvious merit. But again the question arises: which one is best? It may be that rigorous longitudinal experimentation will be required before answers to this question emerge. Also, the admonition offered in an earlier section of this chapter might need to be reiterated: there may indeed be no best method. Rather, we may find that a given method might have superiority over others, depending upon the nature of the learner and of the teacher. However, it might be good to take a brief, critical look at these three major approaches, since each has its own logical and unique ingenuity but carries with it also its own concomitant vulnerability to attack.

The Initial Teaching Alphabet

The rationale of making a temporary complete change in the writing system of English seems like a logical way of postponing the beginning reader's confusion in handling irregular phoneme-grapheme correspondence. Proponents of this method also reason that there is a fundamental perceptual learning that must take place, regardless of orthography, and that this learning transfers somewhat as a primary mental ability to the perceptual learning of new and different printed verbal stimuli.

Informal reports from users of these materials indicate that (1) initial interest in reading is demonstrated early and remains high; (2) use of the initial teaching alphabet results in early speed and fluency in reading; (3) beginning readers demonstrate greater ease of written expression; (4) independent work habits are developed early; (5) there is a noticeable lessening of behavior problems in school; and (6) the transition from the initial teaching alphabet to traditional orthography is made easily and, in many cases, almost automatically.

Skepticism regarding the initial teaching alphabet centers primarily around the problem of transfer of perceptual learning to the recognition of printed forms encountered in traditionally written reading materials or to the reproduction of printed forms required in spelling in the traditional orthography. One other criticism is that considerable time and cost are involved in the translation or the development of materials with special type-setting requirements.

Rather carefully planned research into the effectiveness of the initial teaching alphabet is already under way. In an earlier interim report (Downing, 1964) the following tentative conclusion was drawn: "We may conclude that children who use i/t/a for beginning reading not only can transfer their training to t.o. (i.e., traditional orthography), but, 1½ years after commencing instruction in i/t/a, they can read t.o. with much greater accuracy and comprehension than children who have been attempting to learn t.o. from the very beginning"

Color Coding

The color coding approach appears to have certain advantages over the initial teaching alphabet and the linguistics approach. It avoids the criticism regarding transfer ultimately to traditional orthography that is leveled against the initial teaching alphabet, since color coding requires no change in the structure of word forms. This is also a strength of the linguistics approach. On the other hand, however, color coding has in common with the initial teaching alphabet the avoidance of the problem of unnatural language. This is possible because the phoneme-grapheme consistency imposed upon the written language permits students to handle from the beginning almost any word that is in their spoken vocabulary. The linguistics approach affords no such freedom.

Users of these materials have been very enthusiastic about their results with superior, normal, and severely retarded readers, including dyslexics and adult functional illiterates; they also maintain that color coding aids spelling competence; and they point out that no unlearning is necessary when the reader is weaned away from the use of color, since all along he has had contact with word forms whose structure has remained intact.

A basic question regarding color coding, however, is whether or not the addition of color is an unfeasible addition to the problems of the beginning reader in that it may complicate the initial learning task by adding a chromatic dimension. Might color discrimination or color naming present a problem? If publishers, teachers, or the students themselves must be involved in the color-coding process, does this involve added expense which may not offset the advantages inherent in the method itself? These questions remain to be answered by empirical evidence.

Color blindness of some degree occurs with sufficient frequency to present a stumbling block in any school system using a color coding method alone. According to one survey, eight boys per hundred are color blind, and one girl in two hundred. Obviously, underachievers taught under the color coding method will have to be tested for color blindness, unless all pupils have been screened beforehand for color vision.

The Linguistics Approach

As was true of both the initial teaching alphabet and the color coding, discussed above, so it is also with the linguistics approach that its obvious strengths tend to be somewhat countered by certain weaknesses.

It was mentioned previously that a crucial aspect of the linguistics method was the systematic introduction of letters and letter combinations sequentially and in a manner which permits a one-to-one relationship between sounds and the printed symbols that represent them. The inconsistent sound-symbol relationships are postponed, and even they are introduced gradually. This type of sequencing tends initially to a quite marked limitation on the richness and variety of the reading and writing experiences to which the learner is exposed. Hence, materials for beginning instruction—commercial, teacher-made, or student-written—contain highly unnatural sentences which many critics feel do damage to meaning and destroy interest because of alleged inane content.

Supporters of the linguistics point of view argue, however, that beginning readers regard the content of these materials as whimsical and that interest therefore does not wane. They also argue that the learner's early exposure to order and system, coupled with success in using this method, results in high motivation which sustains him when he later encounters irregularities in the language.

This writer would question criticisms leveled against the so-called inane content of beginning instructional materials based on this method. True, students do enter first grade already armed with a facility in oral language that far outstrips the vocabulary and syntax of most beginning readers. It is agreed, too, that extension of the student's ability to handle the syntax and vocabulary of the English language is highly desirable. Yet the decoding process is difficult enough to justify a postponement of these more sophisticated aspects of language development until basic mastery of sound-symbol relationships has been achieved reasonably well. If a teacher wants the beginning reader to continue his general language development in these other areas simultaneously with the introduction of beginning reading, why not separate reading temporarily from other aspects of language development and enhance syntax, vocabulary, reasoning ability, or whatever else is desired at the oral-language level? This kind of separation would decrease complexity in the learning situation and thereby facilitate learning.

Sophisticated adult readers who react negatively to the content of materials based on the principle of controlled vocabulary input are projecting their own desires for richness of meaning because they have already mastered the decoding process. The beginning reader, on the other hand, is intrigued by the magic of the decoding process, and success in the mastery of this process might well provide adequate motivation at the initial stages of learning to read.

As a case in point, this writer was thirty-five years old when he began to learn the very beautiful but frighteningly different Arabic orthography of the Persian language. However, the mastery of simple sentences like "This is a woman" or "A man should be a breadwinner" yielded indescribable delight and satisfaction. Although the content of Persian beginning readers did not read like a Hemingway novel, the experience of being able to translate this exotic script into its spoken counterparts was reward enough. Hence, extreme caution should be exerted by adults in evaluating methods and materials on the basis of content, since the goal of beginning reading instruction is the development of techniques for the accurate and rapid recognition of words.

Certain proponents of the linguistics method advocate the diminution of illustrations in books and other reading materials designed for beginning readers. Their contention is that the probability of success in the decoding process is based to a significant degree upon the learner's coming to grips with sound-symbol relationships and that, therefore, his attention should be directed toward word forms and their component parts in the act of translating form to sound to meaning. They would not negate totally the role of picture, context, or configuration clues as aids to word recognition. However, their contention is that excessive reliance upon these clues as guessing techniques diminishes the reliability of effective word attack, since sound-symbol relationships in such cases tend to be ignored.

One additional characteristic of many of the variations of the linguistics method is an increased emphasis upon oral reading. The point of this emphasis is that the relationship between a printed form and the sound that it symbolizes can become more clearly established if initially there are oral responses to printed symbols. Detailed arguments have been presented to support this point of view; the assertion is made that the need for this verbalization tends to diminish when word recognition has advanced to the point where almost any word can be perceived at a glance with speed and accuracy (Edwards, 1957). Opponents of this point of view maintain that oral reading should be discouraged from the beginning, since it directs the reader's attention away from meaning and results in verbalizers who pay little heed to what is being read, see word calling as the ultimate in successful reading, and, finally, become adult readers who practice audible vocalization or subvocalization, lip movement, or at least laryngeal activity when totally silent reading would be possible, more appropriate, and faster.

A true rapprochement of the several approaches discussed above would be extremely difficult, if not impossible. As was mentioned previously, two of them—the initial teaching alphabet and color coding—attack the problem of sound-symbol inconsistency by modifying the printed stimulus, the one by changing the structure of word forms and the other by superimposing color upon standard forms. The third, the linguistics approach, ignores form and tackles the problem by a special system of sequencing the symbolic elements presented to the learner so that irregularities are delayed. Here, then, we have teaching medium (i.e., the printed stimuli) in opposition to teaching technique as a crucial difference. This separation must be made in the minds of professional evaluators; otherwise, untenable comparisons will be made, inappropriate criteria will be employed to evaluate various aspects of a new approach, and certain possibilities for combining compatible approaches in the development of even more effective learning systems may be overlooked.

CONSIDERATIONS IN EVALUATING METHODOLOGIES AND MATERIALS

Major emphasis throughout the preceding chapters of this book has been on the problems involved in the teaching of reading. The terms dyslexia, aphasia, or reading disability have been used quite frequently. Such terms often imply that there is a problem inherent in the learner that creates difficulties in reading instruction. With the onus thus placed upon the learner, we can set about guiltlessly to try to help these special cases. Unquestionably, there are special types of genuine learning disability. However, we must recognize that we also have shortcomings as reading specialists, educators, psychologists, or whatever, as we have made faulty assumptions about learners or have predicated our methodologies on faulty hypotheses.

The disabled reader who is bright and who has no discernible physiological impairment is particularly challenging, and it is he who probably has caused us to re-examine ourselves and our methodologies more carefully. As is true in many of the behavioral sciences, explorations of the so-called abnormal cases tend to give us greater insight into the nature even of more typically normal individuals. It is our hope, therefore, that our presentation here of various points of view represents a coming into maturity of the field of reading as we look more critically at what we have been doing and at what we might do more effectively.

One additional characteristic has been typical of the majority of the contributions to this book: the major focus has been upon beginning reading, with much of importance left out regarding more advanced aspects of reading as a complex of behaviors. The following point of view might be kept in mind as we view the reading act as a totality: "continuous development toward greater reading proficiency is a process with many phases, the goal of which is the comprehension of ideas. Success in the process depends on adequate motivation, a substantial background of concepts, word-perception skills, and the ability to reason one's way through small idea elements and to grasp, as a whole, the meaning of a larger unitary idea" (Edwards, 1957).

Unquestionably, primary concern in the preceding chapters has been with the development of word perception or decoding skills, since this is where the beginning of the process of reading actually begins. Without these skills, attention to problems at more advanced levels in the reading hierarchy becomes irrelevant. Yet their existence must not be ignored once the first stage has been completed.

In our evaluation of any program designed for the teaching of reading, we must be cognizant of a number of factors related to learning to read, any one of which may be the *sine qua non* of success for a given learner. The following considerations are therefore itemized and discussed briefly as possible aids in the evaluation of any approach to the teaching of reading.

Prerequisites to Success in Beginning Reading

Often referred to as reading readiness, the prerequisites to success in reading are often assumed to have developed by the time a child enters first grade. However, this is not always the case. When they are not present, the acquisition of beginning reading proficiency may be severely hampered or may not take place at all. Although these prerequisites tend to be absent to a significantly greater degree among the so-called culturally disadvantaged, they may indeed also be absent in the case of allegedly advantaged middle-class children.

It is therefore important to inquire whether or not lack of reading readiness is a problem and, if so, whether a given beginning program takes this deficiency into consideration and provides for it. The difficulty is that we frequently denounce an otherwise excellent reading program without realizing that it simply does not meet the special needs of the individual or group with whom we are working.

Prerequisites common to success in beginning reading are an adequate background of experience, concepts, and general information; visual and auditory discrimination ability; oral language facility (in terms of both production and comprehension); physical and emotional intactness; reasoning ability; interest in learning to read; and, of course, a degree of native intelligence that will permit learning to take place. Certain of these readiness factors are understandably outside of the purview of a beginning reading program. Nevertheless, certain system builders have considered them carefully and woven as many as possible into their programs. When this is not possible, it is futile to impose a beginning reading program upon a child who is not reasonably well armed with these crucial prerequisites.

Auditory Perception and the Decoding Process

The point has been made repeatedly throughout this book that reading is a form of communication that is secondary to and symbolic of speech sounds as a conveyor of meaning. If the beginning reader is to master the symbols of speech sounds, it follows logically that he should first be able to perceive these sounds. Many cannot.

In any analysis of a given methodology for teaching beginning reading, the question should be asked: is adequate provision made to ensure that the speech sounds symbolized by a given letter or combination of letters are already a part of the auditory perception repertoire of the learner? If not, is sufficient auditory practice with a given sound woven into the program prior to any requirement that the symbol for that sound be learned?

Perceptual Learning: Decoding and Reproduction

Perceptual learning might logically and psychologically be divided into two subphenomena. One is recognition, which is the essence of the decoding process. More precisely, recognition may be the instantaneous recognition of a total word form, or it may first require the application of word-analysis skills before it is recognized to be the symbol of a certain word. It is word analysis (often referred to as word attack) which is often the primary goal of the diversified methods for the teaching of reading, with the possible exception of the whole word method. The ultimate goal, obviously, is instantaneous recognition without the need to stop to analyze a word. A second aspect of perceptual learning is somewhat more challenging, as it requires a degree of attention to detail which will permit not only recognition but also reproduction. This is spelling. It should be noted that these two aspects of word perception interact, as exemplified by the fact that we often have to look at a word in order to determine whether or not we have spelled it correctly. In this case, recognition is acting as a check upon accuracy of reproduction.

Some program builders maintain that reproduction (spelling) should be delayed until recognition (reading) has been rather firmly established. Others hold that reproduction in writing provides a type of kinesthetic or motor reinforcement to the recognition. This may be a question open to further investigation. However, any number of educators attest to the combination of recognition and reproduction in perceptual learning in cases commonly labeled as dyslexic (see the chapters by Orton and by Johnson).

This, then, is another consideration that should not be ignored in one's evaluation of a given methodology: Are visual recognition and kinesthetic reproduction combined within a given learning system? Should they be? Is such a combination necessary in all cases or only in those cases involving severe learning disabilities?

Oral Reading and Perceptual Learning

In our discussion, earlier in this chapter, of the linguistics approach to the teaching of reading, the question was raised as to the feasibility of oral reading as an aid to perceptual learning, together with some of its pros and cons. It might be reiterated here that there is some experimental evidence to support the combining of these two sensory modalities—visual and vocomotor—to facilitate perceptual learning of word forms (Edwards, 1956). However, definite qualifications have been added to this point of view, since many teachers have tended to permit audible or subvocalization well beyond the point at which it might have assisted in initial perceptual learning (Edwards, 1957).

Builders and users of reading programs must come to grips with this problem of the possible interrelatedness of perceptual learning with oral and other types of sensory modalities and also with possible reciprocal reinforcement or other types of interaction effects.

Individual Differences in Perceptual Learning Ability: Innate and Environmental

No attempt will be made here to draw the red herring of heredity versus environment across the path. The illustrative cases are replete with evidence of individual differences in the rate, capacity, and nature of learning abilities. Some may be caused by innate endowment, some by uniqueness of learning style, some by the age of the learner when instruction is initiated, some by personality organization, and some by factors yet to be discovered. The fact remains that individuals do differ.

If there is such tremendous variation among individuals in so many dimensions of human makeup—both physiological and psychological—how, then, can we look for the method that will be the universal panacea for problems in the development of reading ability or of any other skill? It must follow that we, like Diogenes, must make a search for an approach which will be appropriate for the individual or group with which we are working, and not for the one and only approach. This, in turn, will require diagnosis, confirmatory diagnosis en route, flexibility in our willingness to shift methods, an awareness of gaps in learning readiness which might preclude any method's working effectively, and an awareness of individual differences which might exist within a given group under our charge and their implications for differentiating instructional approaches and methodologies within such a group.

CONCLUDING COMMENT

The reading field is moving into its adolescent period, with all of the turmoil, indecisiveness, conflict, rebellion against the old, and trial-and-error behavior that is characteristic of a human adolescent. This is fine, since adolescence follows infancy and early childhood and precedes adulthood.

If there is a battle of the methodologies, this too is good, for any school of thought must indeed move into the open arena, flex its muscles, and survive against the onslaught of countering forces or go down because of inadequacy. If other disciplines move into the fray, so much the better, since reading must become increasingly recognized as the overwhelmingly complex behavioral phenomenon that it is. There has been much too much oversimplification of the nature of reading at the cost of untold wasted intellectual manpower due to reading failure and academic dropouts.

Our current war on poverty is revealing the horrendous conditions which daily confront the culturally disadvantaged. Though unsightly educational messes are being laid bare, this is an essential first step in the creation of new curricula which will lessen human intellectual waste.

During the past decade, the ranks of the International Reading Association have swelled within the United States and spilled over to include more than twenty-five foreign countries. This, too, is a good sign, since it is indicative of ever-increasing interest in the problems of better reading instruction and international cross-fertilization in this vital area. So the variety of opinions and approaches, the firm claims, and the struggle for superiority of methodology reflected in the preceding chapters must be viewed by the reader as manifestations of a healthy evolution of the field of reading toward maturity.

APPENDIX TO CHAPTER 10

1. Publications and Materials from the U.S.

Basic Source Materials

Handbook on Writing and Spelling in i/t/a (and Posttransition Spelling Guide). Mazurkiewicz, Tanyzer, and Sir James Pitman. i/t/a Publications, Inc., 20 East 46th Street, New York, New York. $3.50.
To Be or Not to Be. John Downing. The Macmillan Corporation.

Basic Reading Programs

Early-to-Read i/t/a Series. i/t/a Publications, Inc., Revised edition. Basic set about $9.50 for readers, $3.50 for workbooks, $12.00 for guides.

Reader	Workbook	Teacher's Manual
Rides	I	for I and II
Dinosaur Ben	II	
Houses	III	for III, IV, and V
Book 4	IV and V	
Book 5		
Book 6	VI	for VI
Book 7	VII and VIII	for VII and VII
Book 8		
Book 9 (transition)	IX	for IX, transition

Child's Alphabet Book. $1.32.
Teacher's Alphabet Book. $1.32.
Child's Symbol-Sound Cards (2″ by 2″). $0.90.
Teacher's Symbol-Sound Cards (5″ by 5″). $3.95.
Vocabulary Cards for Words through Book 5. $5.95.
Number Books. $1.32
The Experimental Edition. The first-grade basal reader program of Scott, Foresman, Inc.
Downing Readers, Books 1, 2, 3, 4, 4a, 5, 6, 7, 8, 8b, A, B, C, D. No workbooks, rudimentary teaching guide, available from England through i/t/a Publications, Inc.

Remedial Materials in Preparation

Elementary: *A Teacher's Guide for Use with the Early-to-Read i/t/a Series Program.* Shows how to modify the use of this material for remedial reading. C. C. Searle, Indianapolis. Marvin Baker has in production materials which parallel the Early-to-Read program.

Secondary and Adult: *The i/t/a Remedial Reading Laboratory.* Geared to occupational interests, adolescent interests, and the world of the adult. i/t/a Publications, Inc. First materials for experimental use were available as of July 1, 1965.

Tests and Inventories

The Stanford Achievement, Primary I, Form W. Harcourt, Brace and World.
The Metropolitan Achievement Test, Primary I. Harcourt, Brace and World.
Both available June, 1965.
Word Recognition Inventory, by Mazurkiewicz, in i/t/a and T.O. editions; for informal measures; available from O. O. Reading Laboratory, R. D. 1, Coopersburg, Pennsylvania. Instructional and independent levels are identified.

Typewriters

Imperial typewriter in primer-size type, Model 70. Metropolitan Typewriter Company, 18050 James Couzens Highway, Detroit 35, Michigan. $250.00.
Bulletin-size i/t/a type. Remington Rand Corporation, New York. $250.00.
A new model in primer-size type is in production.
An i/t/a ball which fits the Selectric typewriter containing only lower-case characters, in 14-point type. I.B.M. $15.00. Camwell, Inc., Los Angeles, also produces a ball for this I.B.M. typewriter at $42.00 in primer-size type with both upper- and lower-case forms.
Varityper Corporation, Newark, New Jersey, produces a font of type for the Varityper Headliner from which offset plates can be produced.

Supplementary Reading

Scholastic Magazines, Inc., 50 West 44th Street, New York. The following titles as noted in the January, 1965, catalogue are available and by the time of this printing will have been joined by thirty others:

Cat. No.	Title	Price
217	*The Adventures of the Three Blind Mice*	$0.35
495	*The Biggest Bear*	.45
496	*Bird in the Hat*	.45
286	*Clifford, The Big Red Dog*	.35
296	*Indian Two Feet and His Horse*	.35
315	*The Little Fish That Got Away*	.35
316	*Lucky and the Giant*	.35
317	*Olaf Reads*	.35
318	*Tony's Treasure Hunt*	.35
497	*Zany Zoo*	.45

Henry Z. Walck, Inc., New York, produces i/t/a editions of *Mr. Black's Secret*, *The Runaway Chimps*, and *Sammy Seal of the Circus*.

Forty-five titles for supplementary reading in preparation as sets of nine each at various readability levels are available from i/t/a Publications, Inc.

2. Publications and Materials from England

Basal Programs

Old Lob Approach to Reading. Ginn and Co., Ltd., 18 Bedford Row, London, W.C. 1. Also available from Ginn, Canada.

Picture book stage:	Price
Wall pictures of the characters	10*s*. 6*d*.
Picture book, *Old Lob and His Family*	2*s*. 6*d*.
Picture cards and matching sentence strips	7*s*. 10*d*.
Word cards	2*s*. 5*d*.
Introductory book stage:	
Get Ready for "At Old Lob's," a workbook	1*s*. 6*d*.
At Old Lob's, introductory book	3*s*. 3*d*.
Work Book for "At Old Lob's"	1*s*. 6*d*.
Book 1, stage:	
Book 1, Part 1, *Away They Go*	3*s*. 3*d*.
Work Book for "Away They Go"	1*s*. 6*d*.
Book 1, Part 2, *Home They Come*	3*s*. 3*d*.
Work Book for "Home They Come"	1*s*. 6*d*.
In production:	
A Visit to Updown	Prices
What Happened at Updown	to be
Extra readers on Book 1	announced
Stage vocabulary	

Beacon Reading Scheme. Ginn and Co., Ltd., 18 Bedford Row, London, W.C. 1. In production, prices to be announced:

Introductory book, *Kitty and Rover*
Book 1, Part 1, *At Home*
Book 1, Part 2, *At Play*
Book 2, Part 1, *Old Dog Tom*, reader
Book 2, Part 2, *Little Chick Chick*, reader
The Pancake, reader
Careful Hans, reader

The Macmillan Readers. Available from England only.

THE JANET AND JOHN READING SCHEME. James Nisbet and Co., Ltd., Digswell Place, Welsyn, Herts.

Title	Price
Basic books, whole word series:	
Here We Go	2*s*. 8*d*.
Off To Play	3*s*. 0*d*.
Out and About	3*s*. 0*d*.
I Went Walking	3*s*. 8*d*.
Through the Garden Gate	4*s*. 6*d*.
I Know a Story	5*s*. 6*d*.
Extension readers:	
Once Upon a Time	6*s*. 0*d*.
Workbooks:	
Workbook for Here We Go	1*s*. 10*d*.
Workbook for Off To Play	1*s*. 6*d*.
Workbook for Out and About	1*s*. 10*d*.
Workbook for Janet and John Book 1	1*s*. 10*d*.
Janet and John story books:	
Nos. 11, 13, 15, 21, 22, 23, 24, 25, 26, 31, 32, 33, 34, 38	1*s*. 9*d*. paper
Apparatus:	
The First Book of Janet and John Pictures	6*s*. 0*d*.
The Second Book of Janet and John Pictures	6*s*. 0*d*.
The Third Book of Janet and John Pictures	6*s*. 0*d*.
The Fourth Book of Janet and John Pictures	3*s*. 6*d*.
The Fifth Book of Janet and John Pictures	3*s*. 6*d*.
Large Sentence Book	4*s*. 6*d*.
Outline Picture Pads 1–15	1*s*. 3*d*. ea.
Outline Picture Pad 16	1*s*. 4*d*.
Drawing Book	0*s*. 6*d*.
Word Matching Cards, Sets 1–3	1*s*. 5*d*. /set
Picture Word Cards	2*s*. 0*d*.
Picture Sentence Cards	3*s*. 4*d*.
Coloured Cut-Out Pictures, Sets 1 and 2	2*s*. 4*d*. /set

THROUGH THE RAINBOW READING SCHEME. Schofield and Sims, 33 St. John's Road, Huddersfield, Yorkshire. January, 1965.

THE ARNOLD READING SCHEME. Arnold Publishing Co., England. No information available.

APPARATUS (not associated with any reading program). Orders for E.S.A. Apparatus should be sent direct to E.S.A., Ltd., The Pinnacles, Harlow, Essex.

Title	Ref. No.	Price
Large Letter Cards, Set of 44	8952/11	8*s.* 7*d.*
Small Letter Cards, Set of 265	8952/33	5*s.* 11*d.*
Large Letter Cards, Set of 147	8952/22	£1 4*s.* 0*d.*
Alphabet Booklet	8955/10	5*s.* 4*d.*
Small Alphabet Matching Cards	8953	14*s.* 0*d.*
Alphabet Frieze Cards	8954	£1 13*s.* 5*d.*

I.T.A. WORD BUILDING KIT. Two boards and sixteen tiles of each character in an adhering material. Obtainable from Mr. E. Brozon, 1 Riverside Court, Palatine Road, W. Didsbury, Manchester 20. £3 10*s.* 0*d.*

I.T.A. HAND PRINTING OUTFIT. Obtainable from Webb's Rubber Stamps, 79 Roseberry Road, Smethwick, Birmingham 40.

I.T.A. HAND PRINTING OUTFIT. All i/t/a characters, T.O. capitals, and numerals are separately mounted as rubber printing stamps. Orders to Visigraph, Ltd., Holymead Road, Wednesbury, Staffordshire, or through E.S.A., Ltd. £7 15*s.* 0*d.*

I.T.A. FLANNELGRAPHS:

Individual 2″ letters, 150 in sectioned box	42*s.* 0*d.*
Refill packs	15*s.* 0*d.*
Pictorial flannelgraph and word strips, 3 sets in color, 36″ by 24″	
At Home, On the Farm, At School	45*s.* 0*d.* ea.
i/t/a. Bible series with flannelgraph figures, word strips, and matching words	22*s.* 6*d.* ea.
Pupils' flannelgraph boards, 15″ by 12″	2*s.* 0*d.*
Teachers' flannelgraph boards, 36″ by 24″	42*s.* 0*d.*

Book Corner Books

Obtainable from publisher and/or i/t/a Publications, Inc. (N.Y.) as noted.

Code*	Title	Publisher	Price
s	*Gay Color Books*, Nos. 1, 2, 5, 6, 9, 10, 11, 12	Arnold	4*s.* 0*d.* ea.
s	*First Stories*, No. 4	Arnold	4*s.* 0*d.* ea.
s	*Second Stories*, Nos. 3 and 4	Arnold	4*s.* 0*d.* ea.
s	*Jesus the Helper* (E. 2807)	i/t/a Publ., Inc.	3*s.* 6*d.*

* See p. 371 for key.

Available in limited quantities only. Orders should be sent to The i/t/a Scheme, Book Centre, Ltd., North Circular Road, Neasden, N.W. 10.

Code	Title	Publisher	Price
s	*Angus Lost*	Bodley Head	5*s.* 0*d.*
rf	*Timothy's Book of Aircraft*	Collins	2*s.* 6*d.*
s	*The Story of Ferdinand*	Hamilton	7*s.* 6*d.*
vs	*John and Betty*	RoSPA	1*s.* 6*d.*
rf	*Henry the Green Engine*	Ward	5*s.* 0*d.*
rf	*Branch Line Engines*	Ward	5*s.* 0*d.*
s	*Little Bear's Friend*	Worlds Work	10*s.* 6*d.*

In production. Will be obtainable later from the publishers.

Code	Title	Publisher	Price
vs	*The Four Friends*	Benn	7*s.* 6*d.*
vs	*Little Quack*	Benn	7*s.* 6*d.*
vs	*Mabel the Whale*	Benn	7*s.* 6*d.*
vs	*Pearl Goes to School*	Benn	7*s.* 6*d.*
f	Our Book Corner, Third Shelf:	Chambers	
	Men and Women at Work (6 titles)		9*s.* 6*d.*
	Children of Other Times (6 titles)		9*s.* 6*d.*
	Things We Eat and Drink (6 titles)		9*s.* 6*d.*
rf	Our Book Corner, Fourth Shelf:	Chambers	
	Useful Plants (6 titles)		9*s.* 6*d.*
	Nature (6 titles)		9*s.* 6*d.*
	Travel (6 titles)		9*s.* 6*d.*
s	Child Education Readers:	Evans Bros.	
	Timothy Tugboat Book 1		1*s.* 9*d.*
	Timothy Tugboat Book 2		
	Timothy and the Seagull		1*s.* 9*d.*
yr	*Man Makes Towns*	Hamish Hamilton	6*s.* 6*d.* approx.
yr	*Man and Animals*	i/t/a Publ., Inc.	3*s.* 6*d.*
vs	*My Little Book* (E. 2836)	i/t/a Publ., Inc.	3*s.* 6*d.*
vs	*My Book of Pets* (E. 2835)	i/t/a Publ., Inc.	3*s.* 6*d.*
vs	*The Party* (E. 2837)	i/t/a Publ., Inc.	3*s.* 6*d.*
f	People at Work Series: *The Fireman, The Policeman, The Nurse, The Fisherman, The Farmer*	i/t/a Publ., Inc.	3*s.* 6*d.* ea.

Code	Title	Publisher	Price
r	Clearway Readers: *Tom and Pam, The Picnic, A Ride to the Wood, A Day at Home, In the Park, A Holiday by the Sea, The Birthday, The Little Black Car*	i/t/a Publ., Inc.	To be announced
r	Sail Away Series: *Sam the Sailor, Sam Sails On, The Three Sailors*	i/t/a Publ., Inc.	To be announced
s	Let's Read About People: *A Soldier, A Knight, A Cowboy, An Indian, A Squaw, A Nurse, A Bride, A Waitress*	i/t/a Publ., Inc.	To be announced
fr	*Kuma Is a Maori Girl*	Methuen	11*s.* 6*d.* approx.
fr	*Christine Lives in the Alps*	Methuen	11*s.* 6*d.* approx.
fr	*Brendan of Ireland*	Methuen	11*s.* 6*d.* approx.
s	I Can Read a Story (9 titles)	Wheaton	To be announced
s	Andrew and Sally (10 titles)	Wheaton	To be announced

Key

vs—very simple
s—simple
f—for fluency practice
yr—younger remedial
r—remedial
or—older remedial

3: i/t/a Library Books

Available in the U.S. from i/t/a Publications, Inc. All are British materials.

Code*	Title	Publisher	List Price	Net Price
vs	*Puppies and Kittens*, unpaged	Gagg	$0.72	$0.51
vs	*The Farm*, unpaged	Gagg	0.72	0.51
vs	*Telling the Time*, unpaged	Gagg	0.72	0.54
s	*David and Joan on Holiday*, 1–6, paper, two-color	Holland	0.56	0.42
vs	Pitman Picture-Story Books, 16 pages, paper, color: Book 1, *Meet David and Joan* Book 2, *Playing at Mothers and Fathers*	Holland	0.40 ea.	0.30 ea.

* See above for key.

Code*	Title	Publisher	List Price	Net Price
vs	Book 3, *Shopping*	Holland	$0.40 ea.	$0.30 ea.
	Book 4, *Sally the Dog*			
	Book 5, *Sally and the Balloon*			
	Book 6, *Tim, the Rabbit*			
	Book 7, *Tim Goes for a Walk*			
	Book 8, *Thomas, the Tortoise*			
	Book 9, *Thomas Goes for a Walk*			
	Book 10, *Tea in the Garden*			
	Book 11, *Sally and the Cat*			
	Book 12, *Tim and Thomas*			
vs	Creatures of Colder Lands, paper, set of 6 books from Our Book Corner Series: *The Husky Dog, The King Penguin, The Arctic Fox, The Gray Seal, The Reindeer, The Polar Bear*	Wilson	1.60 ea.	1.20 ea.
f	Magic Carpet Books, color:	Mamlock	1.60 ea.	1.20 ea.
	Magic Carpet to Animal-Rhyme Land			
	Magic Carpet to Nursery-Rhyme Land			
	Magic Carpet to Story-Rhyme Land			
	Magic Carpet to Pudding-Pie Land			
vs	*Helping at Home*	Gagg	0.72	0.54
vs	*The Zoo*	Gagg	0.72	0.54
vs	We Play and Grow Series, 24 pages each, full color, 8½ by 11, paper:	Cobby		
	Book 1, *Jingles for Me To Play—I Am 5*		1.40	1.05
	Book 2, *Rhymes for Me To Speak—I Am 5*		1.40	1.05
	Book 3, *Jingles for Me To Play—I Am 6*		1.40	1.05
	Book 4, *Rhymes for Me To Speak—I Am 6*		1.20	0.90
	Book 5, *Jingles for Me To Play—I Am 7*		1.80	1.35

* See p. 371 for key.

Code*	Title	Publisher	List Price	Net Price
	Book 6, *Rhymes for Me To Speak—I Am 7*		$1.80	$1.35
s	*Toby Stays with Jane*, unpaged	Thwaite	1.40	1.05
f	*Sally on Holiday*, 63 pages	Carruth	1.40	1.05
f	*Sally on the Farm*, 63 pages	Carruth	1.40	1.05
f	*Naughty George*, unpaged, paper	Pilgrim	0.48	0.36
f	*The Birthday Picnic*, unpaged, paper	Pilgrim	0.48	0.36
f	*Mrs. Squirrel and Hazel*, unpaged, paper	Pilgrim	0.48	0.36
f	*Tufty Paints His Door*, unpaged, paper	Cloak	0.36	0.27
f	*Merry's New Hat*, unpaged, paper	Cloak	0.36	0.27
f	*Barnaby's Cuckoo Clock*, unpaged, paper	Cloak	0.36	0.27
f	*The Flying Frog*, unpaged, paper	Cloak	0.36	0.27
yr	*Teddy and Mickey at the Seaside*, 28 pages, paper, black and white	Taylor	0.40	0.30
yr	*Teddy and Mickey's Adventures at Brighton*, 28 pages	Taylor	0.40	0.30
s	*The Little Yellow Car*, unpaged, color	Benn	1.60	1.20
f	*The Ugly Duckling*		2.00	1.50
f	*Hansel and Gretel*		2.00	1.50
f	*The Pied Piper*		2.00	1.50
f	*Snow White and the Seven Dwarfs*		2.00	1.50
f	*Puss-in-Boots*		2.00	1.50
or	The Adventures of Captain Roy Series, two-color:	Gardner	0.48 ea.	0.36 ea.
	Book 1, *Diamonds*			
	Book 2, *The Five Men*			
	Book 3, *The Rescue*			
or	Pitman Reference Books, paper, two-color:	Stockbridge and Southam	0.96 ea.	0.72 ea.
	Ships Series, Books 1–4			
	Aircraft Series, Books 1–5			
	Picture and Word Book, Ships Series			
	Picture and Word Book, Aircraft Series			

* See p. 371 for key.

GLOSSARY

VIOLA LEWIS

agnosia: not knowing; inability to recognize or interpret the meaning of familiar objects, events, or sensations, as a result of a brain lesion or dysfunction.

airencephalogram: see pneumoencephalogram.

ambidextrous: both righthanded and lefthanded.

ambihemispheric: in both hemispheres of the brain.

Amharic: the Semitic language which is official in Ethiopia.

angular gyrus: a cerebral convolution which forms the posterior portion of the inferior parietal lobule and arches over the posterior end of the superior temporal sulcus.

anoxia: failure of tissue either to receive or to utilize an adequate amount of oxygen.

aphasia: defect or loss of the power of expression by speech, writing, or signs or of comprehending spoken or written language, as a result of a brain lesion or dysfunction.

aphasic: pertaining to aphasia.

apraxia: inability to perform purposeful movements, in the absence of paralysis or sensory disturbance, as a result of a brain lesion or dysfunction. Constructional apraxia is inability to perform purposeful movements in the use of materials, objects, and tools.

apraxic: pertaining to apraxia.

astigmatism: the faulty vision which results from irregularity in the curvature of one or more refractive surfaces (cornea, anterior and posterior surfaces of the lens) of the eye. When such a condition occurs, rays emanating from a point are not brought into focus at a point on the retina but appear to spread as a line in various directions depending upon the curvature. The condition may be congenital or of later onset.

athetoid: pertaining to athetosis.

athetosis: a derangement of muscular movement, resulting principally from brain lesion, marked by slow, recurring, weaving movements of arms and legs and by facial grimaces.

aura: a premonitory sensation preceding a convulsion, usually experienced by epileptics. A visual aura is experienced as flashing of bright light, whirling or colored light, or sudden darkness in the visual fields.

aural: of the ears or hearing.

autism, infantile: a severe psychiatric disorder in infants and children characterized chiefly by severe disturbance of the ability to communicate in social interaction; such children live in their private or autistic mental world.

autistic: pertaining to autism.

axon: a structural part of the neuron which transmits impulses away from the cell.

basal series: in reading, the series of texts that a class uses for basic study.

bihemispheric: in the two hemispheres (of the brain).

bilateral extensor plantar response(s): Babinski sign; there is extension of the toes instead of flexion on stimulating the sole of the foot. It is an aid to neurological diagnosis.

binaural: pertaining to or having two ears. Hearing with both ears acting together.

binocular: seeing with both eyes in focus together.

blend: a word made by putting together parts of other words, as *dandle*, a blend of *dance* and *handle*. In phonics, the smooth passage from one sound in a word to the next.

blocking: involuntary inhibition of recall, thinking, or communication, including sudden stoppage of speech.

body image: the picture or mental representation one has of one's own body at rest or in motion at any moment. It is derived from internal sensations, postural changes, contact with outside objects and people, emotional experiences, and fantasies. Body image is also a synonym for body concept, meaning one's evaluation of one's own body, with special attention on how one thinks or fantasizes that it looks to others.

body schema: the over-all pattern of one's direct or sensory awareness of one's own body; the characteristic way in which a person is aware of his own body. The body image is an actual experience; the body schema is a pattern, an acquired structure that codetermines the body image in a given situation.

caloric response: in testing the sense of balance, the reaction of positional sense and/or giddiness when warm fluid is irrigated in the ear and affects the organs of balance in the middle ear.

carotid artery: the principal large artery on each side of the neck.

cerebral: pertaining to the cerebrum, or brain.

cerebral cortex: the external gray layer of the brain; areas of the cortex are differentiated histologically by cell patterns.

cerebral dominance: the tendency for one cerebral hemisphere, usually the left, to be better developed in certain functions, especially speech and handedness.

cerebrospinal fluid: the fluid in the canals of the brain; that is, within the cerebral ventricles and between the arachnoid membrane and pia mater of the brain and spinal cord.

cerebrum: the brain.

chromosomal sex: genetic sex as revealed by the chromosome count, which is 44+ XX chromosomes in females and 44+ XY chromosomes in males; chromosomal sex does not always agree with the other sex variables, and in various abnormal conditions a sex chromosome may be missing or duplicated.

chromosomes: the threadlike structures in the nucleus of cells along which are arranged the genes, the heredity-carrying bodies. In man there are 22 pairs of autosomes and 1 pair (XX in the female and XY in the male) of sex chromosomes.

cluttering (speech): speech so rapid, under pressure of excitement, that enunciation is indistinct, words are run together, and syllables are slighted or dropped out.

CNS: central nervous system, that is, the brain, spinal cord, and sensory and motor peripheral nerves.

cochlea: a cavity of the internal ear resembling a snail shell; it contains the essential organs of hearing.

cochlear: pertaining to the cochlea.

comprehension: in reading, the ability to extract meaning from a written selection, especially the meaning and implication of the whole paragraph.

contralateral: opposite; acting in unison with a similar part on the opposite side of the body.

control group: a group as closely as possible equivalent to an experimental group and exposed to all the conditions of the investigation except the experimental variable being studied.

correlation: the fact that two things or variables are so related that change in one is accompanied by a corresponding or parallel change in the other.

cranial nerves: nerves arising directly from the brain stem and making their exit to the periphery via openings in the skull. There are twelve pairs, including the optic and auditory.

critical period: a period in the life history which is particularly important for some or other aspect of growth and maturation. Organs or functions prevented from developing properly during their critical period remain deformed or defective. After the critical period, adverse influences and interferences are more easily resisted.

cursive script: writing or printing type in flowing strokes, with the letters joined together.

cytoarchitectonic: pertaining to the cellular arrangement of a region, tissue, or organ.

decoding (graphic symbols to speech): translating from an unfamiliar to a familiar set of symbols or language.

demographic: pertaining to demography.

demography: the study of human populations, including vital statistics, geographical distribution, causes of increase and decrease, and the like.

dendrite: a structural part of a neuron which carries the nerve impulse to the cell body. It is usually branched, like a tree.

dextrad: progressing from left to right; toward the right side.

dextrality: preferential use of the right hand or of the right side generally, rightsidedness.

digraph: in spelling, the use of two letters to make one sound, e.g., spe*ll*.

diphthong: a composite speech sound made up of two vowels, one, sonantal, blending with the other, consonantal, as *ei* in *vein.*

discrimination: the process of detecting differences in stimuli, especially, sensory discriminations; the detecting of sensory differences; reacting differently to different objects or stimuli.

dominant hemisphere: in the brain, the side on which speech is represented and controlled.

dyscalculia: impairment of the ability to work even the simplest mathematical problems as a result of a brain lesion or dysfunction.

dysgnosia: an incomplete degree of agnosia.

dysgraphia: impairment of the power of writing, less complete than in agraphia, as a result of a brain lesion or dysfunction.

dysgraphic: pertaining to dysgraphia.

dyslexia: imperfectly developed reading skill, or the deterioration of skill, without its total absence (alexia), as a result of a brain lesion or dysfunction.

dyslexic: pertaining to dyslexia.

ecology: the branch of biology which treats of the relations between organisms and their environment; bionomics. In a broad sense most of psychology is ecological, being concerned with responses to stimuli (which are environmental).

ecology of behavior: the behavior of living organisms in relation to their social and physical environment.

EEG: electroencephalogram.

ego identity: the sameness, unity, and persistence of one's individuality, in greater or lesser degree, especially as it is experienced in self-awareness and behavior.

eidetic imagery: a peculiarly vivid type of imagery, almost as though one were actually perceiving an external stimulus, yet one is aware that it is in imagination or memory. Eidetic imagery is common in childhood.

electroencephalogram: brain wave tracing; EEG.

empyema: a term used to indicate the presence of pus in a cavity, hollow organ, or space.

encephalography: X-ray examination of the brain. See also **pneumoencephalogram.**

endocrine: pertaining to the endocrine, that is, to the ductless or hormone-secreting glands.

endocrinology: the medical specialty that deals with the endocrine or ductless glands, particularly the pituitary, thyroid, adrenal, and sex glands and their hormones.

epilepsy: a disorder of the brain characterized by a recurring excessive neuronal discharge, manifested by transient episodes of motor, sensory, or psychic dysfunction, with or without unconscious or convulsive movements. The seizure is associated with marked changes in recorded electrical brain activity.

epileptogenic foci: limited areas of the brain, scarred or otherwise injured, that become the focal, starting points of epileptic seizures. Surgical removal of the defective area may sometimes abolish seizures.

equinus deformity: a deformity of the human foot in which the heel is elevated and the weight thrown upon the anterior portion of the foot.

experience approach: in reading, the use of subject matter that reflects the child's own day-by-day experiences.

finger agnosia: agnosia applying especially to localization and discrimination of stimuli on the fingers, particularly simultaneous ones.

finger differentiation: ability to identify which finger or fingers have been touched, either simultaneously or in sequence.

finger localization: ability to localize tactile sensations on the fingers.

font: a complete assortment of type of one size.

fossa (plural, **fossae**): a depression or pit.

fundus (plural, **fundi**): the base of an organ; the part farthest removed from the opening of the organ; in ophthalmology, the back of the eye.

gastroenteritis: inflammation of stomach and intestine.

gender identity: the sameness, unity, and persistence of one's individuality as male or female (or ambivalent), in greater or lesser degree, especially as it is experienced in self-awareness and behavior. Gender identity is the private experience of gender role, and gender role is the public expression of gender identity.

gender role: everything that a person says and does to indicate to others or to the self the degree to which one is male or female or ambivalent; it includes, but is not restricted to, sexual arousal and response. Gender role is the public expression of gender identity, and gender identity is the private experience of gender role.

genotype: the genetic makeup of an individual or group, as determined by the genes and chromosomes. The genotype shows itself only in interaction with its environment, the observable product being the phenotype.

Gerstmann's syndrome: a complex disorder of cerebral functions accompanying a lesion in the left angular gyrus and the adjoining area of the middle occipital gyrus, classically giving rise to right-left disorientation, finger agnosia, dysgraphia, and dyscalculia.

gestalt (plural, **gestalten** or **gestalts**)**:** a form, a configuration, or a totality that has, as a unified whole, properties which cannot be derived by summation from the parts and their relationships.

gnosis: knowing, including discrimination and recognition.

grapheme: the visual or written counterpart of a phoneme. In English, the same phoneme may be subject to different spellings.

hemianopsia: blindness in one half of the visual field; may be bilateral or unilateral. Homonymous hemianopsia is that form affecting the inner (nasal) half of one field and the outer half of the other.

hemiatrophy: atrophy confined to one side of an organ or region of the body.

hemispheres (of the brain): the left and right halves of the cerebral cortex, separated by the central fissure.

histrionic: of or pertaining to actors or acting; artificial; affected.

hydrocephalus: "water on the brain," a birth condition marked by excess pressure of the cerebrospinal fluid within the skull, causing enlargement of the head.

hyperkinetic: overactive, either in random movement or in purposeful actions.

internal rectus recession: surgery of the internal rectus muscle to correct crossed eyes.

inventory memory: memory for unrelated items in series, as a list of words in a dictionary or entries in an encyclopedia.

ipsilateral: homolateral; occurring on the same side, e.g., the rare association of lefthandedness and ipsilateral brain dominance for speech.

i/t/a: referred to variously as the augmented alphabet, the augmented Roman alphabet, the initial teaching medium, and more correctly called the Initial Teaching Alphabet.

item analysis: in intelligence testing, an examination of the individual responses in order to locate peculiar or pathological responses.

Jaeger test: a chart to be held in the hand and read, used to test visual acuity at reading distance.

kinesthesia: the sensation of movement or strain in muscles, tendons, or joints.

kinesthetic: pertaining to kinesthesia.

kinetic: of or pertaining to motion.

kinetic overshoot: in handwriting, movements of the hand that push the pen beyond the desired position. In kinetic undershoot, the movements stop short of the desired position.

laterality: sidedness; the preferential use of one side of the body, especially in tasks demanding the use of only one hand, one eye, or one foot.

lateral ventricle: the cavity of either cerebral hemisphere communicating with the third ventricle through the interventricular foramen and consisting of a triangular central cavity, or body, and three smaller cavities, or cornua.

law of camouflage: a special instance of the law of form constancy.

law of directional constancy: the meaning or significance of a form or shape is dependent upon the stability of its positional rotation, e.g., from right to left, upside down, or front to back.

law of form constancy: the meaning or significance of a form or shape is dependent upon the absence of various modifications, additions, or subtractions of detail.

law of object constancy: the meaning or significance of a form or shape persists despite positional and morphologic alterations; e.g., a chair is seen as a chair despite considerable differences in the stimulus pattern on the retina as the viewer changes position relative to it.

lesion: the alteration, structural or functional, due to injury; commonly limited to morphological alterations.

lexigraphic: as in a dictionary; of a word, the way it is spelled and written.

linguistics: the study of human speech, including the origin, modification and structure of language.

lobes of the brain: see diagram of the frontal, parietal, temporal, and occipital lobes of the left hemisphere of the cerebral cortex.

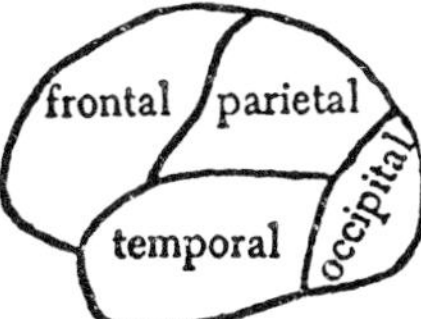

look-say procedure: whole word learning by looking and saying.

manuscript writing: writing, as distinguished from the printed word.

mapping: pattern of symbols that corresponds, point for point, with a physical state or a system of events, especially in the brain.

mixed cerebral dominance: the theoretical construct that speech disorders and some other maladjustments may be due wholly or partly to the fact that one cerebral hemisphere does not consistently lead the other in control of bodily movement.

mnemonics: pertaining to memory or to the art of memorizing; more specifically, pertaining to the art of improving memory.

monohemispheric: in only one hemisphere of the brain.

mutation: in heredity, the change between one generation and the next in the hereditary pattern, as carried by the genes and chromosomes.

neuron: a nerve cell and its threads (axon and dendrites).

neuropathology: disease or defect of the nerve structures.

neuropsychology: the mental or cognitional aspects of the central nervous system's higher functioning.

neurotology: that branch of medical science dealing with the structure and functions of the internal ear, its nervous connections with the brain, and its central pathways within the brain.

nystagmus: an oscillatory movement of the eyeballs. Vestibular (rhythmical) is the form in which the eyes slowly wander a few degrees in one direction and then are jerked back. Optokinetic is the form which occurs in normal individuals when a succession of moving objects traverses the field of vision, or when the individual moves past a succession of stationary objects.

occipital horn: a fluid-filled cavity, part of the ventricular system in the occipital lobe of the brain.

operant behavior: behavior, typically self-initiated, whose rate or form is affected by its consequences.

ophthalmological: pertaining to ophthalmology.

ophthalmology: the medical specialty dealing with vision and the eyes.

orthographic: pertaining to orthography.

orthography: the art of writing words with the proper letters, according to accepted usage; correct spelling; that part of grammar which treats of letters and spelling.

orthoptics: correct eye muscle movements for complete binocular vision.

otology: the science of the ear, its anatomy, functions, and diseases.

paired associate: a procedure used in the study of learning and retention. Items are presented in pairs for learning. Then the first item of each pair (usually not in the original order) is presented for a brief time, and the subject endeavors to reproduce the second item.

paresis: a slight paralysis; incomplete loss of muscular power; weakness of a limb.

paroxysm: the periodic increase or crisis in the progress of a disease; a sudden attack, a sudden reappearance of symptoms, or a sudden increase in the intensity of existing symptoms; a spasm or fit; a convulsion.

paroxysmal: in brain wave tracings, the appearance of wave patterns suggesting epileptic discharge.

pathodynamics: the give-and-take of interaction between people in a group, like a family, that both signifies and induces disturbances or pathology of behavior, feeling, and cognition. The role of one group member complements that of the others and vice versa, so that the behavior of each partly determines that of the others, just as in a ball game the move of each player dictates the moves of the others, and reciprocally.

pedagogy: the principles and methods of teaching.

percentile: for a given score, this value indicates the percentage of subjects tested ranking below that score in the distribution.

perinatal: around the time of birth.

permutations: the act of changing the order of individuals arranged in a particular order (as, abc into acb, bac, etc.), or of arranging a number of individuals in groups made up of equal numbers of the individuals in different orders (as, a and b into ab and ba); any of the resulting arrangements or groups.

phenotype: opposite of genotype (which see).

philology: the science of language.

phone: an individual speech sound.

phoneme: in linguistics, one of the basic sound units of speech from which words are built and meanings construed. There are said to be forty-four phonemes in English. A phoneme like *r* may be pronounced differently without losing its identity. See also grapheme.

phonetic: of or pertaining to speech sounds and their production.

phonemic-graphemic matching: phonetic-graphic matching as applied to the basic units, phonemes and graphemes.

phonetic-graphic matching: the conversion of sound (auditory symbols) into written (visuomotor) alphabetical symbols.

phonic teaching: teaching reading and spelling by analysis of words by their phonetic elements rather than by their individual letters or total visual appearance.

phonogram: a symbol that represents a speech sound; a phonogram may be a larger unit than a phoneme.

phylogenetic: characteristic of the phylogeny, race, or species as contrasted with the individual.

phylogeny: belonging to the race history of a vegetable or animal type, as opposed to ontogeny, which is the history of an individual organism.

physiological jaundice: excessive amount of bilirubin in the blood; constitutional jaundice; physiological hyperbilirubinemia.

pneumoencephalogram: an encephalogram taken after removal of the cerebrospinal fluid and injection of air or gas into the ventricular spaces of the brain.

pneumonia, streptococcal: pneumonia of a type caused by, usually, the Lancefield group A streptococci, either primary or as a complication of an upper respiratory infection. Cf. virus pneumonia.

posterior cranial fossa: the lowest in position of the three cranial fossae; it lodges the cerebellum, pons, and medulla oblongata.

praxis: the doing or performance of an action.

pre-primer level: in American education, the initial stage of reading immediately following reading readiness, and followed by primer level, and first reader level, in that order, in the first grade at the age of six.

primer level: see **pre-primer level.**

proprioceptor: a receptor or sense organ sensitive to the position and movement of the body and its members; such organs are found in the vestibule of the inner ear, the nearby semicircular canals, and in the muscles, tendons, and joints.

psychosexual differentiation: the process whereby a psychosexual identity is established; in human beings differentiation is rudimentary at birth and is complexly dependent on life experience after birth.

quadrant: in vision, one of the four areas in which the visual field is divided according to a right-left and upper-lower (superior-inferior) ordering.

readability: a measure of the difficulty or complexity of any printed material. Various formulas are used to indentify this difficulty, but all formulas generally include the number of words per sentence, the number of words not on a general list and therefore defined as unfamiliar, and sentence length.

reinforcement: a technical term in learning theory and experiment, signifying that learning is strengthened positively by success, or by a reward, and negatively by a penalty for error.

retina: the nerve cells at the back of the interior of the eyeball where light waves are converted to nerve impulses and conducted to the brain.

reversal, mirror: the symmetrical right-left or near-far shift in apparent position perceived when an object is viewed in a mirror. In reading there may be reversal of single letters (*p* for *q*), of the order of letters within a word (*yam* for *may*) or of the order of a whole phrase.

rote memory: reproduction of learned material in which the factor of meaning is absent or disregarded.

schizophrenia: a group of psychotic reactions characterized by fundamental disturbances in reality relationships, by a conceptual world determined excessively by feeling (autism), and by marked affective, intellectual, and overt behavioral disturbances. In many cases there is progressive deterioration. Many varieties are distinguished clinically.

school phobia: an irrational fear of or aversion to attending school, often associated with intense feelings of anxiety.

sedimentation rate: the rate at which red cells settle out of citrated blood; the rate is somewhat more rapid in females than in males. Increases in sedimentation rate occur during menstruation, pregnancy, and in a number of pathological states.

semantics: the study of meaning and changes of meaning of words and other linguistic forms.

semi-vowel: a speech sound of vowel quality used as a consonant, such as *w* in *wet* or *y* in *yet*.

septicemia: a systemic disease produced by microorganisms and their poisonous products in the blood stream.

sequential processing: dealing with items in sequence or serial order.

set for diversity: a mental attitude developed so that, for example, a child begins to be aware that symbols can represent more than one sound.

sex chromatin: a colored spot, revealed by special staining, found on the edge of the nucleus of cells obtained from females of the human and other species; it is believed to represent one of the X chromosomes; it occurs abnormally in males with the XXY syndrome, and is subject to other abnormalities.

sinistrality: preference for using the left side of the body in motor activity, especially the left hand.

soleus neurectomy: cutting of the nerve fibers to the flat muscle of the calf (to correct equinus deformity).

space-form blindness: a condition, analogous to color blindness, in which a person has difficulty discriminating shapes and their relationship. Also called space-form dysgnosia.

spastic diplegia: paralysis with contracted muscles of the legs due to organic changes in the infantile brain, such as diffuse degeneration, malformations or developmental defects, and microscopic cellular alterations. This disorder is sometimes associated with convulsions and mental deficiency.

specific developmental dyslexia: dyslexia of childhood origin, despite schooling, without known trauma to the brain and without parallel deficit in many other skills and activities of play, work, and general living.

stereopsis: stereoscopic vision.

stimulus-response paradigm: a model or pattern based on the observable fact that a certain specified energy change (stimulus) tends to be followed by a specified movement in a given organism.

strabismus: squint; that abnormality of the eyes in which the visual axes do not meet at the desired objective point, in consequence of lack of coordination of the action of the extrinsic ocular muscles. In convergent strabismus (esotropia), the squinting eye is turned to the nasal side.

strephosymbolia: literally, twisted symbols; a term used by Orton for the type of reading disorder characterized by frequent rotations of letters and their serial misplacement.

stuttering: a speech impediment in which the even flow of words is interrupted by hesitations, rapid repetition of speech elements, and spasms of breathing or of the vocal muscles.

supramarginal gyrus: a cerebral convolution which forms the anterior portion of the inferior parietal lobule and arches over the upturned end of the lateral cerebral fissure.

syllabication: breaking a word into its component syllables.

synapse: the region of communication between neurons; the point at which an impulse passes from an axon of one neuron to a dendrite or to the cell body of another. A synapse is polarized, that is, nerve impulses are transmitted only in one direction, and is characterized by fatigability.

syndrome: a group of symptoms and signs which, when considered together, characterize a disease or lesion.

synesthesia: a secondary sensation or subjective impression accompanying an actual perception, as an impression of color or sound aroused by a sensation of taste.

syntactic: pertaining to syntax.

syntax: the patterns of formation of sentences and phrases from words in a particular language.

tachistoscope: an instrument for providing a very brief timed exposure of visual material, such as pictures, letters, or digits. The exposure may be regulated by a shutter, a falling screen, or an interrupted illumination.

tactile procedure: the tracing of a word by children as often as is necessary to learn it, while at the same time, usually, the word is said and looked at.

temporal horn: a fluid-filled cavity, part of the ventricular system in the temporal lobe of the brain. A particular triangular area of this horn is known as the trigone.

temporal lobe epilepsy: epilepsy in which the brain wave pattern of a seizure discharge originates in and spreads from the temporal lobe.

territoriality: the tendency, especially as found in some bird and mammalian species, to establish breeding-territory rights.

theta waves: in brain wave tracings, a frequency range of from 4 to 7 brain waves per second; this is a relatively slow range which is not uncommon in children up to fourteen years of age. In adults, a predominance of theta waves is considered abnormal.

thoracotomy: incision of the thoracic (chest) wall.

T.O.: abbreviation for traditional orthography; embraces both writing and spelling of words using the traditional twenty-six letter alphabet.

transfer of training: a general term for change in ability to perform a given act as a direct consequence of having performed another act relating to it.

trauma: a form of injury; commonly, injury by mechanical agents; broadly, injury produced by any physical agent; also, severe psychic injury.

traumatic: pertaining to trauma.

trigone: triangle.

trigram: a combination of three letters.

visuoconstructional ability: in psychological testing, ability for tasks like writing or block-design building that require joint action of the eyes and hands.

Wada sodium amytal test: a method introduced by Wada in 1949 for determining cerebral dominance. A one-sided intracarotid injection of sodium amytal is carried in the carotid artery directly to the same side of the brain. If it is the side of the dominant hemisphere, there will rapidly be disturbance of speech and a feeling of depression. On the nondominant side, there will be no language disturbance and euphoria instead of depression. In both instances, EEG and other neurological signs are unilateral.

WAIS: Wechsler Adult Intelligence Scale.

Wassermann reaction: specific blood test for the diagnosis of syphilis.

weighting: the determination of the relative influence that each element of a composite score should have in the total by assigning a constant multiplier to each kind of element.

WISC: Wechsler Intelligence Scale for Children.

word-attack skills: a pedagogical term that refers to a child's ability to analyze unfamiliar words by syllables and phonic elements and so arrive at their pronunciation and possibly their meaning.

GENERAL BIBLIOGRAPHY

Ajuriaguerra, J. de, and Hécaen, H. 1960. *Le Cortex Cérébral*, 2d edition. Paris, Masson.

Alexander, D., Ehrhardt, A., and Money, J. 1966. Geometric- and human-figure drawings in Turner's syndrome. *Journal of Nervous and Mental Disease*, 142, in press.

Alexander, D., and Money, J. 1965. Reading ability, object constancy and Turner's syndrome. *Perceptual and Motor Skills*, 20:981–84.

Alexander, D., and Money, J. 1966. Turner's syndrome and Gerstmann's syndrome: neuropsychologic comparisons. *Neuropsychologia*, 4, in press.

Alexander, D., Walker, H. T., and Money, J. 1964. Studies in direction sense. I. Turner's syndrome. *Archives of General Psychiatry*, 10:337–39.

Altus, G. T. 1956. A WISC profile for retarded readers. *Journal of Counseling Psychology*, 20:155–56.

Arthur, G. 1940. Psychotherapy with retarded readers. *Journal of Consulting Psychology*, 4:173–76.

Axline, M. 1947. Non-directive therapy for poor readers. *Journal of Consulting Psychology*, 20:61–69.

Ayllon, T., and Azrin, N. H. 1965. An objective method for the measurement and reinforcement of adaptive behavior of psychotics. *Journal of the Experimental Analysis of Behavior*, 8:357–83.

Bahn, A., Chandler, C., and Eisenberg, L. 1961. Diagnostic and demographic characteristics of patients seen in outpatient clinics for an entire state. *American Journal of Psychiatry*, 117:769–78.

Balow, I. H. 1963. Lateral dominance characteristics and reading achievement in the first grade. *Journal of Psychology*, 55:323–28.

Belmont, L., and Birch, H. G. 1963. Lateral dominance and right-left awareness in normal children. *Child Development*, 34:257–70.

Belmont, L., and Birch, H. G. 1965. Lateral dominance, lateral awareness and reading disability. *Child Development*, 36:57–71.

Bender, L. 1956. *Psychopathology of Children with Organic Brain Disorders*. Springfield, Ill., Charles C Thomas.

Bender, L. 1957. Specific reading disability as a motivational lag. *Bulletin of the Orton Society*, 7:9–18.

Bender, L. 1958. Problems in conceptualization and communication in children with developmental alexia. In P. H. Hoch and J. Zubin (eds.), *Psychopathology of Communication*. New York, Grune and Stratton.

Benton, A. L. 1958. Significance of systematic reversal in right-left discrimination. *Acta Psychiatrica et Neurologica Scandinavica*, 33:129–37.

Benton, A. L. 1959. *Right-Left Discrimination and Finger Localization: Development and Pathology*. New York, Hoeber-Harper.

Benton, A. L. 1961. The fiction of the "Gerstmann Syndrome." *Journal of Neurology, Neurosurgery and Psychiatry*, 24:176–81.

Benton, A. L. 1962. Dyslexia in relation to form perception and directional sense. In J. Money (ed.), *Reading Disability: Progress and Research Needs in Dyslexia*. Baltimore, Johns Hopkins.

Bentzen, F. 1963. Sex ratios in learning and behavior disorders. *American Journal of Orthopsychiatry*, 33:92–98.

Bills, E. 1950. Non-directive play therapy with retarded readers. *Journal of Consulting Psychology*, 14:140–49.

Birch, H. G., and Belmont, L. 1964. Auditory visual integration in normal and retarded readers. *American Journal of Orthopsychiatry*, 34:852–61.

Birch, H. G., and Belmont, L. 1965. Auditory visual integration, intelligence and reading ability in school children. *Perceptual and Motor Skills*, 20:295–305.

Birnbrauer, J. S., Bijou, S. W., Wolf, M. M., and Kidder, J. D. 1965. Programed instruction in the classroom. In L. P. Ullman and L. Krasner (eds.), *Case Studies in Behavior Modification*. New York, Holt, Rinehart, and Winston. Pp. 358–63.

Birnbrauer, J. S., Kidder, J. D., and Tague, C. E. 1964. Programing reading from the teacher's point of view. *Programed Instruction*, 3 (7):1–2.

Birnbrauer, J. S., and Lawler, J. 1964. Token reinforcement for learning. *Mental Retardation Journal*, 2:275–79.

Bishop, C. H. 1964. Transfer effects of word and letter training. *Journal of Verbal Learning and Verbal Behavior*, 3:215–21.

Blanchard, P. 1935. Psychogenic factors in some cases of reading disability. *American Journal of Orthopsychiatry*, 5:361–74.

Blau, A. 1946. The master hand; a study of the origin and meaning of right and left sidedness and its relation to personality and language. Research Monograph No. 5. New York, American Orthopsychiatric Association, Inc.

Bloomfield, L. 1942. Linguistics and reading. *Elementary English Revised*, 19:125–30, 183–86.

Bodmer, F. 1949. *The Loom of Language*. London, Allen and Unwin.

Bond, G. L. 1935. *The Auditory and Speech Characteristics of Poor Readers*. New York, Bureau of Publications, Teachers College, Columbia University.

Bond, G. L., and Tinker, M. A. 1957. *Reading Difficulties: Their Diagnosis and Correction*. New York, Appleton-Century-Crofts.

Botel, M. 1957. Paper read at the Syracuse University meeting, Frontiers of Education.

Bridger, W. H., and Blank, M. 1966. Symbolic mediation deficiencies in retarded readers. Fifty-sixth Annual Meeting of the American Psychopathological Association, Abstracts, pp. 22–23.

Broadbent, D. E. 1958. *Perception and Communication*. New York, Pergamon.

Bronner, A. F. 1917. *The Psychology of Special Abilities and Disabilities*. Boston, Little, Brown.

Brown, H., *et al.* 1958. *Introduction to Geology*. New York, Ginn and Company.

Brown, R. 1958. *Words and Things*. Glencoe, Ill., The Free Press. P. 72.

Buchanan, C. D. 1964. *Teacher's Guide to Programed Reading*. New York, Webster Division, McGraw-Hill.

Buros, O. K. 1961. *Tests in Print*. Highland Park, N.J., Gryphon Press.

Burt, C. 1935. *The Subnormal Mind*. London, Oxford University Press.

Candland, D. K., and Conklyn, D. H. 1962. Use of the "Oddity Problem" in teaching mentally retarded deaf-mutes to read; a pilot project. *The Training School Bulletin*, 59:38–41.

Cattell, J. McK. 1885. Über die Zeit der Erkennung und Benennung von Schriftzeichen, Bildern und Farben. *Philosophische Studien*, 2:635–50.

Childs, B. 1965. Genetic origin of some sex differences among human beings. *Pediatrics*, 35:798–812.

Childs, S. B., and Childs, R. de S. 1962. *Sound Phonics*. Cambridge, Mass., Educators Publishing Service.

Childs, S. B., and Childs, R. de S. 1963. *Sound Spelling*. Cambridge, Mass., Educators Publishing Service.

Cohen, H. L. 1964. *A Two-Year Report on the Experimental Freshman Year Program*. Carbondale, Southern Illinois University.

Cohen, H. L. 1965. Project CASE: *Contingencies Applicable for Special Education*. Institute for Behavioral Research, Silver Spring, Md.

Cohen, J. 1957. A factor-analytically based rationale for the Wechsler Adult Intelligence Scale. *Journal of Consulting Psychology*, 21:451–57.

Cohen, J. 1959. The factorial structure of the WISC at ages 7–6, 10–6, and 13–6. *Journal of Consulting Psychology*, 23:285–99.

Cole, E. M., and Walker, L. 1964. Reading and speech problems as expressions of a specific language disability. In D. McK. Rioch and E. A. Weinstein (eds.), *Disorders of Communication*. Association for Research in Nervous and Mental Disease, Research Publication XLII. Baltimore, Williams and Wilkins.

Coleman, R., and Deutsch, C. 1964. Lateral dominance and right-left discrimination: a comparison of normal and retarded readers. *Perceptual and Motor Skills*, 19:43–50.

Collins, J. E. 1961. The effects of remedial education. Educational Monograph No. 4. Birmingham, England, Institute of Education, University of Birmingham.

Cornell University Cooperative Research Project No. 639. 1963. A basic research program on reading. Final report to the Office of Education, U.S. Department of Health, Education and Welfare. Ithaca, N.Y., Technical Report from Cornell University.

Cravioto, J., and Robles, B. 1965. Evolution of adaptive and motor behavior during rehabilitation from Kwashiorkor. *American Journal of Orthopsychiatry*, 35:499–564.

Critchley, M. 1942. Aphasic disorders of signalling (constitutional and acquired) occurring in naval signalmen. *Journal of Mount Sinai Hospital, New York*, 9:363–75.

Critchley, M. 1953. *The Parietal Lobes*. Baltimore, Williams and Wilkins.

Critchley, M. 1961. Inborn reading disorders of central origin. *Transactions of the Ophthalmological Society of the United Kingdom*, 81:459–80.

Critchley, M. 1964. *Developmental Dyslexia.* London, Heinemann.

Dale, E. (ed.) 1949. *Readability.* Champaign, Ill., National Council of Teachers of English.

Dale, E., and Chall, J. 1948. A formula for predicting readability. *Educational Research Bulletin,* 27:11–20.

Daniels, J. C., and Diack, H. 1958. *Royal Road Readers.* London, Chatto & Windus.

De Hirsch, K. 1963. Psychological correlates of the reading process. *Bulletin of the Orton Society,* 13:59–71.

De Hirsch, K. 1965. Early identification of specific language disability as seen by a speech pathologist. In L. R. Karnes (comp.), *Dyslexia in Special Education.* Pomfret, Conn., The Orton Society, Inc.

De Hirsch, K., Jansky, J. J., and Langford, W. S. 1965. The prediction of reading, spelling and writing disabilities in children: a preliminary study. Final Report to the Health Research Council of the City of New York. New York, Columbia University, Technical Report, Contract U–1270.

Deutsch, M. 1965. The role of social class in language development and cognition. *American Journal of Orthopsychiatry,* 35:78–88.

Dodge, R. 1905. The illusion of clear vision during eye movement. *Psychological Bulletin,* 2:193–99.

Doehring, D. G., and Lacy, J. L. 1963. Programed instruction in beginning reading. Mimeographed report. Indianapolis, Indiana University School of Medicine.

Dolch, E. W. 1945. *A Manual for Remedial Reading.* Champaign, Ill., Garrard.

Downing, J. 1962. Experiments with an augmented alphabet for beginning readers in British schools. Speech presented at Lehigh University, Bethlehem, Pennsylvania.

Downing, J. 1962. The relationship between reading attainment and the inconsistency of English spelling at the infant's school stage. *British Journal of Educational Psychology,* 32:166–77.

Downing, J. 1963. *Experiments with Pitman's Initial Teaching Alphabet in British Schools.* New York, i/t/a Publications.

Downing, J. 1964. The prevention of communication disorder by the use of a simplified alphabet. *Developmental Medicine and Child Neurology,* 6:113–24.

Downing, J. 1964. Pitman's Initial Teaching (augmented Roman) Alphabet. Unpublished interim report, University of London Institute of Education.

Drew, A. L. 1956. A neurological appraisal of familial congenital word-blindness. *Brain,* 79:440–60.

Edfeldt, A. W. 1960. *Silent Speech and Silent Reading.* Chicago, University of Chicago.

Edwards, T. J. 1956. The role of meaning, frequency of contact and auditory-vocomotor stimulation in the visual perception of verbal stimuli. Unpublished doctoral dissertation, Temple University, 1955. *Dissertation Abstracts,* 16:382–83.

Edwards, T. J. 1957. Oral reading in the total reading process. *The Elementary School Journal,* 58:36–41.

Eisenberg, L. 1959. Office evaluation of specific reading disability. *Pediatrics*, 23:997–1003.

Eisenberg, L. 1962. Possibilities for a preventive psychiatry. *Pediatrics*, 30:815–28.

Eisenberg, L. 1964. Behavioral manifestations of cerebral damage in childhood. In H. G. Birch (ed.), *Brain Damage in Childhood.* Baltimore, Williams and Wilkins.

Erdmann, B., and Dodge, R. 1898. *Psychologische Untersuchungen über das Lesen.* Halle a. S., Niemeyer.

Ewing, A. W. G. 1930. *Aphasia in Children.* Oxford, Oxford Medical Publications.

Fabian, A. A. 1951. Clinical and experimental studies of school children who are retarded in reading. *Quarterly Journal of Child Behavior*, 3:15–37.

Fernald, G. M. 1943. *Remedial Techniques in Basic School Subjects.* New York, McGraw-Hill.

Fernald, G. M., and Keller, H. B. 1921. Effects of linguistic factor in development of the word recognition in the case of non-readers. *Journal of Educational Research*, 4:355–77.

Ferster, C. B., and Skinner, B. F. 1957. *Schedules of Reinforcement.* New York, Appleton-Century-Crofts.

Fildes, L. G. 1921. A psychological inquiry into the nature of the condition known as congenital word blindness. *Brain*, 44:286–307.

Flescher, I. 1962. Ocular-manual laterality and perceptual rotation of literal symbols. *Genetic Psychology Monographs*, 66:3–48.

Freedman, M. 1965. Perspectives in youth employment. *Children*, 12:75–80.

Freeman, K. J. 1908. *Schools of Hellas.* London, Macmillan.

Friedlander, B. Z. 1965. Performance differentiation in a child's incidental play for perceptual reinforcement. Paper read at American Psychological Association, Chicago.

Friedlander, B. Z., Lightbody, P. C., and Schwarz, M. E. 1964. The Hawken Letters: a manipulative technique for practicing basic grapheme-phoneme combinations in beginning reading. Cleveland, Western Reserve University, Technical Report, NIMH Grant 08049, USPHS.

Fries, C. C. 1963. *Linguistics and Reading.* New York, Holt, Rinehart and Winston.

Frostig, M. 1965. Corrective reading in the classroom. *The Reading Teacher*, 18(7):573.

Galifret-Granjon, N. 1952. Le Problème de l'organisation spatiale dans les dyslexies d'evolution. In N. Nanent (ed.), *L'Apprentissage de la Lecture et ses Troubles.* Paris, Presses Universitaires de France. Pp. 445–79.

Gallagher, J. 1960. Specific language disability: dyslexia. *Bulletin of the Orton Society*, 10:5–10.

Gates, A. I. 1922. *The Psychology of Reading and Spelling with Special Reference to Disability.* Teachers College Contributions to Education No. 129. New York, Bureau of Publications, Teachers College, Columbia University.

Gates, A. I. 1930. *Interest and Ability in Reading.* New York, Macmillan.

Gates, A. I. 1947. *The Improvement of Reading*, 3rd edition. New York, Macmillan.

Gattegno, C. 1962. *Words in Color*. Chicago, Illinois, 425 North Michigan, Learning Materials, Inc. The following items are included: (a) primer books 1, 2, 3; (b) book of stories; (c) word building book; (d) principles and background; (e) teachers' guide; (f) twenty-one wall charts in color; (g) eight phonic code charts in color; (h) word cards of colored cardboard; and (i) guide for teachers.

Gattegno, C. 1965. *Book of Tales*. Reading, England, Educational Explorers, 11 Crown St.

Gattegno, C. 1965. *Words in Color*. Training film, 39 minutes. Reading, England, Educational Explorers, 11 Crown St.

Gerstmann, J. 1924. Fingeragnosie: Eine umschriebene Störung der Orientierung am eigenen Körper. *Wiener klinische Wochenschrift*, 37:1010–12.

Geschwind, N. 1965. Disconnexion syndrome in animals and man. *Brain*, 88:237–94, 585–644.

Gibson, E. J., Bishop, C. H., Schiff, W., and Smith, J. 1964. Comparison of meaningfulness and pronunciability as grouping principles in the perception and retention of verbal material. *Journal of Experimental Psychology*, 67:173–82.

Gibson, E. J., Gibson, J. J., Pick, A. D., and Osser, H. 1962. A developmental study of the discrimination of letter-like forms. *Journal of Comparative and Physiological Psychology*, 55:897–906.

Gibson E. J., Osser, H., and Pick, A. D. 1963. A study in the development of grapheme-phoneme correspondence. *Journal of Verbal Learning and Verbal Behavior*, 2:142–46.

Gibson, E. J., Osser, H., Schiff, W., and Smith, J. 1963. An analysis of critical features of letters, tested by a confusion matrix. In Cornell University Cooperative Research Project No. 639.

Gibson, E. J., Pick, A. D., Osser, H., and Hammond, M. 1962. The role of grapheme-phoneme correspondence in the perception of words. *American Journal of Psychology*, 75:554–70.

Gillingham, A., and Stillman, B. W. 1956. *Remedial Training for Children with Specific Disability in Reading, Spelling and Penmanship*, 5th edition; reissued, 1964. Cambridge, Mass., Educators Publishing Service.

Gillingham, A., and Stillman, B. W. 1960. *Remedial Training for Children with Specific Disability in Reading, Spelling and Penmanship*, 6th edition. Cambridge, Mass., Educators Publishing Service.

Gloning, I., Gloning, K., and Hoff, H. 1963. Aphasia, a clinical syndrome. In L. Halpern (ed.), *Problems of Dynamic Neurology*. New York, Grune and Stratton.

Goetzinger, C. P., Dirks, D. D., and Baer, C. J. 1960. Auditory discrimination and visual perception in good and poor readers. *Annals of Otology, Rhinology and Laryngology*, 69:121–37.

Goldiamond, I. 1958. Visual signal detection, perception, and response variables as functions of development and mental retardation. In *Perceptual and Response Abilities of Mentally Retarded Children*. Carbondale, Southern Illinois University.

Goldiamond, I. 1962a. Machine definition of ongoing silent and oral reading rate. *Journal of Experimental Analysis of Behavior*, 5:363–67.

Goldiamond, I. 1962b. Perception. In A. J. Bachrach (ed.), *The Experimental Foundations of Clinical Psychology*. New York, Basic Books.

Goldiamond, I. 1964a. Response bias in perceptual communication. In D. McK. Rioch and E. A. Weinstein (eds.), *Disorders of Communication*. Association for Research in Nervous and Mental Disease, Research Publication XLII. Baltimore, Williams and Wilkins.

Goldiamond, I. 1964b. A research and demonstration procedure in stimulus control, abstraction, and environmental programing. *Journal of Experimental Analysis of Behavior*, 7:216.

Goldiamond, I. 1965. Stuttering and fluency as manipulatable operant response classes. In L. Krasner and L. P. Ullman (eds.), *Research in Behavior Modification*. New York, Holt, Rinehart and Winston. Pp. 106–56.

Goldiamond, I. 1966a. Self-control procedures in personal behavior problems. In R. E. Ulrich, T. J. Stachnik, and J. H. Mabry (eds.), *The Control of Human Behavior*. Chicago, Scott, Foresman.

Goldiamond, I. 1966b. Perception, language and conceptualization rules. In B. Kleinmuntz (ed.), *Cognition Symposium: Problem Solving*. New York, Wiley.

Goldiamond, I., Dyrud, J., and Miller, M. 1965. Practice as research in professional psychology. *The Canadian Psychologist*, 6a:110–28.

Goldiamond, I., and Pliskoff, S. S. 1965. Music education and the rationale underlying programed instruction. *Music Education Journal*, 51:43–47, 190–95.

Gooddy, W., and Reinhold, J. 1961. Congenital dyslexia and asymmetry of cerebral functions. *Brain*, 84:231–42.

Gordon, E. 1965. A review of programs of compensatory education. *American Journal of Orthopsychiatry*, 35:640–45.

Gray, W. S. 1956. *The Teaching of Reading and Writing*. Paris, UNESCO.

Gray, W. S. 1957. *The Teaching of Reading*. Burton lecture. Cambridge, Mass., Harvard.

Hallgren, B. 1950. Specific dyslexia: a clinical and genetic study. *Acta Psychiatrica et Neurologica, Supplement 65*. Copenhagen, Munksgaard.

Harlow, H. F. 1949. The formation of learning sets. *Psychological Review*, 56:51–65.

Harrhoff, T. 1920. *Schools of Gaul*. New York, Oxford.

Hécaen, H., and Ajuriaguerra, J. de. 1964. *Left-Handedness: Manual Superiority and Cerebral Dominance*. New York, Grune and Stratton.

Hegge, T. G., Kirk, S. A., and Kirk, W. D. 1940. *Remedial Reading Drills*. Ann Arbor, Mich., George Wahr.

Heimburger, R. F., De Myer, W., and Reitan, R. M. 1964. Implications of Gerstmann's syndrome. *Journal of Neurology, Neurosurgery, and Psychiatry*, 27:52–57.

Herbert, M. 1964. The concept and testing of brain-damage in children: a review. *Journal of Child Psychology and Psychiatry*, 5:197–216.

Hermann, K. 1959. *Reading Disability*. Springfield, Ill., Charles C Thomas.

Hermann, K., and Norrie, E. 1958. Is congenital word blindness an hereditary type of Gerstmann's syndrome? *Psychiatrie et Neurologie*, 136:59–73.

Herrmann, G., and Pötzl, O. 1926. Über die Agraphie und ihre lokaldiagnostischen Beziehungen. *Monatsschrift für Psychiatrie und Neurologie. Supplement 35. Abhandlung Neurologie, Psychiatrie, Psychologie.* Berlin, Karger.

Herrnstein, R. J., and Loveland, D. H. 1964. Complex visual concept in the pigeon. *Science*, 146:549–51.

Hildreth, G. 1932. The success of young children in number and letter construction. *Child Development*, 3:1–14.

Hildreth, G. 1958. *Teaching Reading*. New York, Henry Holt.

Hinshelwood, J. 1917. *Congenital Word Blindness*. London, Lewis.

Hively, W. 1966. A framework for the analysis of elementary reading behavior. *American Educational Research Journal*, 3:89–103.

Hockett, C. F. 1963. The elements of graphonomy. In Cornell University Cooperative Research Project No. 639.

Hoffman, W. C. 1964. Pattern recognition by the method of isoinclines: I. A mathematical model for the visual integrative process. Mathematical Note No. 351, Mathematics Research Laboratory, Boeing Scientific Research Laboratories.

Hofsteater, H. T. 1959. An experiment in preschool education. *Gallaudet College Bulletin*, 8(3):1–17.

Holland, J. G., and Skinner, B. F. 1961. *The Analysis of Behavior*. New York, McGraw-Hill.

Holmes, J. A. 1954. Factors underlying major reading disability at the college level. *Genetic Psychology Monographs*, 49:1–95.

Holz, W. C., and Azrin, N. H. 1961. Discriminative properties of punishment. *Journal of the Experimental Analysis of Behavior*, 4:225–32.

Hunt, J. McV. 1961. *Intelligence and Experience*. New York, Ronald Press.

Ilg, F. L., and Ames, L.B. 1950. Developmental trends in reading behavior. *Journal of Genetic Psychology*, 76:291–312.

Ingram, T. T. S. 1959. Specific developmental disorders of speech in childhood. *Brain*, 82:450–67.

Ingram, T. T. S., and Reid, J. F. 1956. Developmental aphasia observed in a department of child psychiatry. *Archives of Disease in Childhood*, 31:161–72.

Irvine, R., *et al.* 1941. An ocular policy for public schools. *American Journal of Ophthalmology*, 24:779–90.

Issacs, W., Thomas, J., and Goldiamond, I. 1960. Application of operant conditioning to reinstate verbal behavior in psychotics. *Journal of Speech and Hearing Disorder*, 25:8–12.

Jakobsen, R., and Halle, M. 1956. *Fundamentals of Language*. The Hague, Mouton.

Jersild, A. T. 1947. *Child Psychology*. New York, Prentice-Hall.

John, V. 1963. The intellectual development of slum children. *American Journal of Orthopsychiatry*, 33:813–22.

Johnson, G. O. 1963. *Education for the Slow Learners*. New Jersey, Prentice-Hall.

Johnson, M. 1957. Factors related to disability in reading. *Journal of Experimental Education*, 16:1–26.

Joos, L. W. 1964. The phonogram method—a report of an experiment implementing a linguistic approach to reading. Baltimore, Board of Education of Baltimore County.

Joos, L. W., and Jones, V. W. 1964. The phonogram method. *The Maryland Teacher*, 22(2).

Joos, L. W., Leiman, C. J., and Schiffman, G. B. 1961. An investigation of the value of remedial reading with psychotherapy in a public school system. Mimeographed report. Baltimore, Board of Education of Baltimore County.

Kallos, G. L., Grabow, J. M., and Guarino, E. 1961. The WISC profile of disabled readers. *Personnel and Guidance Journal*, 39:476–78.

Karnes, L. R. (ed.) 1965. *Dyslexia in Special Education*. Pomfret, Conn., The Orton Society, Inc.

Kawi, A. A., and Pasamanick, B. 1959. Prenatal and paranatal factors in the development of childhood reading disorders. *Monographs of the Society for Research in Child Development*, XXIV (4).

Kelleher, R. T., and Gollub, L. R. 1962. A review of positive conditioned reinforcement. *Journal of the Experimental Analysis of Behavior*, 5:543–97.

Keller, F. S., and Schoenfeld, W. N. 1950. *Principles of Psychology*. New York, Appleton-Century-Crofts.

Kinsbourne, M., and Warrington, E. K. 1962. A study of finger agnosia. *Brain*, 85:47–66.

Kinsbourne, M., and Warrington, E. K. 1962. A disorder of simultaneous form perception. *Brain*, 85:461–86.

Kinsbourne, M., and Warrington, E. K. 1963. The development of finger differentiation. *Quarterly Journal of Experimental Psychology*, 15:132–37.

Kinsbourne, M., and Warrington, E. K. 1964. Disorders of spelling, with special reference to the Gerstmann syndrome. *Journal of Neurology, Neurosurgery and Psychiatry*, 27:224–28.

Kirk, S. A. 1940. *Teaching Reading to Slow-Learning Children*. New York, Houghton-Mifflin Company.

Kitchen, A. T., Allen, B. F., and Croft, K. (eds). 1964–66. *Reader's Digest Readings for Teaching English as a Second Language*, 6 volumes. Pleasantville, N.Y., Reader's Digest Services, Inc.

Kolers, P. A., and Katzman, M. T. 1963. Naming and reading sequentially presented letters. Paper presented before the Psychonomic Society, Bryn Mawr, Pennsylvania, August, 1963.

Lachmann, F. M. 1960. Perceptual-motor development in children retarded in reading ability. *Journal of Consulting Psychology*, 24:427–31.

Lange, J. 1930. Finger-agnosie und Agraphie (Eine psychopathologische studie). *Monatsschrift für Psychiatrie und Neurologie*, 76:129–88.

Lashley, K. S. 1951. The problem of serial order in behavior. In L. A. Jeffress (ed.), *Cerebral Mechanisms in Behavior*. New York, Wiley.

Lecky, P. 1945. *Self Consistency: A Theory of Personality*. New York, Island Press.

Leonore, Sister N., RSC. 1965. *Words in Color in the Classroom: Creative Writing*. Reading, England, Educational Explorers, 11 Crown St.

Levin, H., Baum, E., and Bostwick, S. 1963. The learning of variable grapheme-to-phoneme correspondence: comparison of English and Spanish speakers. In Cornell University Cooperative Research Project No. 639.

Levin, H., and Watson, J. 1963. The learning of variable grapheme-to-phoneme correspondences: variations in the initial consonant position. In Cornell University Cooperative Research Project No. 639.

Levitt, J., and Levitt, J. 1962. *The Spell of Words*. London, Darwen Finlayson.

Lindsley, O. R. 1962. A behavioral measure of television viewing. *Journal of Advertising Research*, 2(3):2–12.

Lumsdaine, A. A., and Glaser, R. (eds.) 1960. *Teaching Machines and Programed Learning*. Washington, D.C., National Education Association.

Lundin, R. W. 1961. *Personality: An Experimental Approach*. New York, Macmillan.

Lynn, R. 1957. Temperamental characteristics related to disparity in attainments in reading and arithmetic. *British Journal of Educational Psychology*, 27:62–67.

McCarthy, J. J., and Kirk, S. A. 1961. *Illinois Test of Psycholinguistic Abilities*. Urbana, Ill., Institute for Research on Exceptional Children, University of Illinois.

McCready, E. B. 1910. Biological variations in the higher cerebral centers causing retardation. *Archives of Pediatrics*, 27:506–13.

McKim, M. 1955. *Guiding Growth in Reading*. New York, Macmillan.

McNeil, J. D. 1962. Programed instruction as a research tool in reading: an annotated case. *Programed Instruction*, 1:37–42.

Malmquist, E. 1958. *Factors Related to Reading Disabilities in the First Grade of the Elementary School*. Stockholm, Almquist and Wiksell.

Maltzman, E. 1964. An investigation of key tone matching with children and adults. Unpublished doctoral dissertation, Boston University School of Education.

Marks, L. E., and Miller, G. A. 1964. The role of semantic and syntactic constraints in the memorization of English sentences. *Journal of Verbal Learning and Verbal Behavior*, 3:1–5.

Martin, J. H. 1965. Report on automated reading instruction. *Teaching Aids News*, 5(4):6–10.

Maxwell, A. E. 1959. A factor analysis of the Wechsler Intelligence Scale for Children. *British Journal of Educational Psychology*, 29:237–41.

Mazurkiewicz, A. J. 1963–65. Interim reports one through seven, the Lehigh-Bethlehem study. *Journal of the Reading Specialist*, September, 1963, to June, 1965.

Mazurkiewicz, A. J. 1964a. *The Initial Teaching Alphabet. New Perspectives in Reading Instruction*. New York, Pitman.

Mazurkiewicz, A. J. 1964b. A tiger by the tail. *29th Educational Conference Proceedings*. New York, Educational Record Bureau.

Mazurkiewicz, A. J., Dietrick, D., Beauchamp, J., and Ward, B. 1965. i/t/a and learning disorders. In J. Hellmuth (ed.), *Learning Disorders*. Seattle, Special Child Publications.

Mead, G. H. 1934. *Mind, Self, and Society*. Chicago, University of Chicago Press.

Meyer, H., Norgaard, B., and Torpe, H. 1943. *Laesesvage Coerm ag dares*. København, Meddlelser fra Dansklaererforen.

Miller, A. D., Margolin, J. B., and Yolles, S. F. 1957. Epidemiology of reading disabilities. *American Journal of Public Health and the Nation's Health*, 47:1250–56.

Miller, G. A., and Isard, S. 1963. Some perceptual consequences of linguistic rules. *Journal of Verbal Learning and Verbal Behavior*, 2:217–28.

Missildine, W. H. 1946. The emotional background of thirty children with reading disability. *Nervous Child*, 5:263–72.

Money, J. (ed.) 1962. *Reading Disability: Progress and Research Needs in Dyslexia*. Baltimore, Johns Hopkins.

Money, J. 1963. Cytogenetic and psychosexual incongruities with a note on space-form blindness. *American Journal of Psychiatry*, 119:820–27.

Money, J., and Alexander, D. 1966. Turner's syndrome: further demonstration of the presence of specific cognitional deficits. *Journal of Medical Genetics*, 3:47–48.

Money, J., Alexander, D., and Walker, H. T., Jr. 1965. *A Standardized Road-map Test of Direction Sense*. Baltimore, Johns Hopkins.

Monroe, M. 1928. Methods for diagnosis and treatment of cases of reading disability. Foreword by S. T. Orton. *Genetic Psychology Monographs*, 4:335–456.

Montessori, M. 1912. *The Montessori Method*. New York, Frederick A. Stokes.

Moore, O. K. 1963. *Autotelic Responsive Environments and Exceptional Children*. Hamden, Conn., Responsive Environments Foundation.

Moore, R., and Goldiamond, I. 1964. Errorless establishment of visual discrimination using fading procedures. *Journal of the Experimental Analysis of Behavior*, 7:269–72.

Morgan, W. P. 1896. A case of congenital word blindness. *British Medical Journal*, 2:1378.

Morris, J. 1958. Teaching children to read. *Educational Research*, 1:38–39.

Mountcastle, V. B. (ed.) 1962. *Interhemispheric Relations and Cerebral Dominance*. Baltimore, Johns Hopkins.

Murray, W., and Gulliford, R. 1960. Severe reading disability. *Special Education*, 49:28–29.

Namowitz, S. N., and Stone, D. E. 1960. *Earth Science*. Princeton, D. Van Nostrand.

Newman, S. E. 1965. Isolation-effects of paired-associate training. *American Journal of Psychology*, 78:621–26.

Norrie, E. 1960. Word blindness in Denmark—its neurological and educational aspects. *The Independent School Bulletin*, 1959–60(3):8–12.

Olson, W. C. 1949. *Child Development*. Boston, Heath.

Orton, J. L. 1963. The Orton story. *Bulletin of the Orton Society*, 13:1–6.

Orton, J. L. 1964. *A Guide To Teaching Phonics*. Winston-Salem, N.C., Orton Reading Center and Salem College Book Store.

Orton, S. T. 1925. "Word-blindness" in school children. *Archives of Neurology and Psychiatry*, 14:581–615.

Orton, S. T. 1926. Reading disability. *Genetic Psychology Monographs*, 14:335–453.

Orton, S. T. 1928. Specific reading disability—strephosymbolia. *Journal of the American Medical Association*, 90:1095–99.

Orton, S. T. 1931. Special disability in spelling. *Bulletin of the Neurological Institute of New York*, 1:159–92.

Orton, S. T. 1937. *Reading, Writing and Speech Problems in Children*. New York, Norton.

Orton, S. T. 1943. Visual functions in strephosymbolia. *Archives of Ophthalmology*, 30:707–13.

Orton, S. T. 1946. Some disorders in the language development of children. In *Language in Relation to Psycho-motor Development*. Langhorne, Pa., Child Research Clinic of the Woods Schools.

Orton, S. T., and Gillingham, A. 1933. Special disability in writing. *Bulletin of the Neurological Institute of New York*, 3:1–32.

Pasamanick, B., Knobloch, H., and Lilienfeld, A. N. 1956. Socioeconomic status: some precursors of neuropsychiatric disorder. *American Journal of Orthopsychiatry*, 26:594–601.

Pick, A. D. 1965. Improvement of visual and tactual form discrimination. *Journal of Experimental Psychology*, 69:331–39.

Pines, M. 1965. What the talking typewriter says. *The New York Times Magazine*, May 9th.

Pitman, I. J. 1961. Learning to read: an experiment. *Journal of Royal Society of Arts*, 109:149–80.

Plunkett, M. B. 1949. *A Spelling Workbook*. Cambridge, Mass., Educators Publishing Service.

Premack, D. 1959. Toward empirical behavior laws: I. positive reinforcement. *Psychological Review*, 66:219–33.

Rabinovitch, R. D., Drew, A. L., De Jong, R. N., Ingram, W., and Withey, L. 1954. A research approach to reading retardation. *Research Publications of the Association for Research in Nervous and Mental Disease*, 34:363–96.

Raygor, A. L., Wark, D. M., and Warren, A. D. 1964. Operant conditioning of reading rate: the effect of a secondary reinforcer. Minneapolis, University of Minnesota Graduate School.

Reader's Digest Services Editors. 1964–65. *Adult Readers*, 4 volumes for each of three steps, Grades 1–4. Pleasantville, N.Y., Reader's Digest Services, Inc.

Reader's Digest Services Editors. 1965. *Reading Skill Builders*, 19 volumes, Grades 1–6. Pleasantville, N.Y., Reader's Digest Services, Inc.

Reader's Digest Services Editors. 1965–66. *Advanced Reading Skill Builders*, 4 volumes, Grades 7–8. Pleasantville, N.Y., Reader's Digest Services, Inc.

Riesen, A. H. 1950. Arrested vision. *Scientific American*, 183:16–19.

Roberts, R. W., and Coleman, J. C. 1958, Investigation of the role of visual and kinesthetic factors in reading failure. *Journal of Educational Research*, 51:445–51.

Robinson, H. M. 1947. *Why Pupils Fail in Reading*. Chicago, University of Chicago.

Rocha e Silva, M. I., and Ferster, C. B. 1964. An experiment in the teaching of a second language. Technical report. Silver Spring, Md., Institute for Behavioral Research.

Roy, H. L., Schein, J. D., and Frisina, D. R. 1964. New methods of language development for deaf children. Technical report. Washington, D.C., Gallaudet College.

Rubin, H. 1965. Unpublished doctoral dissertation. University of Chicago, Department of Psychology.

Russell, D. H., and Fea, H. R. 1963. Research on teaching reading. In N. L. Gage (ed.), *Handbook of Research on Teaching*. Chicago, Rand McNally.

Schiffman, G. 1963. Correct information on achievement levels in reading. In J. Figurel (ed.), *Reading as an Intellectual Activity. International Reading Association Conference Proceedings*, 8:119–23.

Schilder, P. 1944. Congenital alexia and its relation to optic perception. *Journal of Genetic Psychology*, 65:67–88.

Schonell, F. J., and Schonell, F. E. 1956. *Diagnostic and Attainment Testing*, 3d edition. Edinburgh and London, Oliver and Boyd.

Scrimshaw, N. S., and Behar, M. 1965. Malnutrition in underdeveloped countries. *New England Journal of Medicine*, 272:137–44, 193–98.

Seashore, H. G. 1951. Differences between verbal and performance IQs on the Wechsler Intelligence Scale for Children. *Journal of Consulting Psychology*, 15:62–67.

Shaffer, J. 1962. A specific cognitive deficit observed in gonadal aplasia (Turner's syndrome). *Journal of Clinical Psychology*, 18:403–6.

Silberman, H. F. 1964. Experimental analysis of a beginning reading skill. *Programed Instruction*, 3(7):4.

Silver, A. A., and Hagin, R. 1960. Specific reading disability: delineation of the syndrome and relation to cerebral dominance. *Comprehensive Psychiatry*, 1:126–34.

Skinner, B. F. 1950. Are theories of learning necessary? *Psychological Review*, 57:193–216.

Skinner, B. F. 1953. *Science and Human Behavior*. New York, Macmillan.

Skinner, B. F. 1957. *Verbal Behavior*. New York, Appleton-Century-Crofts.

Skinner, B. F. 1961. Why we need teaching machines. *Harvard Educational Review*, 31:377–98.

Skinner, B. F. 1965. The technology of teaching. *Proceedings of the Royal Society, Section B*, 162:427–43.

Skinner, B. F., and Holland, J. G. 1960. The use of teaching machines in college instruction. In A. A. Lumsdaine and R. Glaser (eds.), *Teaching Machines and Programed Learning*. Washington, D.C., National Education Association. Pp. 159–72.

Slingerland, B. H. 1962. *Screening Tests for Identifying Children with Specific Language Disability*. Cambridge, Mass., Educators Publishing Service.

Smith, D. E. P., and Kelingos, J. M. 1964. *Michigan Successive Discrimination Language Program: A Program for Teachers*. Ann Arbor, Mich., Ann Arbor Publishers.

Spalding, R. B., and Spalding, W. T. 1957. *The Writing Road to Reading*. New York, Whiteside, William Morrow.

Spillane, J. D. 1942. Disturbances of the body scheme: anosognosia and finger agnosia. *Lancet*, 1:42–44.

Spitzer, R. L., Rabkin, B., and Kramer, Y. 1959. The relationship between "mixed dominance" and reading disability. *Journal of Pediatrics*, 54:76–80.

Staats, A. W., Finley, J. R., Minke, K. A., and Wolf, M. 1964. Reinforcement variables in the control of unit reading responses. *Journal of the Experimental Analysis of Behavior*, 7:139–49.

Staats, A. W., Minke, K. A., Finley, J. R., Wolf, M., and Brooks, L. O. 1964. A reinforcer system and experimental procedure for the laboratory study of reading acquisition. *Child Development*, 35:209–31.

Staats, A. W., and Staats, C. K. 1962. A comparison of the development of speech and reading behaviors with implications for research. *Child Development*, 33:831–46.

Staats, A. W., Staats, C. K., Schutz, R. E., and Wolf, M. 1962. The conditioning of textual responses using "extrinsic" reinforcers. *Journal of the Experimental Analysis of Behavior*, 5:33–40.

Stengel, E. 1944. Loss of spatial orientation, constructional apraxia and Gerstmann's syndrome. *Journal of Mental Science*, 90:753–60.

Stone, C. R. 1960. *New Practice Reader*. Books A through G, Grades 2 through 8, respectively. New York, McGraw-Hill.

Stott, D. H. 1962. *Programed Reading Kit*. Glasgow, W. & R. Holmes.

Strang, R. 1943. Relationship between certain aspects of intelligence and certain aspects of reading. *Educational and Psychological Measurement*, 3:355–59.

Strauss, A. P., and Werner, H. 1939. Finger agnosia in children. *American Journal of Psychiatry*, 95:1215–25.

Summers, E. G. 1965. Programed instruction and the teaching of reading. *Teaching Aids News*, V (10):1–13.

Tamm, A. 1943. Ordblindhet has barn. *Pedagogiska Skrifter*, 5:179.

Terrace, H. S. 1963a. Errorless transfer of a discriminative across two continua. *Journal of the Experimental Analysis of Behavior*, 6:223–32.

Terrace, H. S. 1963b. Discrimination learning with and without "errors." *Journal of the Experimental Analysis of Behavior*, 6:1–27.

Venezky, R. 1962. Unpublished master's thesis. Cornell University, Ithaca, N.Y.

Vernon, M. D. 1957. *Backwardness in Reading*. Cambridge, Cambridge University.

Vickery, V. 1962. Reading process and beginning reading instruction. Publication No. 2, Bureau of Educational Research, College of Teacher Education, New Mexico State University, University Park, New Mexico.

Wagner, W. 1932. Über Raumstörung. *Monatsschrift für Psychiatrie und Neurologie*, 84:281–307.

Walker, H. T., Jr. 1965. The reading retardate sample. *A Standardized Road-map Test of Direction Sense*. Baltimore, Johns Hopkins.

Walton, J. N., Ellis, S., and Court, S. D. M. 1962. A study of developmental apraxia and agnosia. *Brain*, 85:603–12.

Washburn, T. C., Medearis, D. N., and Childs, B. 1965. Sex differences in susceptibility to infections. *Pediatrics*, 35:57–64.

Weir, R. H. 1964. Formulation of grapheme-phoneme correspondence rules to aid in the teaching of reading. Report on Cooperative Research Project No. 5–039.

Weisenburg, T., and McBride, K. E. 1935. *Aphasia: A Clinical and Psychological Study*. New York, The Commonwealth Fund.

Whorf, B. L. 1956. *Language, Thought and Reality*. New York, Wiley and The Technology Press of Massachusetts Institute of Technology.

Wilson, A. B. 1963. Social stratification and academic achievement. In A. H. Passow (ed.), *Education in Depressed Areas*. New York, Columbia University.

Woolman, M. 1962a. *The Progressive Choice Reading Program*. Washington, D.C., Institute of Educational Research, Inc. P. 9.

Woolman, M. 1962b. *Programing for Conceptual Understanding*. Washington, D.C., Institute of Educational Research, Inc.

Woolman, M. 1965a. *Reading in High Gear*. Chicago, Science Research Associates, Inc.

Woolman, M. 1965b. Cultural asynchrony and contingency in learning disorders. In J. Hellmuth (ed.), *Learning Disorders*, Vol. I. Seattle, Special Child Publications.

Woolman, M. 1966. *Lift Off to Reading*. Chicago, Science Research Associates, Inc.

SELECTED BIBLIOGRAPHY OF TESTS

I. Alphabetic by Name of Test

Ayres Measuring Scale for Handwriting
Ayres, L. P. 1940. Princeton, Cooperative Test Division, Educational Testing Service.

Bender Visual-Motor Gestalt Test
Bender, L. 1946. New York, The Psychological Corporation.

Benton Visual Retention Test
Benton, A. L. 1955. New York, The Psychological Corporation.

Benton and Kemble Right-Left Discrimination Battery
Benton, A. L. 1959. New York, Hoeber-Harper. Pp. 14–15. Also, Benton, A. L., and Kemble, J. D. 1960. Right-left orientation and reading disability. *Psychiatria and Neurologia*, 139:49–60.

California Achievement Tests
Tiegs, E. W., and Clark, W. W. 1950, 1957. Monterey, Calif., California Test Bureau (2 editions).

California Test of Mental Maturity
Sullivan, E. T., Clark, W. W., and Tiegs, E. W. 1957. Monterey, Calif., California Test Bureau.

Daniels and Diack Standard Reading Tests
Daniels, J. C., and Diack, H. 1964. London, Chatto and Windus.

Detroit Tests of Learning Aptitude
Baker, H. J., and Leland, B. 1959. Indianapolis, Ind., Bobbs-Merrill.

Draw-A-Person Test
Harris, D. B. 1963. New York, Harcourt, Brace and World.

Durrell Analysis of Reading Difficulty
Durrell, D. D. 1955. New York, Harcourt, Brace and World.

Embedded Geometric Figures Test
Thurstone, L. L. 1944. *A Factorial Study of Perception; Psychometric Monographs No. 4.* Chicago, University of Chicago.

Finger Differentiation. See **Kinsbourne and Warrington Finger Tests.**

Gates Basic Reading Tests
Gates, A. I. 1958. New York, Bureau of Publications, Teachers College, Columbia University.

Gates Reading Survey
Gates, A. I. 1960. New York, Bureau of Publications, Teachers College, Columbia University.

Gilmore Oral Reading Test
Gilmore, J. V. 1952. New York, World Book Company.

Gray Oral Reading Tests
Gray, W. S. 1963. Helen M. Robinson (ed.). Indianapolis, Ind., Bobbs-Merrill.

Halstead-Wepman Aphasia Screening Test
Halstead, W. C., and Wepman, J. M. n. d. Chicago, University of Chicago Industrial Relations Center.

Harris Tests of Lateral Dominance
Harris, A. J. 1958. New York, The Psychological Corporation.

Holborn Reading Scale
Watts, A. F. 1948. London, Harrap.

Identification Audiometry
Darley, F. L. (ed.). 1961. *Journal of Speech and Hearing Disorders, Monograph Supplement No. 9.* American Speech and Hearing Association, Washington, D.C., September.

Illinois Test of Psycholinguistic Abilities
McCarthy, J. J., and Kirk, S. A. 1961. Urbana, Ill., Institute for Research on Exceptional Children, University of Illinois.

Informal Graded Reading, Transcription, Dictation and Spelling. See **Money Informal Graded Reading, Transcription, Dictation and Spelling.**

Iota Word Test
Monroe, M. 1929. Chicago, C. H. Stoelting.

Iowa Silent Reading Tests
Greene, H. A., Jorgensen, A. N., and Kelley, V. H. 1956. New York, Harcourt, Brace and World, new edition.

Iowa Tests of Basic Skills
Lindquist, E. F., Hieronymus, A. N., *et al.* 1956. Boston, Houghton Mifflin.

Ishihara Tests for Colour-Blindness
Ishihara, S. 1960. Tokyo, Kanehara Shuppan Company.

Kinsbourne and Warrington Finger Differentiation Tests
Kinsbourne, M., and Warrington, E. K. 1963. The development of finger differentiation. *Quarterly Journal of Experimental Psychology,* 15:132–37. See pp. 133–34.

Lee-Clark Reading Readiness Test
Lee, J. M., and Clark, W. W. 1951. Monterey, Calif., California Test Bureau.

Massachusetts Vision Tests
Titmus Optical Company. 1960. Petersburg, Va.

Money Informal Graded Reading, Transcription, Dictation and Spelling
Money, J. 1965. *Transactions of the Pennsylvania Academy of Ophthalmology and Otolaryngology,* 18:16–24. See pp. 22–24.

Pintner-Cunningham Primary Test
Pintner, R., Cunningham, B. V., and Durost, W. N. 1946. New York, Harcourt, Brace and World.

Psychodiagnostic Plates
Rorschach, H. n. d. New York, The Psychological Corporation.

Raven Standard Progressive Matrices
Raven, J. C. 1956. New York, The Psychological Corporation.

Right-Left Discrimination. See **Benton and Kemble Right-Left Discrimination Battery.**

Road-map Test of Direction Sense
Money, J., Alexander, D., and Walker, H. T., Jr. 1965. Baltimore, Johns Hopkins.

Rogers Test of Personality Adjustment
Rogers, Carl R. 1931. New York, Association Press, 291 Broadway.

Rorschach Test. See **Psychodiagnostic Plates.**

Roswell-Chall Diagnostic Reading Test of Word Analysis Skills
Roswell, F. G., and Chall, J. S. 1959. New York, Essay Press.

SRA Primary Mental Abilities
Thurstone, L. L., and Thurstone, T. G. 1954. Chicago, Science Research Associates, 57 W. Grand Ave.

Stanford Achievement Test
Kelley, T. L., Madden, R., Gardner, E. F., Terman, L. M., and Ruch, G. M. 1953. New York, Harcourt, Brace and World.

Thematic Apperception Test
Murray, H. S. 1943. Cambridge, Mass., Harvard University Press.

Wechsler Adult Intelligence Scale
Wechsler, D. 1955. New York, The Psychological Corporation.

Wechsler Intelligence Scale for Children
Wechsler, D. 1949. New York, The Psychological Corporation.

Wepman Auditory Discrimination Test
Wepman, J. M. 1958. Chicago, Language Research Associates, 950 East 59 Street.

Wide Range Achievement Test
Jastak, J., Bijou, S. W., and Jastak, S. R. 1965. Wilmington, Del., Guidance Associates, 1526 Gilpin Ave.

II. Classified by Function of Test

Intelligence Evaluation

Pintner, R., Cunningham, B. V., and Durost, W. N. 1946. *Pintner-Cunningham Primary Test.* New York, Harcourt, Brace and World.

Raven, J. C. 1956. *Standard Progressive Matrices.* New York, The Psychological Corporation.

Sullivan, E. T., Clark, W. W., and Tiegs, E. W. 1957. *California Test of Mental Maturity.* Monterey, Calif., Monterey Test Bureau.

Terman, L. M., and Merrill, M. A. 1960. *Stanford-Binet Intelligence Scale, Form L-M.* Boston, Houghton Mifflin.

Thurstone, L. L., and Thurstone, T. G. 1954. *SRA Primary Mental Abilities.* Chicago, Science Research Associates, 57 W. Grand Ave.

Wechsler, D. 1949. *Wechsler Intelligence Scale for Children.* New York, The Psychological Corporation.

Wechsler, D. 1955. *Wechsler Adult Intelligence Scale.* New York, The Psychological Corporation.

Brief Personality Evaluation

Murray, H. A. 1943. *Thematic Apperception Test.* Cambridge, Mass., Harvard University Press.

Rogers, Carl R. 1931. *A Test of Personality Adjustment.* New York, Association Press, 291 Broadway.

Rorschach, H. n. d. *Psychodiagnostic Plates.* New York, The Psychological Corporation.

Academic and Reading Evaluation

Ayres, L. P. 1940. *Ayres Measuring Scale for Handwriting.* Princeton, Cooperative Test Division, Educational Testing Service.

Daniels, J. C., and Diack, H. 1964. *The Standard Reading Tests.* London, Chatto and Windus.

Durrell, D. D. 1955. *Durrell Analysis of Reading Difficulty.* New York, Harcourt, Brace and World.

Gates, A. I. 1958. *Gates Basic Reading Tests.* New York, Bureau of Publications, Teachers College, Columbia University.

Gates, A. I. 1960. *Gates Reading Survey.* New York, Bureau of Publications, Teachers College, Columbia University.

Gilmore, J. V. 1952. *Gilmore Oral Reading Test.* New York, World Book Co.

Gray, W. S. 1963. Helen M. Robinson (ed.). *Gray Oral Reading Tests.* Indianapolis, Ind., Bobbs-Merrill.

Green, H. A., Jorgensen, A. N., and Kelley, V. H. 1956. *Iowa Silent Reading Tests,* new edition. New York, Harcourt, Brace and World.

Jastak, J., Bijou, S. W., and Jastak, S. R. 1965. *Wide Range Achievement Test.* Wilmington, Del., Guidance Associates, 1526 Gilpin Ave.

Kelley, T. L., Madden, R., Gardner, E. F., Terman, L. M., and Ruch, G. M. 1953. *Stanford Achievement Test.* New York, Harcourt, Brace and World.

Lee, J. M., and Clark, W. W. 1951. *Lee-Clark Reading Readiness Test.* Monterey, Calif., California Test Bureau.

Lindquist, E. F., Hieronymus, A. N., *et al.* 1956. *Iowa Tests of Basic Skills.* Boston, Houghton Mifflin.

Money, J. 1965. Informal Graded Reading, Transcription, Dictation and Spelling. *Transactions of the Pennsylvania Academy of Ophthalmology and Otolaryngology,* 18:16–24. See Pp. 22–24.

Monroe, M. 1929. *Iota Word Test.* Chicago, C. H. Stoelting.

Roswell, F. G., and Chall, J. S. 1959. *Roswell-Chall Diagnostic Reading Test of Word Analysis Skills.* New York, Essay Press.

Tiegs, E. W., and Clark, W. W. 1950, 1957. *California Achievement Tests,* 2 editions. Monterey, Calif., California Test Bureau.

Watts, A. F. 1948. *Holborn Reading Scale.* London, Harrap.

Special Senses: Screening Tests

Darley, F. L. (ed.) 1961. Identification audiometry. *Journal of Speech and Hearing Disorders,* Monograph Supplement 9, September, 1961. Washington, D.C., American Speech and Hearing Association.

Titmus Optical Company. 1960. *Massachusetts Vision Tests.* Petersburg, Va.

Wepman, J. M. 1958. *Auditory Discrimination Test.* Chicago, Language Research Associates, 950 East 59 Street.

Tests of Specific Cognitional Functions

Baker, H. J., and Leland, B. 1959. *Detroit Tests of Learning Aptitude.* Indianapolis, Ind., Bobbs-Merrill.

Bender, L. 1946. *Visual-Motor Gestalt Test.* New York, The Psychological Corporation.

Benton, A. L. 1955. *The Revised Visual Retention Test.* New York, The Psychological Corporation.

Benton, A. L. 1959. *Right-Left Discrimination and Finger Localization: Development and Pathology.* New York, Hoeber-Harper. Pp. 14–15.

Benton, A. L., and Kemble, J. D. 1960. Right-left orientation and reading disability. *Psychiatria and Neurologia,* 139:49–60.

Halstead, W. C., and Wepman, J. M. n. d. *Halstead-Wepman Aphasia Screening Test.* Chicago, University of Chicago Industrial Relations Center.

Harris, A. J. 1958. *Harris Tests of Lateral Dominance.* New York, The Psychological Corporation.

Harris, D. B. 1963. *Children's Drawings as Measures of Intellectual Maturity: A Revision and Extension of the Goodenough Draw-A-Man Test.* New York, Harcourt, Brace and World.

Ishihara, S. 1960. *Tests for Colour-Blindness.* Tokyo, Kanehara Shuppan Co.

Kinsbourne, M., and Warrington, E. K. 1963. The development of finger differentiation. *Quarterly Journal of Experimental Psychology,* 15:132–37.

McCarthy, J. J., and Kirk, S. A. 1961. *Illinois Test of Psycholinguistic Abilities.* Urbana, Ill., Institute for Research on Exceptional Children, University of Illinois.

Money, J., Alexander, D., and Walker, H. T., Jr. 1965. *A Standardized Road-map Test of Direction Sense.* Baltimore, Johns Hopkins.

Thurstone, L. L. 1944. *A Factorial Study of Perception; Psychometric Monographs, No. 4.* (Includes the Embedded Geometric Figures perceptual test.) Chicago, University of Chicago.

INDEX OF NAMES

INDEX OF SUBJECTS